이것이
독해다

There is only one thing that makes

a dream impossible to achieve – the fear of failure

– *Paulo Coelho (1947)*

꿈을 불가능으로 만드는 데에는 단 한가지 요소가 존재한다.

실패에 대한 두려움이다.

Photo by kazuend on Unsplash

이것이 독해다

이종현 저

PREFACE 머리말

학생들이 편입 영어를 공부하다 보면 독해 부분에서 막힌 기분이 들 때가 많습니다. 영어 구문을 공부해도 무슨 말인지 해석을 못하고 문제를 못 푸는 경우도 허다합니다. 이 이유를 살펴보면 대부분의 경우 문제는 영어 독해력입니다. 이 책은 그런 학생들을 위해 진짜 독해력을 키우기 위한 책입니다.

영어 문장들이 모여 영어 독해 지문을 형성하게 됩니다. 그럼 이 지문들은 일정한 구조를 가지게 됩니다. 이를 글의 구조라고 합니다. 학생들이 가장 먼저 익혀야 하는 것은 바로 이러한 글의 구조입니다. 글의 구조를 알아야 다음에 어떤 내용이 나올지를 정확하게 추론하면서 독해를 할 수 있고 필요한 부분과 필요하지 않은 부분을 나누어서 글을 바라볼 수 있게 됩니다.

그리고 그 이후 학생들에게 필요한 것은 유형별 독해 풀이법입니다. 실제로 편입시험엔 여러 유형의 문제들이 출제가 됩니다. 각각의 유형들을 정확하게 풀이하기 위한 연습이 필요합니다. 모든 유형엔 접근법이라는 것이 있고 이 접근법대로 풀 수 있다면 답을 못 찍는 독해 문제는 없어질 것입니다.

모든 독해 문제의 정답은 지문 속에 있습니다. 이 책을 통해 여러분들이 문제 풀이법을 정확하게 익혀서 어떤 독해 문제를 만나도 정확하게 답을 찍고 편입에 성공하기를 소망합니다.

HOW TO USE 이 교재 학습법

❶ 문제 풀이법을 읽어본 후 먼저 문제 풀어보기

먼저 책에 적혀 있는 문제풀이법을 확실하게 암기한 후에 연습 문제를 풀어본다. 시간은 잴 필요 없이 확실하게 답을 맞춘다는 마음으로만 풀어본다. 풀어본 이후에 정답을 확인한다.

❷ 틀리면 다시 풀어보기

틀렸을 때 바로 해설을 보지 말고 다시 문제를 풀어본다. 5분에서 10분정도 고민을 다시 해보고 다시 정답을 찍어본다. 이렇게 고민을 하는 것이 독해력을 향상시키기 위해선 필수적이다.

❸ 또 틀린 경우 답을 찍어두고 고민해보기

틀린 문제를 또 틀린 경우엔 정답을 찍어두고 고민해본다. 답을 찍어두고 역으로 근거를 찾아보는 것이다. 해설지를 보기 전에 반드시 이 3단계의 과정을 거쳐야 고민을 통해 독해력을 키울 수 있다.

❹ 해설지 확인 + 동영상 강의

책 뒤편에 해설지를 보면 실제 풀이법대로 풀었을 때 어떻게 정답이 나오는지 설명을 적어 놓았다. 따라서 해설지를 확인해보면 된다. 그리고 이 이외에 혹시 완벽하게 공부를 하며 필요한 포인트를 전부 정리하고 싶다면 www.brounedu.co.kr에서 동영상으로도 학습을 할 수 있게 강의를 촬영해두었다. 혼자 공부해도 충분하지만 동영상 강의로 정리하면 완벽하게 정리할 수 있을 것이다. 브라운에듀 홈페이지에서 이것이 독해다! Part1, 2, 3 강의를 수강하면 된다.

CONTENTS 차례

PART 1 기본 유형 총정리

PART 2 복잡한 유형 총정리

PART 3 고난이도 실전 모의고사 5회

정답과 해설

PART 1

기본 유형 총정리

PART 1 기본 유형 총정리

UNIT 0 글의 구조 총정리

- 글의 구조 총정리

01 비교와 대조

→ 핵심 : 비교, 대조의 연결사

대조 비교	in/by contrast, on the other hand, conversely
공통 비교	likewise, similarly, in the same way, by the same token, equally

❶ 둘 중 하나를 강조하는 경우

비교/대조를 통해서 하나의 소재를 강조하고 싶은 경우이다. 이 경우에는 그게 왜 중요한지, 왜 좋은지 등등의 표현이 지문에 있게 된다. 그리고 다른 비교 대상은 주제를 강조하기 위해서 사용한 반대되는 소재라고 볼 수 있다.

❷ 둘 비교 대상을 일반화시키는 경우

비교하는 두 대상을 단순하게 공통점과 차이점을 보여주는 식으로 비교하는 경우이고 이 경우엔 둘의 일반화시킨 이야기가 주제가 된다. 가령 지문의 첫 부분에 일본 음식의 특징이 나오고 중간에 on the other hand라는 연결사 이후로 한국 음식의 특징이 나열되어 있다면, 이 글의 주제는 일본 음식과 한국 음식의 차이점이 될 것이다.

- 예시 지문

1. There is a constant tension between science and politics. From the perspective of science, policies should reflect careful consideration of the scientific data, and should be in line with the findings and recommendations of science. Scientists who offer advice to policy makers, however, often complain that their input is ignored or distorted during the policy making process. Political values and necessities may conflict sharply with the data presented by scientists. A policy may be developed that represents a compromise between the criteria determined by science and the pragmatic needs of politics. An effective policy should be cost-effective and fair, place limited demands on government, and provide assurance to the public that the goals will be met. 7 If an administration's position is not supported by the data, it may ask for further studies rather than accept what is offered. 8 In extreme cases, scientific data might be buried in the face of the apparent demands of politics.

2. Although height and weight are similar in their simplicity, they are very different in how they rule our lives. Our adult height is fixed — there is little one can do about it, and short people are not held responsible for their height as well as for their eye colors. Weight, however, is another matter. We are bombarded with the message that we can control our weight through will power, proper nutrition, and exercise. The diet industry (which includes diet programs, diet foods, and diet magazines and books) is enormous, with revenues of tens of billions of dollars, catering to an American public desperate to slim down. We shop at grocery stores filled with food that isn't food and exercise at gyms packed with people walking furiously on treadmills that take them nowhere. Each morning we step onto the bathroom scale and measure our progress or lack thereof.

02 Myth & Truth

→ Myth의 단서 찾기, Truth의 시작점 찾기

❶ Myth의 단서

1. People(Most/Some) say(think/believe) that ~
   = It is said(thought/believed) that ~

2. People(most/some) argue(claim/insist) that ~

3. There is a tendency to ~
   = S + tend to v ~ = have a tendency to v
   = be inclined/prone/apt to v

4. Common belief ~, commonly

5. as if S 과거동사/had p.p ~

6. may/might, can/could, would v ~의 형태가 들어간 문장

7. sometimes/usually/often

8. generally/in general, theoretically/in theory

9. 과거의 표현
   - S once 과거동사, S have/has/had long p.p, S have/has/had p.p for/since~
   - traditionally, conventionally, existing, historically, initially, stereotype 등이 들어간 문장
   - until recently (최근까지) 가 들어간 문장

❷ Truth의 시작점

1. However, but, still, yet, though 등 역접 연결사

2. In fact, In reality, Indee, As a matter of fact, Actually

3. From my experience, for me, in my opinion 등 내 얘기의 시작점

4. they are mistaken, this is not true, this is not the case
   nothing can be further from the truth

5. 현재 표현
   - now, today, these days, currently, new 등이 들어간 문장

√ 구조에 따른 주제 파악하는 방법!

Myth라는 것을 확실하게 파악한 후 그 Myth와 반대가 되는 주제 문장을 찾아서 주제를 생각해낼 수도 있고, 주제가 보이지 않을 경우엔 Myth라는 확신을 가지고 그 내용의 반대되는 내용이 주제라고 생각해낼 수도 있다.

- 예시 지문

1. It is estimated that people age fifty and older spend about 48 percent of consumer dollars. They buy about 48 percent of all luxury cars, and they are responsible for about 80 percent of luxury travel. They even buy about 25 percent of all toys annually (there are about fifty-five million grandparents age fifty years and older in the United States). Nevertheless, marketing and merchandising programs commonly treat these customers as if they are much older. For example, there is the myth that older consumers are fixed on certain products and are unwilling to try new alternative products. Therefore, why should advertising of a new product be directed at older consumers? In fact, a survey of five hundred people over age fifty in shopping malls revealed that about 80 percent of them were quite willing to try new products.

2. Diet has been known for many years to play a key role as a risk factor for chronic diseases. What is apparent at the global level is that great changes have swept the entire world since the second half of the twentieth century, inducing major modifications in diet, first in industrial regions and more recently in developing countries. Traditional, largely plant-based diets have been swiftly replaced by high-fat, energy-dense diets with a substantial content of animalbased foods. But diet, while critical to prevention, is just one risk factor. Physical inactivity, now recognized as an increasingly important determining factor of health, is the result of a progressive shift of lifestyle towards more sedentary patterns, in developing countries as much as in industrialized ones.

3. We sometimes think of aging as a process applying uniformly to the whole organism, yet physiological studies show that different parts of the body age at different rates. For example, white blood cells die and are replaced within 10 days, but red blood cells last 120 days. The stem cells that produce all blood cells reveal no signs of aging at all. Cells in the brain last as long as the body lives; once the brain is fully formed, neurons do not exhibit significant cell division, and unless damaged by illness, they remain largely intact. But apart from long-living stem cells and brain cells, most parts of the body are constantly subjected to damage and repair. The mechanisms that contribute to this process of aging include wear and tear, the effects of free radicals, and the decline of the immune system.

03 Problem & Solution

➜ 문제점을 알 수 있는 단어들 : 문제, 파괴, 상실, 어려움 등이 들어간 문장이 있을 때

❶ 문제와 해결책

문제가 나오고 그 문제에 대한 해결책이 뒷 부분에 서술이 되어 있는 구조이다. 이 때 주제는 해결책이 된다.

❷ 문제, 문제, 문제

어떤 문제가 나오고 그 문제에 대한 해결책이 등장하지 않는 구조이다. 마지막 부분에서도 그래서 이 내용이 문제다 라는 내용으로 끝나게 된다. 이 때 주제는 문제점이 주제가 된다.

❸ 상황을 먼저 제시하고 문제점을 제시하는 글

문제점을 바로 제시하지 않고 일단 상황을 제시한 후에 중간에 However나 But같은 표현을 통해 문제점 얘기를 시작하는 지문도 있다. 이런 지문을 만났을 땐 중간에 Problem이 나왔다는 것을 인지하면 그 순간부터 Solution이 있나 없나에만 집중하면 된다.

❹ 중간에 해결책이 나왔지만 다시 문제점으로 가는 글

처음에 문제가 제시되고 중간에 해결책이 제시되는 글이라면 그 글 뒤에 다시 뒤집어지면서, 그러한 해결책의 문제점에 관한 얘기, 또는 그런 해결책으론 문제를 해결할 수 없다는 얘기가 나올 수 있다. 그럴 땐 다시 문제점이 주제가 된다.

- 예시 지문

1. One of the most important things that young adults need to understand is that any time you are trying to live a normal and decent life, you will always find people that will hate you for that. That is how most young people compromise in some situations. They give up on what they believe is right and go with the crowd, and later pay the consequences. What you have to understand is the people who hate you are jealous because of the fact that they cannot have such good behaviors, so they choose to hate you. When you have something good, don't give it up for foolish people who never stand for anything good. It's better for them to call you names for your good behaviors than for you to compromise with them. They can call you old-fashioned; whatever they want, it's their business.

2. Our addiction to criticizing others is a huge block to effectively giving feedback. When we criticize, even if we choose our words with care, we are likely to assign others to a specific, potentially harmful, status. We are likely to assign others, for instance, to the status of being "wrong." No one likes to be labeled "wrong." Most people get defensive when they are labeled, even when sure they are not "wrong." And what's more important, defensive people block messages. Unless you are trying not to be understood, then, criticism is not an effective communication strategy. And it doesn't help to call it "constructive" either. Saying something like, "I'm telling you this for your own development, your design is all wrong" isn't going to produce positive results. Criticism is criticism. It blocks understanding.

3. Maps are made from data. These data may be positional, involving the latitude and longitude of a place, an address, a road, or a border. Some maps use statistical data to show such things as population; others use qualitative data such as locations of grasslands or deserts. Errors can enter when data are collected. Maps made by geographic information systems (GIS), maps on the Internet, and GPS units must be digitized. That is, the data must be put in a form that the computer can read. Some of this digitizing is done by humans plotting and entering the information, and thus, there is the potential for human error. On historic maps and even some modern maps there might be a lack of data, gaps in the data, and even erroneous data.

04 실험 & 결과 / 예시 & 나열

❶ 실험 & 결과

어떤 연구팀의 연구 결과를 바탕으로 글의 중심내용을 뒷받침하는 글이다. 크게 두 가지 유형이 있을 수 있다. 첫 번째는 먼저 연구 내용에 대해서 상세한 설명이 나오고 뒤에 그 연구의 결과가 나온 다음 일반화시키는 구조이다. 이 땐 연구 결과가 주제가 된다.

두 번째는 먼저 연구 결과의 내용이 나오고 그 뒤에 어떤 식으로 연구를 진행했는지 부연설명을 해주는 글이다. 이 때에도 마찬가지로 앞 부분에 있는 연구 결과가 주제가 된다.

연구 결과로 뒤쪽에 많이 나오는 패턴은
S Vt that절, 중간에 나오는 But ~ 등의 문장이 있다.

❷ 예시 & 나열

실험 & 결과와 마찬가지로 두 가지 형태가 나올 수 있다. 첫 번째는 먼저 하고 싶은 이야기인 주제가 나오고 그 주제를 뒷받침하는 예시를 적어준다. 이 땐 첫 부분에 일반적인 내용이 주제가 된다.

두 번째로는 예시들로 먼저 시작하는 글이다. 먼저 예시들로 쭉 나열하고 마지막 부분에 일반화된 주제를 적어주는 글이다. 이 때엔 주제가 뒷 부분에 있다. 다만 간혹 일반화된 주제를 안 써주는 경우도 있으므로 이 땐 예시의 핵심 내용을 추론하여 주제를 생각해내어야 한다.

- 예시 지문

1. Before language develops, emotions and touch are the primary means by which parent and child communicate. Consequently, it would not be surprising if preverbal infants had some basic understanding of other people's emotional, nonverbal communications, which research has indicated is indeed the case. For example, infants as young as 14 months understand that emotions are often "about" a particular event (e.g., someone is scared of a dog) and are very adept at identifying what a person is emoting about. In addition, by 18 months, infants begin to appreciate that two people can have a different emotional response about the exact same object (e.g., you like peas, but I hate them). In contrast, 14-month-old infants are still highly egocentric and assume that everyone has the same emotional responses to a particular object or event.

2. A company might find a market attractive if it fits the company's long-term vision and objectives. While short-term profits may be constrained, the long-term profitability picture may look more favorable. General Electric's participation in the market for medical imaging devices (called CT scanners) in the 1970s reflects this mode of thinking. During the 1970s, GE acquired other companies that made CT scanners, but were uninterested in remaining active in the market due to declining sales volumes and market saturation. By purchasing these assets, GE obtained a dominant long-term position in the market. Although the market exhibited no immediate signs of growth at that time, its subsequent return to growth and profitability made GE a powerful player in the CT scanner market, especially in the United States.

05 Question & Answer

질문과 답변으로 이루어진 글이다. 의문문이 등장을 하고 그 의문문에 대한 정답이 나왔을 때 그 부분이 주제가 된다. 항상 지문에서 의문문의 형태가 있다면 이 의문문에 대한 답이 있을 수 있다는 마음으로 글을 읽어야 한다. 질문 바로 뒤에 정답이 나오는 경우가 많다. 그리고 진짜 의문문으로 질문하는 것이 아닌 S + wonder ~ 이런 식으로 의문문을 나타내는 경우도 있으므로 주의해야 한다.

√ Question & Answer 구조의 패턴 총정리

- 예시 지문

1. If you kept a list of things observed in the sky, it might include birds, smoke, clouds, rainbows, halos, lightning, stars, the Moon, the Sun, and comets. One of the first ideas that might occur to you is that the sky has depth. Some things in it appear closer, and some appear farther away. Why? Perspective! From everyday experiences you know that closer objects block your view of more distant objects. For example, if you hold your hand in front of your eyes, you cannot see a more distant tree. Therefore, if a bird flying by blocks your view of a cloud, you logically conclude that the bird is closer to you than the cloud. Then you see a cloud move "in front of " the Sun, and you conclude that the cloud is closer to you than the Sun. Or perhaps you see a solar eclipse, and you conclude that the Moon is closer to you than the Sun. In this way, all of the objects on your list could be put in order of distance from an observer.

2. Literature students often wonder if there is a rule about how much you should quote. The answer is that you should quote what will best serve to illuminate your point, neither more nor less. Sometimes a single sentence, or a single line of verse, will be enough; sometimes you will need a whole paragraph or a whole sonnet. When quoting, you must take care to pick precisely the right passage. Neither the random chunk of text with the image you want to draw attention to buried somewhere inside it, nor the stray line which may perhaps remind the reader of the relevant couplet you fail to quote, will make your point effectively. You must be careful, too, not to quote in such a way that you distort your author's meaning. It is sensible to avoid the really obvious quotation, which may be a jewel of our literature in its proper place, but in the context of your essay will strike the reader as a cliché.

3. Does music change technology, or does technology change music? History says the latter. The advent of the phonograph record (1877) ended the monopoly of the live performance; the fidelity wasn't as good as live music, but millions of new listeners would soon enjoy it nonetheless. In the 1940s, the advent of the electric guitar caused the end of swing music and made headbanging rock music possible decades later. In our day, the digital delivery of sound on YouTube and other streaming sites has changed how we receive music as well as its quality. And, just as the digital revolution has altered our contemporary musical landscape, so did technological advancements lead to the modern symphony orchestra.

06 설명문 or Story Telling

이런 종류의 글은 어떤 특정한 주제가 나오는 것이 아닌 여러 정보들을 나열하는 글이다. 따라서 주제를 잡는 것이 아니라 세부적인 내용들의 핵심을 잡아두는 것이 중요하다. 어떤 주제가 아닌 디테일한 내용 일치/불일치, 추론 등을 묻는 문제가 많이 출제될 수 있다.

- 예시 지문

1. Van Gogh's paintings instilled the objects he painted with a soulful quality. When he painted a pair of worn-out shoes, it spoke volumes of the long day life's hardship the wearer might have had. The melancholy atmosphere of the kitchen in The Potato Eaters, bleakly lit by a simple lamp, deliberately hints at the painter's chronic agony and the nature of his disease. The painting has undertones of his notion of family. Sitting on the far right, the old woman with the sad look on her face is his mother. It seems that the painter intended to isolate her from the others. The young man on the far left could very well be van Gogh, who is looking at his mother even though she has averted her son's eyes.

His landscapes and self-portraits imply a subdued solitude and unease. In May of 1889, van Gogh checked himself into a mental hospital. As he worked on what would become his magnum opus, The Starry Night, he grew ill. During this time, he finished a unique Self-Portrait. In the earlier self-portraits, he usually looked a decade older than he was because of his nomadic lifestyle and financial difficulties, but in this last painting he looked young. It is probable that he wanted to start anew and overcome his mental difficulties. Ten months after his last self-portrait, in July, 1890, he shot himself dead. As seen in his paintings, van Gogh's youth can be symbolized by despair and the specter of death.

2. Irish writer George Orwell's life and literature can be summarized by his faith in one thing: human decency. Although the definition can be ambiguous, it does contain a sense of fundamental dignity, and above all, honesty and tolerance. Orwell was opposed to dogma, ideological political doctrines, planned social reformation, and religious absolutism. He instead preferred to support the individual's right of expression, particularly the rights of minorities, and the freedom of press.

Orwell's sense of human decency was based on the idea of liberation and expression. It was not something that could be enjoyed passively, but must be worked for and sought after. The phrase "The secret of freedom is courage" implies that people have an obligation to be brave in their speech and courageous in their tolerance of other opinions. For Orwell, decency meant, above all else, communality, common sense, and respect for the common man. He was adamantly opposed to Marxism, which dictates that freedom is denied by equality. He believed true socialism was possible not by seizing power but by guaranteeing fair and open discussions.

Orwell loathed abstract theories such as communism, which necessitated ideology. This can be seen in his anti-totalitarian work Animal Farm and his dystopia classic 1984, in which he pursues an anti-dictatorial, anti-class, and anti-discriminatory society. Orwell believed that it was the obligation of human beings to fight against these systems not just for the sake of society, but for the progression of a society.

UNIT 1 내용 일치 / 불일치 (True / Not True)

- 일치/불일치, 추론 문제, 지칭 추론 문제 접근법

일치/불일치 유형, 추론 유형의 핵심은 글의 주제를 먼저 생각하면서 접근하는 것이다.
글의 큰 내용을 보면서 먼저 답을 찾아주는 것이 중요하다.

❶ 주제와 밀접한 연관이 있는 유형

일치/불일치, 추론 문제이지만 이 유형같은 경우는 주제와 밀접한 연관이 있는 내용을 일치/불일치 문제로 출제를 하게 된다. 이런 유형에선 일치하는 문제, 즉 True를 물어보는 문제라면 주제와 부합하는 선지가 정답이 되는 경우가 많고 나머지 선지들은 지문과 반대되는 형식으로 많이 나온다. 반대로 Not True 문제의 경우는 나머지가 주제와 같은 내용이고 정답이 되는 선지만 주제와 반대되는 경우로 많이 출제가 된다.

❷ 하나하나 찾는 유형

찾을 때도 그냥 찾는 것이 중요한게 아니라 선지의 소재간의 관계를 보는 눈이 중요하다. 가령 선지에 A 때문에 B가 된다 라고 써있을 때, 지문에 A 얘기도 써있고 B 얘기도 써있지만 A와 B는 인과관계가 아니어서 불일치인 경우가 있다. 따라서 이 부분부터 접근할 필요가 있다. 이걸로도 안된다면 이제 인물, 상황, 집단, 숫자, 비교급 등으로 찾아야 한다.

- 세부적인 선지의 출제 방식

❶ 일치, 추론 문제에서

① 정답이 되는 선지가 주제, 나머지 선지가 주제랑 반대

② 정답이 되는 선지가 주제, 나머지 선지는 찾는 유형

③ 정답이 되는 선지가 찾는 유형, 나머지가 주제와 반대 or 찾는 유형

④ 모두 찾는 유형

❷ 불일치, 추론할 수 없는 것을 묻는 문제에서

① 정답이 되는 선지가 주제와 반대, 나머지 선지가 주제

② 정답이 되는 선지가 주제와 반대, 나머지 선지가 찾는 유형

③ 정답이 되는 선지가 찾는 유형, 나머지 선지가 주제, or 찾는 유형

④ 모두 찾는 유형

- 연습 문제

1.

Back in the 1980s and 1990s, tax rates were far higher, and my percentage rate was in the middle of the pack. According to a theory I sometimes hear, I should have thrown a fit and refused to invest because of the elevated tax rates on capital gains and dividends.

I didn't refuse, nor did others. I have worked with investors for 60 years and I have yet to see anyone — not even when capital gains rates were 39.9 percent in 1976-1977 — shy away from a sensible investment because of the tax rate on the potential gain. People invest to make money, and potential taxes have never scared them off. And to those who argue that higher rates hurt job creation, I would note that a net of nearly 40 million jobs were added between 1980 and 2000. Unfortunately, you know what's happened since then: lower tax rates and far lower job creation.

1. 위 글의 내용과 맞지 않는 것을 고르시오

① Investors are reluctant to invest when tax rates rise.

② Capital gains rates are lower than they were in 1977.

③ The writer invests regardless of the tax rate for him.

④ The writer's present tax rate is lower than in the 1990s.

2.

The status of a character trait depends on the reference point. For instance, for an ape fingernails are considered primitive in relation to other primates because all other primates have fingernails. Thus, fingernails would not serve to distinguish apes from, for example, monkeys. Fingernails are a derived character for primates as a whole, however, because no other mammals have them. Thus, fingernails serve to distinguish primates from other mammals. The second character illustrated here — brow ridges — is found only in hominoids, not in other primates, and is therefore derived for hominoids. This character distinguishes apes from monkeys. In a chimpanzee, however, brow ridges would be considered to be primitive with respect to other hominoids; that is, the character would not distinguish a chimpanzee from, for example, a gorilla.

2. 위 글의 내용과 맞지 않는 것은?

① All primates have fingernails

② Some primates have brow ridges

③ Neither apes nor monkeys belong to hominoids

④ Both chimpanzees and gorillas belong to hominoids.

3.

People from cultures on polychronic time live their lives quite differently than do those who move to the monochronic clock The pace for P-time cultures is more leisurely than the one found in M-time cultures. One reason for this is that people and human relationships, not tasks, are at the center of polychronic cultures. These cultures are normally collective and deal with life in a holistic manner. For P-time cultures, time is less tangible; hence, feelings of wasted time are not as prevalent as in M-time cultures. Their members can interact with more than one person or do more than one thing at a time, while people from M-time cultures suppress spontaneity and tend to focus on one activity at a time. This explains why there are more interruptions in conversations carried on by people from Arabic, Asian, and Latin American cultures compared to the ones from Germany, Austria, Switzerland, and the U.S.

3. 다음 글의 내용과 일치하는 것은?

① Feelings of wasted time are more prevalent in P-time cultures

② People in Polychronic cultures can do multiple things simultaneously

③ People in monochronic cultures think highly of relationships with others.

④ Arabic, Asian, and American cultures are categorized as M-time cultures.

4.

Why are you reading Spinoza's Ethics? Perhaps it is assigned reading on a university course. Maybe you are a philosopher who wants to brush up on a neglected area. Or perhaps you are led by curiosity about the nature of reality, the mind and human behaviour. If you fall into any of these categories, this book—and indeed, Spinoza's Ethics itself—was written for you.

It may surprise you to hear that Spinoza's Ethics was written just as much for a non-expert audience in the twenty-first century as for the philosophical world of the seventeenth. Spinoza anticipated that his book would be read largely by those steeped in the philosophical traditions of the time. (If you do have some philosophical background, you may hear echoes of Plato, Aristotle, the Stoics, Descartes and Hobbes in his work, as well as anticipations of Nietzsche, Sartre, Foucault and Deleuze.) But Spinoza would be delighted to learn of non-experts reading his work more than 300 years later, for his aim is to help as many people as possible understand the truth. The Ethics is a workbook designed to enable the reader to develop his or her own understanding. Spinoza thinks that if more people read the Ethics, then reason and virtue amongst human beings will increase, leading to more peaceful and tolerant societies.

That is not to say that the Ethics is a kind of early self-help manual. Spinoza's Ethics is a rich and complex work of metaphysics, epistemology and ethics. Undoubtedly, it is one of the most difficult philosophical books you will ever read. You will grapple with language and concepts that are unfamiliar and encounter ideas with which you may disagree profoundly. But it is also one of the most exciting philosophy books ever written. Spinoza gives us a programme for being human beings in the best way possible—a programme based on a deep understanding of the nature of reality that anyone can attain. He leads us on a journey that reveals to us the truth about what we are and our place in the universe. Understanding the truth about ourselves is the basis for positive human relationships, true scientific knowledge and good political organisation. Spinoza can lead you to think differently about yourself and your life, about nature, about God, about freedom and about ethics. So perhaps the best reason for reading Spinoza's Ethics is this: it is a book that may change your life.

4. 위 글의 내용과 일치하지 않는 것을 고르시오.

① Understanding the truth about ourselves is prerequisite for true scientific knowledge.

② As a whole, Spinoza's Ethics is committed to influencing its readers' lives.

③ The author of the Ethics aimed to help as many people as possible understand the truth.

④ Those who were stuck with the philosophical tradition of the time did not like the Ethics.

5.

Let us assume that crises are a necessary precondition for the emergence of novel theories and ask next how scientists respond to their existence. Part of the answer, as obvious as it is important, can be discovered by noting first what scientists never do when confronted by even severe and prolonged anomalies. Though they may begin to lose faith and then to consider alternatives, they do not renounce the paradigm that has led them into crisis. They do not, that is, treat anomalies as counter-instances, though in the vocabulary of philosophy of science that is what they are. In part this generalization is simply a statement from historic fact, based upon the examples which hint what our later examination of paradigm rejection will disclose more fully: once it has achieved the status of paradigm, a scientific theory is declared invalid only if an alternate candidate is available to take the place. No process yet disclosed by the historical study of scientific development at all resembles the methodological stereotype of falsification by direct comparison with nature. That remark does not mean that scientists do not reject scientific theories, or that experience and experiment are not essential to the process in which they do so. But it does mean—what will ultimately be a central point—that the act of judgment that leads scientists to reject a previously accepted theory is always based upon more than a comparison of that theory with the world. The decision to reject one paradigm is always simultaneously the decision to accept another, and the judgment leading to that decision involves the comparison of both paradigms with nature and with each other.

5. 위 글의 내용과 가장 일치하는 것을 고르시오.

① Scientists give up the existing theories when they begin to consider alternatives.

② Scientists think that a new scientific theory should usually be tested with the falsification stereotype through direct comparison with nature.

③ The final decision to accept one scientific paradigm used to be made after the comparison of both paradigms with nature as well as with each other.

④ The advantages and disadvantages of a scientific theory are well revealed by a study of anomalous scientific phenomenon in which the theory becomes invalid.

6.

Depression is more than just feeling a bit down or overwhelmed; at its worst, it is a debilitating illness, leaving its sufferers unable to sleep or eat and filled with feelings of immense sadness and guilt. It is sometimes thought of as a modern affliction, a result of the rich world's leisurely preoccupation with the self. But that couldn't be further from the truth. Depression was one referred to as 'melancholia', a diagnosis recorded around the 5th century BC by philosophers like Hippocrates. Arateus described symptoms that sound all to familiar to modern clinicians: 'the patients become dull or stern, dejected or unreasonably torpid ... they also become peevish, dispirited and start up from a disturbed sleep'. Depression is a reality for people in the developing world, too: one survey of Aids-stricken regions in Uganda showed that 21 percent of residents were clinically depressed, while studies in a Pakistani village showed that 44 percent of the population were suffering from some kind of depressive disorder.

6. According to the passage, which of the following is true?

① Depression was diagnosed recently in human history.

② People nowadays suffer more from depression than in the past.

③ The symptoms of depression seem similar both in the past and in the present

④ Depression is more serious in developing countries than in the rich world.

7.

Individuals who are genetically predisposed to any type of addiction have a defective gene in the part of the brain responsible for the manufacture of dopamine, which is the neurotransmitter involved with drugs, according to the experts. Cocaine, heroin, nicotine, amphetamines and other addictive drugs alter the brain's pleasure circuit, producing a feel-good sensation. Eating cheesecake or nachos or any other food you love activates it. So does winning a competition, acing a test, receiving praise and other pleasurable activities. The pleasure circuit communicates in the chemical language of dopamine, and this neurotransmitter zips from neuron to neuron in the brain to produce feelings of mild happiness to euphoria. But chronic use of these addictive drugs produces enduring changes in the brain. The most important is a reduction in the number of dopamine receptors that are simply little molecular baseball gloves that sit on neurons, grab passing neurotransmitters like fly balls and reel them in.

7. 위 글의 내용과 일치하지 않는 것을 고르시오.

① The genes of a drug addict become more fecund by chronic use of drugs.

② Eating delicious food and getting flattered trigger the brain's pleasure circuit.

③ Long term use of addictive drugs reduces the number of receptors of neurotransmitters.

④ Dopamine is a chemical language to activate the pleasure circuit.

8.

Asian carp were originally brought to the U.S. to control algae in southern aquaculture farms and, unfortunately, made their way into the Mississippi River through flooding. Over time, the carp swam north, up the Mississippi and into the river's tributaries. All eyes are now on the fish as they move toward the Great Lakes. In fact, an unprecedented binational effort between the U.S. and Canada has been launched to prevent the carp from invading the lakes. These fish are voracious predators of the tiniest prey, plankton, which is the basis of the entire Great Lakes food system. Given that Asian carp can eat up to 20 percent of their body weight in one day, their hefty appetities could harm the food web native species need to survive.

8. According to the passage, which of the following is not true about Asian carp?

① They were imported to America to control algae

② Flooding allowed them into the Mississippi

③ They are abundant throughout the Great Lakes.

④ They are outcompeting native fish species for food.

9.

If Silicon Valley had its way, all humans would have abandoned analog products by now. We would be consuming music from the cloud, reading stories online, and sketching designs on battery-powered devices. And indeed, many of us do. And yet, we have also started an analog revolution. Sales of objects like vinyl records and paper notebooks have consistently grown over the past decade, as has their cultural relevance. Meanwhile, big brands in e-commerce like Amazon are rushing to open brick-and-mortar stores. Many assume it is nostalgia driving the switch, led by the wistful romance of aging Luddites. But in fact, many of analog's newest fans are millennials drawn to its raw utility; the designer who uses a paper notebook, for example, to sketch out a website's early look. Opting for less-modern technology might seem to make no sense. But humans are not machines. We are complex creatures, driven by emotions beyond our comprehension. And at its core, the human experience remains a deeply, truly analog one, no matter how many virtual platfroms we embrace.

9. According to the passage, which of the following is NOT true?

① Although we accept virtuality, human experiences are analog.

② The cultural relevance of analog products has been increasing.

③ It is largely older generations who drive the analog revolution.

④ Many people read stories online and consume music from the cloud.

10.

Famed for its amazingly intricate sculptures and massive replicas of global icons, the Harbin International Snow and Ice Festival is now underway. Made up of several themed zones, the event area covers an area of about 750,000 square meters, say organizers. Works are mostly inspired by Chinese fairy tales and famous landmarks, such as the Great Wall of China and the Egyptian Pyramids. It's best seen at night when sculptures are lit up from the inside, giving the whole area a fairyland feel. Harbin is a bitingly cold city with January daytime temperatures ranging from minus 13-23 Celsius. Nevertheless, a lot of tourists enjoy this magnificent festival in Harbin.

10. Which of the following in NOT correct about the Harbin Snow and Ice Festival?

① Its view is far better at night than during the daytime.

② It exhibits many works reminiscent of China and other countries.

③ When the weather is severely cold, its visitors sharply decrease.

④ It is very famous for its exquisite sculptures and huge replicas.

11.

Back in 1967, Scottish inventor John Shepherd-Barron thought getting cash should be as easy as getting a chocolate bar. He is credited with pioneering the first cash machine or ATM in a Barclays Bank in London, UK. But the difficulties lay in ensuring that you were who you said you were.

To prevent problems, Shepherd-Barron developed a special type of paper cheque that acted as a precursor to the debit cards we have today. Each cheque would cause his cash machine to request a personal identification number - or PIN - that only the account holder knew. Shepherd-Barron was going to make the machine require a six-digit PIN, but he was overruled ... by his wife. She believed that six digits were too many to remember, and four became the standard.

11-1. Which is NOT included in the passage?

① What PIN was for

② When the ATM was invented

③ How popular the first ATM was

④ Where the ATM was first in service

11-2. Which is NOT true according to the passage?

① It was in the end Shepherd-Barron's wife who decided that PIN should be four digits.

② Shepherd-Barron thought earning money should be as easy as eating a chocolate bar.

③ Identification of the account holder was a main problem in introducing the cash machine.

④ A special type of paper cheque developed by Shepherd-Barron was a primitive type of the debit card.

12.

One hundred and two Pilgrims, after a four-month journey, landed at Plymouth in 1620. Confronted with severe weather and a plague, they lost forty-six members during the first year. The survivors, though, had something to be thankful for. A bountiful crop had been harvested. They were alive, in part thanks to the assistance of an English-speaking Pawtuxet Indian named Squanto. He had helped them build houses and plant crops. In the fall of 1621, the Pilgrims proclaimed a day of thanksgiving. The Pilgrims invited the chief of the Wampanoag tribe and his tribesmen and women. They prepared the first Thanksgiving Day meal with many of the elements that have since come to be traditional holiday fare. The establishment of the day we now celebrate was the result of the efforts of magazine editor Sarah Hale. Mrs. Hale started her crusade for a Thanksgiving celebration in 1827. Her editorials argued for the observance of a national Thanksgiving holiday. She wrote hundreds of letters to politicians. She requested that the last Thursday in November be set aside to "offer God a tribute of gratitude." Finally, Mrs. Hale's dreams became a reality.

12. Choose the one that is not mentioned in the passage.

① the amount of food offered at the first Thanksgiving feast

② how many of the original members perished in the first year

③ the Pilgrims' relationship with the neighboring tribes

④ Sarah Hale's strategy for making Thanksgiving a national holiday

13.

The Fertile Crescent, a fertile land between the Tigris and Euphrates Rivers, was labeled by the Greeks as Mesopotamia, which means "land between the rivers." Though the region's rainfall was minimal, snow melt fed the rivers and flooding made the valley fertile, which led to the birth of organized civilization. The people in the region near the mouths of the rivers are called Sumerians. In the region of Sumer that created theocratic city-states they invented many things that we still use today, including the wheel, schools, arches, bricks, and the system of time based on the number 60 and the circle. Today we are still reliant on wheels to get us from place to place, schools to educate us, and clocks that they invented for time.

13. Which of the following is true according to the passage?

① In the region of Sumer, the city-states were ruled by religious authority.

② The mouths of the Tigris and the Euphrates were barren with no residents.

③ There was a fair amount of rainfall in Mesopotamia.

④ Today's long-distance education dates back to the Sumerian era.

14.

In the very first decades following the discovery of the diode in 1939 and the transistor in 1947 germanium was used almost exclusively because it was relatively easy to find and was available in fairly large quantities. It was also relatively easy to refine to obtain very high levels of purity, an important aspect in the fabrication process. However, it was discovered in the early years that diodes and transistors constructed using germanium as the base material suffered from low levels of reliability due primarily to its sensitivity to changes in temperature. At the time, scientists were aware that another material, silicon, had improved temperature sensitivities, but the refining process for manufacturing silicon of very high levels of purity was still in the development stages. Finally, however, in 1954 the first silicon transistor was introduced, and silicon quickly became the semiconductor material of choice. Not only is silicon less temperature sensitive, but it is one of the most abundant materials on earth, removing any concerns about availability.

14. 본문 내용과 일치하지 않는 것을 고르시오.

① The germanium diodes and transistors were popular in the early years.

② Germanium transistors were not reliable as they were sensitive to temperature changes.

③ Silicon replaced germanium immediately after it was found to be temperature sensitive.

④ Silicon is available in large quantities, probably as abundant as germanium.

15.

Perhaps no musical innovation has generated as much puzzlement, dismay, and anger among its critics as rap music, which was popular in some urban African-American and Latino communities for years before becoming nationally visible beginning in the early 1980s. Unlike many earlier forms of black music that have attracted broad audiences, rap has relatively little melodic content. Indeed, many rap songs use almost identical musical and instrumental elements - sometimes even literally identical elements. Rap recordings often copy pieces of instrumental backgrounds from other recordings through a technique known as "sampling." Rap's most important element is its words. It is as much a form of language as a form of music.

15. 본문 내용과 일치하지 않는 것을 고르시오.

① Rap caused anger among its singers.

② Rap recordings often borrow melodic content from other recordings.

③ Rap's words are more important than its melody.

④ Rap is one form of African-American music.

⑤ one of rap's common techniques is sampling.

16.

The modern mall is the direct descendant of an earlier retail innovation, the automobile-oriented shopping center, which strove to combine a number of different shops in a single structure, with parking for customers. The first modern shopping center, the Country Club Plaza, opened in Kansas City in 1924. By the mid-1950s, shopping centers - ranging from small "strips" to large integrated complexes - had proliferated throughout the country and were challenging traditional downtown shopping districts, which suffered from lack of parking and from the movement of middle-class residents to the suburbs.

16. 본문 내용과 일치하지 않는 것을 고르시오.

① The middle-class people moved to the suburbs.

② The traditional downtown shopping centers were not convenient for the driving shoppers.

③ The modern malls were competing with the traditional shopping centers.

④ The modern mall had increased slowly throughout the country.

⑤ The traditional shopping centers had not enough parking lots.

17.

In the Middle Ages the inn was supplemented to some extent by the monastic houses, but these, as a rule, entertained only two classes, the very rich and the very poor. The first were received by the monks because they did not dare to refuse them, but many were their complaints regarding the excesses of their unwelcome guests. The monastery door, however, was always open to the poor man, who was never turned empty away.

The inns were used by the people between these two extremes, for they were too miserable for the nobility, and too expensive for the poor. They were frequented by the smaller gentry, merchants, packmen, and other traders. The entertainment was poor enough; a number of beds were spread out in one room on the floor, and each guest bought what food he required.

17. According to the passage, which of the following is true?

① Merchants could afford to stay in an inn.

② The monastic houses had more guests than the inns.

③ The rich were very welcome guests at the monastic houses.

④ The poor could not stay in an inn because it was not open to them.

18.

The potlatch was a ceremonial distribution of property practiced by the indigenous communities of the Pacific Northwest in the United States and in the province of British Columbia in Canada. This custom, usually held in long houses or large outdoor areas, served as markers for certain social events such as the birth of a new child, the marriage of a young couple, or a successful hunting season. It could be used to commemorate the transfer of ownership or serve as a record of payment in lieu of written records in addition to providing a public display of military alliances or familial bonds. The primary purpose of the potlatch, however, was to provide a means to re-distribute wealth among the tribe in an equitable and ethical manner, allowing the host to rid himself of the spiritual burden that he felt as the sole owner of material items in an essentially communal environment.

18. 본문 중에서 potlatch의 이유로 언급되지 않은 것을 고르시오.

① It honored relationships between different social units.

② It was held to celebrate major events in people's lives.

③ It made it mandatory for the wealthy to distribute their valuables.

④ It served as public notice of a change in proprietorship.

⑤ It displayed social bonds publically.

19.

Everything about Titanic was as epic as the original ship. To begin with, the budget - the largest of any movie, at the time. What did writer/director James Cameron do with $200 million? First, he took 11 deep-sea expeditions down to the original wreck. Next, he assembled an all-star cast led by Leonardo DiCaprio and Kate Winslet, and put them in a 17 million gallon water tank. Above deck a sumptuous set was built, meticulously modeled after the Titanic's original blueprints, down to the grand staircase and the logo on the china. Was it money well spent? Shooting Titanic was notoriously rough sailing, but it was a critical hit that won the 11 Oscars it was up for, including Best Picture and Best Director. It also made boatloads of money, the first film to hit the billion dollar mark at the box office.

19. Choose the one that is mentioned in the passage.

① the dangers involved in sailing the Titanic

② the location of the original Titanic wreck

③ James Cameron's scrupulous attention to detail

④ how well Titanic did in DVD sales worldwide

20.

For twenty-three years, thousands of Maryland families and visitors have gathered at the Chesapeake Bay Bridge to join in an annual rite of spring. For one day only - this year, May 4th - the eastbound span of the bridge is open solely to pedestrians, allowing walkers of all ages to stroll for 4.3 magnificent miles. The scenic walk takes about an hour and a half, but most families make a day of it, taking time out for a picnic on the bridge to watch the boats float by. Pedestrians can start their trek between 9 A.M. and 2 P.M. Baby strollers are welcome, but please leave your pets and in-line skates at home. Although the walk is free, the Transportation Authority requests a $1 donation per person to cover the cost of the shuttle buses that bring families back to their starting point.

20. Which is NOT true about 'Bay Waling' according to the passage?

① People are allowed to take pets while walking.

② People participate in walking only for one day a year.

③ Shuttle buses are provided by the Transportation Authority.

④ Walking can begin in the morning and may take more than an hour.

21.

I had initially intended this to be an analysis of the styles of each of the participants individually, but the conversation itself made this impossible. It turned out that the non-New York participants had perceived the conversation to be "New York" in character, and they had felt out of their element. Because the New Yorkers present tended to expect shorter pauses between speakers' turns at talk, the non-New Yorkers had a harder time saying something before a faster speaker had begun to talk. Furthermore, because the New Yorkers had different ideas about how talk proceeded from topic to topic, the non-New Yorkers were often puzzled about what would be an appropriate comment, or what was appropriate about others' comments. Therefore, this book ended up as a study of one style, what I call a "high-involvement" style, which tended to characterize the speakers from New York, in contrast to the style of the non-New Yorkers, which I call "high-considerateness." (Bear in mind, again, that although aspects of the participants' styles justify grouping them in this way, each speaker's style is unique: there are many New Yorkers whose styles are very different from those of the speakers in this study, and there are many people, not from New York, whose styles are similar to that of these New Yorkers.)

21. Which of the following is a true description of the New Yorkers according to the passage?

① They began to talk more quickly than the non-New Yorkers did.

② They interrupted others less often than the non-New Yorkers did.

③ They did not express their disagreement as often as the non-New Yorkers did.

④ They had more difficulties in starting a new topic than the non-New Yorkers did.

정답과 해설 p.228 ~

UNIT 2 추론 (inferred / cannot be inferred)

- 일치/불일치, 추론 문제, 지칭 추론 문제 접근법

일치/불일치 유형, 추론 유형의 핵심은 글의 주제를 먼저 생각하면서 접근하는 것이다.
글의 큰 내용을 보면서 먼저 답을 찾아주는 것이 중요하다.

❶ 주제와 밀접한 연관이 있는 유형

일치/불일치, 추론 문제이지만 이 유형같은 경우는 주제와 밀접한 연관이 있는 내용을 일치/불일치 문제로 출제를 하게 된다. 이런 유형에선 일치하는 문제, 즉 True를 물어보는 문제라면 주제와 부합하는 선지가 정답이 되는 경우가 많고 나머지 선지들은 지문과 반대되는 형식으로 많이 나온다. 반대로 Not True 문제의 경우는 나머지가 주제와 같은 내용이고 정답이 되는 선지만 주제와 반대되는 경우로 많이 출제가 된다.

❷ 하나하나 찾는 유형

찾을 때도 그냥 찾는 것이 중요한게 아니라 선지의 소재간의 관계를 보는 눈이 중요하다. 가령 선지에 A 때문에 B가 된다 라고 써있을 때, 지문에 A 얘기도 써있고 B 얘기도 써있지만 A와 B는 인과관계가 아니어서 불일치인 경우가 있다. 따라서 이 부분부터 접근할 필요가 있다. 이걸로도 안된다면 이제 인물, 상황, 집단, 숫자, 비교급 등으로 찾아야 한다.

- 세부적인 선지의 출제 방식

❶ 일치, 추론 문제에서

① 정답이 되는 선지가 주제, 나머지 선지가 주제랑 반대

② 정답이 되는 선지가 주제, 나머지 선지는 찾는 유형

③ 정답이 되는 선지가 찾는 유형, 나머지가 주제와 반대 or 찾는 유형

④ 모두 찾는 유형

❷ 불일치, 추론할 수 없는 것을 묻는 문제에서

① 정답이 되는 선지가 주제와 반대, 나머지 선지가 주제

② 정답이 되는 선지가 주제와 반대, 나머지 선지가 찾는 유형

③ 정답이 되는 선지가 찾는 유형, 나머지 선지가 주제, or 찾는 유형

④ 모두 찾는 유형

- 연습 문제

1.

The presence and operation of the <u>binary code</u> in a modern computer are not apparent to the user. Personal computers may be used for a variety of functions - playing music, editing photos, writing documents, or performing financial accounting. The user performs each of these activities by entering unrelated commands into different software programs. Yet, each of these applications uses the same components in the computer to perform its functions. In order to achieve this, the functions of each program must be converted to the binary code used by the computer's processor, memory, and storage hardware.

1. 본문을 통해 binary codes에 대해 바르게 유추한 것을 고르시오.

① The conversion of commands into binary code is not visible to a computer user.

② The functions behind commands in different applications are actually quite similar.

③ Central processing units and storage components perform similar functions.

④ Applications would perform more effectively if the user entered binary code.

⑤ The similar coding system is a key for consistent performance.

2.

Several states in America are converting one lane of some of the nation's busiest highways into a toll lane. These pay-as-you-go routes allow drivers to buy their way out of traffic jams and sail past nonpaying motorists stuck in congestion. Some states are allowing private companies to build the new toll lanes in exchange for the revenue generated from them. Other states are simply designating existing lanes as toll lanes. However, many people consider this trend unfair. Several driver advocacy groups claim that tolls amount to yet another tax on people who have no choice but to drive. As AAA spokesperson Mantill Willians put it, "Our overall philosophy is tolls are a regressive tax on motorists." Others have dubbed the new routes "Lexus Lanes" and criticize them as a luxury for only those who can afford to pay. Advocates of toll lanes, however, say that they are just like any other convenience that some people choose to pay for and some people don't. "It offers a model of personal choice for drivers," says John Horsley of the American Association of State Highway and Transportation Officials. "If you're willing to pay a bit more, you can get there faster."

2. What is implied by "Lexus Lanes"?

① Toll lanes are for the rich only.

② Toll lanes have been funded by Lexus.

③ The term "Lexus Lanes" was coined by AAA.

④ Only those who own a Lexus can use toll lanes.

3.

When we consider what, to use the words of the catechism, is the chief end of man, and what are the true necessaries and means of life, it appears as if men had deliberately chosen the common mode of living because they preferred it to any other. Yet they honestly think there is no choice left. But alert and healthy natures remember that the sun rose clear. It is never too late to give up our prejudices. No way of thinking or doing, however ancient, can be trusted without proof. What everybody echoes or in silence passes by as true today may turn out to be falsehood tomorrow, mere smoke of opinion, which some had trusted for a cloud that would sprinkle fertilizing rain on their fields. What old people say you cannot do you try and find that you can. Old deeds for old people, and new deeds for new. Old people did not know enough once, perchance, to fetch fresh fuel to keep the fire a-going; new people put a little dry wood under a pot, and are whirled round the globe with the speed of birds, in a way to kill old people, as the phrase is. Age is no better, hardly so well, qualified for an instructor as youth, for it has not profited so much as it has lost. One may almost doubt if the wisest man has learned any thing of absolute value by living. Practically, the old have no very important advice to give the young, their own experience has been so partial, and their lives have been such miserable failures, for private reasons, as they must believe; and it may be that they have some faith left which belies that experience, and they are only less young than they were.

3. What does the underlined "our prejudices" imply?

① We are born free.

② We follow the law of nature.

③ We have no future.

④ We have no choice but to live this way.

⑤ We can do whatever we can.

4.

Consider the balance that we are told needs to be struck between security and civil liberties. In the abstract, there is some truth in this claim. But in some specific policy areas, the right balance might mean tilting the scales entirely to one side. There is, for instance, arguably no balance that needs to be struck between incarcerating people without trial for years on end and national security; the former just should not happen. No balancing is required when the scales come firmly down on one side.

4. What can be most likely inferred from the above passage?

① One set of concerns just overrides the other.

② Poverty with security is better than plenty in the midst of uncertainty.

③ The ground of liberty must be gained by inches.

④ Just scales and full measure injure no man.

⑤ Truth finds no asylum.

5.

Most obviously, cheaper energy prices will incrementally increase the temptation to fritter away precious power - to leave the car engine idling , or to fail to go upstairs to switch off that light. Little habits matter, because, with the clock ticking remorselessly down towards climate catastrophe, every little hurts. How much damage the great oil crash will do here depends on what happens next. In the past, the world has been stunned not only by the waning but also the waxing of the price. If what comes down soon goes back up, such direct effects may not prove so profound. What will matter more in the longer term is the dynamic effect on the energy infrastructure.

5. What can be most likely inferred from the above passage?

① Cheap oil will discourage investment in alternative energy.

② High energy prices will help to push inflation lower.

③ Manufacturers of electric cars will expand their production lines.

④ Oil-exporters will be the obvious winners from sliding oil prices.

⑤ The most exploitative schemes to extract fossil fuels will become more economic.

6.

All science is subject to human bias. This is especially true for social scientists. Since human behavior is their area of study, they are actually part of the subject matter. Furthermore, human behavior patterns vary from one place to another and from one group to another. This is in contrast to the subject matter of the natural sciences. When a chemist studies hydrogen, he can assume that one hydrogen atom is very much like another, wherever it is found, and that the conditions surrounding it can be quite accurately controlled. The same is true when a physicist measures a metal bar; he can be quite sure that it will not stretch or shrink in length as long as natural conditions are the same. This is why Earl Babbie quotes economist Daniel Suits, who calls the natural sciences the "easy sciences" because of the predictable nature of their subject matter.

6. What can be most likely inferred from the above passage?

① Human bias is the subject matter that social scientists mainly study.

② The conditions surrounding human behavior can be accurately controlled.

③ Social sciences may be called hard because of their stubborn subject matter.

④ Daniel Suits is quoted to support that natural sciences are subject to bias.

⑤ A metal bar may change in length according to natural conditions.

7.

A smartphone app will soon serve as an official driver's license for many people in Iowa, USA. "We are really moving forward on this," Paul Trombino, director of the state's Department of Transportation, announced during an agency budget hearing this week. "The way things are going, we may be the first in the nation." The new license will be accepted by police during traffic stops as well as at the state's airports. "It is basically your license on your phone," he said, according to the newspaper. A pin number will be needed for verification, making it secure. Iowans will still have the option of keeping their traditional licenses. The new app license will be available in 2015 at no additional cost to drivers.

7. What can be most likely inferred from the above passage?

① The app license costs drivers a registration fee.

② The new license on the phone is vulnerable to identification theft.

③ The Iowa state government actively makes use of new technologies.

④ People in Iowa are required to carry a traditional license in the state airport

8.

While comparing economic date, a group of sociologists concluded that, among all people at a certain income level, individuals in rural areas have greater purchasing power than those living in urban or suburban regions. The group factored in several data points, including the population density within a certain radius of city centers, the number of people per household, and the percentage of those households that included two working parents. Ultimately, However, the main premise was that the money spent by urban and suburban dwellers on their fundamental need for food and shelter could be spent by rural households on discretionary items.

8. Which of the following can be inferred from the passage?

① Suburban households have more purchasing power than urban households.

② The father away from a city center, the less purchasing power a rural household has.

③ The average urban or suburban household contains fewer people than the average rural household.

④ Rural households spend less on food and housing than either urban or suburban households do.

9.

The ultimate failure Bohr and Einstein to continue their dialogues together symbolizes the degree of fragmentation that exists in the field of physics today. Despite their close friendship and the energy they brought to their encounters, the two men eventually reached the point where they had nothing more to say to each other. This break in communication was a result of the different incompatible ways in which the informal language of physics was being used. Each protagonist was using certain terms in particular ways and laying stress on different aspects of the interpretation. A deeper analysis of this whole question shows that what was really at issue was the different notions of order involved. Bohr and Einstein both held to subtly different ideas of what the order of physics, and of nature, should be and this led to an essential break in their dialogue, a break which is reflected in the distance that lies between relativity and quantum theory today. In particular, Bohr believed that the order of movement of a particle would admit ambiguity while Einstein felt that such a possibility was too absurd to contemplate. The source of this failure in communication between the two giants of modern physics therefore lay in their incompatible notions of order.

9. What can be inferred from the passage?

① Einstein's relativity theory and Bohr's quantum theory can be seen as two different interpretations of order.

② The break in communication between the two scientists was due to the different orders contained in their theories

③ Today it is generally acknowledged that science may not be the proper tool with which we can grasp reality

④ Bohr and Einstein were fundamentally different in their methods of physics research.

10.

In the Philippines, television has become all things to all people: friend, teacher, lover, mother. With the decline in local movie production, viewers now have the biggest stars of Philippine cinema in their homes every single day. The two largest TV networks now advertise themselves as kapuso(of the same heart) and kapamilya(member of the family), underscoring their intimate personal relationships with the viewers. News anchors don't just read the day's news, they also blast erring government officials, often without benefit of any investigation. They host public-service programs that provide everything from medical assistance to scholarships to karaoke machines(apparently a basic necessity)

In a country where about half of the population lives in poverty, TV is the easiest avenue of escape. Not only does it offer variety shows, soap operas and superhero fantasies, but it also gives away millions of cash in game shows and contests. Of course, the ultimate escape is via the new "American Idol" type shows, in which viewers pick the winner by text-message voting, This is democracy in action: unfiltered and instantaneous.

10. Which is implied by the underlined part?

① reliable excuse

② final destination

③ safe fire exit

④ becoming rich

11.

Writing helps us to record and communicate ideas. It is a definitive and essential part of daily human experience. Whether we write a shopping list or a great novel, we use a tool without which we would find ourselves isolated. Without writing we cut ourselves off from vital processes like the expression of political opinions, the description of medical emergencies, and the examination of our feelings in diaries and letters.

Writing crosses many cultures. Whether we consider historic cave drawings or the transmission of fax messages after the World Trade Center disaster, we find evidence of the human instinct to communicate to other people.

In the past, writing brought about change. African American slaves were frequently forbidden to learn to read or write, but some managed to find ways to gain literacy anyway. Their narratives of slave life helped fire the abolition movement. Women in the nineteenth century used writing to advance the cause of suffrage, winning votes with passionate speeches and articles in newspaper. Immigrants struggled to learn English in order to find a better life in the New World.

11. 위의 글이 제시하거나 암시하는 내용과 일치하는 것을 고르시오.

① As we write something, we usually stay alone, separated from others.

② Before the abolition of slavery, none of African Americans could read or write

③ While drawings are universal communication tools across various cultures,
writing is confined in a certain culture.

④ Women were not allowed to vote before the 19th century

⑤ To write a brief note or long prose, we need a tool.

12.

The guard's reluctance to let the foreigner continue on is understandable. Other than a handful of scientists bound for the government-run observatory in Hanie, most Westerners have been denied access since the end of the Chinese-Indian war of 1962. Fearing that spies from China might slip over the border into Hanie, which sits just 12 miles from the disputed frontier, the Indian government declared the area off-limits.

12. 위의 글이 제시하거나 암시하는 내용과 일치하지 않는 것을 고르시오.

① Hanie belongs to the Indian territory

② Hanie is located near the borderline.

③ People in Hanie do not like Chinese people.

④ There are a lot of Westerners staying in Hanie

⑤ There is a government-run observatory in Hanie

13.

The subway system's famous announcement, "Stand clear of the closing doors, please," could be approaching the end of the line. The Metropolitan Transportation Authority(MTA) is starting to replace its familiar warning to straphangers with the tighter phrase "Please stand clear" on the No. 2 train to see if brevity will speed rail traffic, according to an MTA spokesperson. The four-word difference between "Stand clear of the closing doors, please" and the new "Please stand clear" announcement saves about one second. When combined with other announcements that also will be edited down, trains could get moving about three to four seconds faster. The new words may soon spread to other subway lines.

While many New Yorkers will miss hearing "Stand clear of the closing doors, please" in the instant before the doors shut and the train moves on, the man who speaks those words is philosophical about the change. "What an incredible run I've had in New York City," said Bloomberg Radio reporter Charlie Pellett, who recorded the announcement in 2001. "Broadway shows don't last that long." He said that although the announcement is one of the most famous catchphrases in New York City, he wasn't paid for the recording. "If I made a penny for every announcement, I could retire," Pellett joked.

13. Which is implied or stated in the passage?

① The new announcement is now heard on all the subway lines

② Charlie Pellett has been paid for every announcement

③ The MTA hopes the new, shorter message decreases dwell times at stations

④ Straphangers in New York City need more instruction to get a train quicker

⑤ Transit riders got tired of the old announcement, which caused its change.

14.

The sacrosanct status of unfettered sovereignty is being increasingly questioned. Part of the assault has come from the traditional critics of sovereignty; for instance, opponents of war argue that armed conflict is an integral, inevitable, and regrettable consequence of a world in which sovereignty reigns. From this view, dismantling sovereignty is the necessary prerequisite for world peace. At the same time, the rise of other concerns such as human rights collides with state sovereignty. Why? Because a major historical justification for mistreatment of individuals and groups within states is that sovereign states possess absolute authority over their citizens, and that how states act within their sovereign jurisdiction is strictly their own business.

14. 주어진 글의 내용과 가장 거리가 먼 것을 고르시오.

① Opponents of war point to the link between armed conflict and sovereignty

② Conflict may sometimes arise between human rights and state sovereignty

③ Critics of sovereignty argue that world peace can better be promoted by the abolition of sovereignty.

④ The author suggests that a sovereign state should posses an unfettered license to limit its citizen's rights.

15.

In any given society, the transmission of privilege is "mis-recognized." Individuals tend to see their society's social arrangements as legitimate. Status, privilege, and similar social rewards allegedly are "earned" by individuals; that is, they are perceived as resulting from intelligence, talent, effort, and other strategically displayed skills. Pierre Bourdieu makes clear that individuals' social position is not the result of personal attributes such as effort or intelligence. In particular, he argues that individuals in privileged social locations are advantaged in ways that are not a result of the intrinsic merit of their cultural experiences. Rather, cultural training in the home is awarded unequal value in dominant institutions because of the close compatibility between the standards of child rearing in privileged homes and the standards proposed by these institutions.

15. 주어진 글의 내용과 가장 거리가 먼 것을 고르시오.

① Individuals tend to wrongly accept their social position as legitimate

② Bourdieu sees a pattern of domination and inequality at the heart of social structure.

③ Bourdieu points to the close relationship between cultural training in the home and dominant institutions, in the case of children in privileged homes.

④ Bourdieu argues that individuals' social locations result from their intelligence, talent and effort.

16.

Modernization is clearly not an unambiguous boon from every reasonable perspective, even when it is successful in the narrow sense that its objectives are fulfilled without unanticipated, unintended, or unwelcome consequences. No one celebrates when tyrants modernize their repressive apparatuses or their military capabilities; even the successful modernization of entirely civilian activities can prove to be a wasteful dead end, having to be replaced by other modernizations that may prove more durable platforms for sustained development. Although modernization has been hugely attractive to policy-makers at various times, it has not always been viewed as a trump card, and other rhetorical justifications have been used for a wide range of reforms.

16. 주어진 글의 내용과 가장 거리가 먼 것을 고르시오.

① Modernization reforms have often resulted in some kind of unintended or unanticipated consequences.

② Modernization is a one-way road to disappointment, failure, and unhappy surprise.

③ Sometimes, a once successful modernization needs to be replaced by more durable reform

④ Tyrants' repressive apparatuses and their military capabilities may be unwelcome consequences of modernization.

17.

A very different conception of order emerges from the writings of socialists and anarchists. Anarchists, for instance, advocate the abolition of the state and all forms of political authority, including, of course, the machinery of law and order. Marxist socialists have also sympathized with this utopian vision. Marx himself believed that the state — and with it law and other forms of social control — would gradually "wither away" once social inequality was abolished. Parliamentary socialists and modern liberals have made more modest proposals, but they have nevertheless been critical of the belief that order can only be maintained by strict laws and stiff penalties. Although such views are critical of the conventional notion of "law and order," they do not amount to an outright rejection of "order" itself. Rather, they are based upon the alternative belief that social order can take the form of spontaneous harmony, regulated only by the natural good sense of individuals themselves.

17. 주어진 글의 내용과 가장 거리가 먼 것을 고르시오.

① Marxists sympathize with arguments of anarchists on the concept of social order.

② Anarchists advocate that all forms of political authority should be abolished to solve the problem of social inequality.

③ Socialists are critical of the belief that social order can more easily be maintained in a society which encourages spontaneous harmony by individuals.

④ Anarchists and Marxists have more radical views on the conception of order than parliamentary socialists and modern liberals.

18.

Pulling into my service station 45 minutes late one morning, I shouted to the customers, "I'll turn the gas pumps on right away!" What I didn't know was that the night crew had left them on all night. This means that any car could have been filled up for free. By the time I got to the office, most of the cars had filled up and driven off. Only one customer stayed to pay. My heart sank. Then the customer pulled a bunch of cash from his pocket and handed it to me. "We kept passing the money to the last guy," he said. "We figured you'd get here sooner or later.

18. Which of the following can be inferred from the passage?

① The gas pumps had been broken overnight

② The customers were as honest as the author

③ The last customer paid his own money for the gas taken by other customers

④ Once the gas pumps are on, any car can be for free filled up.

⑤ The author was paid for the gas with which some of the cars had been filled up.

19.

The normative position of the liberal paradigm follows straightforwardly from its explanatory theories. Liberals reject the realist notion that progress in international affairs is impossible. They argue that collaboration can make all participants better off and that it should therefore be a priority in international affairs. Much of the substantive discussion of issues in contemporary international politics concerns the perceived need for states to work together to solve problems. In security, economic, health, and environmental affairs, much of the discussion concerns what international collaboration should look like and how best to promote it.

19. 다음 글을 바탕으로 유추할 때 적절하지 않은 것을 고르시오.

① Liberals suggest that progress in international politics is possible

② Liberals argue that collaboration should be a priority in international affairs

③ Liberals provide a much less pessimistic outlook on international affairs than do the realists

④ Liberal believe that the basic characteristics of international relationships have not changed over the many past years.

20.

In reality, each generation starts its life in the traditional settings the past has left to it, and, however much it strives to fashion these settings in its own image, it will never succeed, even by the end of its life, in completely modernizing them. Sites, therefore, are in the main architectural settings inherited from the past, which, whether we like it or not, we must accept as existent factors and develop in our turn. Hence any human settlement necessarily means coexistence between past and future and this coexistence, which will vary according to date and location, will invariably reflect, within a site, the latter's personality as geographically, socially and historically determined. The most outstanding features of this personality will be embodied in the historical monuments of the place, which are thus an integral part of that structure in space which reaches from the past towards the future, and as such must be preserved and survive together with it.

20. 다음 글을 바탕으로 유추할 때 적절하지 않은 것을 고르시오.

① We need to protect monuments by seeking the means of revitalizing them.

② It is impossible to modernize the architectural settings from the past completely.

③ Historical monuments should be treated as an encumbrance to progress.

④ A contemporary community is recognized to be the continuous coexistence of past and present

UNIT 3 지칭 추론

지칭 추론 유형은 밑줄 친 부분이 무엇을 나타내는지를 찾는 문제이다. 여기에는 크게 2가지 유형이 있다.

❶ 밑줄 친 부분의 의미를 찾는 유형

밑줄 친 부분의 내용을 추론하는 유형이다. 밑줄 친 부분을 기준으로 앞 뒤 문장의 소재와 내용을 그대로 이어주거나 반대로 뒤집어준다고 생각을 하면서 보는 것이 좋다. 밑줄 친 말의 해석과 의미에 집착하기 보단 그 앞과 뒤의 내용에 나오는 소재와 내용으로 근거를 잡는다는 사실을 기억하자!

• 문제 유형

Which of the following does the underlined Ⓐ__ refer to?

Which is closest in meaning to the underlined Ⓐ__ ?

❷ 가리키는 대상이 다른 하나를 찾는 유형

이 유형은 다섯 개의 밑줄이 지문에 있고 밑줄 친 것들 중 다른 것을 지칭하는 명사를 하나 찾아내는 유형이다. 각각의 밑줄이 어떤 것을 나타내는지 확실하게 잡아가면서 푸는 것이 중요하다.

• 문제 유형

Which of the following does not refer to the same?

√ 풀이의 핵심

밑줄 친 부분의 내용을 추론하는 유형이다. 밑줄 친 부분을 기준으로 앞 뒤 문장의 소재와 내용을 그대로 이어주거나 반대로 뒤집어준다고 생각을 하면서 보는 것이 좋다. 밑줄 친 말의 해석과 의미에 집착하기 보단 그 앞과 뒤의 내용에 나오는 소재와 내용으로 근거를 잡는다는 사실을 기억하자! 그걸로 안된다면 그 지문의 주제, 핵심소재를 가지고 답을 찍겠다고 생각하면 된다.

- 연습 문제

1.

Before the American Revolution most people in the British North American Colonies considered Ⓐ themselves loyal subjects of the British Crown, with the same rights and obligations as people in Britain. However, under the doctrine of mercantilism the British considered the Colonies more as a resource to be utilized for the benefit of Ⓑ their own economy and had little respect for the Colonialists. The difference in perception led to a vicious circle of Colonialists acting against what Ⓒ they saw as unfair policies, harsh British reaction, followed by stronger Colonial reaction, leading to even harsher British reaction — all of this spiraling into the revolution. As the Colonialists started rejecting the Crown, Ⓓ they also started becoming more radicalized in other ways, paying more attention to the idea of broad democracy.

1. 위의 Ⓐ~Ⓓ 중 의미가 다른 것을 고르시오.

① Ⓐ themselves　　② Ⓑ their

③ Ⓒ they　　④ Ⓓ they

2.

The heroine of the novel, Isobel, has spent the last ten years nursing her disabled father, whose Catholic funeral takes place at the beginning of the book. Ⓐ Her only rival was Margaret, their former housekeeper, who had hoped to become her father's wife. But Isobel, detecting her designs, had persuaded Ⓑ her father to dismiss Ⓒ her and had thus become the victor. After her father's burial, Isobel at first appears to be serene: she buys herself some clothes, sells the family home, and enters into a passionate liaison with a married man. But her newfound happiness is shattered by a sudden tirade from her lover's wife. Baffled by grief, the only penitence Isobel can imagine for Ⓓ her crimes is to devote herself to the repulsive Margaret.

2. 위의 Ⓐ~Ⓓ 중 의미가 다른 것을 고르시오.

① Ⓐ　　② Ⓑ

③ Ⓒ　　④ Ⓓ

3.

In travelling by land there is a continuity of scene and a connected succession of persons and incidents, that carry on the story of life, and lessen the effect of absence and separation. We drag, it is true, "a lengthening chain," at each movement of our pilgrimage; but the chain is unbroken: we can trace it back link by link; and we feel that Ⓐ the last still grapples us to home. But a wide sea voyage severs us at once. It makes us conscious of being cast loose from the secure anchorage of settled life, and sent adrift upon a doubtful world. It interposes a gulf, not merely imaginary, but real, between us and our homes — a gulf subject to tempest, and fear, and uncertainty, rendering distance palpable, and return precarious.

3. Which of the following does the underlined Ⓐ the last refer to?

① the last story

② the last chain

③ the last world

④ the last person

4.

What is the insight in which the scientist tries to see into nature? Can it indeed be called either imaginative or creative? To the literary man the question may seem merely silly. He has been taught that science is a large collection of facts; and if this is true, then the only seeing which scientists need to do is, he supposes, seeing the facts. He pictures them, the colorless professionals of science, going off to work in the morning into the university in a neutral, unexposed state. Ⓐ They then expose themselves like a photographic plate. And then in the dark room or laboratory they develop the image, so that suddenly and startingly it appears, printed in capital letters, as a new formula for atomic energy.

4. Which of the following does the underlined Ⓐ They refer to?

① literary men

② professors

③ scientists

④ photographers.

5.

Young potential leaders should gain exceptional command, in both writing and speaking, of their own language. In addition, they should have workable knowledge of a second language. Leadership requires strong public speaking skills. Courses in public speaking do not enjoy high status in the academic world today; moreover, many bright young people are poor speakers, and they must develop their ability in <u>this area</u>.

5. 밑줄 친 this area와 부합하는 것은?

① a second language

② leadership

③ public speaking

④ high status

⑤ the academic world

6.

When I was 25, I attended a youth conference in the summer of 2008. I thought it would just be a refreshing weekend in the city. On the first day, I was a little nervous when the youth group went swimming. A burst appendix four years earlier had left me with a 12cm scar on my abdomen and I couldn't stand people staring at me and wondering what had happened. This was made worse knowing that a guy I'd met might see it.

Little did I know that he was nervous about swimming too. When he was 17 he had a serious car accident and was left with a 15cm scar on his abdomen. Talk about an icebreaker. Almost identical scars and so much in common, Ⓐ <u>it was meant to be.</u> We have just celebrated our sixth wedding anniversary.

6. Which is closest in meaning to the underlined Ⓐ it was meant to be?

① we felt as if we were twins

② it did mean a lot to both of us

③ we were destined to get married to each other

④ we could understand each other even without words

7

Those who are regarded as inferior elements of society may play an important role in the shaping of history. Their importance lies in the readiness with which Ⓐ <u>they</u> are collectively swayed in any direction. Ⓑ <u>They</u> can be easily persuaded to take risks and to plunge into some united action.

7. Choose the one that is closest in meaning the the underlined parts Ⓐ they and Ⓑ they in common.

① historians

② social leaders

③ risk-takers

④ inferior people

8.

Science is often defined inadequately as an organized body of knowledge. This would make cook-books, catalogues, and telephone books science, Ⓐ <u>which</u> they are not. Sometimes science is defined simply as rationality, but that would make much of theology and metaphysics science, Ⓑ <u>which</u> they are not. Rationality is logical consistency, lack of contradiction. It is to be distinguished from reasonableness, the quality of a mind open to arguments and evidence opposed to its beliefs: a willingness to reconsider. Rationalists can be quite unreasonable or dogmatic.

8. Choose the one that is closest in meaning to the underlined parts Ⓐ which and Ⓑ which in common.

① science

② books

③ knowledge

④ rationality

9.

In a society that worships at the altar of supermodels like Claudia, Christy and Kate, white teenagers are obsessed with staying thin. But there's growing evidence that blacks and white girls view their bodies in dramatically different ways. The latest findings come in a study to be published in the journal Human Organization this spring by a team of black and white researchers at the University of Arizona. While 90 percent of the white junior-high and high-school girls studied voiced dissatisfaction with their weight, 70 percent of African-American teens were satisfied with their bodies.

In fact, even significantly overweight black teens described themselves as happy. That confidence may not carry over to other areas of black teens' lives, but the study suggests that, at least here, it's a lifelong source of pride. Asked to describe women as they age, two thirds of the black teens said they get more beautiful, and many cited their mothers as examples. White girls responded that their mothers may have been beautiful — back in their youth. Says anthropologist Mimi Nichter, one of the study's coauthors, Ⓐ "In white culture, the window of beauty is so small."

9. Which is the closest in meaning to the underlined Ⓐ "In white culture, the window of beauty is so small"?

① In general, black girls are slimmer than the whites

② The white people are less interested in their appearance than the black people.

③ White teens have more strict standards for the beauty

④ Most beautiful women are described as white girls

⑤ The black girls are perceived to be more beautiful than the white.

10.

Although it's been a long time, I vividly recall my reaction when I learned that I had been admitted to Amherst College: the admissions office must have made a terrible mistake. I had graduated from a Long Island high school where most students didn't go to college, so I was convinced that at Amherst I would be overmatched by my better-educated, more sophisticated classmates and sliced to ribbons by my brilliant professors. To my surprise, I fared well academically, but I never entirely got over the feeling of <u>being an imposter</u>. Only decades later, at a class reunion, did I discover that many of my peers had felt exactly the same way.

Regardless of their credentials, many freshmen doubt that they have the necessary brainpower or social adeptness to succeed in college. This fear of failing hits poor, minority and first-generation college students expecially hard. If they flunk an exam, or a professor doesn't call on then, their fears about whether they belong may well be confirmed. The cycle of doubt becomes self-reinforcing, and students are more likely to drop out.

10. What does the underlined 'being an imposter' imply?

① Receiving terrible grades

② Setting an unrealistic goal

③ Being admitted due to luck

④ Having disadvantaged backgrounds

11.

To explain how and in what way cuisines are different or similar, and how they change over time, I propose a theory called the "grammar of cuisine," which suggests that a cuisine is like a language. The metaphor comes from linguistic grammar. The grammar of English, for example, consists of implicit rules that specify that adjectives tend to come before nouns(we say "hot fudge," not "fudge hot"), or objects come after verbs("eat chocolate," not "chocolate eat"). A grammar defines how linguistic parts are structured into a linguistic whole.

Just as a language has an implicit grammar that native speakers know even if they can't explain, a cuisine has an implicit structure, a set of rules about which foods go together, what constitutes a "grammatical" dish or meal in that cuisine. This implicit structure of cuisine consists of rules about how dishes are structured out of ingredients, meals are structured out of dishes, and entire cuisines out of particular flavor combinations and required cooking techniques. Each of these kinds of structuring helps explain the nature of cuisines and their similarities and differences.

11. According to the passage, what does the underlined 'grammatical' imply?

① Delicious

② Linguistic

③ Appropriate

④ Classical

UNIT 4 주제 / 제목 / 요지

- 주제, 제목, 요지 유형 문제 해결 전략

❶ 첫 두 문장에서 소재 + 글의 구조에 대한 단서를 잡는다.
→ 글의 구조에 대한 단서가 보이지 않는다면 첫 두 문장의 소재가 핵심소재라고 생각한다.

❷ 지문을 읽어 내려가면서 글의 구조가 갑자기 바뀔 수 있는 Point를 찾는다.
→ 없으면 여전히 첫 두 문장의 소재를 핵심이라고 생각한다

❸ 주제문에 해당할 수 있는 표현을 본다면 그 부분이 첫 두 문장에 해당하는 얘기와 같은 얘기인지를 계속 확인해준다.

❹ 선지로 가기 전에 지문 전체의 핵심 소재를 잡는다.
* 정답엔 반드시 핵심소재가 들어가 있어야 한다.

- 주제문이 될 수 있는 표현 총정리

❶ 중간에 새로운 상황/시점, 인물 등이 등장할 때

❷ 중간에 문제점, 통념의 단서, 질문 등이 나올 때

❸ 1) that s v ~(완전한 문장)
2) 깔고가는 표현 ~~~ but ~~~(이 부분이 주제문)

√ 깔고가는 표현 총정리
① 물론(of course), 확실히(to be sure, surely, certainly), 명백히/분명히(obviously, clearly)
② S may/might S, S can/could V, S would V ~의 표현
③ 부정문, 가정법, 갑자기 나오는 반대집단, 가정법, at first, 갑자기 나오는 과거의 표현 등

- 연습 문제

1.

In travelling by land there is a continuity of scene and a connected succession of persons and incidents, that carry on the story of life, and lessen the effect of absence and separation. We drag, it is true, "a lengthening chain," at each movement of our pilgrimage; but the chain is unbroken: we can trace it back link by link; and we feel that the last still grapples us to home. But a wide sea voyage severs us at once. It makes us conscious of being cast loose from the secure anchorage of s settled life, and sent adrift upon a doubtful world. It interposes a gulf, not merely imaginary, but real, between us and our homs — a gulf subject to tempest, and fear, and uncertainty, rendering distance palpable, and return precarious.

1. Which of the following is the passage mainly about?

① merits of being settled
② drawbacks of travelling by land
③ the meaning of pilgrimage in one's life
④ the sense of uncertainty caused by a voyage

2.

An examination of our class structure reveals that gambling is more the concern of the lower and upper social classes than of the middle classes, and there is a very good reason for this if we accept it as an expression of a basic hunting drive. Work has become the major substitute for primitive hunting, but as such it has most benefited the middle classes. For the average lower-class male, the nature of the work he is required to do is poorly suited to the demands of the hunting drive. It is too repetitive, too predictable. It lacks the elements of challenge, luck and risk so essential to the hunting male. For this reason, lower-class males share with the (non-working) upper-class males a greater need to express their hunting urges than do the middle classes, the nature of whose work is much more suited to its role as a hunting substitute.

2. What is the passage mainly about?

① evolutionary view of social structure in human history
② common and distinct features of hunting and gambling
③ relationship between social stratification and the division of labor
④ reasons for levels of predisposition to gambling across social classes

3.

The accuracy and speed of real-time automatic translation is undoubtedly going to improve dramatically in the near future, but it is going to take much longer before this medium becomes globally widespread and economically accessible to all. This poses a threat to the current availability and appeal of a global language. All the evidence suggests that the position of English as a global language is going to become stronger. By the time automatic translation matures as a popular communicative medium, that position will very lively have become impregnable. It will be very interesting to see what happens then — whether the presence of a global language will eliminate the demand for world translation services, or whether the economics of automatic translation will so undercut the cost of global language learning that the latter will become obsolete.

3. What is the best title for the passage?

① What Are the Dangers of a Global Language?

② Why Computers Will Never Be a Smart Translator

③ The Battle Between Technology and Global Language

④ Automatic Translation and the End of Language Learning

4.

Art is much more than decoration, for it is laden with meaning, even if that content is sometimes shallow or obscure. Art enables us to communicate our understanding in ways that cannot be expressed otherwise. Truly a picture is worth a thousand words, not only in its descriptive value but also in its symbolic significance. In art, as in language, human being is above all an inventor of symbols to convey complex thoughts in new ways. We must think of art not in terms of everyday prose but as poetry, which is free to rearrange conventional vocabulary and syntax in order to convey new, often multiple meanings and moods. A painting likewise suggests much more than it states. Like a poem, the value of art lies equally in what it says and how it says it. It does so partly by implying meanings through allegory, pose, facial expression, and the like or by evoking them through the visual elements: line, form, color, and composition.

4. What is the main point of the passage?

① The ultimate value of art is the beauty of description

② Semantics take a priority over syntax in art appreciation.

③ Artwork resembles a personal essay rather than a complex poem.

④ As in poetry, representation is as important as meaning in art.

5.

Plant breeders who choose genetic engineering over traditional cross-breeding are able to get desired traits faster and with more consistency. The safety of genetically engineered foods, however, has been a critical issue in bringing these products to markets. Consumers who have food allergies are concerned that genetically altered foods will cause allergic reactions. For example, if a gene from a wheat plant is used to provide resistance to disease in corn plants, will a person who is allergic to wheat products have an allergic reaction after eating the genetically altered corn?

5. 다음 글의 주제로 가장 적절한 것은?

① Recent development of genetic engineering

② Advantages of genetic engineering technology

③ Potential danger of genetically altered foods

④ Conflicts between consumers and food market

⑤ Genetic similarities between wheat and corn

6.

When your paper is returned to you, spend time examining the comments your teacher made. This is a good time to compare your classmates' responses to your teacher's, taking into account the changes you made between the original draft and revised paper. Did you improve on the parts of your original paper that your classmates encouraged you to work on? Did your teacher comment on aspects of your paper that your classmates did not comment on? Share this information with the classmates you did peer-editing with. For each paper you looked at, compare the comments you made to the teacher's comments. Keep in mind the ideas you and your teacher had in common about each paper. Also notice comments that your teacher made that you missed. This is valuable information. You'll use it the next time you write and the next time you do peer-editing.

6. 위 글의 주제로 가장 적절한 것은?

① Advantages and disadvantages of peer feedback

② Several tips for efficient drafting and proofreading

③ Importance of sharing ideas in peer-editing projects

④ Using wisely teacher's and peer's feedback in writing

⑤ Why we should consider others' feeling in peer-editing

7.

In a fascinating experiment, researchers investigated the impact of photos on children's memories for events that had actually happened (true memories) and events that had never happened (false memories). In each of three interview sessions, 10-year-old children were shown a series of four photographs: three real photos provided by parents depicting events that occurred when the children were about 6 years old and one false photo (a photo of a hot air balloon). For half the children, the photo showed a group of unknown people in the balloon's basket (child-absent condition). For the other half, the photo had been doctored using Adobe Photoshop so that an image of the child along with some family members was inserted among other people in the basket (child-present condition). In reality, of course, none of the children had actually been in a hot balloon. The researchers found that almost all of the children reported memories for the events pictured in the real photos. More importantly, many of the children also reported memories of riding in the hot air balloon, whether their picture appeared in the photo or not. False memories occurred significantly more often, however, when children had seen themselves in the photo (about 47%) than when they had not (about 18%).

7. 위 글의 주제로 가장 적절한 것은?

① Riding in a Hot Air Balloon

② Memorizing Events in Photos

③ Interviewing Children with Photos

④ Creating False Memories in Children

⑤ Investigating Photos with Technologies

8.

Why don't we run out of oxygen to breathe or water to drink? Many organisms produce oxygen during a process called photosynthesis, which constantly replenishes the oxygen consumed by all aerobic organisms. The physical materials on which life depends are limited to what is presently on earth. Water, for example, is naturally recycled from the atmosphere to the surface of Earth, through food webs and back to the atmosphere. Nitrogen, carbon, and other essential substances are cycled in a similar manner. A natural resource that is replaced or recycled by natural processes is called a renewable resource. Other examples of renewable resources include plants, animals, food crops, sunlight, and soil.

8. 위 글의 제목으로 가장 적절한 것은?

① Limits of Natural Processes

② Preservation or Consumption

③ Recycling Natural Resources

④ What if Oxygen is Run Out

⑤ Substances Essential for Life

9.

A cork pops. The sudden change in pressure in the champagne bottle releases carbon dioxide. Bubbles form. Once in a glass, a million of them cling to its edges before rising to the top and bursting. The explosions release tiny droplets that dart across your tongue. Researchers follow carbon dioxide from where it first forms in harvested grapes until it bursts in your glass. Each bubble's spray has droplets full of intense aromas and flavors.

9. 윗글의 제목으로 가장 적절한 것은?

① The Way to Open a Champagne Bottle

② Preservation of Bubbles in Champagne

③ Process of Carbon Dioxide to Make Bubbles

④ Dynamic Nature of Bubbles in Champagne

⑤ Maximizing Aromas and Flavors of Bubbles

10.

'The Fourth Industrial Revolution.:__________'

This Revolution will change not only what we do but also who we are. It will affect our identity and all the issues associated with it: our sense of privacy, our notions of ownership, our consumption patterns, the time we devote to work and leisure, and how we develop our careers, cultivate our skills, meet people and nurture relationships. It is already changing our health and leading to a "quantified" self. The list is endless because it is bound only by our imagination. One of the greatest individual challenges posed by new information technologies is privacy. Debates about fundamental issues such as the impact on our inner lives of the loss of control over our data will only intensify in the years ahead. Similarly, the revolutions occurring in biotechnology and artificial intelligence (AI), which are redefining what it means to be human by pushing back the current thresholds of life span, health, cognition, and capabilities, will compel us to redefine our moral and ethical boundaries.

10. 윗글 'The Fourth Industrial Revolution'의 부제목으로 가장 적절한 것은?

① Its Impact on Human

② Toward a Quantified Self

③ New Information Technologies

④ Debates on Human Lives

⑤ Biotechnology and AI

11.

Within the set of gestures that accompany speech, we can distinguish between those that echo the content of the spoken message and those that indicate something being referred to. Iconics are gestures that seem to be a reflection of the meaning of what is said, as when we trace a square in the air with a finger while saying "I'm looking for a small box." By itself, an iconic gesture doesn't 'mean' the same as what is said, but it may add 'meaning.' For example, a woman was moving her forearm up and down, with a closed hand, as if holding a weapon, while she was saying, "I chased the dog again." The communicated message, including the weapon, was accomplished through speech and gesture combined. Another common group of gestures can be described as deictics. The term deictic' means 'pointing' and we often use gestures to point to things or people while talking. We can use deictics in the current context, as when we use a hand to indicate a table (with a cake on it) and ask someone, "Would you like some cake?" We can also use the same gesture and the same table (with a cake no longer on it) when we later say, "That cake was delicious." In this case, the gesture and the speech combine to accomplish successful reference to something that only exists in shared memory rather than in the current physical space.

11. Which is the best title of the passage?

① The Essence of Human Gestures

② Types of Gestures Used with Speech

③ The Role of Physical Space in Communication

④ The Ability of Humans to Talk about the Past

12.

The nature of time seems to be very tied up with the way we perceive it. The universe that we perceive is, in the most fundamental way, the creation of our sensory apparatus. When you touch a wooden table top with your fingertips you are actually 'feeling' the tiny repulsive forces of trillions and trillions of electrons; you are not actually 'touching' anything at all. When you 'see' objects you are simply making sense of reflected and emitted photons which your brain has, in a probably rather arbitrary and contingent way, evolved to interpret as light and dark, colours and so on. It is the same with time. The strange and elastic nature of perceived time is well illustrated by a quote from Albert Einstein: 'When a man sits with a pretty girl for an hour, it seems like a minute. But let him sit on a hot stove for a minute and it's longer than any hour. That's relativity'.

12. Which is the best title of the passage?

① From Nothing to Something

② Time Depends on the Way You Perceive It

③ What You Perceive Is What the Universe Is

④ The Development of Our Sensory Apparatus

⑤ Linear Notion of Time: A Single Path at a Time

13.

In 1986, musician Paul Simon befriended a homeless woman named Marie whom he saw every morning as he walked to his recording studio in New York City. Then one day, Marie wasn't there — and he had no way of finding out whether she was okay. He became interested in the problem of homelessness and met child advocate Irwin Redlener, a professor of pediatrics at Columbia University. Simon spent a day visiting homeless shelters with him, and didn't find Marie though they discovered another disturbing fact: "We saw what was essentially a warehouse for a thousand homeless kids and their families," Dr. Redlener remembers. "And nobody was paying attention to whether they were receiving even the most basic medical care." Together with Dr. Redlener's wife, Karen, they launched the Children's Health Fund in a "big blue bus" that housed a state-of-the-art mobile medical clinic. Today, the organization runs a network of 50 mobile health clinics, as well as more than 200 fixed-site health centers, in underserved, low-Income neighborhoods across the country, reaching more than 350,000 poor and homeless children to date.

13. Which is the best title of the passage?

① Establishing Children's Health Fund

② Proposing Laws for Homeless Families

③ Ways of Remodeling Homeless Shelters

④ Cause and Effect of Children in Poverty

⑤ Developing Medical Care through Mobile Clinics

14.

Occam's razor is based on the notion that simplicity equals perfection. It fits perfectly with the scientific method — the series of steps scientists take to prove or disprove something. Indeed, you could make the case that the scientific method was built upon Occam's razor. It serves as a heuristic device — a guide or a suggestion — that states that when given two explanations for the same thing, the simpler one is usually the correct one.

Here's a classic example of the use of Occam's razor. A pair of physicists — Lorentz and Einstein — both concluded mathematically that things tend to go a little unstable within the space-time continuum. For example, the closer we get to moving at the speed of light, the more we slow down. While both arrived at the same results from their equations, Einstein and Lorentz had different explanations for them. Lorentz said that it was because of changes that take place in "the ether." The problem is that science doesn't hold that "the ether" exists, thereby introducing a problematic element of the equation. Einstein's explanation used no references to the ether, and, therefore, his explanation eventually won out over Lorentz's.

14. Which is the best title of the passage?

① Perfection for Simplicity

② Einstein's Explanation vs. Lorentz's Explanation

③ The Base of Modern Science

④ Occam's Razor as a Scientific Method

⑤ The Importance of a Heuristic Device

15.

Professor Westbury has been doing important work, exploring the connections between language difficulties and brain function. As part of his inquiry, Westbury presents patients suffering from aphasia — whose comprehension of words and speech is often impaired — with a string of letters and asks whether or not it constitutes a real English word. One day, a graduate student pointed out something curious: certain nonsense words consistently made patients smile and sometimes even laugh out loud. "Particularly," Westbury says, "snunkoople." He started checking with friends and colleagues to see whether they had the same reaction, and the response was nearly unanimous. Snunkoople was funny. But why? Westbury presents what he believes could be the answer: the inherent funniness of a word, or at least of context-free non-words, can be quantified — and not an nonsense is created equal. According to Westbury, the less statistically likely it is for a certain collection of letters to form a real word in English, the funnier it is. The playwright Neil Simon seemed to grasp this implicitly in his 1972 work The Sunshine Boys, in which an old character tells his nephew, "If it doesn't have a 'k' in it, it's not funny!" — "k" being one of the least frequently used letters in the alphabet.

15. 위 글의 제목으로 가장 적절한 것은?

① Aphasia: The Way We Laugh

② Why Certain Words Are Funny

③ Humor as an Art of Equivocation

④ "Snunkoople." an Unusual Cluster of Letters

16.

Those firms and industries that are not participating in the world market have to recognize that in today's trade environment isolation has become impossible. Willing or unwilling, more and more firms are becoming participants in global business affairs. Even if not by choice, most firms and individuals are affected directly or indirectly by economic and political developments that occur in the international marketplace. Those firms that refuse to participate are relegated to reacting to the global marketplace and therefore are unprepared for harsh competition from abroad.

Some industries have recognized the need for international adjustments. Farmers understand the need for high productivity in light of stiff international competition. Computer makers and firms in other technologically advanced industries have learned to forge global relationships to stay in the race. Firms in the steel, textile, and leather sectors have shifted production, and perhaps even adjusted their core business, in response to overwhelming onslaughts from abroad. Other industries in some countries have been caught unaware and have been unable to adjust. The result is the extinction of firms or entire industries, such as VCRs in the United States and coal mining and steel smelting in other countries.

16. 위 글의 제목으로 가장 적절한 것은?

① Road Not Taken: Entrepreneurship in the Future

② New Challenges Looming over the Global Market

③ Different Players, Different Rules in the Business World

④ Two Faces of Global Business: A Dilemma of Being "Global/Local“

17.

The status of a character trait depends on the reference point. For instance, for an ape fingernails are considered primitive in relation to other primates because all other primates have fingernails. Thus, fingernails would not serve to distinguish apes from, for example, monkeys. Fingernails are a derived character for primates as a whole, however, because no other mammals have them. Thus, fingernails serve to distinguish primates from other mammals. The second character illustrated here — brow ridges — is found only in hominoids, not in other primates, and is therefore derived for hominoids. This character distinguishes apes from monkeys. In a chimpanzee, however, brow ridges would be considered to be primitive with respect to other hominoids; that is, the character would not distinguish a chimpanzee from, for example, a gorilla.

17. 위 글의 제목으로 가장 알맞은 것을 고르시오.

① Relative Status of Species

② Absolute Status of Species

③ Relative Status of Characters

④ Absolute Status of Characters

18.

There is a stark reality increasingly facing American orchestras: They are now charities, relying more, on average, on philanthropy than on the ticket sales that used to buttress them. While orchestras have always required subsidies — whether from monarchs, the church, governments or patrons — the balance has shifted to the point where they generally get more revenue from donations than from selling tickets, according to a report released Tuesday by the League of American Orchestras, an industry association. The report also found that orchestras had reached a tipping point in how they sell tickets: In 2013 for the first time, ensembles no longer earned a majority of their ticket revenue from the subscription packages they have depended on for decades. These changes have forced orchestras to change everything from how they organize their staffs to how they define their missions.

18. 위 글의 제목으로 가장 적절한 것은?

① American Orchestras' Subscription Package Sale on the Rise

② American Ensembles' Increasing Demand for Budget Cuts

③ The Debacle of Classical Music in the United States

④ American Orchestras and the Winds of Change

19.

Most industry discourse about convergence begins and ends with what I call the black box fallacy: sooner or later all media is going to be flowing through a single black box in our living rooms and all we have to do is to figure out which black box it will be. Media convergence is not an endpoint; rather, It is an ongoing process occuring at various intersections between media technologies, industries, content, and audiences. Thanks to the proliferation of channels and the increasingly ubiquitous nature of computing and telecommunications, we are entering an era where media will be everywhere and we will use all kinds of media in relation to each other.

Media convergence is more than simply a technological shift; it alters the relationship between existing technologies, industries, markets, genres, and audiences. This initial wave of media changes exerts a destabilizing influence, resulting in a series of lurches between exhilaration and panic. Yet, media convergence is also sparking creative innovation in almost every sector of popular culture; our present media environment is marked by a proliferation of differences.

19. What is the most appropriate title of the passage above?

① Black Box Fallacy: The Beginning and the Ending of Media Convergence

② Black Box Fallacy and the Technological Shift

③ Media Convergence and Its Destabilizing Influence

④ Media Convergence and the Changing Environment

⑤ The Intersections of Media and the Fallacy of Convergence

20.

Plants protect themselves from the ravages of herbivores by producing poisons. In the forests of Madagascar, for example, there is a type of bamboo that is highly toxic. The tips of its shoots contain cyanide in quantities that should deter even the most tolerant of vegetarians — about 1/500 oz for every pound of bamboo. Yet there is one animal that eats it — the golden bamboo lemur, one of three lemurs known to eat bamboo. The other two species, the grey gentle lemur and the greater bamboo lemur, feast on bamboo leaves and the thick bamboo trunks, leaving the poisonous shoots to the golden bamboo lemur. It eats and digests 17.5 lb of poisonous shoots per day — which is equivalent of 12 times the lethal dose for humans. How it manages to do this is something of a mystery, although there are some possible explanations. One is that the lemur has learned, probably by some process of trial and error, that by eating the iron-rich soil in its home range it can neutralise the poison. Irons in the soil combine with the cyanide to prevent the formation of the poison. Clay in the soil also acts much like kaolin in human medicine. It binds with substances in the gut to lessen their detrimental effects.

20. 윗글의 제목으로 가장 적합한 것을 고르시오.

① Potential Accounts of How Lemurs of Madagascar Take Cyanide arid Survive

② Protective Roles of Bamboo Poisons in Madagascar Forests

③ Discovery of Bamboo Shoots as Novel Natural Medicine for Humans

④ Mysterious Learning Patterns of Golden Bamboo Lemurs

PART 2
복잡한 유형 총정리

PART 2 복잡한 유형 총정리

UNIT 5 빈칸 유형

- 빈칸 추론 유형을 접근하는 방법

√ 빈칸 유형 풀이 핵심 Point!

❶ 빈칸이 있는 문장에 어떤 관계성이 있는지를 파악한다. (지문에서 뭘 찾을지를 정하기 위해)

- 빈칸이 원인 자리인지
- 빈칸이 결과 자리인지
- 빈칸과 반대될만한 요소가 있는지

❷ 빈칸 바로 앞 뒷 문장에서 관계성에 맞게 근거를 찾는다.

❸ 보이지 않을시 지문 전체를 보며 주제문에 해당하는 부분에서 빈칸의 근거를 찾는다.

❹ 근거를 찾았으면 빈칸을 주관식으로 만들어준다.

❺ 그 주관식 답을 기준으로 선지를 걸러낸다.

√ 선지 분석법

❶ 내가 잡은 주관식과 정반대 내용

→ 주관식으로 잡고 보면 선지에 내가 잡은 주관식과 반대 내용을 써둔 선지가 있다. 이를 반대선지라 한다.

❷ 내가 잡은 주관식과 아무 상관없는 내용

→ 내가 잡은 주관식과 아무 상관없는 내용의 선지가 있기도 하다. 주관식을 잡지 않으면 상식적이고 교훈적인 얘기가 있어서 헷갈릴 수 있지만 주관식을 잡을 수 있다면 아무렇지도 않게 걸러낼 수 있다.

❸ 역추론

→ 이래도 저래도 안되는 경우 빈칸에 헷갈리는 두 선지를 각각 넣어보고 역으로 지문 속에서 근거를 찾아본다.

- 연습 문제

※ 1~22. 빈칸에 어울리는 답을 찾으시오.

1.

While the frontier idealized the rugged and tough individuals as the great American hero, the need for self-reliance on the frontier encouraged ___________. Frontier men and women not only had to provide most of their daily life essentials, but they were also constantly facing new problems and situations that demanded creative solutions. Observers from other countries were very impressed by the frontiersman's ability to make up new useful farm tools. They were equally impressed by the pioneer woman's ability to make unique clothing, candles, soap, and many other items needed for their daily life of her family.

① an adventurous lifestyle

② a spirit of inventiveness

③ the concept of gender equality

④ a strong sense of individualism

2.

The Japanese are fanatics for fresh food. As a result, Japanese food-processing companies enjoy local monopolies. A milk producer in northern Japan cannot hope to compete in southern Japan, because transporting milk there would take an extra day or two, a fatal disadvantage in the eyes of consumers. These local monopolies are reinforced by the Japanese government, which obstructs the import of foreign processed food by imposing a 10-day quarantine, among other restrictions. Hence Japanese food-producing companies __________.

① are compelled to rely heavily on imported food

② strategically optimize their operations on a global level

③ are preoccupied with ways to prolong the shelf life of food

④ are not exposed to either domestic or foreign competition

3.

Is there a way to tackle low entrepreneurship rates and high unemployment rates by using a policy that addresses both challenges? The answer may lie in ________. A case supporting this idea is found in a large-scale reform implemented in France in 2002. The reform allowed self-employed individuals who started their own businesses to keep their access to unemployment benefits program for three years in case their business venture failed. The program was successful. The overall positive benefits included shorter unemployment spells and the reallocation of labor to more productive and higher-paying jobs.

① introducing tax exemption schemes for new startup companies

② adjusting unemployment insurance to encourage entrepreneurial ventures

③ providing skill training programs to stimulate productive entrepreneurship

④ offering government funding in the early stage of venture startup development

4.

Discussions between the United States and the Soviet Union concerning a ban on nuclear testing began in the mid-1950s. Officials from both nations came to believe that the nuclear arms race was reaching a dangerous level. In addition, public protest against the atmospheric testing of nuclear weapons was gaining strength. Nevertheless, talks between the two nations dragged on for years, usually collapsing when ________. The Americans wanted on-site inspections, something the Soviets vehemently opposed. In 1960, the two sides seemed close to an agreement, but the downing of an American spy plane over the Soviet Union in May of that year brought negotiations to an end.

① the effects of radioactive fallout were questioned

② hard-liners set high demands in negotiation

③ the Soviets insisted on underground testing

④ the issue of verification was raised

5.

In love with whole numbers, the Pythagoreans believed that all things could be derived from them, certainly all other numbers. ___________ when they discovered that the square root of two(the ratio of the diagonal to the side of a square) was irrational, that √2 cannot be expressed accurately as the ratio of any two whole numbers. Ironically this discovery was made with the Pythagorean theorem as a tool. “Irrational” originally meant only that a number could not be expressed as a ratio. But for the Pythagoreans it came to mean something threatening, a hint that their world view might not make sense, which is today the other meaning of “irrational”.

① The public were dubious

② A crisis in doctrine arose

③ They became even more convinced

④ The uncertainties finally cleared up

6.

People use the phrase “Middle Ages” to describe Europe between the fall of Rome in 476 CE and the beginning of Renaissance in the 14th century. The phrase “Middle Ages” tells us more about the Renaissance that followed it than it does about the era itself. Starting around the 14th century, European thinkers, writers and artists began to look back and celebrate the art and culture of ancient Greece and Rome. Accordingly, they dismissed the period after the fall of Rome as a “Middle” or even “Dark” age in which no scientific accomplishments had been made, no great art produced, no great leaders born. This way of thinking about the era prevailed until relatively recently. However, today’s scholars note that ___________. In fact, great intellectual and artistic development in the Renaissance had its roots in the Middle Ages.

① the starting point for the era needs to be revised

② the era was as complex and vibrant as any other

③ the Renaissance was the cultural bridge leading to modern history

④ the term for the era helps us understand European history as a whole

7.

The cliche outfit may in some cases become so standardized that it is spoken of as a "uniform": the pin-striped suit, bowler and black umbrella of the London City man, for instance, or the blue jeans and T-shirts of highschool students. Usually, however, these costumes only look like uniforms to outsiders; ______________. The London businessman's tie will tell his associates where he went to school and the cut and fabric of his suit will allow them to guess at his income. Highschool students, in a single glance, can distinguish new jeans from those that are fashionably worn, functionally or decoratively patched or carelessly ragged; they grasp the fine distinctions of meaning conveyed by straight-leg, flared, boot-cut and peg-top.

① we all desperately strive to fit in

② their range of expression is fairly limited

③ peers will be aware of significant differences

④ such outfits are not uncommon in major cities

8.

In the spring of 1918, a deadly flu virus attacked the world. The virus infected as much as 40 percent of the global population. The pandemic became commonly known as the "Spanish Flu" or the "Spanish Lady" in the United States and Europe. Many assumed that this was because the sickness had originated from the Iberian Peninsula, but the nickname was actually the result of a widespread misunderstanding. Spain was one of only a few major European countries to remain neutral during World War 1. Unlike in the Allied and Central Powers nations, where wartime censors suppressed news of the flu to avoid affecting morale, the Spanish media was free to report on it in gory detail. Since nations undergoing a media blackout could only read in depth accounts from Spanish news sources, they naturally assumed that ______________.

① the country was the pandemic's ground zero

② Spain would stay neutral until the end of the war

③ Spain's media enjoyed more freedom than any other country

④ the country was falsely branded as the major disseminator of the flu

9.

Consider the tragic tampering case in which eight people died from swallowing cyanide-laced capsules of Tylenol. Although Johnson & Johnson believed that the pills had been altered in only a few stores, not in the factory, it quickly recalled all of its product. The recall cost the company $240 million in earnings. In the long run, however, the company's swift recall of Tylenol strengthened consumer confidence and loyalty, and Tylenol remains as the nation's leading brand of pain reliever. Johnson & Johnson management found that ____________.

① the costs of attracting new customers are fast rising
② satisfying customer needs is the top priority in marketing
③ it is crucial to create profitable relationships with customers
④ doing what's right benefits both customers and the company

10.

We live in a sea of images conveying the culture and learning of modern civilization. Fostered by an unprecedented media expansion, this visual background noise has become so much a part of our daily lives that we take it for granted. In the process, we __________. Anyone can buy cheap paintings and reproductions to decorate a room, where they often hang virtually unnoticed, perhaps deservedly so. It is small wonder that we also look at the art in museums with equal casualness. We pass rapidly from one object to another, sampling them like a smorgasbord. We may pause briefly before the famous masterpiece we are supposed to admire, then ignore the galleryful of equally beautiful and important works around it.

① have become desensitized to art
② have responded to art on many levels
③ become to appreciate the true meaning of art
④ learn how to make a meaningful individual choice

11.

Fear is, of course, a normal response to danger, i.e., real danger, and results in a conditioned mode of response — flight, anxiety, or caution, etc. But the little child is most intensively afraid of many imaginary dangers as well as real dangers. There has been a considerable amount of argument among psychologists as to what may constitute _____ to a young child.

① a fear-provoking situation

② the non-committal imagination

③ the conscious levels of the mind

④ a response to inner stimuli

12.

Parasitic plants are plants that survive by using food produced by host plants rather than by producing their own food from the Sun's energy. Because they do not need sunlight to survive, parasitic plants are generally found in ______ areas rather than in areas exposed to direct sunlight. Parasitic plants attach themselves to host plants, often to the stems or roots, by means of haustoria, which the parasite uses to make its way into the food channels of the host plant and absorb the nutrients that it needs to survive from the host plants. The world's heaviest flower, a species of rafflesia, is a parasite that lives off of the roots of jungle vines. Each of these _____ blooms can weigh up to 15 pounds and can measure up to 3 feet across.

① fertile - bulky

② parched - exuberant

③ alluvial - meager

④ umbrageous - ponderous

13.

Today laws govern the number of hours that young people may work as well as the conditions in which they work. This was not always so, however. For example, until the twentieth century, the children of poor families in England were often exploited for inexpensive labor. This exploitation took a number of forms. Children as young as nine years old were forced to work for fourteen to sixteen hours a day. Poor working conditions seriously impaired the children's health. Although many parents tried to envelop their children with protection and care, the families needed the money and could not fight the factory and mine owners. Many children must have felt ______. English writers criticized such mistreatment of children. For example, Charles Dickens, the famous novelist, often described the _____ waste of young lives.

① pampered - brutal

② forsaken - inhumane

③ redeemed - critical

④ abandoned - insipid

14.

Inflation did ______ because of government spending cuts and continued high interest rates, but the "cure" _______ the business recession under way since 1979, leading to the worst downturn in the economy since the 1930s. Factories closed, businesses went bankrupt, and farm mortgages were foreclosed at an increasing rate. By the end of 1982, more than 12 million Americans were out of work, more than 10 percent of the labor force. Double-digit inflation had been ended at the cost of double-digit unemployment.

① occur - exacerbated

② abate - accelerated

③ ripple - quashed

④ decline - appeased

15.

Political Economy or Economics is a study of mankind in the ordinary business of life; it examines that part of individual and social action which is most closely connected with the attainment and with the use of the material requisites of wellbeing. Thus it is on the one side a study of ______; and on the other, and more important side, a part of the study of ______. For man's character has been moulded by his every-day work, and the material resources which he thereby procures, more than by any other influence unless it be that of his religious ideals.

① wealth - man

② welfare - capitalism

③ society - religion

④ class - parity

16.

Many linguistics researchers are excited about the possibility of humans using language to communicate with chimpanzees, our close cousins in the animal world. Some scientists believe that chimpanzees, and in particular Bonobo chimpanzees, may have the comprehension skills of two-and-a-half-year-old children. With dedicated training, the scientists claim, these chimpanzees are able to understand complicated sentences and to communicate on an advanced level with human beings. In a recent and rather astonishing episode, ________, a Bonobo chimpanzee pressed symbols on a special keyboard in order to tell her trainers about a fight between two chimpanzees in a separate facility.

① for example

② additionally

③ nevertheless

④ on the other hand

17.

The human brain contains approximately one trillion nerve cells and so it might seem that trying to understand the neural machinery of our own behavior is a task that is beyond our abilities. Fortunately nerve cells are all remarkably similar to one another in terms of their mode of operation across the whole of the animal kingdom. This means that the neurobiological and technical breakthroughs that are currently being made in this exciting and fast moving aea of animal behavior ________ a real impact upon our understanding of our own machinery for behavior.

① did have
② does not have
③ could have
④ could not have

18.

The mola sunfish uses its fins to steer its rather awkwardly-shaped body through the water. Its body has a very narrow cross-section — it is basically a flattened oval with a head at the front, and very high top and bottom fins at the back. In fact, the mola's height I often equal to its length, which is unusual in fish, which are typically ________.

① buoyant
② elongated
③ hydraulic
④ rectangular

19.

This should have been a happy century for Detroit, given the U.S. auto industry's past record sales and profits. But "_______________," and this is a sad reality for me: Although the industry is still thriving, more and more American cars are built outside of the country.

① every rose has its thorn

② strike while the iron is hot

③ even Homer sometimes nods

④ the grass is greener on the other side of the fence

20.

Heidegger is a notoriously difficult philosopher to understand. The way he wrote was, in part, a result of the fact that he was deliberately trying to break with the philosophical tradition. One way of breaking with the tradition is to coin neologisms, that is, to invent words which will, by virtue of their _______, be free of any philosophical baggage. This is a method that Heidegger frequently employed, but at the cost of considerable ___________. In addition, Heidegger believed his task was to provoke his readers to thoughtfulness rather than provide them with a facile answer to a well defined problem.

① originality - originality

② originality - intelligibility

③ intelligibility - intelligibility

④ intelligibility - originality

21.

A myth about sign languages is that they are the same language as spoken by their broader community, just done on the hands and face. This is not true. Actual sign languages have grammars that differ markedly from spoken languages in contact with them. _______, countries which use essentially the same spoken language do not necessarily have mutually intelligible sign languages. The sign languages used in the United States, England, and Ireland, for example, are quite different from each other. Sign languages do not develop according to the grammatical rules of the spoken languages of their communities. _________, they have their own complex morphology, phonology, syntax, and semantic rules.

① Instead - Nevertheless

② Instead - In fact

③ In fact - Nevertheless

④ In fact - Instead

22.

This year, the Arctic sea ice over experienced relatively slow rates of melt in June, which is the month the Arctic receives the most solar energy. _______, the rate of ice loss picked up during July, when the sun is still strong. Faster than normal ice loss rates continued through August, a transition month when ice loss typically begins to slow. A big "hole" appeared in August in the ice pack in the north of Alaska, when thinner seasonal ice surrounded by thicker, older ice __________. The huge opening allowed for the ocean to absorb more solar energy, accelerating the process.

① However - melted

② However - froze

③ Consequently - melted

④ Consequently - froze

UNIT 6 무관한 문장

* 무관한 문장 유형 문제 해결 전략

밑줄 문장을 기준으로 바로 앞뒤 문장과의 비교를 통해 푸는 문제이다. 즉 밑줄 문장을 기준으로 앞 뒷 문장간의 소재 비교를 통해 소재가 끊어진 점을 찾는 것이다. 이걸 위해 우리가 집중적으로 봐야할 부분은 밑줄 문장과 그 다음 문장에 써있는 내용이다.

- 예시 1

❶ 정우성은 현빈처럼 잘생겼다.
❷ 현빈은 많은 영화에 출연했다.
❸ 정우성은 이목구비의 비율이 완벽하다.

→ 이 문장들에서 보면 1번과 3번은 정우성의 외모에 대해서 얘기하고 있고 2번 혼자 1번 문장에 잠깐 등장했던 현빈에 대해 이야기하고 있으므로 2번 문장이 소재가 끊어진 점이 된다. 그래서 정답은 2번이다.

- 예시 2

❶ 정우성은 현빈처럼 잘생겼다.
❷ 그런데, 정우성은 연기력이 조금 아쉽다.
❸ 정우성은 이목구비의 비율이 완벽하다.

→ 이렇게 나왔을 때가 더 어려운 유형이 된다. 이 경우엔, 1번과 3번은 정우성의 외모에 대해서 이야기하고 있고 2번 문장은 정우성의 연기력에 대해서 이야기하고 있다. 즉 2번 혼자 소재가 연기력이고, 1번 문장과 3번 문장은 외모 얘기가 이어진다. 그래서 외모 얘기를 바로 이어지게 하려면 2번이 무관한 문장이 되어야 한다.

- 연습 문제

※ 1~6. 글의 내용과 무관한 문장을 찾으시오.

1.

Although scattered local airline companies began offering flights to passengers as early as 1913, scheduled domestic flights did not become widely available in the United States until the 1920s. Ⓐ During the early years of commercial aviation, U.S. airline travel was limited to a small population of business travelers and wealthy individuals who could afford the high ticket prices. Ⓑ The majority of travelers relied instead on more affordable train services for their intercity transportation needs. Ⓒ Over ninety-five years later, the airlines have grown to be one of the most important and heavily used transportation options for American business and leisure travelers. Ⓓ Following deregulation of the airline industry by the U.S. government in 1978, airline routes increased, ticket fares decreased, and discount carriers prospered, thus making airline travel accessible to a much broader segment of the U.S. population. Ⓔ Plane tickets were generally prepared by hand using carbon paper and were given to passengers upon their arrival at the airports. In 2008 alone, 649.9 million passengers traveled on domestic flights on U.S. airlines.

① Ⓐ ② Ⓑ
③ Ⓒ ④ Ⓓ
⑤ Ⓔ

2.

The 2012-13 flu season took a serious toll on families: 158 children — most of them younger than 11 — died. Sadly, about 90 percent of those who died missed out on the one thing that could have saved them: a flu vaccination. Ⓐ Despite studies proving that flu vaccinations are a lifesaver, less than half of all children in the U.S. are immunized each year. Ⓑ One recent survey from a social-research company found that 16 percent of Americans consider the vaccine to be unsafe and 35 percent believe the vaccine causes the flu. Ⓒ "The tragedy is that children continue to die from an illness that is largely preventable," says Dr. Blumberg. Ⓓ Doctors want moms and dads to understand that children ages 6 months to 5 years are at a high risk of serious diseases like diarrhea and dehydration. Ⓔ Because awareness and education are key to making smart decisions about your family's health, it's of primary importance for parents with children to get clear-cut information about the flu and the vaccine.

① Ⓐ ② Ⓑ

③ Ⓒ ④ Ⓓ

⑤ Ⓔ

3.

John Henry was an ex-slave who went to work on the railroad as a steel-driver for the Chesapeake & Ohio (C&O) Railroad. His job was hitting steel spikes into rocks, and he was the fastest and strongest worker on the line. Ⓐ When the owners of the C&O decided to drill right through Big Bend Mountain in West Virginia instead of building the railroad around it, many workers lost their lives because of the dangerous work. But not John Henry. Ⓑ Thousands of African-Americans worked on the railroad, with hundreds perishing during the drilling of the Great Bend Tunnel. He drove spike after spike, digging his way through the mountain. Ⓒ One day a salesman appeared, touting the efficiency and speed of a new steam-powered drill. The workers arranged a contest: John Henry versus the machine. Ⓓ When the dust settled, John Henry dug a 14-foot(4-meter) hole, but the machine made it only 9 feet (nearly 3 meters). Ⓔ As the rail workers celebrated, John Henry toppled over and died from exhaustion.

① Ⓐ ② Ⓑ

③ Ⓒ ④ Ⓓ

⑤ Ⓔ

4.

Vigorous activity is usually a healthful pursuit but it can become maladaptive when carried to extremes. Ⓐ There are runners and body builders, for instance, who use their obsessive workouts to avoid taking responsibility for other aspects of their lives, allowing little time for family, friends, or additional interests. Ⓑ Rather than enjoying their fitness endeavors, they feel powerless to make any adjustments in their routines except to try to do more. Ⓒ Pursuing pleasurable fitness endeavors can be a great coping strategy for lessening daily pressures. Ⓓ Unfortunately, the exercise patterns of some adolescents and adults reflect deep=seated psychological problems. Ⓔ They become dangerously fixated on trying to change their bodies by a combination of exhausting exercise and dieting, increasing their risk of serious health problems including substance abuse and eating disorders.

① Ⓐ ② Ⓑ

③ Ⓒ ④ Ⓓ

⑤ Ⓔ

5.

Ⓐ Teotihuacan was one of the first true urban centers in the Western Hemisphere, covering nearly eight square miles at its heyday. Ⓑ Precious artifacts recovered from the Pyramid of the Moon and other structures reveal that this was a wealthy trade metropolis with far-reaching connections. Ⓒ Inexplicably, the city suffered sudden and violent collapse in about A.D. 600 and many people fled. Ⓓ Assuming that some of the buildings were tombs, they called the boulevard Street of the Dead. Ⓔ They left few written records, just the ruins of their city and intriguing clues about a once powerful culture.

① Ⓐ ② Ⓑ

③ Ⓒ ④ Ⓓ

⑤ Ⓔ

6.

According to study experts, one tip for exam success is regular daily and weekly study. Another tip is to focus on, in your study sessions, ideas that the instructor has emphasized in class. Ⓐ In addition, use the night before an exam for a careful review rather than a stressful cramming. Ⓑ Then get up a bit early the next morning and review your notes one more time. Ⓒ Study skills are tools and strategies used to make learning more efficient, organized, and successful. Ⓓ Last, once the test begins, the advice of experts is to answer the easiest question first; go back and tackle the hard ones.

① Ⓐ　　② Ⓑ

③ Ⓒ　　④ Ⓓ

정답과 해설 p.278 ~

UNIT 7 문장 삽입

- 문장 삽입 유형 접근법

* 문장 삽입 유형 문제 해결 전략

❶ '제시문'이 중요하다. '제시문'을 보고 '제시문'의 앞/뒤에 나올 수 있는 내용을 추론해본다.

→ 추론 방법

앞 내용 : 연결사, 대명사, 지시사, 형 + 명 등에 집중 (ex) a cheap product

뒷 내용 : 명사에 집중(소재에 집중)

❷ 소재에 집중한다. 정답이 되는 부분은 앞 뒷 문장과 소재가 맞으면서,
제시문부터 새로운 이야기가 시작되거나 제시문까지로 그 소재에 대한 이야기가 끝나고
제시문 다음 문장부터 새로운 내용이 나온다. (시작점과 끝점의 개념)

→ 따라서 각 선지 바로 다음 문장에 어떤 소재가 써있는지에 집중한다.

• 소재 잡는 방법

① 인물/집단, 상황 설정(in 명사, when/if 절)

② 문장 끝 전명구

③ 인과 관계 중 뒤

④ 주어(S)

√ 문장 삽입에서 답으로 많이 나오는 Point!

1) 지시사/대명사는 바로 앞 문장에서 이어지는 것이 원칙이다.

2) 연결사 앞 선지는 정답일 확률이 높다.

- 연습 문제

1. 글의 흐름으로 보아, 주어진 문장이 들어가기에 가장 적절한 곳은?

In the 11th century, the Chinese government began issuing these receipts which became the world's first paper money.

Coins were very convenient to use, but they were heavy. (①) In 10th century China, iron coins had square holes in the middle, and string was used to tie them together in heavy bundles of one hundred. (②) People began leaving these bundles with merchants in exchange for receipts. (③) The receipts could be used over time to purchase goods from the merchants. (④) The money would be worthless if the government did not guarantee its value. (⑤) Paper currency has no value if the people do not have confidence in its worth.

2.

(A) Social media such as Facebook rapidly expanded as smartphones were widely used and communications technology developed. (B) They have increased influence in creating public opinion as a news platform. (C) Fake information is being produced and distributed through social media. (D) In the U.S. presidential election, fake news like the pope endorsing one of the candidates became controversial, and problems with fake news are still rampant.

(E) News shared on social media sites such as Facebook are hard to filter, and fake news could become a problem anytime. Responses on distribution and expansion of fake news and fake information and their influences need to be studied while guaranteeing freedom of speech. Stony Brook University in New York is offering a free six-week online course to distinguish fact from fiction.

2. 다음 밑줄 친 표현이 들어갈 가장 적절한 곳은?

<u>Concerns grow as social media's influence increases.</u>

① A ② B

③ C ④ D

⑤ E

3. Choose the best place for the sentence given in the box.

Michelangelo attended dissections to perfect his understanding of surface form, while Leonardo opened the body to see and discover for himself our physical mechanisms.

Artists are thought to have begun drawing from the nude during the Italian Renaissance. In this period, the junior workshop apprentices posed as part of their duties. Drawings were usually made from the male nude to avoid offending the church. (①) Look closely at Renaissance drawings of the female body and you will see that most are actually young men with minor adjustments. (②) During this time, artists also tried to define ideal proportions in the body; Leonardo drew a man within a circle and square, while Durer took his research further — he sought perfection in the infinitesimal measurement of the body and produced four volumes of illustrated explanation. (③) Renaissance artists studying anatomy from dissection were decades ahead of their medical counterparts. (④) Leonardo even believed he had located the soul in the pituitary fossa beneath the brain and behind the eyes, giving physical foundation to the theory that the eyes are the windows of the soul.

4.

In the late 1890s two German psychologists, Georg Miiller and Alfons Pilzecker, found out that it takes an hour or so for memories to become fixed, or "consolidated", in the brain. Subsequent studies confirmed the existence of short-term and long-term forms of memory and provided further evidence of the importance of the consolidation phase during which the former are turned into the latter. In the 1960s, University of Pennsylvania neurologist Louis Flexner made a particularly intriguing discovery. After injecting mice with an antibiotic drug that prevented their cells from producing proteins, he found that the animals were unable to form long-term memories but could continue to store short-term ones. The implication was clear: long-term memories are not just stronger forms of short-term memories. ⓐ Storing long-term memories requires the synthesis of new proteins. Storing short-term memories does not. More recent research turned to the issue of the physical workings of both short-term and long-term memory. ⓑ The results demonstrated that the more times an experience is repeated, the longer the memory of the experience lasts. Repetition encourages consolidation. Particularly, when researchers examined the physiological effects of repetition on neuronal signals , they discovered something amazing. ⓒ Not only did the concentration of neurotransmitters in synapses change, altering the strength of the existing connections between neurons, but the neurons grew entirely new synaptic terminals. The formation of long-term memories, in other words, involves not only biochemical changes but anatomical ones. ⓓ That explains why memory consolidation requires new proteins. Proteins play an essential role in producing structural changes in cells.

4. 아래의 문장이 들어갈 위치로 가장 적합한 곳을 고르시오.

The two types of memory entail different biological processes.

① ⓐ　② ⓑ

③ ⓒ　④ ⓓ

5. 다음 문장이 들어갈 위치로 가장 적합한 곳을 고르시오.

Or encourage him to entertain an even more forgiving listener.

To truly enjoy reading, it needs to become second nature. ⓐ "Children should read both silently and aloud," says Judy Cheatham. ⓑ That's where a child's fluency —— the ability to read smoothly and expressively— comes in, says Dr. Cheatham. ⓒ Since kids gain fluency by practicing familiar text, don't worry if your child chooses the same book over and over again. ⓓ If your kid is anxious about reading aloud to you, let him read to himself or into a recording device and then play it back for himself or a younger sibling. ⓔ A study from the University of California, Davis showed that second-graders who read aloud to the family dog improved reading skills by 12 percent over ten weeks.

① ⓐ　② ⓑ

③ ⓒ　④ ⓓ

⑤ ⓔ

6. 다음 문장이 들어갈 위치로 가장 적합한 곳을 고르시오.

He can just picture how she'll give a little shout of joy when she opens the box.

A 2016 paper based on prior research of gift giving notes a discrepancy in the way a gift giver and the recipient think about the gift. ⓐ Gift givers typically select a present by picturing how it will be received, often going for a "wow" factor or a complete surprise. ⓑ Yet recipients are more practical when they open a gift, focusing on its usefulness and long-term desirability. Here's an example. ⓒ A husband purchases pricey diamond earrings for his wife, going for that "wow" factor. ⓓ But she doesn't. She'd asked for slippers, a blender or a pair of leather gloves, and would have preferred those to the diamond earrings, no matter how beautiful, ⓔ Another scenario: A woman buys her coffee-loving dad a gift card to a coffee shop, something she deems a very thoughtful present. While her dad does enjoy coffee, he wishes he had received a more versatile credit card gift card.

① ⓐ ② ⓑ
③ ⓒ ④ ⓓ
⑤ ⓔ

7. 다음 문장이 들어갈 위치로 가장 적합한 곳을 고르시오.

Further, they claim the right to defend specific geographical boundaries against real or imaginary aggressors, irrespective of the persons who actually govern them.

The state itself has, of course, changed its form over time. ⓐ In Europe, the embryonic nation-state emerged from around the fifteenth century, and largely achieved a full-grown form by the nineteenth century. ⓑ The nation-state that has emanated since then largely consists of a 'people' or 'peoples', expressing their right to self-determination, and within a 'sovereign' territory, ⓒ Moreover, within the modern nation-state, a government is seen to have authority over the area and is the ultimate power within it. ⓓ The modern nation-state marks the replacement of absolutist rulers by a set of rules administered by a state-organized bureaucracy. ⓔ It is in this that the state is seen to achieve legitimacy.

① ⓐ ② ⓑ
③ ⓒ ④ ⓓ
⑤ ⓔ

8. 다음 문장이 들어갈 위치로 가장 적합한 곳을 고르시오.

And yet, though much changed, Old English did in fact survive.

It was the invasion of the Norman French that changed everything. The defeat of King Harold at the Battle of Hastings in 1066 resulted in the installation of a dynasty of French kings on the throne in London (the first, the Hastings victor William Ⅰ, actually spending very little time in England). ⓐ And for the next 300 years the French held sway over almost all areas of English power, governance, and culture. ⓑ Norman French became the language of England's administration and in time settled as the country's politer forms of intercourse. ⓒ Old English came briefly to be despised, regarded haughtily as the language of the peasant and the pleb. ⓓ After a century-and-a-half of linguistic mystery when no one is certain quite what happened to the language, Old English miraculously lived on, transmuted itself into what is now called Middle English, adopted thousands of new loanwords from the French and became stronger by doing so. ⓔ Finally it emerged, fully established, to be displayed to greatest advantage for all time in the writings of that most impressive of the early figures of English literature, Geoffrey Chaucer.

① ⓐ　② ⓑ
③ ⓒ　④ ⓓ
⑤ ⓔ

9. 다음 문장이 들어갈 위치로 가장 적합한 곳을 고르시오.

Instead, Athena persuades them to join the city, giving them a place of honor beneath the earth, in recognition of their importance for those same legal institutions and the future health of the city.

At the end of Aeschylus' Oresteia, two transformations take place in the archaic world of the characters. In the famous transformation, Athena introduces legal institutions to replace and terminate the seemingly endless cycle of blood vengeance. ⓐ Setting up a court with established procedures of reasoned argument and the weighing of evidence, an independent third-party judge, and a jury selected from the citizen body of Athens, she announces that blood guilt will now be settled by law, rather than by the Furies, ancient goddesses of revenge. ⓑ But the Furies are not simply dismissed. ⓒ Typically this move of Athena's is understood to be a recognition that the legal system must incorporate the dark vindictive passions and honor them. ⓓ Thus the great Hellenist Hugh Lloyd-Jones concludes, "Far from wishing to abolish the prerogatives of the Erinyes, Athena is anxious to conserve them."

① ⓐ　② ⓑ

③ ⓒ　④ ⓓ

10. 다음 문장이 들어갈 위치로 가장 적합한 곳을 고르시오.

He formulated the concept of regional parallelism , according to which vegetation responses to climate change were parallel in different parts of the world.

In 1916, Swedish geologist Lennart von Post showed that by identifying and counting pollen preserved at different depths in Swedish peat bogs he could infer changes in forest composition through time. Following his pioneering work, pollen analysis quickly became established as a key tool for understanding past vegetation, climate, and ecosystems. ⓐ Today, it is used widely to reconstruct past ecosystems and test hypotheses about drivers of ecosystem change. Using pollen analysis, von Post explored the temporal changes in postglacial forest composition at many sites in southern Sweden. ⓑ He then demonstrated the spatial patterns of change by mapping his pollen data at selected times. ⓒ He also developed pollen analysis as a relative-dating technique for resolving postglacial sea-level changes. ⓓ In the 1930s to 1950s, pollen-analytical studies around the world were performed to establish vegetation history, estimate pollen-accumulation rates, elucidate the relationship of modern pollen spectra to vegetation, and map pollen data through time.

① ⓐ　② ⓑ

③ ⓒ　④ ⓓ

11. 다음 문장이 들어갈 위치로 가장 적합한 곳을 고르시오.

> Professor Case insists his death could have been prevented if students had better access to school counselors and support groups.

Both the general public and parents of school age children have been slow to recognize how damaging cyberbullying can be. ⓐ According to Professor Case, a leading expert on cyberbullying at Pacifica Central University, victims experience a sense of alienation and low self-esteem. ⓑ He points to the recent suicide of teenager Jerome Farthing who committed suicide after receiving countless threatening text messages and emails mocking him for being overweight. ⓒ A review of his phone and email records showed a staggering 563 text messages and 1,465 emails taunting and threatening him. ⓓ Statistics show that schools and communities with dedicated counselors and cyberbullying policies have higher rate of reported incidents but a lower rate of severe cases.

① ⓐ ② ⓑ

③ ⓒ ④ ⓓ

12.

Like any epidemic, Ebola is best stopped early. ⓐ It kills health workers by exposing them to patients who, by the end, excrete up to ten liters of virus-laden fluids a day. The number of infections tends to double every two to four weeks. ⓑ As healthcare workers fall ill and the infection grows exponentially, a society's defences against Ebola are rapidly overwhelmed. ⓒ One reason is that an epidemic had never been seen in that part of Africa. The disease may also have been helped by urbanization and development, which strengthen the transport links that shuttle the virus from villages to cities and back into uninfected rural areas. ⓓ Perhaps it was only a matter of time before Ebola would find its way into a slum too chaotic and vast to cope with.

12. Choose the most suitable position of the following sentence in the above passage.

In this case the response has been fatally slow.

① ⓐ ② ⓑ
③ ⓒ ④ ⓓ

13.

There is a common belief that many Americans get fat because they eat too many carbohydrates. ⓐ The idea is that a high-carbohydrate, low-fat diet leads to weight gain, higher insulin and blood glucose levels, and more diabetes, even if the calories are the same as in a higher-fat diet. That did not happen in the study. Others have said the opposite: that low-fat diets enable people to lose weight naturally. ⓑ As for heart disease risk factors, the only one affected was LDL cholesterol, which increases heart disease risk. ⓒ The levels were slightly higher in women eating the higher-fat diet , but not high enough to make a noticeable difference in their risk of heart disease. ⓓ Although all the study participants were women, the results should also apply to men.

13. Choose the most suitable position of the following sentence in the above passage.

But again, that belief was not supported by the data in the study.

① ⓐ ② ⓑ
③ ⓒ ④ ⓓ

14.

Modern forecasting methods are fairly accurate when it comes to short-range predications, but the longer the forecast, the more chances there are that the forecasts are going to be incorrect. ⓐ The current metho d of mathematically calculating weather conditions confine s accurate predictions to about five days in advance due to the chaotic nature of the weather. ⓑ Meteorologists combine the results of the computational data collection methods with the actual atmospheric conditions occurring in th e present. ⓒ Current information concerning the temperature, dew point, and winds at various levels is gathered throughout the day all around the world to provide clues that are compared to computer models based on past conditions to come up with probable weather patterns. ⓓ As a result, an experienced meteorologist who has seen a great variety of weather conditions and is knowledgeable about the changes and shifts that they are likely to make stands nearly as good of a chance at accurately predicting future weather conditions as a computer-generated model does.

14. Choose the most suitable position of the following sentence in the above passage.

> However, though the science and methodology of meteorological methods have improved, there are still large gaps in the understanding of atmospheric and weather-related activity.

① ⓐ ② ⓑ

③ ⓒ ④ ⓓ

UNIT 8 순서 배열

- 순서 배열 유형 문제 해결 전략

순서 배열 문제를 풀 땐 3가지 원칙을 정확하게 활용하면 된다.

- 제시문이 있는 순서 배열

❶ 같은 소재끼리 묶어준다

❷ 가능하다면 글을 둘로 나눈다.

❸ 소재의 시작점

- 제시문이 없는 순서 배열

❶ 같은 소재끼리 묶어준다

❷ 가능하다면 글을 둘로 나눈다.

❸ 소재의 시작점

가장 중요한 Point는 소재가 바로바로 이어지는 부분을 찾는거지 어떻게 해석하면서 연결하는게 더 자연스러울까를 따지는 것이 아니다. 그리고 절대 제일 처음에 뭐가 오면 좋을까에 집착해선 안 된다.

- 소재의 시작점

❶ S call O O.C(O.C의 시작점)

❷ S be called A(A의 시작점)

❸ S Vt O as A(A의 시작점)

❹ S be p.p as A(A의 시작점)

❺ A (후치수식) → A의 시작점
명사

- 연습 문제

1.

If we lived on a planet where nothing ever changed, there would be little to do. There would be nothing to figure out. ⓐ And if we lived in an unpredictable world , where things changed in random or very complex ways, we would not be able to figure things out. ⓑ Again, there would be no such thing as science. © But we live in an in-between universe, where things change, but according to patterns, rules, or, as we call them , laws of nature. ⓓ There would be no impetus for science. If I throw a stick up in the air, it always falls down. If the sun sets in the west, it always rises again the next morning in the east. And so it becomes possible to figure things out. We can do science , and with it we can improve our lives.

1. Which of the following is the best order?

① A - C - D - B

② A - D - C - B

③ D - A - B - C

④ D - C - A - B

2.

Alzheimer's disease is, perhaps, the classic illness of old age. Physical frailty is expected, and can be coped with. Mental frailty is much scarier for the sufferer and more demanding for those who have to look after him. It is expensive, too. ⓐ The number of people suffering from the disease is expected to triple by 2050. ⓑ Effective treatments would thus be embraced with enthusiasm by sufferers and society alike. © And it is getting commoner as average lifespans increase. ⓓ Alzheimer's is estimated to cost America alone some $170 billion a year.

2. Which is the proper order of the sentences A - D ?

① C - D - B - A

② A - C - D - B

③ D - C - A - B

④ B - A - C - D

3.

Within the set of gestures that accompany speech, we can distinguish between those that echo the content of the spoken message and those that indicate something being referred to. Iconics are gestures that seem to be a reflection of the meaning of what is said, as when we trace a square in the air with a finger while saying , "I'm looking for a small box." By itself, an iconic gesture doesn't 'mean' the same as what is said, but it may add 'meaning. , For example, a woman was moving her forearm up and down, with a closed hand, as if holding a weapon, while she was saying, "I chased the dog again." The communicated message, including the weapon, was accomplished through speech and gesture combined. Another common group of gestures can be described as deictics.

[A] In this case, the gesture and the speech combine to accomplish successful reference to something that only exists in shared memory rather than in the current physical space.
[B] The term deictic' means 'pointing' and we often use gestures to point to things or people while talking.
[C] We can also use the same gesture and the same table (with a cake no longer on it) when we later say, "That cake was delicious."
[D] We can use deictics in the current context, as when we use a hand to indicate a table (with a cake on it) and ask someone, "Would you like some cake?"

3. Which is the proper order of the sentences A - D?

① A - C - D - B

② B - D - C - A

③ C - A - D - B

④ D - A - B - C

4.

Laurence is the creator of 'Pavegen, a paving tile for which he now holds apatent,that turns the force of people's footsteps into clean, renewable energy. "My vision is for Pavegento be to cities what 'Intel inside' is for PCs," he says. "I want to cover every single city in the world with our tiles. I want to turn every bridge, road and building into a kinetic-energy device." The idea first came to him while he was studying industrial design and technology at Loughborough University. As part of his course he was sent to work at the energy company E.ON.

[A] "I was really upset. Then one day I was walking through Victoria Station in London and I thought about all the people there. I'd read that 38,000 people an hour walked through the station. What if we could © harness that energy as a power source?"

[B] "They said, 'Laurence, can you design a street light that's powered by solar or by wind?'" he recalls. "But when the sun , s not shining there's no power and when the wind's not blowing there's no power. So I tried for a year and I failed."

[C] Laurence took a different route. The weight of a footstep on his tile makes a horizontal flywheel inside it rotate. "The more people walk, the more this flywheel spins," he explains. "Then we withdraw the power from the flywheel as we need it. We can suck it out bit by bit."

[D] Laurence admits, "The idea of generating energy from footsteps isn't new and other people have tried it. They're using things such as the piezoelectric crystals you find in cigarette lighters to create a charge. But the power is so low that you can never do anything meaningful with that energy."

Every pedestrian that passes over a tile generates around seven watts in energy. These tiles generate electricity with a hybrid solution of mechanisms that include the piezoelectric effect and induction, which uses copper coils and magnets.

4. Which is the proper order of the four paragraphs A - D?

① C - B - D - A

② A - C - B - D

③ B - A - D - C

④ D - B - C - A

5. Choose the best order after the sentences given in the box.

Julie Mennella, a biologist who studies the sense of taste in babies and toddlers, often records her experiments on video. When I visited her recently at the Monell Chemical Senses Center in Philadelphia, she showed me a video of a baby in a high chair being fed something sweet by her mother.

[A] The baby grimaces, gags, and shudders. He pounds the tray of his high chair. He makes the sign language gesture for "stop." Human breast milk contains lactose, a sugar. "What we know about babies is that they're born preferring sweet," Mennella said.

[B] Almost as soon as the spoon is in the baby's mouth, her face lights up ecstatically, and her lips pucker as if to suck. Then Mennella showed me another video, of a different baby being given his first taste of broccoli, which, like many green vegetables, has a mildly bitter taste.

[C] The aversion to bitter foods is inborn too,she said, and it also has survival value: It helps us avoid ingesting toxins that plants evolved to keep from being eaten — including by us.

① A - C - B

② B - A - C

③ B - C - A

④ C - A - B

6. Choose the most logical order of the following sentences.

[A] All readers of Charlotte Perkins Gilman's work know that she tells the same stories over and over again. [B] In Gilman's fiction the use of the analogue is more than the mere repetition of particular plots or themes. [C] For example, it is especially effective when she is dealing with the relationship between the individual and the social health. [D] This feature of her writing I would like to describe as the writing of the analogue. [E] It is crucial to any understanding of the way in which she organized and expressed both her art and her ideology.

① A - C - E - B - D
② A - C - D - E - B
③ A - E - C - D - B
④ A - D - B - E - C
⑤ A - D - E - B - C

7.

The ancient Greeks pursued mathematics and astronomy for their own sake. They did not study them out of their wish to be accountants or season predictors. Their sole desire was to gain a better understanding of the world. We read Shakespeare's Hamlet and Walt Whitman's poetry. Their lines strike us as beautiful as a comet across the sky — so much so that we are compelled to recite all the famous verses.

(A) But I find there is something praiseworthy about the Greeks. They were not ashamed to be eccentric when their curiosity demanded it. They always valued the intrinsic interest of knowledge over its material benefit. There was no practical reason for their scrutiny of mathematical knowledge, or even knowledge of how we should live. They suggest that useless knowledge is essential in making civilisation possible, by cultivating what is desirable in life.

(B) How then does the study of stars and other useless knowledge make civilisation possible? The study of stars suggests that there is something inherently elegant and wonderful in the night sky other than city lights. The splendour of the stars, whose light originated perhaps millions of years ago, confronts us with a natural work of art. Yet the study of stars doesn't only allow us to appreciate the beauty of nature, it also produces in us a contemplative habit of mind.

(C) Snap back to reality, and what use are those verses? Does remembering a beautifully-written line of Shakespeare's get us a brand new Mercedes? Does it help to highlight the ills of capitalism, or get us to the top of the social hierarchy? I'm afraid not. Knowledge, as I have been told, is merely a tool for providing us with a good career. Therefore I must bow to the necessities of practical knowledge, and neglect the arts and humanities in their uselessness.

City life is fast, and makes people nervous. The day of a businessman is dense with meetings. He seldom has the time to engage in serenity and scrutinise himself and everything that happens around him. By looking at the stars, he discovers the beauty he previously neglected. As the stars stand still and look upon him, he is in awe of their remote beauty and able to obtain the peace of mind essential for meditation. Through the study of them, the pleasure we derive from appreciating the world becomes fuller and richer. It enhances our sensitivity and purifies our soul. civilising us.

7. 윗 글의 단락을 논리적 흐름에 맞게 순서대로 배열한 것으로 가장 적합한 것을 고르시오.

① (A) — (B) — (C)

② (A) — (C) — (B)

③ (B) — (A) — (C)

④ (C) — (A) — (B)

8. Choose the best order after the sentences given in the box.

> After the war, and in response to Roosevelt being elected to third and fourth terms, the Twenty-second Amendment was adopted in 1951.

[A] Since the amendment's adoption, four presidents have served two full terms: Dwight D. Eisenhower, Ronald Reagan, Bill Clinton , and George W. Bush. Jimmy Carter and George H. W. Bush sought a second term, but were defeated. Richard Nixon was elected to a second term, but resigned before completing it.

[B] Harry S. Truman, president when this amendment was adopted, was exempted from its limitations and briefly sought a third (a second full) term before withdrawing from the 1952 election.

[C] The amendment prohibits anyone from ever being elected to the presidency for a third term. It also prohibits a person from being elected to the presidency more than once if that person previously had served as president, or acting president, for more than two years of another person's term as president.

① A - C - B

② B - A - C

③ B - C - A

④ C - A - B

⑤ C - B - A

9. Choose the best order after the sentences given in the box.

> The clock, as Lewis Mumford has pointed out, is the key machine of the machine age, both for its influence on technology and for its influence on the habits of men.

[A] It is true that the Greeks had invented a number of primitive automatic machines, but these were used, like Heron's steam engine, either for obtaining "supernatural" , effects in the temples or for amusing the tyrants of Levantine cities.

[B] But the clock was the first automatic machine that attained public importance and a social function. Clock-making became the industry from which men learnt the elements of machine-making and gained the technical skill that was to produce the complicated machinery of the industrial revolution.

[C] Technically, the clock was the first really automatic machine that attained any importance in the life of man. Previous to its invention, the common machines were of such a nature that their operation depended on some external and unreliable force, such as human or animal muscles , water or wind.

① A - C - B

② B - A - C

③ B - C - A

④ C - A - B

⑤ C - B - A

10.

[A]

In 1950 , after training for two years, a 32-year-old long-distance swimmer named Florence Chadwick swam the English Channel in 13 hours and 20 minutes, from France to England, breaking Gertrude Ederle's 24-year-old world record. Soon she became the first woman to swim the Channel both directions — not only from France to England but from England to France. She then attempted to become the first woman to swim across the Catalina Channel.

[B]

Later, when she was warm and dry, newspaper reporters asked her if she knew that she had been only a short distance from the shore when she gave up her courageous effort to break the record. She responded that even though her trainers told her the same thing, it simply hadn't made a difference to her. "You see," she said, "I lost sight of my goal. I'm not sure I ever had it firmly in mind." On a clear day two months later, however, Florence Chadwick swam the Catalina Channel, breaking a 27-year-old record by more than two hours and becoming the first woman ever to complete the swim.

[C]

On the day scheduled for the Channel swim, Chadwick faced heavy seas. However, because she had trained in the Persian Gulf, she was in peak condition and prepared to do battle with the surging waves. Chadwick also encountered chilling cold. That was a problem, but, again, her training made a big difference. She was accustomed to cold water and her trainers had greased her body to help insulate her from the elements. In addition, Chadwick's trainers, rowing alongside her, were able to sustain her with comforting words of encouragement as she fought the cold, rough sea.

[D]

Yet, with all her planning and superior training, the one thing Chadwick and her trainers had not anticipated was fog. As a fog bank descended, the distance she could see decreased to only a few feet, obscuring the horizon and the distant shore. Chadwick started to flounder. With____ , the ice-cold, heavy waves seemed to grow to towering proportions. Chadwick began to suffer cramps in her arms, legs, feet, and hands from the severe cold. Her muscles screamed in pain as she battled the huge waves. Finally, she asked her trainers to bring her onboard and take her ashore.

10. Given A as the beginning of the entire passage, choose the best order of B, C and D .

① B - D - C ② C - B - D

③ C - D - B ④ D - B - C

⑤ D - C - B

11. 아래의 단락을 논리적 흐름에 맞게 순서대로 배열한 것으로 가장 적합한 것을 고르시오.

Many people have trouble starting their cars on a cold winter morning. In a cold car, the engine turns over more slowly, and it sometimes does not turn over at all. Car owners may blame their cold engines, but the real problem is a cold battery, which powers the starter motor. This motor is generally connected to its circuit by using a battery.

[A] Increasing the number of electrons moving increases the current and so increases the amount of power available to the motor.
[B] When a motor is hooked up in a circuit with a battery, electrons move through the circuit, creating a current.
[C] Likewise, decreasing the number of electrons moving will decrease the amount of power available.

① A - B - C
② A - C - B
③ B - A - C
④ B - C - A

12. 아래의 단락을 논리적 흐름에 맞게 순서대로 배열한 것으로 가장 적합한 것을 고르시오.

A number of diseases are due to faulty genes. The goal of gene therapy is to insert the correct genes into the cells of a patient in order to remedy the disorder. Some initial treatments have been successful. However, gene therapy does have some drawbacks.

[A] For one, the treatments must be given repeatedly.

[B] Despite these obstacles, scientists believe that gene therapy offers the potential for medical treatments to be tailored for individual patients.

[C] In addition, there is a chance the body's immune system will respond negatively and reject the treatment, causing the patient to die.

More recent efforts have been successful in restoring sight to patients with retinal disease.

① A - B - C

② A - C - B

③ B - C - A

④ B - A - C

13. Choose the most logical order of the following sentences.

[A] At the height of European colonialism, Creole could be found spanning all across the globe, in cultures form West Africa to Australia.

[B] When we hear the word "creole , " many of us tend first to think of the unique folk musical style native to southern Louisiana that gave rise to zydeco.

[C] Creole in its true sense, however, is a much more general and encompassing term, with a history that spreads far beyond the Gulf Coast or the Caribbean.

[D] Others, understandably, often mistake “Creole” for one of the two national languages of Haiti.

① B - C - A - D

② A - B - D - C

③ B - D - A - C

④ B - D - C - A

14. Choose the most logical order of the following sentences.

[A] Generally speaking, probability theory is used for decision-making if the consequences of future events have to be estimated.

[B] The cost of accident insurance, for example, should not be too high but must be enough to cover the expenses of the insurer.

[C] It actually developed from questions about chance in gambling.

[D] Probability theory is one of a few disciplines in mathematics that was oriented toward practical applications right from the start.

① A - B - C - D

② A - C - B - D

③ D - C - A - B

④ D - A - C - B

15. Choose the best order after the sentences given in the box.

The mouse was invented by Douglas Engelbart in 1964 and consisted of a wooden shell, circuit board and two metal wheels that came into contact with the surface it was being used on.

[A] This mouse was produced for $17 and sold for $35. Despite this, it wasn't until 10 years later around 1998 that optical mice became a commercially viable alternative to the ball mouse and infiltrated the mass consumer market.

[B] An optical mouse was developed 8 years later in 1980, eliminating the ball which often became dirty from rolling round the desktop, negatively affecting its operation. In another 8 years, US patent no. 4751505 was issued for an optical mouse invented by Lisa M. Williams and Robert S.Cherry.

[C] Bill English developed the design further 8 years later by inventing what is k6nown as the "Ball Mouse." The ball replaced the wheels and was capable of monitoring movement in any direction. It came into contact with two rollers that in turn spun wheels with graduations on them that could be turned into electrical pulses representing direction and speed.

① A - B - C

② B - A - C

③ C - B - A

④ B - C - A

⑤ C - A - B

16. Choose the best order after the sentences given in the box.

December is here : store fronts are festooned with holiday decorations, the cold is setting in, and another year is reaching its close. December has marked the end of the year and the beginning of winter since the ancient Romans established their first calendar. As its etymology indicates, December is formed from the Latin root decem- "ten," though December is our twelfth month.

[A] This is because the ancient Roman calendar had only ten months in the year, which began in March. Eventually January and February were added to the end of the year after December, though by the time the Julian calendar was established in 45 B.C.

[B] The strange numbering discrepancy is also present for the months of September, October, and November, which mean "seven," "eight," and "nine," even though they are our ninth, tenth, and eleventh months, respectively.

[C] January and February appeared at the beginning of the year, bumping all of the original months back by two, and leaving the names as they were originally assigned.

① A - B - C

② A - C - B

③ B - A - C

④ B - C - A

⑤ C - B - A

17. Which is the best order from [A] to [C] for a paragraph starting with the sentence in the box?

Women and men feel interrupted by each other because of the differences in what they are trying to accomplish with talk.

[A] Women who yield to these efforts do so not because they are weak or insecure or deferential but because they have little experience in deflecting attempts to grab the conversational wheel.

[B] Unlike men, they see steering the conversation in a different direction not as a move in a game, but as a violation of the rules of the game.

[C] Men who approach conversation as a contest are likely to expend efforts not to support the other's talk but to lead the conversation in another direction, perhaps one in which they can take center stage by telling a story or displaying knowledge. But in doing so, they expect their conversational partners to mount resistance.

① A - B - C

② A - C - B

③ B - C - A

④ B - A - C

⑤ C - A - B

18.

For the first time in history, global economic prosperity has placed the world within reach of eliminating extreme poverty altogether. This prospect will seem fanciful to some, but the dramatic economic progress made by China, India , and other low-income parts of Asia over the past 25 yers demonstrates that it is realistic. Although economic growth has shown a remarkable capacity to lift vast numbers of people out of extreme poverty, progress is neither automatic nor inevitable. Market forces and free trade are not enough.

[A]

Such theories have waned as societies of an ever-widening range of religions and cultures have achieved relative prosperity. Moreover, certain supposedly unchangeable aspects of culture do in fact change, often dramatically, as societies become urban and develop economically. Most recently, commentators have zeroed in on "poor governance," or corruption. They argue that extreme poverty persists because governments fail to open up their market, provide public services and eliminate bribetaking.

[B]

Although the debate continues, the weight of the evidence indicates that governance makes a difference but it is not the sole determinant of economic growth. According to surveys conducted by Transparency International , business leaders actually perceive some fast-growing countries to be more corrupt than some slow-moving African ones. A second common misunderstanding concerns the extent to which corruption is likely to eat up the donated money. Some foreign aid in the past has indeed ended up this way. That happened when the funds were provided for political reasons during the Cold War. On the other hand, when assistance has been targeted at development rather than political goals, the outcomes have been favorable.

[C]

Many of the poorest regions are still caught in a poverty trap; they lack the financial means to make the necessary investments in infrastructure, education, health care systems, and other vital needs. Public opinion in affluent countries often blames extreme poverty on faults within the poor themselves —— or at least with their governments. Culture was once thought to be the deciding factor: religious divisions and taboos, caste systems, a lack of entrepreneurship, gender inequalities, etc.

18. 위 글의 단락을 논리적 흐름에 맞게 순서대로 배열한 것으로 가장 적합한 것을 고르시오.

① A - B - C　　② A - C - B

③ B - A - C　　④ C - A - B

19. Choose the best order after the sentence given in the box.

In the early 1900s, a course of study at the London School of Hygiene and Tropical Medicine might have meant traveling to a hut in Italy for several months to study the causes of malaria.

[A] Today, medical academics say that in an interconnected world, the study of such illnesses has become more complex. Researchers have realized that factors outside biology contribute to patients' well-being. Addressing public health goes beyond microbes and pathogens, they say, to factors like socioeconomic status and politics.

[B] Or it might have included sailing to the West Indies to help a team of researchers investigate something called filariasis , a pathogen that seemed to be spread by mosquitoes. It could even have meant heading to Africa to help combat outbreaks of bubonic plague or dysentery.

[C] "The colonial legacy gave rise to schools of tropical medicine," explained Dr. Peter Riot, who has been the director of the school since 2010. "Belgium, Germany, France, Portugal — all colonial powers had them." Such schools' main purpose, according to Dr. Piot, was to study sicknesses endemic to overseas territories before the diseases reached the European countries' shores, usually carried by sailors returning home.

① A - C - B

② B - A - C

③ B - C - A

④ C - A - B

20. 아래의 단락을 논리적 흐름에 맞게 순서대로 배열한 것으로 가장 적합한 것을 고르시오.

[A] Hundreds of millions of people have joined Facebook, KakaoTalk, and other sites so that they can communicate with those friends online.

[B] However, the meaning of the word "friend" seems to have changed.

[C] Social networking makes it very easy to have friends — lots and lots of friends.

In the past, a friend was someone you had a close personal relationship with. Now, anyone in the world can be your friend online! Some people have thousands of friends, but what do you do if you don't want so many friends? Easy! You can dump an unwanted friend with just one press of your finger.

① A - B - C

② A - C - B

③ C - B - A

④ C - A - B

21. 아래의 단락을 논리적 흐름에 맞게 순서대로 배열한 것으로 가장 적합한 것을 고르시오.

The Unites States Army has fought many enemies over the nation's history. Not all those foes were human. Some of the Army's toughest enemies were tiny organisms that caused disease. In 1898 , the Army fought the Spanish-American War in Cuba. It was not a pleasant place to be. Many American soldiers died from yellow fever -- so called because it turned the skin yellow. It was a greater enemy than the Spanish. Something had to be done, and the Army had the right person to do it: a brilliant physician named Major Walter Reed.

[A] Believing in his ability , the Army assigned Reed to study yellow fever and find out how it was transmitted. Did yellow fever spread from person to person, as colds did, or was something else involved?

[B] Reed had gotten his medical degree before he was 20 years old. Then he joined the Army. While in the Army, he helped solve the mystery of how typhoid fever was transmitted. Flies carried the disease.

[C] Reed watched medics who cared for patients with yellow fever. They rarely got the disease. So, Reed figured yellow fever did not spread directly from person to person. What else could spread the disease?

The answer was mosquitoes: They carried a virus which caused yellow fever. Reed discovered that mosquitoes carried the illness when he performed experiments on volunteers.

① A - B - C

② B - A - C

③ B - C - A

④ C - B - A

UNIT 9 어휘 유형

- 어휘 유형 풀이법

빈칸 문제 풀 듯이 하나하나의 근거를 찾아가며 그 어휘가 적절한지 아닌지 판단하는 것이다. 여기서의 핵심은 근거를 찾았을 때 반대어휘에 대해 생각하는 것이다. 이러한 어휘 유형엔 2가지가 있다.

❶ 밑줄형

다섯 개의 밑줄이 있는 선지가 있고 이 중 문맥상 알맞지 않는 단어를 찾는 유형이다. 문법적으로 틀린 것이 아니고 잘못된 의미의 단어를 찾는 유형이다.

여기서 핵심은 정답이 되는 선지는 주제와 반대가 되는 의미의 단어를 써둔 경우라는 것이다. 그래서 밑줄을 보면서 항상 반대되는 의미가 와야하는 건 아닌지에 대해서 생각을 하며 읽는 것이 중요하다.

❷ 선택형

둘 중 문맥상 알맞은 의미를 고르는 유형이다. 이렇게 나왔을 때의 핵심은 제시되는 두 단어가 서로 반대되는 의미를 지니고 있는 단어라는 점이다. 그래서 그 반대되는 의미의 두 단어중 주제와 맥락에 맞는 유형을 찾는 것이 중요하다.

- 기출 문제로 확인해보자!

※ 1~4. 다음 글의 밑줄 친 부분 중, 문맥상 낱말의 쓰임이 적절하지 않은 것은?

1.

Scientific evidence suggests that humans have a biological desire to help others, including strangers.

① Altruistic behavior towards strangers is uniquely human and observed at a very young age. Researchers have shown that children as young as 18 months want to help strangers. When their 18-month-old subjects saw a stranger throw a pencil on the floor, none of them picked it up. ② However, when the same subjects saw someone "accidentally" drop a pencil, nearly all of the children picked it up in the first ten seconds, The researchers say that the results are ③ natural because these children are so young. They still wear diapers and are ④ barely able to use language, but they already show helping behavior. Because altruistic behavior ⑤ appears in children so young, the researchers hypothesize that the human brain is designed to be altruistic.

2.

One is tempted, in heated argument, to disparage the character of one's opponents, to deny their intelligence or reasonableness, to question their understanding, or their seriousness, or even their integrity. But the character of an adversary is logically relevant to the truth or falsity of what that person asserts, or to the correctness of the reasoning employed.

① tempted

② disparage

③ adversary

④ relevant

⑤ employed

3.

Some historians believe that the study of history will reveal the existence of a single cosmic purpose or pattern, either religious or naturalistic, which accounts for or explains the entire course of recorded history. Others deny the existence of any such cosmic design but insist that the study of history will reveal certain historical laws that explain the actual sequence of past events and can be used to predict the future. On either of these views, the historian seeks explanations that must account for and be confirmed by the recorded events of the past. On either of these views, therefore, history is a theoretical rather than a merely descriptive science, and the role of hypothesis must be admitted as marginal in the historian's enterprise.

① single

② entire

③ any

④ actual

⑤ marginal

4.

When a chain of causes leads to an event (e.g., an injury for which compensation is sought) the elements in the actual chain closest to the injury, the proximate causes, are most likely to be assigned legal responsibility for the outcome. Those whose actions are further back in the causal chain, and who therefore could not foresee the injurious result, are much more likely to be held responsible for it. But how far back must we trace the causal chain?

① closest

② most

③ further

④ more

⑤ far

UNIT 10 연결사 유형

- 연결사 문제 총 정리

※ 빈출 연결사 정리

- 인과관계 : 같은 소재, 같은 내용 or [Problem → Solution]의 관계
  therefore, thus, accordingly, in conclusion, consequently, so, hence, as a result
  as a consequence, eventually

- 역접/대조/강조 : However, But, Yet

- 역접 : still, even so, nevertheless, nonetheless, unfortunately, fortunately

- 대조 : in/by contrast, on the other hand, conversely
  cf) on the one hand(뒤에 on the other hand, 또는 But, However가 있어야 가능)

- 재진술, 역접이 가능한 것
  in fact, in reality, as a matter of fact, indeed, actually

- not A but B같은 관계를 만들어주는 연결사(앞 문장이 부정문 or 해석상 부정문)
  Instead, Rather, On the contrary

- 첨가 : 같은 소재, 같은 맥락의 다른 내용
  also, besides, moreover, furthermore, what is more, still more, in addition

- 공통 비교 : 다른 소재, 같은 내용
  likewise, similarly, in the same way, by the same token, equally, in a similar fashion, also

- 앞에 있는 걸 하지 않았을 때의 결과 : otherwise

- 예시 : for example, for instance

- 재진술 : 같은 소재 같은 내용
  In other words, that is (to say), so to speak,
  to put it (in) another way, namely
  in brief, in short, in summary, to sum up, in a nutshell,
  in sum

- 기타 연결사

  meanwhile, in the meantime (한편, 그 동안에) → 다른 소재, 다른 내용(대조 포함)

  all the while (그 동안에) → 동시동작(뒤에가 진행형) / 다른 소재, 다른 내용

  by the way (그런데) → 대조에 가까운 연결사(소재 다름, 다른 내용)

  Ironically, Paradoxically (역설적으로) → 예상/의도와는 반대의 결과가 뒤에 나온다.

- 연습 문제

1.

It is difficult for travellers to become strategic buyers. As buyers make their choices from the wide selection of travel times and ticket prices offered by airlines and independent retailers, they believe the Internet is giving them good insight into the comparative pricing of tickets by competitors. Ⓐ ________ , the systems are not as transparent as they appear. Most users are unaware of the airline industry's use of sophisticated revenue management systems designed to benefit the airlines, not passengers. The pricing algorithms these systems use enable airlines to anticipate user behavior and prevent travellers from strategic buying. Ⓑ________ , the Web permits airlines to continually adjust the number of seats available for various fare rates — ensuring maximum profit. In 1977 United Airlines alone made ten million fare changes, and with the Internet today, dynamic pricing strategies have become more popular with airline carriers.

1. Which is the most appropriate for the blanks Ⓐ and Ⓑ?

① For example - Meanwhile

② However - For example

③ For example - Therefore

④ However - In contrast

⑤ However - Nonetheless

2.

According to researchers, gossip has some benefits. Exchanging information can create a healthy connection. It can build rules for acceptable and unacceptable behavior. It can improve society. Ⓐ__________, gossip is useful in the business world. Gossip researcher Professor Frank McAndrew says, "If people are talking about good things others do, we want to emulate that good behavior. It is a nice way of socially controlling people." When a company faces bad times, gossip about the future of the employees can reduce fear and uncertainty. It can also create a feeling of fellowship. Ⓑ__________, bad gossip, the negative talk about other people's lives, can be destructive. Disappointingly enough, the researchers spend little time on this form of malice. People engage in negative gossip for several reasons. They may do it to bond with another person. They may do it to pass the time or to deny problems. They may gossip to build themselves up through comparisons with others, or they may want to hurt others.

2. Which is the most appropriate for the blanks Ⓐ and Ⓑ?

① Nevertheless - However

② However - Similarly

③ However - Nevertheless

④ Similarly - However

3.

Our understanding of the physical universe has deepened profoundly during the past century. The theoretical tools of quantum mechanics and general relativity allow us to understand the physical happenings from the atomic and subatomic realms all the way through phenomena occurring on the scales of galaxies and beyond to the structure of the whole universe itself. This is a monumental achievement. It is truly inspiring that beings confined to a small planet in the far edges of a galaxy have been able to ascertain and comprehend some of the most mysterious characteristics of the physical universe. Ⓐ ___________ , physicists by their nature will not be satisfied until they feel that the deepest and the most fundamental understanding of the universe has been unveiled. This is what Stephen Hawking has alluded to as a first step toward knowing "the mind of God."

3. Which of the following is most appropriate for the blank Ⓐ?

① By the same token

② Nevertheless

③ To sum up

④ As a result

4.

Unusual patterns of financial transactions can clue in investigators about a terror suspect. However, there are always exceptions to these patterns, and potential terrorists might do something unusual just to avoid looking suspicious. Ⓐ __________, the profile of your "average" terrorist might not always be accurate. Although the poor and uneducated are considered the most likely to become terrorists, the would-be terrorist on Christmas Day in the U.S was the son of a distinguished Nigerian family.

4. Which of the following is most appropriate for the blank Ⓐ?

① Instead

② On the other hand

③ By the way

④ Likewise

5.

The theory that skin color adapts to the level of ultraviolet radiation makes some sense. The ancestors of modern humans who lived predominantly near the equator in Africa had darker skin because it was more efficient at reflecting heat, helping the body cool down and preventing the skin from receiving harmful ultraviolet rays. Ⓐ ____________, less exposure to ultraviolet rays can lead to a deficiency in Vitamin D, also known as the "sunshine vitamin." This is the main reason why black people are at higher risk of contracting rheumatoid arthritis due to vitamin D deficiency.

5. Which of the following is most appropriate for the blank Ⓐ ?

① For instance

② Therefore

③ However

④ In conclusion

PART 3

고난이도 실전
모의고사 5회

정답과 해설 p.303 ~

PART 3 고난이도 실전 모의고사 5회

UNIT 11 Test 1

1~2.

Perhaps the most significant problem with the media hyperbole concerning cloning is the easy assumption that humans simply are a product of their genes — a view usually called "genetic essentialism." Television hosts and radio personalities have asked whether it would be possible to stock an entire basketball team with clones of Michael Jordan. In response, philosophers, theologians, and other experts have reiterated wearily that, although human behavior undeniably has a genetic component, a host of other factor — including uterine environment, family dynamics, social setting, diet, and other personal history — play important roles in an individual's development. Consequently, a clone produced from the DNA of an outstanding athlete might not be interested in sports. What's more, the cloning issue reveals the way in which the mass media foster attitudes of technological and scientific determinism by implying that scientific 'progress' cannot be halted. Of course, many scientists share these attitudes, and, too often, they refuse to accept moral responsibility for their participation in research that may contribute
to human suffering.

1. The best title of the passage would be ______.

① Benefits of Scientific Progress

② Media and the Ethics of Cloning

③ Media's Contribution to Anti-cloning Campaigns

④ Sports and Scientific Determinism

⑤ Regulation of Cloning through Laws

2. According to the passage, which of the following is true?

① Scientists are entitled to adopt the objective attitude towards moral controversy.

② The media seem to be obsessed with the idea of DNA as fate.

③ Most scientists admit that cloning research needs to be limited.

④ Most theologians have very little knowledge of science.

⑤ There has been too much negative media attention on human cloning.

3~5.

The camera is the means by which we stamp ourselves on everything we see, under cover of recording the Wonders of the World already wonderfully recorded by professionals and on sale at every corner bookshop and newsagent. But what use to us an illustrated book of perfect photographs? What use to show our friends, back home, postcards of the Taj Mahal, the Coliseum, the Leaning Tower of Pisa since ______? No temple is of interest without our faces beside it, grinning. Most amateur photographers show no interest in the world as it is, only in the world as it ideally should be. For example, you want a picture of the Real Morocco — a scene as old as time. Unfortunately for you, a glassy modern building edges up to the mosque; behind the minaret television aerials spike the sky; beside the camel two Moroccans in unsuitable Western suits stand discussing business. So you must stand and twist your camera, hold it up sideways, shift your position so that the little yellow lines just clear the building, just cut out the aerials and the telegraph wires, just exclude the business men while retaining the rest. And when all these alien elements have, for a precious moment, been obliterated, click. There, the Real Morocco. That is the summit of the amateur photographer's art — total unreality. The World As It Isn't.

3. What is the tone of the passage?

① informative

② sentimental

③ apologetic

④ satirical

⑤ gloomy

4. Which of the following would be best for the blank?

① our pictures are out of focus

② we don't visit the real places

③ we are not in the picture

④ we forget to bring the cameras

⑤ we are not the professional photographers

5. According to the passage, which of the following is true?

① In Morocco, it is very hard to find the real Moroccans.

② The poor skill of amateur photographers often distorts the reality.

③ Tourists tend to prefer modern Morocco to old-fashioned one.

④ Travelling with camera encourages tourists to experience the unexpected things.

⑤ Travelling with camera often narrows the minds of tourists.

6~8.

The managing director in a client company booked two of his middle managers on a team building seminar. This prestigious event was held in the opulence of a posh Manhattan hotel. The attendance fee was not much under $1,000 apiece, so the direct cost was over $2,000, plus the opportunity cost of their time. He had singled them out because they were both keen on and normally receptive to the idea of self development, they were hard workers and high flyers, and he wanted to send a clear message to them about how pleased he was with their performance. When he handed over their tickets, he received a response that could generously be described as lukewarm, and the only feedback he had from them after the event was that it had been 'all right.' When he probed further, he discovered simmering resentment which could be paraphrased as 'We head up two of the best and smoothest functioning teams in the place. Why pick on us? What have we done wrong?' Hardly able to credit such ingratitude our man went off in a huff and with the silent resolve to be less generous in the future. What went wrong? A major part of the answer is Ⓐ '__________.' It is not a question of pandering to egalitarianism. It is common sense. This approach is no more than a special case of the general principle: Where possible, involve everyone who is going to be affected by a decision. We operate in an age where Ⓑ ________ is, or should be, part of the fabric of work. This case shows that no matter how unfair it seems, it is a terrible mistake to think that it can be bypassed just because we are doing something 'nice.'

6. The managing director eventually got angry with the middle managers because ______.

① they rejected his generous offer outright

② they were not open to the new ideas

③ their performance did not meet the company's requirements

④ they did not seem to appreciate his benevolent gesture

⑤ they did not present the follow-up report in time

7. Which of the following would be best for the blank Ⓐ?

① No one complained

② No one decided

③ No one thanked me

④ No one asked me

⑤ No one helped mes

8. Which of the following would be best for the blank Ⓑ?

① consultation

② self development

③ team building

④ profit-making

⑤ hierarchy

9~11.

An interesting aspect of graphic symbolism is the extent to which individual variations in letter formation can reliably be interpreted. The term graphology, which refers to the psychological study of handwriting, has been practised for over a century. It was the French abbot, Jean Hippolyte Michon, who first set this branch of scholarship in train. Graphologists claim that careful and detailed analysis of an individual's handwriting can reveal important information about an individual's personality and can indicate, for example, whether they are suitable for a particular job or not. In recent years they have been employed in several professional contexts and in forensic science, where questions of handwriting identity and imitation are critical. The subject plainly has the scope for scientific development, as variables such as letter size, shape, angle, line direction and consistency of stroke all lend themselves, in principle, to precise scientific description. ______ Graphology has suffered from scepticism generated by its popularity at agricultural shows and seaside resorts, where characters are described and fortunes foretold on the basis of little more than a scribbled signature. The subject has also been heavily biased towards the famous or infamous, discerning the basis of success in a signature — but without objective controls.

9. The best title of the passage would be ______.

① History of Handwriting Analysis

② Recent Popularity of Graphology among Job-seekers

③ Mythical Origin of graphic Symbolism

④ Digital Signatures as a Replacement for Handwriting

⑤ Use of Graphology in Criminal Investigation

10. Which of the following is most appropriate for the blank?

① Moreover

② Therefore

③ Obviously

④ Officially

⑤ Yet

11. According to the passage, which of the following is true?

① The government controlled handwriting practices because they often misled the general public.

② Michon was the first person to receive the research grant for the new field.

③ Identifying the difference between the famous and the infamous is the most important task for graphologists.

④ Graphology contributed to changing the superstitious minds of rural people.

⑤ Graphology was often regarded as a simple fortune-telling skill.

12~14.

The nation has lived with TV for more than 50 years now. We are not, as it was once predicted we would be, fantastically well-informed about other cultures or about the origins of life on earth. ⓐ People do not remember much from television documentary beyond how good it was. Only those who knew something about the subject in the first place retain the information. ⓑ Documentaries are not what most people want to watch anyway. Television is at its most popular when it celebrates its own present. Its ideal subjects are those that need not be remembered and can be instantly replaced, where what matters most is what is happening now and what is going to happen next. ⓒ Sports, news, panel games, cop shows, long-running soap operas, situation comedies — these occupy us only for as long as they are on. ⓓ However good or bad it is, a night's viewing is wonderfully forgettable. It's a little sleep, it's Entertainment; our morals remain intact. ⓔ The box is further neutralized by the sheer quantity people watch. Of course, some programs are infinitely better than others. ⓕ There are gifted people working in television. But seen from a remoter perspective — say, four hours a night viewing for three months — the quality of individual programs means as much as the quality of each car in the rush-hour traffic.

12. When the above passage can be divided into three paragraphs, which would be the best boundaries?

① ⓐ and ⓒ ② ⓑ and ⓒ

③ ⓑ and ⓔ ④ ⓒ and ⓔ

⑤ ⓓ and ⓕ

13. The underlined expression implies that the longer you watch TV, ______.

① the more informed you become

② the less moral you become

③ the more excited you become

④ the more of its content matters

⑤ the less of its content matters

14. According to the passage, the author argues that ______.

① TV industry needs more intelligent program makers

② many people avoid TV documentaries because they do not contain any moral messages

③ TV turns out to be no transformer of our minds and societies

④ TV will have the greater impact on human civilization in the future

⑤ TV is getting more and more successful as a moral educator

15~16.

In modern developed societies, there is one variety of language that ranks above the others. This superposed variety is employed by the government and communications media, used and taught in educational institutions, and is the main or only written language. It is more fixed and resistant to change than any other variety in the community and is something of a yardstick against which other varieties are measured. It is to the written standard that prescriptivists, those who seek to regulate how others use language, usually appeal when they condemn some usage as incorrect, improper, or even barbarous.

15. Which of the following would be the best title of the passage?

① Language Varieties in Social Contexts

② The Status of the Standard Variety of a Language

③ Government Policies and Language Use

④ Influence of Government and Media on Language

16. Which of the following best characterizes the author's attitude towards the standard language?

① patronizing

② neutral

③ inciting

④ deprecating

17.

Historicism is a critical movement insisting on the prime importance of historical context to the interpretation of texts of all kind. It has enjoyed a long tradition of influence upon many disciplines of thought, recently experiencing a lively renewal in contemporary literary criticism. ⓐ______ The most prominent late 20th-century critical fashions, poststructuralism and postmodernism, have ended up being understood through the images of history they imply. Yet this historical turn rejoins a well-worn tradition of historicism. ⓑ______ At present, historicism is tempted to present itself as "new," the latest way forward for literary theory.

Historicism emerges in reaction to the practice of deducing from first principles truths about how people are obliged to organize themselves socially and politically. The natural laws governing human behavior at all times are formulated, and cultures evaluated by the degree to which they approximate to this ideal pattern. ⓒ______ They argue that human nature is too various for such legislation to be universally applicable. ⓓ______ They therefore have to evolve a model for apprehending social and cultural diversity different from the scientific, law-governed paradigm of the Enlightenment.

17. Which of the four blanks in the passage is the most appropriate place for the following sentence?

Historicists oppose this tradition.

① ⓐ

② ⓑ

③ ⓒ

④ ⓓ

18.

ⓐ In many countries, however, forest clearance is continuing at a rapid rate. ⓑ Deforestation is currently threatening wildlife in forests throughout the Tropics. ⓒ International efforts are being made to preserve forest — in Costa Rica, for example, almost 30 percent of the country has been designated as national park. ⓓ Nearly half of the world's original tropical rainforest cover has been destroyed during the last 40 years.

18. Choose the most logical order of the following sentences.

① ⓐ — ⓒ — ⓑ — ⓓ

② ⓑ — ⓓ — ⓒ — ⓐ

③ ⓓ — ⓒ — ⓑ — ⓐ

④ ⓒ — ⓐ — ⓑ — ⓓ

19.

ⓐ The vocal folds also constrict the airway, a critical concept for phonation. ⓑ As the airstream passes between the vocal folds, they may be made to vibrate, much as a flag flaps in the wind. ⓒ Vocal folds are located in the airstream at the upper end of the trachea. ⓓ The larynx is the cartilaginous structure that houses the two bands of tissue we call the vocal folds or vocal cords.

19. Choose the most logical order of the following sentences.

① ⓒ — ⓓ — ⓐ — ⓑ

② ⓑ — ⓒ — ⓓ — ⓐ

③ ⓐ — ⓒ — ⓑ — ⓓ

④ ⓓ — ⓒ — ⓑ — ⓐ

20.

ⓐ Gottlieb Mittelberger was a Lutheran minister who migrated to Pennsylvania with thousands of other Germans in the 1740s.

ⓑ In Journey to America, a book published in Germany in 1750, Mittelberger examined America with a critical eye.

ⓒ He warned his readers of the difficulties of migration, the danger of indentured servitude, and the hazards of life in a competitive society.

ⓓ Dismayed by the lack of piety among the colonists and the lack of state support for religious authority, he returned to his homeland after a few years.

20. Choose the most logical order of the following sentences.

① ⓐ — ⓑ — ⓒ — ⓓ

② ⓐ — ⓒ — ⓑ — ⓓ

③ ⓐ — ⓓ — ⓑ — ⓒ

④ ⓐ — ⓑ — ⓓ — ⓒ

UNIT 12 Test 2

1~2.

In early childhood, we come to know the denotations of our first words in the course of close encounters with the world, painstakingly mediated by our caregivers, sometimes with point-and-say demonstrations of the kind called ostension. But once we have a start in a language, we learn the meanings of most other words through language itself: by having them explained to us or by inference from the constructions words are put into. One of the focuses of linguistic studies is the systematic description of meaning relationships within a language, between the senses of expressions. The aim is to state economically and insightfully which expressions are equivalent in meaning to which others or contrast with them in various ways according to the linguistic knowledge of individuals ______ in the language.

1. Which of the following would be the best title for the passage?

① The Significance of Caregivers in Language Acquisition

② Different Aspects of Children's Language Learning

③ Meaning Relationships among Words in a Language

④ Linguistic Studies of Abilities of Language Speakers

2. Which of the following is the most appropriate for the blank?

① capable ② competent

③ intellectual ④ eminent

3~4.

In the study of literature, common sense is never Ⓐ ________. For most of a class hour, a professor once rhapsodized about the arrangement of the contents of W. H. Auden's Collected Poems. Auden, he claimed, was a master of thematic continuity, who had brilliantly placed the poems in an order that best complimented each other. Near the end of the hour, his theories were Ⓑ ________ — with a great inaudible pop — when a student, timidly raising a hand, pointed out that Auden had arranged the poems in the book not by theme but in alphabetical order according to the first word of each poem. The professor's jaw dropped: "Why didn't you say that sooner?" The student was Ⓒ ________: "I — I was afraid I'd sound too ordinary."

3. Which of the following sets of words would best fit in the three blanks in the passage?

① out of place — punctured — apologetic

② out of line — buttressed — conceited

③ out of place — exalted — poised

④ out of line — expounded — light-headed

4. Which of the following would be the theme of the passage?

① Poetry is hard to analyze.

② There are excellent old ideas as well as new.

③ Don't be afraid to state a conviction, though it seems obvious.

④ It does not matter that you may be repeating something that has been said before.

5. Which statement cannot be inferred from the passage?

Whereas beef and chicken appear in many New Mexican recipes, in Massachusetts, fish is very popular because of the nearby seacoast. New England is famous for its clam chowder, lobster, cod, scallops, and fish cakes. English herbs and spices are the seasonings used in New England dishes, which might taste rather bland to people accustomed to hot and spicy New Mexican food. Each region of the United States is unique. Louisiana has a French influence. Many Germans populate the Midwest. In traveling around America, a tourist has the opportunity not only to visit a variety of places and see diverse landscapes, but to taste a variety of foods as well.

① One may taste authentic German sausages and beers in the Midwest.

② Food in Massachusetts has been influenced by its geographical conditions.

③ It is uncommon to find top-quality beef dishes in New England.

④ Beef and chicken are frequently used in a traditional meal in New Mexico.

6. Which statement cannot be inferred from the passage?

Limits must be placed on the biofuels industry. The North cannot shift the burden of overconsumption to the South because the tropics have more sunlight, rain, and arable land. If biofuels are to be forest- and food-friendly, the grain, cane, and palm oil industries need to be regulated, and not piecemeal. Strong, enforceable standards based on limiting land planted for biofuels are urgently needed, as are anti-trust laws powerful enough to prevent the corporate concentration of market power in the industry. Sustainable benefits to the countryside will only accrue if biofuels are a complement to plans for sustainable rural development, not the centerpiece. A global moratorium on the expansion of biofuels is needed to develop regulatory structures and foster conservation and development alternatives to the transition. We need the time to make a better transition to food and fuel sovereignty.

① Powerful anti-trust laws are needed to promote the corporate concentration of market power in the biofuels industry.

② The South cannot be exploited to solve the North's problem of overconsumption.

③ Under the condition in which biofuels are used complementarily for rural development, sustainable benefits to the countryside will be possible.

④ Suspending the expansion of biofuels globally is required to promote development alternatives to the transition to biofuels.

7~9.

ⓐ______ A movable host of metaphors, metonymies, and anthropomorphisms: in short, a sum of human relations which have been poetically and rhetorically intensified, transferred, and embellished, and which, after long usage, seem to a people to be fixed, canonical, and binding. Truths are illusions which we have forgotten are illusions; they are metaphors that have become worn out and have been drained of sensuous force, coins which have lost their embossing and are now considered as metal and no longer as coins. Only by forgetting this primitive world of metaphor can one live with any repose, security, and consistency: only by means of the ⓑ______ of a mass of images which originally streamed from the primal faculty of human imagination like a fiery liquid, only in the invincible faith that this sun, this window, this table is a truth in itself, in short, only by forgetting that he himself is an artistically creating subject, does man live with any repose, security, and consistency.

7. Which is true according to the passage?

① Truth is like a fiery liquid that only poets truly understand.

② The idea of truth entails the fossilization of language.

③ Truth can only be found outside of language.

④ Life is hopeless without stable truths.

8. Choose the best topic sentence for blank ⓐ above.

① Truth is impossible to grasp.

② Language helps us understand the world.

③ What is entailed in the discourse?

④ What then is truth?

9. Choose the best phrase for blank ⓑ above.

① petrification and coagulation

② empathy and sympathy

③ subtle nuance and poetic fervor

④ sturm and drang

10~12.

History is necessary because it helps to explain current events. How do cultures rise and how do they fall? History will not give us the answers, but it will certainly help to focus our questions and our understanding of the forces at work in the world today. Of course history is easily manipulated, though that makes it even more important for us to know what actually happened. We need a knowledge of history to spot the delusions of leaders and the media. As voters and citizens, we have to be able to see through these dangerous distortions. Besides, history is — or should be — interesting. The chain of cause and effect is fascinating, as are the details. ______, many teachers who lack historical training themselves are naturally defensive, fearing that their subject may be boring to their pupils. I would never argue that historians or history teachers have a moral role. Their main obligation is to understand the mentality of the time and to pass on that understanding. Nor should they simplify for moral effects. History offers the richest imaginable source of moral examples and moral dilemmas, which are themselves the essence of great fiction, great drama, and life itself. Without an understanding of history, we are politically, culturally and socially impoverished.

10. Which of the following cannot be inferred from the passage?

① Understanding history helps us resist untruths propagated by power.

② Morals of past events should be diluted through history education.

③ Some teachers today do not seem confident about the appeal of history.

④ History enables us to form a perspective required for understanding the present.

11. Choose the one that best fills in the blank.

① Repulsed by this

② Motivated by this

③ In concordance with this

④ Shying away from this

12. What is the best title for the passage?

① Pitfalls of History

② Competing Interpretations of History

③ What History Tells

④ Historical Insights for the Future

13~15.

Mr. Makari's highly engaging story begins with Rene Descartes. Ever since Greek philosophy had merged with Christianity, the soul had been regarded as the "unifying link between nature, man and God." Mr. Makari writes. By the 17th century, however, Christendom was in crisis, and many found it hard to reconcile the notion of an incorporeal soul with a mechanical world that was increasingly understood as made up of matter. Descartes tried to satisfy the demand of skeptical naturalists by narrowing the concept of the soul to a "thing that thinks," yet that was separate from the body. The French philosopher thus breathed new life into the Christian belief in an immortal soul. At the other end of the Ⓐ ________ stood Thomas Hobbes, who thought there was no such thing as "immaterial substance." In his view the soul, rather than being rational and Godlike, was "material, prone to illness and errors." Ⓑ __________. And they were to demonstrate the importance of Mr. Makari's narrative as more than just an intellectual exercise. After Hobbes concluded that men were controlled by animal feelings that inevitably produced conflict, his proposed solution was to hand over power to an absolute monarch.

13. Select the statement most consistent with the passage.

① European philosophy became increasingly religious in the seventeenth century.

② Mr. Makari charts the rise of modern secular philosophy.

③ Hobbes advocated modern forms of demagoguery based on humans' tendency to "illness and errors."

④ Descartes emphasized the insignificance of the mechanical world.

14. Choose the best sentence that fits blank Ⓑ above.

① Hobbes's views were consistent with those of Descartes but extrapolated them one step further

② Hobbes corroborated Descartes's ideas by translating his notion of the immaculate soul into material terms

③ The disparate views on the nature of the "thing that thinks" were to have monumental implications

④ Rather than "I think, therefore I am," Hobbes famously posited, "I think, therefore I am." but "I am, therefore I think, too"

15. Choose the best word for blank Ⓐ above.

① diaspora

② bulwark

③ obscurity

④ gamut

16~19.

It makes little sense to imagine the scene of culture as one that one might enter to find bits and pieces of evidence that show an Ⓐ ________ abiding faith in a~~n al~~ready established notion of universality. If one were to enter various domains of culture in order to find examples of world citizens, one would Ⓑ ________ from those various examples the selfsame lesson, the selfsame universal bearing. But is the relation between culture and the universal appropriately construed as that between an example and the moral dictum it is said to support? In such cases, the examples are subordinate to the universal, and they all indicate the universal in the same way. The future articulation of the universal, however, can happen only if we find ways fo effect cultural translations between those various cultural examples in order to see which versions of the universal are proposed, on what exclusions they are based, and how the entry of the excluded into the domain of the universal requires a radical transformation in our thinking of universality. When competing claims to the universal are made, it seems imperative not to presume that the cultural moments at issue exemplify a(n) Ⓒ ________ universal. The claim is part of the ongoing cultural articulation of universality, and the complex process of learning how to read that claim is not something any of us can do outside of the difficult process of cultural translation. This translation will not be an easy one in which we reduce every cultural instance to a presupposed universality, nor will it be the enumeration of radical particularisms between which no communication is possible.

16. Choose the answer that has the closest meaning to the underlined word Ⓐ above.

① staunch

② coruscating

③ subsiding

④ appending

17. How does the author define the “universal”?

① a religious belief that opposes modern androcentric culture

② a perennial truth that can only be discovered through numerous cultural translations

③ an ideology to be debunked

④ an ongoing approximation of perspectives in a single articulation

18. According to the author, why are cultural translations important for the future expression of the universal?

① It is central to the articulation of a multicultural society based on mutual respect for one another.

② It is needed to recognize and incorporate excluded aspects into better approximations of the universal.

③ It is essential for actualizing timeless truths that can only be articulated through cultural comparisons.

④ An abiding faith should be reinforced by adopting a universal truth that reflects all cultures.

19. Choose the best words for blanks Ⓑ and Ⓒ above.

① Ⓑ cull - Ⓒ ready-made

② Ⓑ rile up - Ⓒ protean

③ Ⓑ foment - Ⓒ excremental

④ Ⓑ prod - Ⓒ nascent

UNIT 13 Test 3

1~4.

Ⓐ _____; rather, gender is an identity tenuously constituted in time, instituted in an exterior space through a stylized repetition of acts. The effect of gender is produced through the stylization of the body and, hence, must be understood as the mundane way in which bodily gestures, movements, and styles of various kinds constitute the illusion of an abiding gendered self. This formulation moves the conception of gender off the ground of a substantial model of identity to one that requires a conception of gender as a constituted Ⓑ _____. Significantly, if gender is instituted through acts which are internally discontinuous, then the Ⓒ _______ is precisely that, a constructed identity, a performative accomplishment which the mundane social audience, including the actors themselves, come to believe and to perform in the mode of belief. Gender is also a norm that can never be fully internalized; "the internal" is a surface signification, and gender norms are finally Ⓓ _____, impossible to embody. If the ground of gender identity is the stylized repetition of acts through time and not a seemingly seamless identity, then the spatial metaphor of a "ground" will be displaced and revealed as a stylized configuration, indeed, a gendered corporealization of time. The abiding gendered self will then be shown to be structured by repeated acts that seek to approximate the ideal of substantial ground of identity, but which, in their occasional discontinuity, reveal the temporal and contingent groundlessness of this "ground." The possibilities of gender transformation are to be found precisely in the arbitrary relation between such acts.

1. Choose the best phrase for blank Ⓐ above.

① Gender roles vary little from culture to culture

② Gender should not be seen as performative

③ Gender ought not to be construed as a stable identity

④ One cannot assume gender identity to be mimetic

2. Choose the best phrase for blanks Ⓑ and Ⓒ above.

① cultural construction - diaphanous transcendence

② patriarchal illusion - perceived existence

③ spatial anomaly - gendered subjectivity

④ social temporality - appearance of substance

3. Choose the best word for blank Ⓓ above.

① feckless

② phantasmatic

③ opprobrious

④ saturnine

4. Which statement CANNOT be inferred from the passage?

① Gender can only be fully internalized through the recognition of a mundane social audience.

② Gender only approximates a grounded identity.

③ Gender is constituted through repeated temporal iterations.

④ Gender gives the illusion of unity through inherently discontinuous bodily movements, gestures, and styles.

5~7.

Many of the early experimenters believed that they had devised tests that did not depend on acquired knowledge but were essentially a measure of ⓐ______ mental ability. Hence, they thought, the scores of individuals on such tests could not be affected by any ordinary differences in environment. However, various studies and experiments have demonstrated beyond a reasonable doubt that factors such as differences in family environment and schooling may have a substantial effect on the scores individuals make on standard intelligence tests. For example, when identical twins are separated early and reared in different types of homes, the twin reared by parents of superior social, economic, and educational status almost ⓑ______ does better on an intelligence test than the other of the pair, and sometimes the difference is fairly substantial.

Another example is that people who take the same test thirty years after entering high school will score in direct relation to how much education they have received in that span of time. Yet another chink in the armor of IQ test infallibility comes from Robert Rosenthal of Harvard University and Lenore Jacobsen, an elementary school principal in San Francisco, who successfully convinced a group of teachers that certain students were gifted. According to Pygmalion in the Classroom, in which the study is published, the students, ⓒ______, surpassed their classmates and became high-level achievers. These "brighter" students scored an average of 12.22 points higher on achievement tests administered at the beginning and end of the year, compared with only an 8.42 point improvement from their classmates. The only difference between the two groups was how the teachers responded to their learning needs.

5. What is the most appropriate title of the passage above?

① The History of Intelligence Tests

② Limitations of Intelligence Tests

③ Precursors to Intelligence Testing

④ How Do Intelligence Tests Work?

⑤ How to Interpret Intelligence Test Scores

6. Which pair best fits ⓐ and ⓑ?

① extrinsic - specifically

② innate - invariably

③ superior - marginally

④ mediated - uncommonly

⑤ incidental - allegedly

7. Which expression best fits ©?

① who were academically successful

② who were extraordinarily motivated

③ who were largely minority and at risk

④ who actually were chosen at random

⑤ who were learning in the traditional classrooms

8. Choose the best order after the sentences given in the box.

> Instead, Athena persuades them to join the city, giving them a place of honor beneath the earth, in recognition of their importance for those same legal institutions and the future health of the city.

At the end of Aeschylus' Oresteia, two transformations take place in the archaic world of the characters. In the famous transformation, Athena introduces legal institutions to replace and terminate the seemingly endless cycle of blood vengeance. ⓐ Setting up a court with established procedures of reasoned argument and the weighing of evidence, an independent third-party judge, and a jury selected from the citizen body of Athens, she announces that blood guilt will now be settled by law, rather than by the Furies, ancient goddesses of revenge. ⓑ But the Furies are not simply dismissed. © Typically this move of Athena's is understood to be a recognition that the legal system must incorporate the dark vindictive passions and honor them. ⓓ Thus the great Hellenist Hugh Lloyd-Jones concludes, "Far from wishing to abolish the prerogatives of the Erinyes, Athena is anxious to conserve them."

① A

② B

③ C

④ D

9. Choose the best order after the sentences given in the box.

December is here : store fronts are festooned with holiday decorations, the cold is setting in , and another year is reaching its close. December has marked the end of the year and the beginning of winter since the ancient Romans established their first calendar. As its etymology indicates, December is formed from the Latin root decem- "ten," though December is our twelfth month.

[A] This is because the ancient Roman calendar had only ten months in the year, which began in March. Eventually January and February were added to the end of the year after December, though by the time the Julian calendar was established in 45 B.C.

[B] The strange numbering discrepancy is also present for the months of September, October, and November, which mean "seven," "eight," and "nine," even though they are our ninth, tenth, and eleventh months, respectively.

[C] January and February appeared at the beginning of the year, bumping all of the original months back by two, and leaving the names as they were originally assigned.

① A - B - C

② A - C - B

③ B - A - C

④ B - C - A

⑤ C - B - A

10~12.

The West thought it was winning the battle against Jihadist terrorism. A few months ago Barack Obama declared that al-Qaeda was "on the path to defeat." Its surviving members, he said, were more concerned for their own safety than with plotting attacks on the West. Terrorist attacks of the future, he claimed, would resemble those of the 1990s — local rather than transnational and focused on "soft targets." His overall message was that it was time to start winding down George Bush's war against global terrorism. Mr Obama might argue that the assault on the Westgate shopping mall in Nairobi by al-Qaeda's Somali affiliate, the Shabab, was just the kind of thing he was talking abou: lethal, shocking, but a long way from the United States. Yet the inconvenient truth is that, in the past 18 months, despite the relentless pummelling it has received and the defeat it has suffered, al-Qaeda and its jihadist allies have stages an extraordinary comeback. The terrorist network now holds sway over more territory and its recruiting more fighters than at any time in its 25-year history.

10. Which would be the best title of the above passage?

① Mr Obama's Triumph over Terrorism

② Al-Qaeda's Counterattack in Nairobi

③ Mr Obama's Attack on al-Qaeda

④ Local vs Global Terrorists

⑤ The New Face of Terror

11. What is the main argument of the author?

① The West must cooperate with al-Qaeda.

② Al-Qaeda should not celebrate its success.

③ The West should not underestimate al-Qaeda.

④ The West is returning to its old system.

⑤ Al-Qaeda does not know what to do.

12. Which is not true of the above passage?

① Mr Obama expects that terror wouldn't happen in the US.

② Mr Obama thinks the terror in the future would be local

③ George Bush is responsible for the war against global terrorism

④ Al-Qaeda is planning a terror like 9/11 attacks against the US.

⑤ Al-Qaeda is recovering from its defeats these days.

13~15.

In most countries bereaved spouses or partners can expect only a fraction of the deceased's public pension, typically half, and it often comes with conditions attached, such as having dependent children or being close to retirement age themselves. In Brazil survivors of any age get almost the full sum for the rest of their lives. Even if the deceased person has not yet retired, the pension starts straight away. As a result, Brazil spends an unmatched 3% of GDP on survivors' pensions. Rich OECD countries on average spend less than 1%.

The pensioners themselves, too, do remarkably well. Men can retire at 65 and women at 60, on full pay up to a high cap, as long as they have contributed for 15 years. All but recently hired civil servants can retire on full pay with no cap. Men over 65 and women over 60 living in poor households get a pension equal to the minimum wage, currently 678 reais a month, even if they have never contributed. Rural workers, poor or not, enjoy the same privilege five years younger. Terms for early retirement are same privilege five years younger. Terms for early retirement are particularly generous. Greeks, whose pension system almost bankrupted their country, on average work on until they are 61. The average Brazilian draws a pension of 70% of final pay at 54.

13. The topic of the above passage is __________.

① Brazil's welfare system

② irrational pension system of Brazil

③ Brazil's ascension to a developed country

④ corruption of the Brazilian officers

⑤ average working hours of Brazilians

14. In Brazil, you can receive a full pay pension only if ________.

① you register for the pension

② you are born in Brazil

③ you work for 15 years

④ your spouse is dead

⑤ you are over working age

15. What does the underlined part "with no cap" mean?

① without any protection

② without any fund

③ without any clothes

④ without any limit

⑤ without any capability

16~18.

Vogelstein, a cancer geneticist, and Cristian Tomasetti, an applied mathematician, put forth a mathematical formula to explain the genesis of cancer in a research paper. Here's how it works: Take the number of cells in an organ, identify what percentage of them are long-lived stem cells, and determine how many times the stem cells divide. Ⓐ With every division, there's a risk of a cancer-causing mutation in a daughter cell. Thus, Tomasetti and Vogelstein reasoned, the tissues that host the greatest number of stem cell divisions are those most vulnerable to cancer. Ⓑ Although the randomness of cancer might be frightening, those in the field see a positive side, too. When Tomasetti crunched the numbers and compared them with actual cancer statistics, he concluded that this theory explained two-thirds of all cancers.

"Using the mathematics of evolution, you can really develop an engineerlike understanding of the disease," says Nowak, who has worked with Tomasetti and Vogelstein. "It's a baseline risk of being an animal that has cells that need to divide." The idea emerged during one of the pair's weekly brainstorming sessions in Vogelstein's office. They returned to an age-old question: How much of cancer is driven by environmental factors, and how much by genetics? Ⓒ To solve that, Tomasetti reasoned, "I first need to understand how much is by chance and take that out of the picture."

By "chance" Tomasetti meant the roll of the dice that each cell division represents, leaving aside the influence of deleterious genes or environmental factors such as smoking or exposure to radiation. He was most interested in stem cells because they endure - meaning that a mutation in a stem cell is more likely to cause problems than a mutation in a cell that dies more quickly. Tomasetti searched the literature to find the number of stem cell divisions over a lifetime risk of cancer in 31 different organs revealed a correlation. Ⓓ As the number of divisions rose, so did risk.

Colon cancer, for example, is far more common than cancer of the duodenum, the first stretch of the small intestine. This is true even in those who carry a mutated gene that puts their entire intestine at risk. Tomasetti found that there are about stem cell divisions in the colon over a lifetime, compared with in the duodenum. Mice, by contrast, have more stem cell divisions in their small intestine - and more cancers - than in their colon. The line between mutations and cancer isn't necessarily direct. "It may not just be whether a mutation occurs," says Bruce Ponder, a longtime cancer researcher.

16. 위 글의 흐름상 가장 적합하지 않은 것을 고르시오.

① Ⓐ

② Ⓑ

③ Ⓒ

④ Ⓓ

17. 위 글을 통해 추론할 수 있는 것으로 가장 적합한 것을 고르시오.

① The number of stem cell divisions has to do with the productivity of their daughter cells.

② For mice, more stem cell divisions lead to less risk of cancers.

③ Cells with short life span do not incur cancer-causing mutation as often as stem cells.

④ In rodents, colon cancer is more frequently observed than duodenum cancer.

18. 위 글의 제목으로 가장 적합한 것을 고르시오.

① The Simple Math that Explains Why You May Get Cancer

② The Proactive Research Agenda that Intrigue Extensive Arguments

③ The Best Solution to Prevent You from Having Cancer

④ The Effective Method to Explore the Stem Cell that Causes Cancer

19~20.

A best-selling book offers "Seven Ways to Become a Better Person." A radio ad promises you will feel great in 30 days or less just by taking some pills. If you buy our exercise equipment, a TV ad guarantees, you will have the body you have always wanted. In today's society, we are continually bombarded with the latest techniques of how to better ourselves, a focus which some feel is unhealthy. (A) A better approach would be to help people grow in character. (B) Building character involves taking a person's strengths and building on them. Such strengths as unselfishness can be developed into a lifelong habit of generosity, a positive spirit into an unfailing compassion for others. Everyone has strength in character and the ability to build on these strengths through self-improvement. (C) For example, impatience can be turned into determination to accomplish goals. Strong will turns into perseverance. (D) If a person can just find a way to capitalize on a weakness, it can be turned into a strength. Self-improvement is the best way to do this.

19. 아래의 문장이 들어갈 가장 알맞은 곳은?

Weakness are not flaws, but rather negative traits that, through self-improvement, can be developed into more positive traits.

① (A)
② (B)
③ (C)
④ (D)

20. 윗글의 다음에 올 내용으로 가장 알맞은 것은?
① steps to get rid of weaknesses
② a discussion about what defines character
③ a book review of a book titled, Seven Ways to Become a Better Person
④ a guide to improving character through strengths and weaknesses

21~23.

We can sometimes observe people whose general intellectual abilities are much lower than average but whose talent in a certain area is extraordinary. They are often called "savants." One interesting example of savants is 'language savant.' Christopher had a lot of difficulty doing routine things due to his low general intelligence. He needed help even when he buttoned his shirt or vacuumed the carpet. However, there was one thing he could do extremely well; he was able to speak and write more than 10 languages. He had not been taught those languages by language teachers or any specialists. Rather, he acquired them in his own way, like reading grammar books by himself. How can we reconcile the conflict between his poor intelligence and superb linguistic ability? One possibility seems to be to propose that language faculty has little do to with general intelligence. In other words, linguistic ability neither reflects nor presupposes general intellectual ability. In fact, such a proposal has been made by some linguists and psychologists. _______, little has been known so far about what makes it possible for language savants to have extraordinary talent. To know the truth, lots of research would be necessary on the ability of savants.

21. Fill in the blank.

① However

② In addition

③ To sum up

④ For instance

22. What is the passage about?

① The necessity of foreign language education for the disabled

② The definition of savants and their limitations in language learning

③ The importance of self-study in savants' language acquisition

④ The mystery of language savants' talent and low intelligence

23. Which of the following is correct about Christopher?

① He had an average nonverbal IQ while his language skills are unusual

② He could do only simple jobs by himself such as vacuum cleaning.

③ Grammar books were helpful for him to learn many languages by himself.

④ He had a chance to learn more than 10 languages from language specialists.

24~25.

We've all seen animals playing. But are they having fun? (A) In the past, most scientists believed that only humans could have fun. But today, those beliefs are changing. More and more scientists are studying animal emotions and play. (B) And what they are finding out might surprise you. For example, scientists have done experiments to show that some animals laugh. They have learned that chimpanzees, dogs, and rats, among other animals, all laugh. Their laughs might not sound like human laughter, but they are laughing. The idea of laughing chimpanzees and dogs may not be difficult to imagine. (C) And anyone who has a dog knows that dogs like to play. However, rats? Have you ever played with a rat? Have you ever tickled one? (D) Scientists at a university in Ohio did. What happened? The rats laughed! Actually, they chirped, which is the sound that rats make. And like humans, the rats chirped only when someone they knew and liked tickled them. But how do the scientists know that the rats were really laughing? (E) They studied their brains. When humans laugh, one part of the brain is very active. When a rat chirps, that part of its brain is active, too.

24. Which is the best place for the following sentence?

We know that there are many similarities between humans and chimps.

① (A) ② (B) ③ (C)

④ (D) ⑤ (E)

25. What is the most suitable title for the passage?

① Why Do Humans Laugh?

② How Do Animals Have Fun?

③ Do Animals Have Emotions?

④ Are Animal Experiments Reliable?

⑤ Do Animals Laugh?

UNIT 14 Test 4

1~2.

Nobody believes that media by themselves cause aggression. But Leonardo Eron and Rowell Huesmann of the University of Michigan found in a 22-year study following kids from third grade through adulthood that the single best predictor of later aggression - better than poverty, grades, a single-parent home or exposure to real violence - is a heavy childhood diet of TV carnage. "Of course not every youngster is affected," say Eron. "Not everyone who gets lung cancer smoked cigarettes. And not everyone who smokes cigarettes gets lung cancer. But nobody outside the tobacco industry denies that smoking causes lung cancer." Much of the most effective research has been done on children because they are considered most _____. As Centerwall puts it, " Later variations in exposure, in adolescence and adulthood, do not exert any additional effect." In the early 60's, Albert Bandura at Stanford was the frist to show four theories of learning to describe how TV violence may influence kids: they learn to imitate what they see on TV, especially when the behavior is rewarded; from the frequency of violence on TV they learn that violence is normal; they become desensitized to real people's suffering; and they become aroused by images on television, triggering violent responses.

1. Which of the following is inferred from the above passage?

① Media can cause copycat crimes.

② Smoking always gives rise to lung cancer.

③ The poverty in childhood plays the most important role in later violence.

④ Exposure to violence on TV leads kids to be sensitive to people's suffering.

⑤ Bandura believes that kids do not learn violent behavior from their parents.

2. Which best fits in the blank?

① susceptible

② immature

③ rebellious

④ influential

⑤ aggressive

3~4.

Sentimentality, notoriously, is entirely compatible with a taste for brutality and worse. (Recall the canonical example of the Auschwitz commandant returning home in the evening, embracing his wife and children, and sitting at the piano to play some Schubert before dinner.) People don't become inured to what they are shown — if that's the right way to describe what happens — because of the quantity of images dumped on them. It is passivity that dulls feelings. The states described as Ⓐ ___________, moral or emotional anesthesia, are full of feelings; the feelings are rage and frustration. But if we consider what emotions would be desirable, it seems to simple to elect sympathy. The imaginary proximity to the suffering inflicted on others that is granted by images suggests a link between the far-away sufferers — seen close-up on the television screen — and privileged viewer that is simply untrue, that is yet one more mystification of our real relations to power. So far as we feel sympathy, we feel we are not accomplices to what caused the suffering. Our sympathy proclaims our innocence as well as our impotence. To that extent, it can be (for all our good intentions) an impertinent — if not an inappropriate — response. To set aside the sympathy we extend to others beset by war and murderous politics for a reflection on how our privileges are located on the same map as their suffering, and may — in ways we might prefer not to imagine — be linked to their suffering, as the wealth of some may imply the destitution of others, is a task for which the painful, stirring images supply only an initial spark.

3. Choose the best word for blank Ⓐ.

① pathos

② sympathy

③ apathy

④ inertia

4. Choose the statement most consistent with tha passage.

① The author calls for sympathy for the suffering caused by war and murderous politics

② An innate tropism toward the gruesome is as natural to human beings as is sympathy

③ The increase of information in media about calamities taking place in another country makes the spectator a better citizen of the world.

④ Journalism driven by mercantile values and its hunt for more dramatic images is a quintessential feature of modern experience.

5.

All human beings, in their understanding of themselves, build sets of defenses to protect the ego. The newborn baby has no concept of its own self; gradually it learns to identify a self that is distinct from others. Ⓐ In childhood, the growing degrees of awareness, responding, and valuing begin to create a system of affective traits that individuals identify with themselves. Ⓑ In adolescence, the physical, emotional, and cognitive changes of the pre-teenager and teenager bring on mounting defensive inhibitions to protect a fragile ego, to ward off ideas, experiences, and feelings that threaten to dismantle the organization of values and beliefs on which appraisals of self-esteem have been founded. Ⓒ Some persons - those with higher self-esteem and ego strength - are more able to withstand threats to their existence, and thus their defenses are lower. Ⓓ those with weaker self-esteem maintain walls of inhibition to protect what is self-perceived to be a weak or fragile ego, or a lack of self-confidence in a situation or task.

5. Which is the best place to fill the following sentence in?

The process of building defenses continues into the next phase.

① Ⓐ

② Ⓑ

③ Ⓒ

④ Ⓓ

6. Choose the best order after the sentence in the box.

In 1979, when Ken Ross was eight, his family moved from Scotland to France for his father's job with IBM.

Ⓐ During the past quarter-century, according to the International School Consultancy Group(ISG), based in Britain, their number has grown from under 1,000 to more than 7,300. In the 2013-14 academic year they generated $41.6 billion in revenue and taught 3.75 million pupils globally. Twenty-two countries have more than 100 international schools, headed by the UAE, with 478, and China, with 445.

Ⓑ The computer firm paid the fees at the English School of Paris, where his classmates were mostly children of expats from Britain and elsewhere: managers, army officers, diplomats and the like. A couple were Saudi princes. For the most recent class reunion, old boys and girls, flew in from as far afield as China and South Africa.

Ⓒ Since then, there has been a boom in such "international schools," which teach in English in non-Anglophone countries, mostly offering British A-levels, American APs and SATs, or the International Baccalaureate.

① Ⓐ - Ⓒ - Ⓑ

② Ⓑ - Ⓐ - Ⓒ

③ Ⓑ - Ⓒ - Ⓐ

④ Ⓒ - Ⓐ - Ⓑ

7~9.

One of this year's top-selling Christmas presents is a drone. For $50 you can buy a tiny quadcopter with a video camera, perfect for snapping a bird's-eye view of your garden; for $700, one equipped with a gyroscopically stabilised camera which, when paired with a wireless tracking device on your wrist, will film you while you ski, cycle or kite-surf. More significantly still, drones could revolutionize all sorts of businesses.

Initially developed for military use, drones are taking off in civilian life largely thanks to the falling costs of commodity electronics. A smartphone contains a raft of devices that can be deployed in drones, including gyroscopes, accelerometers, wireless transmitters, signal processors and GPS units.

One immediate commercial use is surveying land cheaply and effectively. A drone can photograph a road to a resolution of 2cm, compared with the 30cm that a satellite offers - and it can do so at a third of the cost. Already farmers are using them to monitor crop growth, which in turn enables modern farm machinery to deliver exactly the right amount and type of fertilizer. Ⓐ Drones also improve safety: they can be used to do jobs, such as inspecting power lines, that currently require dangling a man from a helicopter. And they can deliver goods faster. DHL, a logistics firm, already uses a "parcelcopter" to deliver medicine to Just, a small island off the coast of Germany. But their potential depends on regulation. Ⓑ Since they can be dangerous - there are increasing numbers of reports from nervous airline pilots of drones flying near them - governments need to set rules for their use. And treatment of the commercial drones varies between countries.

America's Federal Aviation Authority (FAA) bans almost all commercial drone use. Ⓒ That will soon change, as Congress has ordered it to come up with rules for commercial drone flights by September 30th 2015. Ⓓ The drone industry suspects that this is regulatory capture - that the FAA is acting as a lobby for pilots.

The right way to balance safety and innovations is to create a set of rules for commercial drones that depend on their size, use and so on. The rules should also vary according to location, since surveying the outside of a building in a city is more hazardous than flying over a field. Like any disruptive technology , commercial drones will hurt existing business. Some pilots will lose their jobs as more farmers and logistics firms use drones instead of hiring a helicopter or aircraft. The incumbents' opposition to the drone industry is understandable. The FAA's is not. It should take a more objective view, and free commercial drones.

7. Choose the one that does not agree with the passage.

① Reduced cost in producing drones in part boosts the current booming of drones.

② Besides personal use, drones have potential to change current businesses drastically.

③ Germany is the first to use a drone for medicine delivery to remote islands.

④ Drones can be used for land survey and power line inspection.

8. Choose the best place for the sentence in the box.

But draft proposals due in the next few weeks are expected to show that the FAA continues to take a restrictive view, requiring drone operators to have experience flying manned aircraft and to keep drones within sight at all times.

① Ⓐ

② Ⓑ

③ Ⓒ

④ Ⓓ

9. Which of the following best describes the author's position?

① Despite all the benefit of commercial drones, law makers should consider job security for pilots and existing business such as logistics firms.

② Drones have immense commercial potential, so long as regulators don't try to tether them to the ground.

③ Commercial use of drones should be restricted due to latent dangers in unmanned manoeuvre.

④ Drone operators are required to have experience of flying manned aircraft and to keep drones within sight at all times.

10. Choose the best order after the sentences given in the box.

There is no duty we so much underrate as the duty of being happy. By being happy we sow anonymous benefits upon the world, which remain unknown even to ourselves, or when they are disclosed, surprise nobody so much as the benefactor.

Ⓐ One of these persons, who had been delivered from more than usually black thoughts, stopped the little fellow and gave him some money with this remark: 'You see what sometimes comes of looking pleased.'
Ⓑ The other day, a ragged, barefoot boy ran down the street after a marble, with so jolly an air that he set everyone he passed into a good humor.
Ⓒ If the boy had looked pleased before, he had now to look both pleased and confused. For my part, I justify this encouragement of smiling rather than tearful children.
Ⓓ I do not pay for tears anywhere but upon the stage; but I am prepared to deal largely in the opposite commodity. A happy man or woman is a better thing to find than a five-pound note.

① Ⓐ - Ⓑ - Ⓓ - Ⓒ
② Ⓑ - Ⓐ - Ⓒ - Ⓓ
③ Ⓒ - Ⓑ - Ⓐ - Ⓓ
④ Ⓓ - Ⓒ - Ⓑ - Ⓐ

11. Which is the best place for the following sentence?

It does mean that you can be sure they'll be safe and potent at least until the expiration date.

The FDA requires that drug manufacturers test their products to see how long they last and then include an expiration date on the packaging. Ⓐ That doesn't necessarily mean that the products are no good the day after the expiration date. Ⓑ Most manufacturers just don't keep testing forever to see when their products lose potency. Ⓒ Companies may test only for a year or two, and if the product is okay, they stamp an expiration date of one year or two - whatever applies - after the date of manufacture. Ⓓ The question of expiration dates may seem tricky, but there are guidelines that can help consumers keep medications and foods safe.

① Ⓐ　② Ⓑ　③ Ⓒ　④ Ⓓ

12~13.

A former mortgage consultant, Chris Ihle, had just parked his motorcycle in front of his office in Ames, Iowa, last July when he noticed a Pontiac Bonneville sedan with disabled-person tags stalled on railroad tracks. Then he heard a train whistle from next intersection.

Chris threw down his glasses and keys near his bike and ran toward the car. An elderly man in a neck brace, Jean Papich, 84, sat in the driver's seat, turning the key and hitting the gas. Jean's wife, Marion, 78, was peering nervously at him from the passenger's seat. Ⓐ Chris ducked under the crossing gates, got behind the car, and pushed, but his boots slipped on the warm asphalt. He could see the train approaching fast. Ⓑ He ran around to the front of the vehicle and shouted at Jean to put the car in neutral. Chris could feel the ground rumbling beneath his feet as the locomotive was bearing down on them, brakes squealing and horn blaring. He wedged his boots into the track grooves and shoved. Finally, the car rolled off the tracks.

When Chris looked up, the Union Pacific train's towering grill was just a few feet away. Ⓒ He flattened himself against the side of the sedan as the train roared past. Ⓓ Stunned and speechless, Chris staggered back to work and poured himself a cup of coffee as a crowd gathered at the scene. Weeks later, Marion called to thank Chris. He responded, "There's a time to talk and a time to act."

12. Which is the best place for the following sentence?

It might be easier to push the car backward, Chris thought.

① Ⓐ ② Ⓑ
③ Ⓒ ④ Ⓓ

13. Which is the best title for the passage?

① An Unhappy car Accident on Railroad Tracks
② Pushing or Pulling? Which One is More Effective?
③ Quick Thinking Saves a Couple Stalled in a Train's Way
④ A Former Mortgagc Consultant Met a Disabled Couple on a Train

14. Choose the best order after the sentences given in the box.

> Therefore in a just society the liberty of equal citizenship is taken as settled: the rights secured by justice are not subject to the calculus of interests or to political bargaining.

Justice is the first virtue of social institutions, as truth is of systems of thought. (A) A theory, however elegant and economical, must be rejected or revised if it is untrue: likewise, laws and institutions, no matter how efficient and well-arranged, must be reformed or abolished if they are unjust. (B) Each person possesses an inviolability founded on justice that even the welfare of society as whole, cannot override. (C) For this reason justice denies that the loss of freedom for some is made right by a greater good shared by others. It does not allow that the sacrifices imposed on a few are outweighed by the larger sum of advantages enjoyed by many. (D) The only thing that permits us to acquiesce in an erroneous theory is the lack of a better one; analogously, an injustice is tolerable only when it is necessary to avoid an even greater injustice. Being the first virtues of human activities, truth and justice are uncompromising.

① (A)

② (B)

③ (C)

④ (D)

15~16.

The sugar industry was expanded with cane from two different parts of the Orient: India and the islands of the Southwest Pacific. Cane cultivation eventually spread westward and was introduced to the Mediterranean region by the Arabs. In about 703 the sugar industry was established in Sicily and in about 755 it spread to Spain. Ⓐ As early as 1150, Spain had at least 75,000 acres of cane field. The Crusades were partly responsible for the further expansion and improvement of the sugar industry. During the early period, sugarcane was grown mainly to meet local demand.

Since sugarcane was transported through the western regions of Asia into Arabia and later into the counties adjacent to the Mediterranean, it gave rise to a cane sugar industry that flourished there until the late 1500's. Ⓑ After syrup was made from the evaporation of the juice, the sugarmakers determined when sugar crystals had formed, using rule-of-thumb technology. In 1493 Columbus brought sugarcane to the New World on his second voyage, and it was first planted on the island of Hispaniola. Ⓒ During the 16th and 17th centuries, the Spanish, English, and French established sugar production in their Caribbean island colonies. By the late 18 century, the French colony of St. Dominique (present-day Haiti) became one of the most important sugar producers in the Caribbean as demand for sugar was rising rapidly across many nations.

In the early 1700's American colonies tried to plant sugarcane from St. Dominique along the southern Mississippi, but the attempt failed. Ⓓ A little over a decade later, the first administrator of France's Louisiana colony transported sugarcane from Martinique and successfully grew it in New Orleans. The French Jesuits introduced and raised cane from St. Dominique at their New Orleans plantation in the 1750's. During the late 1750's and early 1760's, a few colonists succeeded in producing sugar for commercial purposes in the New Orleans area with cane brought from St. Dominique or the Jesuits.

15. 위 글에서 논지의 흐름상 가장 적합하지 않은 것을 고르시오.

① Ⓐ ② Ⓑ

③ Ⓒ ④ Ⓓ

16. 위 글의 주제로 가장 적합한 것을 고르시오.

① Early history of the sugar industry

② Cane cultivation in the Mediterranean

③ Use of human resources in the sugar industry

④ Contribution of sugar to the modern world

17~19.

The birth of Dolly the sheep seemed one of those moments in scientific research that would change the world forever. The cloning of the first animal from an adult cell was a remarkable scientific achievement. It promised new treatments for debilitating diseases. But it also raised fears of cloned human beings, designer babies and a dystopian future.

Dolly was created from DNA taken from a cell taken from a sheep. There were 277 attempts to clone Dolly and many miscarriages on the way. There were also genuine concerns that it would not be long before cloned humans would be walking the Earth. The airwaves were filled with conversations about what it meant to be human, whether the clones would be exactly the same as the person from which they were cloned and what kind of world the scientists were tumbling us into.

Dolly's creator, Prof Ian Wilmut, was acutely aware of ________. And he knew it was important to be clear, open and honest about his work. He promoted the term "therapeutic cloning": his vision was to develop treatments for heart disease, Parkinson's Disease and rheumatism by taking cells from patients and using cloning technology to create healthy tissues which could then be transplanted to heal their damaged cells.

The raised further concerns from some church and anti-abortion groups, who were concerned that the process involved the creation, and then destruction, of human embryos. They wanted the technology banned but, following strong lobbying by the medical research community. British parliament permitted therapeutic cloning but banned the cloning of human beings.

Since then, the much hoped-for benefits from therapeutic cloning have not emerged. But scientists have proved that animal cells could be reprogrammed. They can now be rejuvenated and redirected to form any cell in the human body. Scientists may not have reaped the clinical benefits just yet but, at a stroke, Dolly's birth changed scientific thinking forever.

17. Which of the following is most appropriate for the blank?

① official denunciation

② communal decision

③ professional opinion

④ partisan slander

⑤ public suspicion

18. The best topic of the above passage would be ________.

① The History of Dolly the Sheep

② Dolly's Legacy

③ An Exact Genetic Copy of the Human

④ Fear of Modern Frankenstein

⑤ Therapeutic Cloning

19. According to the passage, which of the following is NOT correct?

① Some church groups showed strong worry about the destruction of viable embryos for medical use.

② Therapeutic cloning refers to the use of cloning technology in regenerating human cells to restore their normal function.

③ Dolly the sheep was the first successful case of the reproductive cloning of a mammal.

④ British parliament finally prohibited the cloning of the living organism after the birth of Dolly.

⑤ There is growing concern that in the foreseeable future it would be possible to use the current cloning technique to produce a human clone.

20~21.

By studying instinctive and learned fear in people and in experimental animals, we have gained much insight into both the behavioral and the biological mechanisms of instinctive and learned fear in people. One of the first behavioral insights was stimulated by the theories of Freud and the American philosopher William James, who realized that fear has both conscious and unconscious components. What was not clear was how the two components interact. Traditionally, fear in people was thought to begin with conscious perception of an important event, such as seeing one's house on fire. This recognition produces in the cerebral cortex an emotional experience — fear — that triggers signals to the heart, blood vessels, adrenal glands, and sweat glands to mobilize the body in preparation for defense or escape. Thus, according to this view, a conscious, emotional event initiates the later Ⓐ________ defensive responses in the body.

James rejected this view. In a highly influential article published in 1884 and entitled "What is Emotion?" he proposed that the cognitive experience of emotion is secondary to the physiological expression of emotion. He suggested that when we encounter a potentially dangerous situation — for example, a bear sitting in the middle of our path — our evaluation of the bear's ferocity does not generate a consciously experienced emotional state. We do not experience fear Ⓑ________ we have run away from the bear.

20. Which does NOT fit in the blank Ⓐ?

① cognitive

② reflexive

③ biological

④ physiological

21. Which does NOT fit in the blank Ⓑ?

① because

② so that

③ until after

④ irrespective of

UNIT 15 Test 5

1~3.

The elegance of the brain lies in its inelegance. For centuries, neuroscience attempted to neatly assign labels to the various parts of the brain: This is the area for language, this for morality, this for tool use, color detection, face recognition, and so on. The search for an orderly brain map started off as a viable endeavor but turned out to be misguided.

The deep and beautiful trick of the brain is more interesting: It possesses multiple, overlapping ways of dealing with the world. It is a machine built of conflicting parts. It is a representative democracy that functions by competition among parties who all believe they know the right way to solve the problem. Ⓐ _____, we can get mad at ourselves, argue with ourselves, curse at ourselves, and contract with ourselves. We can feel conflicted. These sorts of neural battles lie behind marital infidelity, relapses into addiction, cheating on diets, breaking of New Year's resolutions - all situations in which some parts of a person want one thing and other parts another.

These are things that modern machines simply do not do. Your car cannot be conflicted about which way to turn: It has one steering wheel commanded by one driver, and it follows directions without complaint. Brains, on the other hand, can be of two minds, and often many more. We don't know whether to turn toward the cake or away from it, because there are several sets of hands on the steering wheel of behavior.

Take memory. Under normal circumstances, memories of daily events are consolidated by an area of the brain called the hippocampus. But in frightening situations - such as a car accident or a robbery - another area, the amygdala, also lays down memories along an independent, secondary memory track. Amygdala memories have a different quality to them: They are difficult to erase and they can return to "flash-bulb" fashion - a common description of rape victims and war veterans. Ⓑ _____, there is more than one way to lay down memory. We're talking not about memories of different events but about different memories of the same event. According to the unfolding picture, there may be even more than two factions involved, all writing down information and later competing to tell the story. The unity of memory is an illusion.

1. 밑줄 친 Ⓐ와 Ⓑ에 들어가기에 가장 적절한 것을 고르시오.

① Under the circumstances - Notwithstanding

② As an illustration - For instance

③ However - Without doubt

④ As a result - In other words

2. 위 글을 통해 추론할 수 있는 것으로 가장 적절한 것을 고르시오.

① The existence of the hippocampus may account for individual variations in one's response to emotionally stressful events.

② Unusual tragic events can be recorded in multiple memory tracks.

③ Various parts of the brain coordinate with one another via amygdala.

④ The illusory nature of the structure of the human brain can be examined in far greater detail when more sophisticated tools are available.

3. 위 글의 제목으로 가장 적절한 것을 고르시오.

① Brain Mapping: Decades of the Research and Recent Findings

② The Future of Brain: Challenges and Groundbreaking Advances

③ Functional Architecture of Brain: Modularity and Domain Specificity

④ Information Encapsulation in Brain: An Evolutionary Account

4~5.

As the world's largest emitter of carbon, China has decided that one of the best ways to clean up its polluted air is through solar power. (A) The country has led the world in solar installations for the last two years and will likely do so again in 2015. (B) It's on pace to reach 33 gigawatts of solar power capacity by the end of 2014, 42 times more than it had in 2010 and more than exists in Spain, Italy, and the U.K. combined, according to Bloomberg New Energy Finance(BNEF). Most of China's solar power comes from sprawling utility-scale solar farms in the country's rural west. (C) Now the idea is to distribute solar panels in Ⓐ _____ areas, putting them on top of office buildings and factories and connecting them to the grid without building miles of costly transmission lines. In 2015, BNEF estimates that China will add as much as 15 gigawatts of solar capacity, enough to power roughly 16 million homes. (D) If the 2015 projection holds, China will have installed twice more solar power in factories and office towers in one year than currently exists in all of Australia, one of the world's sunniest countries.

4. Which best fits into the blank Ⓐ?

① urban

② deserted

③ forgotten

④ encamped

5. Which is the best place for the following sentence?

More than half of that increase will come from cheap panels installed on commercial buildings.

① (A)　② (B)

③ (C)　④ (D)

6~8.

For the first time in history, across much of the world, to be foreign is a perfectly normal condition. It is no more Ⓐ _____ than being tall, fat, or left-handed. Nobody raises an eyebrow at a Frenchman in Berlin, a Zimbabwean in London, a Russian in Paris, a Korean in New York. The desire of so many people, given the chance, to live in countries other than their own makes nonsense of a long-established consensus in politics and philosophy that Ⓑ _____. The error of philosophy has been to assume that man, because he is a social animal, should belong to some particular society. No doubt many people do feel most at ease with a home and a homeland. But what about the others, who find home Ⓒ _____ and foreignness Ⓓ _____?

Theirs is a choice that gets both easier and more difficult to exercise with every passing year. Easier, because the globalisation of industry and education tramples national borders. More difficult, because there are ever fewer places left in this globalised world where you and go and feel utterly foreign when you get there.

6. Which best fits into the blank Ⓐ?

① positive

② ludicrous

③ distinctive

④ vulnerable

7. Which best fits into the blank Ⓑ?

① the human animal is best off at home

② nonsense can sometimes make consensus

③ the human desire is always self-contradictory

④ it is good to human nature to live in foreign countries

8. Which best fits in to blanks Ⓒ and Ⓓ?

① comfortable - disconcerting

② agreeable - disagreeable

③ unsatisfactory - unpleasant

④ oppressive - liberation

9~10.

We know all this well enough when we contemplate the dictatorships. But when we try to picture our own system, by way of contrast, what picture do we have in our minds? It is, is it not, that anyone may stand up on his own soapbox and say anything he pleases, like the individuals in Kipling's poem who sit each in his separate star and draw the Thing as they see it for the God of Things as they are. Kipling, perhaps, could do this, since he was a poet. But the ordinary mortal isolated on his separate star will have an hallucination, and a citizenry declaiming from separate soapboxes will poison the air with hot and nonsensical confusion. It is not true that liberty has developed among civilized men when anyone is free to set up a soapbox, is free to hire a hall where he may expound his opinions to those who are willing to listen. __________, freedom of speech is established when different opinions are expounded in the same hall to the same audience.

9. Which of the following is most appropriate for the blank?

① Therefore

② In addition

③ Finally

④ On the contrary

10. Which of the following is most true according to the passage?

① We should respect different opinions on the same base in a democratic society.

② The freedom of speech is important in its separate situation.

③ Dictatorships don't allow any kind of soapbox to declaim one's opinion.

④ Ordinary people want to keep their originality in their isolated stars.

11~13.

Thomas Hardy's impulses as a writer, all of which he indulged in his novels, were numerous and divergent, and they did not always work together in harmony. Hardy was to some degree interested in exploring his characters' psychologies, though impelled less by curiosity than by sympathy. Occasionally he felt the impulse to comedy (in all its detached coldness) as well as the impulse to farce, but he was more often inclined to see tragedy and record it. He was also inclined to literary realism in the several senses of that phrase. He wanted to describe ordinary human beings; he wanted to speculate on their dilemmas rationally (and, unfortunately, even schematically); and he wanted to record precisely the material universe. Finally, he wanted to be more than a realist. He wanted to transcend what he considered to be the banality of solely recording things exactly and to express as well his awareness of the occult and the strange.

In his novels these various impulses were sacrificed to each other inevitably and often. Inevitably, because Hardy did not care in the way that novelists such as Flaubert or James cared, and therefore took paths of least resistance. Thus, one impulse often surrendered to a fresher one and, unfortunately, instead of exacting a compromise, simply disappeared. A desire to throw over reality a light that never was might give way abruptly to the desire on the part of what we might consider a novelist-scientist to record exactly and concretely the structure and texture of a flower. In this instance, the new impulse was at least an energetic one, and thus its indulgence did not result in a relaxed style. But on other occasions Hardy abandoned a perilous, risky, and highly energizing impulse in favor of what was for him the fatally relaxing impulse to classify and schematize abstractly. When a relaxing impulse was indulged, the style — that sure index of an author's literary worth — was certain to become verbose. Hardy's weakness derived from his apparent inability to control the comings and goings of these divergent impulses and from his unwillingness to cultivate and ⓐ______ the energetic and risky ones.

11. What is the most appropriate title of the passage above?

① Divergent Impulses: The Issue of Unity in the Novel

② The Real and the Strange: Two Areas of Interest to Hardy

③ Hardy's Novelistic Impulses: The Problem of Control

④ The Role of Ordinary People in Hardy's Fiction

⑤ Verbosity: Hardy's Fatal Weakness

12. Which expression best fits ⓐ?

① sustain

② subordinate

③ suppress

④ supplant

⑤ subsidize

13. Which statement can not be inferred from the passage above?

① The term "literary realism" is susceptible to more than a single definition.

② A writer's style is considered to be a reliable means by which to measure the writer's literary merit.

③ The indulgence of a relaxing impulse led Hardy into a wordy style.

④ Flaubert and James indulged more impulses in their novels than did Hardy in his novels.

⑤ Comedy appeared less frequently in Hardy's novels than did tragedy.

14~15.

In addition to the belief that machines reduce the demand for skilled workers, there is an even more persistent notion that has little foundation in past experience — the idea that advances in machine technology, by replacing labor, progressively decrease total job opportunities and total employment. This belief had a strong appeal in the 1930s when millions were out of work. At that time, many writers argued that our economy had come "mature" and that in order to provide enough jobs in the future, it would be necessary either to spread the work around by progressively shortening the work week or else to have the government keep creating more jobs through an expanding program of public works. In addition to shortening the work week, it was often proposed that young people should be kept in school longer and that older workers should be retired at earlier ages.

No one questions that machines displace individual workers from certain jobs and that in the short run this often creates difficult problems. For example, the use of diesel engines and electric power by railroads has made ⓐ________ the position of "fireman" — the employee who shoveled coal into the locomotive boiler that produced the steam for the train's steam engine — but because of union support, railroads had to fill this position for many years after steam power ceased being used by trains. However, such problems are ⓑ________. Ultimately, advances in machine technology tend to reduce costs and prices or to hold them down, and by enabling people to buy more goods, they create new employment opportunities. If some industries employ fewer workers, others employ more. At the same time, new products are introduced and new industries are established.

14. What is the main idea of the passage above?

① Technological change will alter the composition of the demand for labor.

② New technologies frequently require specific new skills that schools don't teach.

③ Technology creates more problems than it solves and may threaten the quality of life.

④ Technological change does not increase overall unemployment, even though some types of workers may temporarily lose their jobs.

⑤ Although technological progress has conferred great benefits on the human population, it also has created many problems.

15. Which pair best fits ⓐ and ⓑ?

① unsullied - contemporary

② indispensable - insoluble

③ obsolete - temporary

④ invaluable - recurring

⑤ sporadic - staggering

16~18.

Human Acts is a book that could easily founder under the weight of its subject matter. Neither inviting nor shying away from modern-day parallels, Han Kang neatly unpacks the social and political catalysts behind the massacre and maps its lengthy, toxic fallout. But what is remarkable is how she accomplishes this while still making it a novel of blood and bone. The characters frequently address themselves to an unnamed 'You.' Sometimes 'You' is the dead, occasionally it is the reader but often, and most disturbingly, Ⓐ "You" is who people were before the violence and have now become irrevocably exiled from. This sense of Ⓑ________ is most obvious when a dead boy's soul converses with his own rotting flesh; it is here that the language comes closest to the gothic lyricism of Han's previous book, The Vegetarian. At least the boy possesses a soul. Many of the other victims are no longer certain that they do, and their shame at having survived is palpable. By choosing the novel as her form, then allowing it to do what it does best, take readers to the very center of a life that is not their own, Han prepares us for one of the most important questions of our times: "What is humanity? What do we have to do to keep humanity as one thing and not another?" She never answers, but this act of unflinching Ⓒ________ seems as good a place to start as any.

16. Which of the following is closest in meaning to Ⓐ?

① 'You' is the offspring of violent confrontation.

② 'You' is transformed into previous selves.

③ 'You' is characters prior to a permanent change.

④ 'You' is an exiled refugee in another country.

17. Which one of the following ordered pairs best fits into Ⓑ and Ⓒ?

① confirmation - withdrawal

② engagement - attestation

③ dislocation - witness

④ compatibility - spectacle

18. Which of the following is NOT true of the passage?

① The passage is a critical review of a literary work.

② The subject matter of the work is rather serious and disturbing

③ In this novel, Han keeps the grotesque and poetic style of the earlier one.

④ Han focuses on analyzing an event and clearly answers an important question.

19~21.

We use the terms "college" and "university" interchangeably. "She went to Michigan," we say, or "he goes to Oberlin" — not bothering with the noun that follows the name as if a college and a university were the same thing. They are not. Thet are, to be sure, interconnected and a college may exist as a division of "school" within a university. But a college and a university have a different purposes. Ⓐ The former is about transmitting knowledge of and from the past to undergraduate students so they may draw upon it as a living resource in the future. The latter is mainly an array of research activities conducted by faculty and graduate students with the aim of creating new knowledge in order to supersede the past. Ⓑ <u>Both of these</u> are worthy aims, and sometimes they converge, as when a college student works with a scholar or scientist doing cutting-edge or groundbreaking research. More often, however, these purposes come into competition if not conflict, especially as one moves up the ladder of prestige. Ⓒ As the man who created one of the world's great universities, the University of California, acknowledged with unusual honesty, "a superior faculty results in an inferior concern for undergraduate teaching." Ⓓ It has been nearly fifty years since Clark Kerr identified this <u>"cruel paradox"</u> as one of our more pressing problems. Today it is more pressing than ever. Ⓔ But what, exactly, is at stake in college, and why should it matter how much or little goes on there? Ⓕ At its core, a college should be a place where young people find help for navigating the territory between adolescence and adulthood. It should provide guidance, but not coercion, for students trying to cross that treacherous terrain on their way toward self-knowledge. It should help them develop certain qualities of mind and heart requisite for reflective citizenship.

19. The underlined "Both of these" refer to ________.

① college and university

② graduate and undergraduate

③ education and research

④ past and future

⑤ tradition and cutting-edge science

20. The underlined "cruel paradox" means that ________.

① a college might be better than a university

② great scholars are not necessarily great teachers

③ college diploma does not guarantee a decent job

④ a university professor may teach better than a college one

⑤ students don't learn much from their college life

21. If the above passage is divided into three paragraphs, the best boundary would be ________.

① Ⓐ - Ⓒ

② Ⓐ - Ⓓ

③ Ⓑ - Ⓓ

④ Ⓑ - Ⓔ

⑤ Ⓒ - Ⓕ

정답과 해설

정답과 해설

UNIT 0 글의 구조 총정리

1. 비교와 대조

1) 정치와 과학 사이엔 끊임없는 긴장 관계가 있다. 과학의 관점에서, 정책들은 과학적 데이터를 신중하게 고려한 것을 반영해야만 하고 과학의 발견과 추천하는 것들과 맞춰야 한다. 그러나, 정책 입안자들에게 조언을 제공하는 과학자들은 그들의 조언이 정책 입안 과정에서 무시되거나 왜곡된다고 종종 불평한다. 정치적인 가치와 필수적인 것들은 과학자들에 의해 제시된 데이터들과 극명하게 대립할지도 모른다. 과학에 의해 결정된 기준과 정치의 실용적인 필요성 사이의 절충을 보여주는 정책이 개발될지도 모른다. 효과적인 정책은 비용이 효율적이고 공평해야만 하고, 정부에 한정된 요구를 해야 하며, 대중에게 그 목표가 이루어질 것이라는 확신을 줘야 한다. 정부의 입장이 데이터에 의해 뒷받침되지 않으면 정부는 제안된 것을 받아들이기보다는 추가의 연구를 요구할 수도 있다. 극단적인 경우에는 정치의 분명한 요구에 직면하여 과학적 데이터가 묻힐 수도 있다.

2) 신장과 체중은 단순함에 있어서는 유사하지만 그것들이 어떻게 우리의 생활을 지배하는지에 있어서는 매우 다르다. 우리의 성인 신장은 고정되어 있고 그것에 대해 우리가 할 수 있는 것이 거의 없어서 키가 작은 사람들은 그들의 눈 색깔에 대해서뿐만 아니라 신장에 대해서도 책임이 있지 않다. 그러나 체중은 또 다른 문제이다. 우리는 의지력, 적절한 영양 섭취, 운동을 통해서 우리의 체중을 조절할 수 있다는 메시지의 공세를 받고 있다. 다이어트 산업은 (다이어트 프로그램, 다이어트 식품, 그리고 다이어트 잡지와 서적을 포함하는) 군살을 빼는 것을 간절히 원하는 미국 대중에 영합하여 수백억 달러의 수익을 가지며 규모가 엄청나다. 우리는 음식이 아닌 음식으로 가득 찬 식료품점에서 물건을 사고 그들을 어디로도 데려다주지 않는 러닝머신에서 미친 듯이 걷는 사람들로 가득 찬 체육관에서 운동한다. 매일 아침 우리는 욕실의 체중계 위에 서서 우리의 진전 또는 그것의 부재(진전이 없음)를 측정한다.

2. Myth & Truth

1) 50세 이상의 사람들은 소비자가 쓰는 돈의 약 48퍼센트를 쓴다고 추정된다. 그들은 전체 고급 승용차의 약 48퍼센트를 구매하고 호화로운 여행의 약 80퍼센트를 책임진다. 그들은 심지어 매년 전체 장난감의 약 25퍼센트를 구매한다.(미국에는 약 5천 5백만 명의 50세 이상의 조부모들이 있다.) 그럼에도 불구하고 마케팅 및 판매 촉진 프로그램은 보통 이러한 소비자들을 훨씬 더 나이가 많은 것처럼 취급한다. 예를 들어 나이 많은 소비자들은 특정 상품에 고정되어 있고 새로운 선택 가능한 상품을 써보려고 하지 않는다는 근거 없는 믿음이 있다. 그러니 왜 신상품의 광고가 나이 많은 소비자들을 겨냥해야 한단 말인가? 사실 쇼핑몰에 있는 500명의 50세가 넘는 사람들의 설문 조사는 그들의 약 80퍼센트가 신상품을 써 보고자 하는 의지가 꽤 있다는 것을 보여주었다.

2) 오랫동안 음식은 만성 질환의 위험 요인으로서 핵심적인 역할을 하는 것으로 알려져 왔다. 범지구적 수준에서 분명한 것은 20세기 후반이래 큰 변화가 전 세계를 휩쓸어 처음에는 산업이 발달된 지역에서, 그리고 보다 최근에는 개발도상국에서 음식에서의 주요한 변화를 야기했다는 것이다. 대체로 식물성인 전통 음식은 상당량의 동물성 음식으로 이루어진, 지방이 많은 고칼로리의 음식으로 빠르게 대체되었다. 그러나 음식은 질병 예방에 중요하기는 하지만 하나의 위험 요소일 뿐이다. 오늘날 점점 중요한 건강 결정 요인으로 인식되고 있는 신체적 비활동은 산업화된 국가에서만큼 개발도상국에서도 더 주로 앉아서 생활하는 방식으로 바뀌어 가는 생활양식의 점진적인 변화로 인해 나타난 결과이다.

3) 우리는 때때로 노화가 생물(인간) 전체에게 획일적으로 적용되는 과정이라고 생각하지만, 생리학 연구들은 신체의 서로 다른 부위들이 서로 다른 속도로 노화한다는 것을 보여준다. 예를 들어 백혈구는 10일 이내에 죽고 교체되지만, 적혈구는 120일 동안 살아남는다. 모든 혈구를 만드는 줄기세포는 노화의 징후가 전혀 없다. 뇌세포는 신체가 살아 있는 한 생존하는데, 일단 뇌가 완전히 형성되면, 신경세포들은 주목할 만한 세포 분열을 일으키지 않고, 질환에 의해서 손상되지 않는다면, 대체로 온전하게 유지된다. 그러나 수명이 긴 줄기세포와 뇌세포를 제외하고는, 신체의 대다수 부위들은 지속적으로 손상과 복구를 겪어야 한다. 노화의 이러한 과정에 원인이 되는 기제는 마모, 유리기의 영향, 그리고 면역 체계의 쇠퇴를 포함한다.

3. Problem & Solution

1) 청소년이 알아야 하는 가장 중요한 것 중 한 가지는, 여러분이 정상적이고 품위 있는 삶을 살려고 할 때마다 그것 때문에 여러분을 싫어하게 될 사람들을 늘 발견하게 될 것이라는 것이다. 그렇게 해서 대부분의 젊은이들이 어떤 상황에서 타협하게 된다. 그들은 자신들이 옳다고 생각하는 것을 포기하고 대세를 따르다가, 나중에 대가를 치른다. 여러분이 알아야 하는 것은, 여러분을 싫어하는 그 사람들은, 자신들이 그런 훌륭한 행동을 할 수 없다는 사실 때문에 시샘을 해서 여러분을 싫어하기로 결심한다는 것이다. 여러분에게 좋은 것이 있다면, 훌륭한 그 어떤 것도 결코 용납하지 않는 어리석은 사람들 때문에 그것을 포기하지는 마라. 여러분이 그들과 타협하는 것보다 그들이 여러분의 훌륭한 행동에 대해 여러분의 험담을 하는 것이 더 낫다. 그들이 여러분을 구식이라고 할 수 있지만, 그들이 무엇을 원하든지, 그것은 그들의 소관이 아니다.

2) 다른 사람들을 비판하는 데 중독되는 것은 효과적으로 피드백을 제공하는 데 커다란 장애물이다. 우리가 비판할 때, 비록 우리가 신중하게 단어들을 선택한다 하더라도, 우리는 다른 사람들을 특정한, 잠재적으로 해로운 상태로 분류할 가능성이 있다. 예를 들어, 우리는 다른 사람들을 '틀렸다'라는 상태로 분류할 가능성이 있는 것이다. 그 누구도 '틀린'이라는 꼬리표가 붙는 것을 조항하지 않는다. 대부분의 사람들은 그들에게 꼬리표가 붙을 때, 심지어 '틀리지' 않았다고 확신할 때조차 방어적으로 된다. 그리고 더욱 중요한 것은, 방어적인 사람들은 메시지를 차단한다는 것이다. 만약 여러분이 이해받지 않으려고 애쓰는 것이 아니라면, 그런 경우 비판은 효과적인 의사소통 전략이 아니다. 그것을 '건설적'이라고 부르는 것도 역시 도움이 되지 않는다. "나는 당신의 발전을 위해서 당신에게 이것을 이야기하는 거에요. 당신의 디자인은 모두 틀렸어요."와 같이 말하는 것은 긍정적인 결과를 낳지 않을 것이다. 비판은 비판이다. 그것은 이해를 막는다.

3) 지도는 데이터로 만들어진다. 이 데이터는 어떤 장소, 주소, 도로, 혹은 국경의 위도와 경도를 포함하는 위치와 관련된 것일 수 있다. 어떤 지도는 인구 같은 것을 보여주는 통계 데이터를 사용하고, 또 어떤 것은 초원이나 사막의 위치와 같은 정성적 데이터를 사용한다. 데이터가 수집될 때 오류가 생길 수 있다. 지리정보시스템으로 만들어진 지도, 인터넷상의 지도, GPS 장치는 '디지털화되어야' 한다. 다시 말해서, 컴퓨터가 읽을 수 있는 형태로 그 데이터가 입력되어야 한다. 이런 디지털화 작업의 일부는 그 정보를 표시하고 입력하는 사람에 의해 이루어지는데, 그런 까닭에 사람에 의한 오류의 가능성이 존재한다. 역사적으로 중요한 지도와 심지어 몇몇 현대의 지도에도 데이터의 부족, 데이터의 공백, 심지어 잘못된 데이터가 존재할 수 있다.

4. 실험 & 결과 / 예시 & 나열

1) 감정과 접촉은 언어가 발달하기 전에 부모와 아이가 의사소통하는 주요 수단이다. 따라서 말을 할 수 있기 전의 아기가 다른 사람들의 감정적, 비언어적 의사소통을 어느 정도 기본적으로 이해한다고 해도 놀라운 것이 아니며, 그것이 정말 사실이라는 것을 연구가 보여 주었다. 예를 들면, 14개월 정도 된 어린 아기는 감정이 흔히 특정 사건에 '대한' 것(예를 들면, 누군가가 개를 무서워한다)이라는 것을 이해하고 한 사람이 무엇에 대해 감정을 드러내고 있는지를 식별하는 데 매우 능숙하다. 또한 18개월 무렵에 아기들은 두 사람이 정확히 동일한 사물에 대하여 상이한 감정적 반응을 할 수 있다는 것(예를 들면, 너는 완두콩을 좋아하지만, 나는 그것을 싫어한다)을 인식하기 시작한다. 대조적으로 14개월 된 아기들은 여전히 매우 자기중심적이며 모든 이가 특정 사물이나 사건에 동일한 감정적 반응을 보인다고 생각한다.

2) 회사는 어떤 시장이 자기의 장기 비전과 목표에 꼭 맞으면 그 시장을 매력적이라고 생각할 수 있다. 단기적인 수익은 제한되어 있을 수 있지만, 장기적인 수익성 상황은 더 유리하게 보일 수 있다. General Electric이 1970년대에 (CT 스캐너라고 불리는) 의료 영상 장비 시장에 진입한 것은 이런 사고방식을 반영한다. 1970년대에 GE는, CT 스캐너를 만들기는 했지만 감소하는 판매량과 시장 포화 상태 때문에 그 시장에서 계속 이익을 내는 데는 무관심했던 다른 회사들을 인수했다. 이들 자산을 매입함으로써 GE는 그 시장의 단기적인(→ 장기적인) 지배적 지위를 획득했다. 그 당시에는 그 시장이 즉각적인 성장의 조짐을 보이지 않았지만, 그 시장이 그 이후에 다시 성장하고 수익을 내면서 GE는 특히 미국에 서 CT 스캐너 시장의 강력한 회사가 되었다.

5. Question & Answers

1) 만일 여러분이 하늘에서 관찰되는 것들의 목록을 작성한다면, 그것은 새, 연기, 구름, 무지개, (해나 달의) 무리, 번개, 별, 달, 태양, 그리고 혜성이 그 목록에 포함될 것이다. 여러분에게 떠오를 첫 번째 생각들 중 하나는 하늘에는 깊이가 있다는 것이다. 하늘에 있는 어떤 것들은 더 가까이 있는 것처럼 보이고, 어떤 것들은 더 멀리 떨어져 있는 것처럼 보인다. 왜 그럴까? 원근감 때문이다! 일상생활의 경험을 통해 더 가까운 물체가 더 먼 물체에 대한 여러분의 시야를 가로막는다는 것을 여러분은 알고 있다. 예를 들어 손을 여러분 눈앞에 둔다면, 더 멀리 있는 나무를 볼 수 없다. 따라서 만일 날아가는 새가 구름에 대한 여러분의 시야를 가로막는다면, 여러분은 논리적으로 새가 구름보다 여러분에게 더 가까이 있다고 결론을 내리게 된다. 그리고 여러분은 구름이 태양 '앞으로' 지나는 것을 보면서, 여러분은 구름이 태양보다 여러분에게 더 가까이 있다고 결론을 내리게 된다. 또는 아마도 일식을 보면서 여러분은 달이 태양보다 여러분에게 더 가까이 있다고 결론을 내리게 된다. 이런 식으로, 여러분의 목록에 있는 모든 것들은 관찰자로부터의 거리의 순서에 따라 놓일 수 있다.

2) 흔히 문학을 공부하는 학생들은 얼마나 많이 인용해야 하는가에 대한 규칙이 있는지 궁금하게 여긴다. 해답은, 요점을 설명하는 데 가장 도움이 될 것을 더 많지도 더 적지도 않게 인용해야 한다는 것이다. 때로는 단 한 문장, 혹은 단 한 행의 시구가 충분할 것이고, 또 때로는 한 개의 단락 전체나 한 편의 소네트 전체가 필요할 것이다. 인용할 때는 꼭 맞는 구절을 정확하게 고르도록 유의해야 한다. 글 안의 어딘가에 묻혀 있는, 여러분이 주목하게 하고 싶은 이미지를 담고 있는 자의적으로 고른 어구의 덩어리도, 여러분이 인용하지 못한 관련된 대구를 독자에게 혹시라도 상기시킬지도 모르는 따로 떨어진 행도 여러분의 논점을 효과적으로 밝히지는 못할 것이다. 또한 여러분은 저자의 의미를 왜곡하는 방식으로 인용하지 않도록 조심해야 한다. 정말로 뻔한 인용구를 피하는 것이 현명한 데, 그런 인용구는 적절한 자리에서는 우리 문학의 보석일 수 있지만, 여러분이 쓴 글의 문맥 속에서는 상투적 문구라는 인상을 독자에게 줄 것 이다.

3) 음악이 기술을 바꾸는가, 아니면 기술이 음악을 바꾸는가? 역사는 후자라고 말한다. 축음기 음반의 출현(1877년)은 라이브 공연의 독점을 종식시켰는데, (재생음의) 충실도는 라이브 음악만큼 좋지는 않았지만, 그런데도 불구하고 수백만의 음악을 듣는 새로운 사람들은 이내 그것을 즐길 것이었다. 1940년대에 전기 기타의 출현은 스윙 음악의 종말을 초래했고, 수십 년 후에 머리를 세차게 흔드는 록 음악을 가능하게 했다. 오늘날 YouTube와 여타의 스트리밍 사이트에서의 소리의 디지털 방식의 송출은 우리가 음악의 질뿐만 아니라 음악을 받아들이는 방식 또한 바꾸어 놓았다. 그리고 디지털 혁명이 우리의 현대 음악계를 바꾸어 놓은 것과 꼭 마찬가지로 기술적 진보가 현대 교향악단을 낳았다.

6. 설명문 or Story Telling

1) 반 고흐의 그림은 그가 그렸던 물체들에게 혼을 불어넣었다. 그가 닳아해진 신발 한 켤레를 그렸을 때, 이것은 그 신발을 신었던 사람이 가졌을지도 모르는 긴 삶의 고난의 양을 말해줬다. 한 등에 의해 적막하게 비춰지는 The Potato Eaters에서 주방의 우울한 분위기는 의도적으로 그의 만성적인 괴로움과 그의 질병의 본질을 암시한다. 그 그림은 그의 가족 개념에 대한 숨은 의미를 가지고 있다. 오른쪽 멀리에 앉아있는 우울한 얼굴을 하고 있는 늙은 여성은 그의 어머니이다. 그는 그녀를 다른 사람들로부터 고립시키려는 의도인 것처럼 보인다. 왼쪽 멀리 있는 젊은 남성은 거의 반 고흐일 것이다, 그리고 그는 비록 그녀가 그녀의 아들의 눈을 피했을지라도 그의 어머니를 보고 있다.

그의 풍경과 자화상은 우울한 고독감와 불편함을 암시한다. 1889년 5월에, 반 고흐는 스스로 정신병원에 입원을 했다. 그가 그의 최고의 작품이 되었던 The Starry Night를 작업하면서, 그는 병들게 되었다. 이 기간 동안에, 그는 특별한 자화상을 완성했다. 초기의 초상화들에서, 그는 그의 유목민적인 생활스타일이나 재정적인 어려움 때문에 보통 그보다 10년정도 더 나이가 들어보였다, 그러나 이 마지막 그림에서 그는 어려보였다. 아마도 그는 새로 시작하고 그의 정신적인 어려움을 극복하기를 원했을 것이다. 그의 마지막 자화상 이후로 10달 후에, 1980년 7월에, 그는 자살을 했다. 그림에서 보여졌던 것처럼, 반 고흐의 젊음은 절망과 죽음의 망령으로 상징화될 수 있다.

2) 아일랜드의 작가인 George Orwell의 삶과 문학은 한가지, 즉 인간의 품위에 대한 그의 믿음으로 요약될 수 있다. 비록 그 정의는 애매할 수 있을지라도, 이것은 근본적인 품위에 대한 인식을 포함하고, 무엇보다도, 정직함과 관용을 포함한다. Orwell은 독단적인 견해, 이대올로기적인 정치 교리, 계획된 사회 변혁, 그리고 종교적 절대주의를 거부했다. 그는 대신에 인간의 표현할 수 있는 권리, 특히 소수의 권리, 그리고 언론의 자유를 지지하는걸 선호했다.

Orwell의 인간의 품위에 대한 인식은 자유와 표현에 대한 생각에 기초했다. 이것은 수동적으로 즐겨질 수 있는 것이 아니라, 수행되어져야하고 추구되어져야만 한다. “자유의 비결은 용기입니다”라는 구절은 사람들이 그들의 말에 있어서 용기를 내고 다른 사람의 의결들의 수용에 있어서 용기를 내야할 의무가 있다는 것을 의미한다. Orwell에게 있어서, 품위라는 것은, 무엇보다도, 단결심, 상식, 그리고 사람에 대한 존중을 의미했다. 그는 단호하게 마르크스 주의를 반대했다, 그리고 그 마르크스 주의는 평등함을 이유로 자유를 부정했다. 그는 진정한 사회주의가 권력을 잡음으로써가 아닌 공평하고 열린 토론을 보장함으로써 가능하다고 믿었다.

Orwell은 공산주의같은 추상적인 이론들을 혐오했다, 그리고 그것은 이데올로기를 필요하게 만들었다. 이것은 그의 반-전체주의적인 작품인 동물 농장과 1984년 디스토피아에서 보여줄 수 있다. 그리고 그 작품들에서 그는 독재를 반대하는, 계층을 반대하는, 그리고 차별을 반대하는 사회를 추구했다. Orwell은 이런 시스템에 반대해서 투쟁하는 것이 사회 그자체를 위해서 뿐만 아니라, 사회의 발전을 위해서도 인간의 의무라고 믿었다.

UNIT 1 내용 일치 / 불일치 (True / Not True)

1.

해석 : 1980년대와 1990년대에는 세율이 훨씬 높았고, 내 비율도 중간 수준이었다. 내가 가끔 듣는 이론에 따르면, 나는 시세차익과 배당금에 대한 높은 세율 때문에 발작을 일으키고 투자를 거절했어야 했다.

나는 거절하지 않았고, 다른 사람들도 거절하지 않았다. 나는 60년 동안 투자자들과 함께 일해왔고 심지어 1976년~1977년에 자본 이득률이 39.9퍼센트였을 때도, 잠재적 이익에 대한 세율 때문에 합리적인 투자를 꺼려하는 사람을 아직 보지 못했다. 사람들은 돈을 벌기 위해 투자하는데, 잠재적 세금은 결코 그들을 겁먹게 한 적이 없다. 그리고 더 높은 금리가 일자리 창출에 타격을 준다고 주장하는 사람들에게, 나는 1980년에서 2000년 사이에 거의 4천만 개의 일자리가 추가되었다는 것을 지적하고 싶다. 불행히도, 당신은 그 이후로 무슨 일이 일어났는지 알고 있다: 세율을 낮추고 훨씬 더 낮은 일자리 창출이 생겼다.

이종현T의 독해 Point!

이 글의 핵심은 세금 비율이 높다고 해도 투자자들은 투자하는 것을 두려워하지 않는다는 내용이다. 그런데 1번 선지는 세금 비율이 올라가면 투자하는 것을 꺼린다고 되어 있으므로 지문의 핵심적인 내용과는 반대되는 내용이다. 따라서 정답은 1번이 된다.

① 세율이 상승할 때, 투자자들은 투자를 꺼린다.

② 자본소득세율은 1977년보다 더 낮다.

③ 저자는 자신에 대한 세율에 상관없이 투자를 한다.

④ 저자의 현재 세율은 1990년대보다 더 낮다.

2.

해석 : 성격 특성의 상태는 기준점에 따라 달라진다. 예를 들어, 유인원의 손톱은 다른 영장류들과 관련하여 원시적인 것으로 간주된다. 왜냐하면 다른 영장류들은 모두 손톱을 가지고 있기 때문이다. 그러므로 손톱은 예를 들어 원숭이와 원숭이를 구별하는 역할을 하지 않을 것이다. 그러나 다른 포유류들은 그것을 가지고 있지 않기 때문에, 손톱은 영장류의 전체에서 파생된 특성이다. 따라서 손톱은 영장류와 다른 포유류를 구별하는 역할을 한다. 여기에 설명된 두 번째 문자(바람의 굴곡)는 다른 영장류가 아닌 호미노이드에서만 발견되며, 따라서 호미노이드의 경우 파생된다. 이 성격은 원숭이와 원숭이를 구별한다. 그러나 침팬지에서는 눈썹의 굴곡이 다른 호미노이드와 관련하여 원시적인 것으로 간주될 수 있다. 즉, 그 캐릭터는 침팬지와 고릴라를 구별하지 못한다.

이종현T의 독해 Point!

여기서 지문의 중간에 원숭이와 유인원은 눈 두덩이(blow ridges)의 여부로 구별할 수 있다고 했다. 눈 두덩이는 직립보행 유인원(hominoids)만의 특징이라고 했으므로 유인원은 직립보행 유인원에 속하고 원숭이는 그렇지 않다는 것을 알 수 있다. 따라서 둘 다 속하지 않는다고 하는 3번이 정답이 된다.

① 모든 영장류는 손톱을 가지고 있다.
② 몇몇 영장류는 '눈두덩이'을 가지고 있다.
③ 유인원과 원숭이는 모두 직립보행 영장류에 속하지 않는다.
④ 침팬지와 고릴라는 모두 직립보행 영장류에 속한다.

3.

해석 : 다원시계의 문화권 사람들은 단원시계로 이동하는 사람들과는 전혀 다른 삶을 산다. P시간문화의 속도는 M시간문화에서 발견되는 속도보다 더 느긋하다. 그 한 가지 이유는 업무가 아닌 사람과 인간관계가 다원적 문화의 중심에 있기 때문이다. 이러한 문화들은 보통 집단적이고 전체주의적인 방식으로 삶을 다룬다. P-타임 문화의 경우, 시간은 덜 구체적이다. 따라서, 시간 낭비의 느낌은 M-타임 문화에서처럼 널리 퍼져 있지 않다. 그들의 멤버들은 한 번에 한 명 이상의 사람과 교류하거나 한 가지 이상의 일을 할 수 있는 반면, M 타임 문화 사람들은 자발성을 억압하고 한 번에 한 가지 활동에 집중하는 경향이 있다. 독일 오스트리아 스위스 미국 등에 비해 아랍, 아시아, 중남미 문화권 사람들이 벌이는 내화에서 더 많은 방해 요소가 있는 것도 이 때문이다.

이종현T의 독해 point!

여기서 핵심은 P-time의 문화는 여러 가지 일을 할 수 있고, M-time 문화는 한 번에 한 가지 일에 집중한다는 내용으로 둘을 대조하고 있다는 것이다. 따라서 2번은 P-time 문화에 대한 설명이 맞으므로 정답은 2번이 된다.

① 시간 낭비라는 느낌은 P-time 문화에서 더 만연하다.
② P-time 문화의 사람들은 동시에 여러 가지 일들을 할 수 있다.
③ M-time 문화의 사람들은 다른 사람들과의 관계를 몹시 중시한다.
④ 아랍, 아시아, 그리고 라틴 아메리카 문화들은 M-time 문화로 분류된다.

4.

해석 : 당신은 왜 스피노자(Spinoza)의 『윤리학(Ethics)』을 읽고 있는가? 그것은 아마 대학 과정에서 지정돼 있는 읽기 과제일 수 있다. 당신은 소홀히 해왔던 한 분야를 다시 공부해보기 원하는 철학자일 수도 있다. 어쩌면 당신은 실재와 마음과 인간 행동의 본성에 대한 호기심에 이끌렸을 수도 있다. 당신이 이들 범주 어디에라도 해당된다면, 이 책 스피노자의 『윤리학』은 정말로 당신을 위해 써진 책이 맞다.'

당신은 스피노자의 『윤리학』이 17세기 철학계를 위해서는 물론, 21세기의 일반인 독자들을 위해서도 집필되었다는 사실을 듣고 놀랄 수도 있다. 스피노자는 자신의 책이 그 당시 철학적 전통에 열중해있는 사람들에 의해 널리 읽혀질 것이라고 기대했다. (만약 당신이 철학적 배경이 조금 있다면 그의 이 책에서 플라톤, 아리스토텔레스, 스토아학파, 데카르트, 홉스 등의 울림을 들을 수 있을 것이며 니체, 사르트르, 푸코와 들뢰즈를 예상할 수도 있을 것이다.) 그러나 스피노자는 300년도 더 지나서 비전문가들이 자신의 책을 읽고 있다는 사실을 알게 되면 기뻐할 것이다. 가능한 한 많은 사람들이 진리를 이해하도록 돕는 것이 그의 목적이기 때문이다. 『윤리학』은 독자가 스스로 자신의 이해력을 개발할 수 있도록 의도된 일종의 워크북이다. 스피노자는 더 많은 사람들이 『윤리학』을 읽을수록, 인류의 이성과 미덕은 증가하고, 결국 더 평화롭고 관대한 사회를 이룩할 수 있을 것이라 생각했다.

『윤리학』이 일찍이 나온 일종의 자기계발 매뉴얼이라는 말은 아니다. 스피노자의 『윤리학』은 형이상학, 인식론 및 윤리학을 다룬 풍부하고 복잡한 저서이다. 이것은 당신이 읽게 될 가장 난해한 철학 저서들 가운데 하나임이 분명하다. 당신은 낯선 용어 및 개념들과 씨름하고, 정말 동의하기 힘든 사상들과 마주치게 될 것이다. 하지만 이 책은 철학서 사상 가장 흥미로운 저술들 가운데 하나이기도 하다. 스피노자는 우리에게 가능한 최선의 방법으로 인간다워질 수 있는 프로그램, 누구든지 달성할 수 있는 실재의 본질에 관한 깊은 이해에 토대를 둔 프로그램을 제공한다. 그는 우리는 누구이며, 우주 속에서 어떤 지위에 있는가에 관한 진리를 밝혀주는 여정으로 우리를 이끈다. 우리 자신에 관한 진리를 이해하는 것은 긍정적인 인간관계, 참된 과학적 지식 및 선한 정치조직의 토대가 된다. 스피노자는 당신 자신과 당신의 삶, 자연과 신에 관해 당신이 다르게 생각하도록 이끌 것이다. 아마도 스피노자의 『윤리학』을 읽는 가장 훌륭한 이유는 바로, 이 책이 당신의 삶을 바꿀 수 있는 책이라는 것이다.

이종현T의 독해 Point!

세 번째 단락에 That is not to say ~ 문장과 Undoubtedly ~의 문장들이 계속 깔고가는 표현이고, But부터 핵심이 나온다 라고 볼 수 있다. 따라서 But 뒷 문장부터 주제라고 생각하고 선지를 보면 1~3번은 전부 주제에 관련된 선지이다. 그리고 4번은 2번째 단락의 Spinoza anticipated that ~ 부분의 깔고가는 표현을 보면 철학적 전통에 빠져있던 사람들이 좋아할 것이다 라고 되어있으므로 4번은 불일치가 된다.

5.

해석 : 위기가 새로운 이론이 출현하기 위한 필수 전제조건이라고 가정하고, 위기의 존재에 대해 과학자들이 어떻게 반응하는지 살펴보자. 매우 심각하고 장기적인 변칙들에 직면했을 때 과학자들이 결코 하지 않는 것이 무엇인지 살펴봄으로써, 중요하면서도 분명한 해답의 단초를 발견할 수 있을 것이다. 그들은 신념을 잃고 대안적 이론들을 고려하기 시작하지만, 그들을 위기로 이끈 그 패러다임을 포기하지는 않는다. 다시 말해, 과학철학의 용어로 말하자면 변칙은 분명 반례인데도, 과학자들은 변칙들을 반례로서 다루지 않는다는 것이다. 부분적으로는, 이러한 일반화는 패러다임 폐기에 대해 우리가 나중에 해볼 논의를 통해 한층 더 온전히 드러날 것 — 즉 어떤 과학적 이론이 패러다임의 지위를 획득하면, 오로지 대체 후보가 그 자리를 대체하는 것이 가능한 경우에만 그 이론이 무효라고 선언된다는 것 — 을 암시하는 사례들을 바탕으로 한 역사적 사실에 기초한 진술일 뿐이다. 지금껏 과학 발달의 역사적 연구에 의해 밝혀진 어떠한 과정도 자연과의 직접적 비교에 의해 반증(허위증명)이 이루어진다는 방법론적 고정관념과는 다르게 전개된다. 이 말이 곧 과학자들은 과학적 이론을 폐기하지 않는다거나, 과학자들의 연구 과정에서 경험과 실험이 본질적인 것이 아니라는 말은 아니다. 이 말은, 궁극적으로 핵심적인 요점이겠지만, 과학자들이 이전에 수용했던 어떤 이론을 폐기하도록 이끄는 판단 행위는 언제나 그 이론을 자연과 비교하는 것 이상에 토대를 두고 있다는 말이다. 하나의 패러다임을 폐기하는 결정은 언제나 그와 동시에 다른 패러다임을 수용하는 결정인 것이며, 그러한 결정으로 이끄는 판단에는 그 두 패러다임들을 자연과 비교하는 것은 물론, 패러다임들끼리 서로 비교하는 과정이 포함된다는 것이다.

이종현T의 독해 Point!

이 글의 주제문을 찾겠다고 생각하고 본다면 마지막 부분에 But it does mean ~ 부분이 주제문이 되는 부분이다. 그 문장과 마지막 문장까지를 주제문이라고 생각하고 선지로 가면 정답은 3번이 된다.

6.

해석 : 우울증은 조금 감정이 다운되거나 지치는 것 이상이다; 최악의 경우에는, 이것은 쇠약하게 하는 질병이다, 우울증으로 고통을 겪는 사람들이 잠을 자거나 먹을 수 없고 엄청난 슬픔과 죄책감으로 가득차게 두기 때문이다. 이것은 때때로 현대의 고통의 원인이라고 여겨진다, 즉 부유한 나라의 한가로움 자신에 대한 몰두의 결과로서 생기는 질병이라는 뜻이다. 그러나 그것은 전혀 사실이 아니다. 우울증은 히포크라테스 같은 기원전 5세기 철학자들에게서도 기록된 질병인 melancholia라고 여겨졌다. 아라테우스는 현대 의사들에게 모두 친숙하게 들리는 증상을 설명했다: 환자들은 둔하고 심각해지고, 낙담하거나 매우 무기력하다. 그들은 또한 짜증도 잘내고 낙담하고 불면증으로 시작하게 된다. 우울증은 개발도상국에 있는 사람들에게도 현실이다: 우간다에서 병이 발생되는 지역들에 대한 한 조사는 21퍼센트가 의학적으로 우울증이라는 것을 보여줬다, 파키스탄 마을에 대한 연구들이 44퍼센트의 인구가 우울증으로 고통받고 있는 것을 보여주는 동안에.

이종현T의 독해 Point!

이 지문에서의 핵심은 우울증은 과거에도 거의 비슷한 형태로 있어왔다는 내용이다. 따라서 정답은 3번으로 가는 것이 가장 좋다.

① 인간의 역사에서 우울증은 최근에서야 진단이 이루어졌다.

② 오늘날 사람들은 과거보다 우울증에 더 많이 걸린다.

③ 우울증의 증상은 과거와 현재에서 모두 유사한 것으로 보인다.

④ 우울증은 부유한 국가들보다 개발도상국에서 더 심각하다.

7.

해석 : 전문가들에 따르면 그 어떤 유형의 중독이든 중독 성향을 유전적으로 가진 사람들은 약물과 관련된 신경 전달 물질인 도파민의 생성을 관장하는 뇌 부위에 유전자 결함이 있다고 한다. 코카인, 헤로인, 니코틴, 암페타민 및 여타 중독성 약물들은 기분 좋은 느낌을 일으키는 뇌의 쾌감 회로를 변화시킨다. 치즈케이크, 나초 등 당신이 좋아하는 다른 어떤 음식을 먹어도 쾌감회로가 활성화된다. 경쟁에서 이기거나, 시험에서 A를 받거나, 칭찬을 받거나 여타 유쾌한 경험을 하여도 마찬가지다. 이 쾌감 회로는 도파민이라는 화학적 언어(매개)를 통해 의사 전달을 하는데, 이 신경 전달 물질은 뇌 속의 신경 세포들 사이를 쏜살같이 오가며 가벼운 행복감에서부터 희열에 이르는 감정들을 일으킨다. 그러나 이러한 중독성 약물들을 만성적으로 사용하면 뇌 속에 영구적인 변화가 일어난다. 도파민 수용기들은 신경 세포에 자리 잡은 작은 분자적 야구 글러브와 같아서, 공처럼 날아다니는 신경 전달 물질들을 붙잡아 당겨 넣는데, 그 수가 감소한다는 점이 가장 중요하다.

이종현T의 독해 Point!

마지막에 나오는 But chronic ~ 부분을 주제문이라고 본다면 중독 약물의 만성적 사용이 뇌의 변화를 만들어낸다는 것이고 그 변화는 도파민 수용체의 감소라고 써 있다. 따라서 유전자가 풍부해진다고 써 있는 1번 선지는 불일치가 된다.

8.

해석 : 아시아의 잉어를 미국에 처음 도입한 것은 남부지방 양식장의 조류를 억제하려는 의도에서였다. 그러나 불행하게도 홍수가 나서, 이 잉어가 미시시피 강으로 흘러들어갔다. 시간이 지나면서 아시아 잉어는 북쪽으로 올라가 미시시피 강 상류와 강의 여러 지류 쪽으로 이동했다. 이 잉어가 오대호 쪽으로 나아가게 되면서, 모든 사람이 이 잉어를 주목하고 있다. 사실, 잉어가 오대호로 들어가지 못하도록, 미국과 캐나다 양국은 전례 없는 협력을 경주하고 있다. 아시아 잉어는 먹성이 왕성한 포식어종으로, 오대호 전체 먹이 시스템의 기반이며 가장 작은 먹이인 플랑크톤을 먹어치운다. 아시아 잉어가 하루에 자기 체중을 20%까지 먹어치울 수 있다는 점을 감안한다면, 그 엄청난 식욕은 토종 어종이 생존하는 데 필요한 먹이망에 피해를 줄 수 있다.

이종현T의 독해 Point

4, 5번째 줄에 Great lakes로 흘러들어가는 것을 막으려고 한다는 내용이 있으므로 풍부하다는 얘기인 3번이 정답이다.

① 그들은 조류를 통제하기 위해 미국으로 수입되었다.

② 홍수는 그들이 미시시피 강으로 흘러들어가게 했다.

③ 그들은 Great Lakes 전체에 걸쳐서 풍부하다.

④ 그들은 음식에 대해서 다른 원래 그 지역 물고기 종들보다 뛰어났다.

9.

해석 : 만약 실리콘 밸리가 자신의 길을 나아갔다면, 모든 인간들은 지금까지 아날로그 제품들은 버렸을 것이다. 우리는 클라우드로부터 음악을 소비하고, 온라인으로 이야기들을 읽고, 배터리로 충전된 장치들로 디자인들을 스케치할 것이다. 그리고 사실상, 우리들 중 많은 사람들은 그렇게 한다. 그러나, 우리는 또한 아날로그 혁명도 시작했다. 그들의 문화적인 적절성이 생기면서 노트나 레코드판같은 물건들의 판매들도 지난 십년동안 꾸준히 성장해오고 있다. 한편, 아마존과 같은 전자상거래에서의 대기업들도 서둘러서 오프라인 매장을 개장하고 있다. 많은 사람들은 늙어가고 있는 기술 혁신 반대자들의 과거에 대한 낭만에 의해 스위치를 작동시키는 향수병이라고 가정한다. 그러나 사실상, 많은 아날로그의 최신의 팬들은 가공하지 않은 효용성에 끌리는 밀레니엄 세대이다. 즉 예를 들어, 종이 공책을 이용하여 웹사이트의 초기 화면을 드리는 디자이너가 있다. 덜 현대적인 기술을 선택하는 것은 이치에 맞지 않는 것 같을지도 모른다. 그러나 인간은 기계가 아니다. 우리는 이해할 수 없는 감정에 의해 이끌리는 복잡한 생명체이다. 그리고 이 핵심에서, 아무리 우리가 많은 가상 플랫폼을 받아들일지라도, 인간의 경험은 깊게, 진정으로 아날로그 제품인 채로 있다.

이종현T의 독해 Point!

이 글의 핵심은 중간에 But in fact가 들어간 문장에 있다. 그 문장에선 아날로그 제품의 인기가 높아지는 이유는 나이가 있는 사람들의 향수 때문이 아니라, 밀레니엄 세대들이 이 효용성을 좋아하기 때문이라고 나와 있다. 따라서 정답은 3번이 된다.

① 가상현실을 수용하지만, 인간의 경험은 아날로그적이다.

② 아날로그 제품의 문화적 관련성이 증가하고 있다.

③ 아날로그 혁명을 일으키는 사람은 대체로 노년층이다.

④ 많은 사람이 온라인상에서 글을 읽고, 클라우드를 통해 음악을 소비한다.

10.

해석 : 놀랍게도 복잡한 조각상들과 세계적인 상징물들에 대한 거대한 복제품으로 유명한 Harbin International Snow and Ice Festival은 현재 진행중이다. 몇몇 테마 존들로 구성된 그 이벤트 지역은 대략 75만 평방미터 정도의 지역을 포함한다고 조직위원이 말했다. 작품들은 대부분 중국 우화와 유명한 만리장성이나 이집트 피라미드같은 유명한 건축물들의 영감을 받았다. 이것은 밤에 조각상들이 안에서 불빛이 켜질 때 가장 잘 보인다. 그러면서 동시에 전체 지역에 요정의 나라같은 느낌을 주게 된다. Harbin은 영하 13에서 23도까지의 범범위에 이르는 낮 온도를 1월에 지니고 있는 아주 추운 도시이다. 그럼에도 불구하고, 많은 여행객들은 Harbin에서의 이 웅장한 축제를 즐긴다.

이종현T의 독해 Point!

이 지문에서는 마지막 문장에서 날씨가 굉장히 춥지만 사람들은 많이 온다고 했으므로 3번 선지와는 정반대가 되는 내용이 된다. 따라서 정답은 3번이 된다.

① 새로운 고객들을 유치하는 비용이 빠르게 증가하고 있다

② 고객의 욕구를 만족시키는 것은 마케팅에서 최우선 사항이다

③ 고객들과 수익성이 있는 관계를 형성하는 것이 중요하다

④ 올바른 일처리가 고객들과 회사에 모두 이롭다

11.

해석 : 1967년, 스코틀랜드 발명가 ‘John Shepherd-Barron'은 돈을 얻는 것은 초콜렛바를 얻는 것만큼이나 쉽다고 생각했다. 그는 영국의 'Barclays Bank'에서 최초의 현금 기계 또는 ATM을 개척한 것으로 명성을 얻었다. 그러나 어려움은 당신이 당신이 누구라고 말했는지를 확인하는 데 있다. (신분증명의 어려움)

문제를 해결하기 위해서, ‘Shepherd-Barron‘은 오늘날 우리가 가지고 있는 직불카드의 선구자 역할을 하는 특별한 유형의 종이수표를 만들었다. 각각의 수표는 그의 현금 기계에게 계좌 소유자가 알고 있는 개인식별번호(PIN)를 요청하게 됩니다. 'Shepherd-Barron'은 기계가 6자리의 숫자 PIN이 필요하도록 만들었지만, 그의 아내에 의해 무효화되었다. 그녀는 6자리 숫자는 기억하기에 너무 많은 숫자이고, 4자리 숫자가 표준이 될 것이라 믿었다.

이종현T의 독해 Point

11-1번 : 전반적인 내용은 현금인출기의 발명 과정과 문제점, 해결과정 순서로 나열이 되어 있다. 3번의 최초의 현금인출기의 인기는 본문의 흐름에 맞지 않다.

11-2번 : 첫 번째 문장에서 돈을 얻는 것과 초콜렛바를 얻는 것을 비교하였다. 2번은 돈을 버는 것이므로 현금인출기로 인해 돈을 얻는 것과 돈을 버는 것은 다른 범주에 속한다. 그러므로 정답은 2번이다.

11-1번 :

① 개인 식별 번호는 무엇을 위한 것이었는

② 현금인출기는 언제 발명 되었는가

③ 최초의 현금인출기는 얼마나 인기가 있었는가

④ 현금인출기는 어디에서 최초로 사용되었는가

11-2번 :

① 개인 식별 번호가 네 자리 숫자여야 한다고 결정한 사람은 결국 쉐퍼드-배런의 아내였다.

② 쉐퍼드-배런은 돈을 버는 것이 초콜릿 바를 먹는 것만큼 쉬운 일이 되어야 한다고 생각했다.

③ 현금 인출기를 도입하는 데 있어서 주된 문제점은 예금주의 신원을 확인하는 것이었다.

④ 쉐퍼드-배런이 개발한 특별한 종류의 종이 수표는 직불카드의 모태가 되었다.

12.

해석 : 4개월의 여정을 마치고 102명의 순례자들은 1620년 'Plymouth'에 도착했다. 악천후와 전염병에 마주친 그들은 첫 해에 46명의 동료들을 잃었다. 그럼에도 불구하고, 생존자들은 감사해야 할 것이 있다. 풍부한 농작물이 경작되었다. 그들은 부분적으로는 영어를 사용하는 'Squanto'라고 이름 붙여진 'Paxtuxet Indian'의 도움으로 살아남았다. 그는(인디언) 그들이(순례자들) 집을 짓고 농작물을 경작도록 도와주었다. 1621년 가을, 순례자들은 추수감사절을 선포하였다. 순례자들은 'Wampanoag' 부족의 족장과 부족민과 여자들을 초대하였다. 그들은 첫 추수감사절 식사를 이 이후로 전통적인 휴일식사가 된 많은 구성요소들로 준비하였다. 우리가 지금 기념하는 이 설립된 날은 잡지 편집가 'Sarah Hale'의 노력의 결과이다. 'Sarah Hale'여사는 1827년 추수감사절 기념운동을 시작하였다. 그녀의 사설들은 국가적인 추수감사절 휴일의 기념(국경일)을 주장한다. 그녀는 정치인들에게 수백개의 편지를 썼다. 그녀는 11월 마지막 목요일을 "신께 감사의 찬사를 바치는" 날로 지정해야 한다고 주장하였다. 마침내, Hale여사의 꿈은 현실이 되었다.

이종현T의 독해 Point

이 글의 전반적인 내용은 추수감사절이 탄생하게 된 과정(순례자들의 여정, 원주민들의 도움)과 Sarah Hale여사의 추수감사절에 대한 주장에 대한 글이다. 1번의 제공된 음식의 양이 아니라 글의 중간 부분에 지금의 전통휴일의 식사가 된 음식의 종류를 말한다. 그러므로 정답은 1번이다.

① 첫 번째 추수감사절 연회 때 제공된 음식의 양

② 처음에 함께 했던 일행 가운데 얼마나 많은 사람들이 이주 첫해에 죽었는지

③ 청교도와 이웃 부족들 간의 관계

④ 추수감사절을 국경일로 만들려는 사라 헤일의 전략

13.

해석 : Tigris와 Euphrates강들의 사이의 비옥한 땅인 'The Fertile Crescent'(비옥한 초승달)는 그리스인들에 의해 "강 사이의 땅"을 의미하는 Mesopotamia(메소포타미아)로 분류되었다. 비록 그 지역(비옥한 초승달)의 강우량은 적을시라노, 녹은 눈이 강에 흘러 들어가고 홍수는 그 계곡을 비옥하게 만들었다. 그 결과로 조직화된 문명의 탄생을 이끌었다. 이 강들의 어귀근처에 사는 사람들은 'Sumerians'(수메르인)라고 불린다. 신권정치의 도시국가들을 만든 수메르 지역에서 오늘날 여전히 우리가 사용하는 많은 것들(바퀴, 학교, 아치형 구조물, 벽돌 그리고 60진법과 원을 기반으로 한 체계)을 발명하였다. 오늘날 우리는 여전히 장소를 이동하기 위해 바퀴를, 우리를 가르치기 위해 학교를 그리고 그들이 시간을 알기 위해 발명한 시계에 의지하고 있다.

이종현T의 독해 Point

수메르지역은 '신권정치의 도시국가'라고 하였으므로 1번이 정답이다. 이 문제는 신권정치의 정확한 뜻을 모른다면 충분히 헷갈릴 수 있는 문제이다. 이로 인해 어휘의 진짜 의미를 파악하는 중요성을 다시 한번 새기길 바랍니다.

*신권정치 : 지배자가 '신' 또는 '신의 대리인'으로 간주되고, 절대적인 권력으로써 인민을 지배하는 정치체제

① 수메르 지역에서, 도시국가들은 종교적 권위에 의해 지배되었다.

② 티그리스강과 유프라테스강의 어귀는 사람들이 살지 않는 불모의 땅이었다.

③ 메소포타미아에는 강수량이 상당이 많았다.

④ 오늘날의 원격교육은 수메르인의 시대까지 거슬러 올라간다.

14.

해석 : 1939년 다이오드가 발견 된지 수십 년 후인 1947년에 트랜지스터(게르마늄)는 거의 독점적으로 사용되었는데, 그 이유는 그것(germanium)은 상대적으로(다이오드와 비교하였을 때) 발견하기가 쉽고 상당히 많은 양을 이용할 수 있기 때문이다. 그것(germanium)은 또한 상대적으로(다이오드와 비교하였을 때) 제조 공정에서 중요한 부분인 매우 높은 수준의 순노를 얻는 것은 비교적 쉽습니다. 그러나 초기에 게르마늄을 기본 재료로 사용하여 제작 된 다이오드와 트랜지스터는 주로 온도 변화에 대한 민감성으로 인해 낮은 수준의 신뢰성에 대한 어려움을 겪었습니다. 그 당시, 과학자들은 또 다른 물질인 '실리콘'이 온도 민감성을 개선하였음을 알고 있었지만, 매우 높은 순도의 실리콘을 제조하는 정제 공정은 아직 개발 단계에 있었다. 그러나 마침내, 1954년에 첫 번째 실리콘 트랜지스터가 도입되었고 실리콘은 반도체 소재로 신속하게 선택되었다. 실리콘은 온도에 덜 민감할뿐만 아니라 지구상에서 가장 풍부한 재료 중 하나이며 이용가능성에 대한 우려를 제거하였다.

이종현T의 독해 Point

중간 부분 이후에, 정제 공정은 아직 개발단계에 있다고 하였다. 그러므로 3번의 즉시 대체되었다는 올바르지 않다. 항상 문제의 immediately, always 등 확실성을 나타내는 의미는 주의하면 좋다.

① 게르마늄 다이오드와 트랜지스터는 초기에 인기가 있었다.

② 게르마늄 트랜지스터는 온도변화에 민감하기 때문에 신뢰할 수 없었다.

③ 게르마늄이 온도에 민감하다는 것이 발견된 후 즉시 실리콘이 게르마늄을 대체했다.

④ 실리콘은 다량으로 이용가능하며, 아마도 게르마늄과 같이 풍부할지도 모른다.

15.

해석 : 아마도, 어떤 음악적 혁신도 몇몇 도시 흑인과 라틴 공동체에게 인기를 끌다가 1980년대 초반부터 전국적으로 눈에 띄게 된 랩 음악만큼 비평가들 사이에서 당황, 실망, 그리고 분노를 일으킨 것은 없을 것이다. 폭넓은 청중들을 끌어들이던 흑인음악의 많은 초기 형태들과는 달리, 랩은 상대적으로(초기 흑인음악과 비교) 멜로디가 거의 없다. 확실히 많은 랩 노래들은 거의 동일한 음악 및 악기의 요소들을 사용하는데, 때로는 문자 그대로 똑같은 요소를 사용한다. 랩 음반은 'sampling'으로 알려진 기술을 통하여 다른 음반들에게 악기로 연주되는 배경음악의 일부를 종종 복사한다. 랩의 가장 중요한 요소는 가사이다. 랩은 음악의 형태인 만큼 언어의 형태이다.

이종현T의 독해 Point

첫 번째 문장에서 랩 음악이 가장 비평가들의 당황, 실망, 분노를 일으켰다고 되어있다. 가수가 아니라 비평가이다. 1번이 난해한 보기이긴 하지만 가수들의 반응에 대한 언급을 해주어야지 1번 보기가 성립할 수 있다.

① 랩은 가수들 사이에서 분노를 일으켰다.

② 랩 음반은 종종 다른 음반에서 멜로디를 따온다.

③ 랩의 가사들은 멜로디보다 더욱 중요하다.

④ 랩은 미국 흑인 음악의 한 가지 형태이다.

⑤ 랩의 흔한 기술들 중 하나는 샘플링이다.

16.

해석 : 현대의 쇼핑몰은 초기 소매 혁신의 직접적인 후손으로 고객들을 위한 주차시설을 갖추고 많은 수의 다른 상점들을 하나의 단일 구조로 결합하는데 매진한 자동차 이용객 중심의 쇼핑센터였다. 최초로 현대적인 쇼핑센터, 'Country Club Plaza'는 1924년에 Kansas City에서 개점했다. 1950년대 중반까지 이미 작은 'strip(번화가)'에서 대규모 복합단지에 이르기까지 다양한 쇼핑센터가 전국적으로 급증했고, 주차장 부족과 중산층 거주자들의 교외 이주로 타격을 입은 전통적인 시내중심가 상업 지구에 도전장을 내밀고 있었다.

이종현T의 독해 Point

마지막 부분 쪽에 다양한 쇼핑센터가 전국적으로 급증했다고 하였다. 이 부분으로 4번의 천천히 증가했다는 옳지 않다. 게르마늄 지문처럼 부사의 뜻을 정확히 파악하여 실수하지 않도록 주의하자! 되게 실수하기 좋은 보기이지만 다른 보기를 보고 아니라는 확신을 갖는 것도 매우 중요하다.

① 중산층은 교외로 이주했다.

② 전통적인 시내중심가의 쇼핑센터는 자동차를 이용하는 쇼핑객들에게 불편했다.

③ 현대의 쇼핑센터는 전통적인 쇼핑센터와 경쟁했다.

④ 현대의 쇼핑센터는 전국적으로 천천히 증가했다.

⑤ 전통적인 쇼핑센터는 주차장이 충분치 않았다.

17.

해석 : 중세시대에 여관은 수도원에 의해 어느 정도는 보완이 되었지만, 이들 수도원(여관이 되려면 these(복수)가 되면 안된다.)들은 대체로 오직 두 부류(매우 부유한 사람들과 매우 가난한 사람들)만을 손님으로 접대했다. 전자(매우 부유한 사람들)는 수도사들에 의해 손님으로 맞이되었는데, 왜냐하면 수도사들이 감히 부자들을 거부하지 못했기 때문이었다. 그러나 그 반갑지 않은 손님들(부자들)의 지나친 행동과 관련하여 수도사들은 불만이 많았다. 그러나 수도원의 문은 가난한 사람들에게 항상 열려 있었고, 그리고 그 가난한 사람들은 결코 빈손으로 돌려 보내지지 않았다.

여관들은 이러한 양극단 사이에 있는 사람들에 의해 이용되었는데, 그들(여관들)은 귀족에게는 너무나 형편없는 것이었고, 가난한 사람들에게는 너무 비싼 것이었기 때문이었다. 그들(여관들)은 보다 작은 상류층, 상인, 행상인, 그리고 무역업자에 의해 방문되었다. 여관의 접대는 충분히 열악해서, 한 방에 수많은 침대가 바닥의 공간을 차지하고 있었으며, 그리고 각각의 손님은 자신이 필요로 하는 음식을 모두 사서 먹었다.

이종현T의 독해 Point

두 번째 단락의 중간 부분을 보면 여관은 상인, 행상인, 무역업자들이 방문하였다고 한다. 그러므로 1번의 진술은 옳은 진술이다.

① 상인들은 여관에 머무를 형편이 되었다.

② 수도원들은 여관보다 더 많은 손님을 수용했다.

③ 부자들은 수도원에서 매우 환영받는 손님이었다.

④ 여관이 가난한 사람들을 허용하지 않아 가난한 사람들은 여관에 숙박할 수 없었다.

18.

해석 : 'Potlatch'는 북서부 태평양 연안의 미국과 캐나다 'British Columbia'주의 토착사회에서 실행 된 의식적인 재산 분배였다. 보통 공동주택 또는 대규모 야외지역에서 열린 이러한 관습은 신생아의 출생, 젊은 커플의 결혼, 또는 성공적인 수렵과 같은 특정한 사회적 사건을 표지 역할을 하였다. 그것(관습)은 소유권 이전을 기념하는 데 쓰이거나 문서기록을 대신한 지불기록의 역할을 할 수 있으며, 더 나아가 군사동맹이나 가족 유대를 공개적으로 과시해주었다. 그러나 'Potlatch'의 주된 목적은 부족 사이에서의 재산을 공평하고 윤리적인 방식으로 재분배하여, 주인으로 하여금 본질적으로 공동의 환경에서의 물품들의 단독 소유자로서 느꼈던 정신적인 부담을 그로부터 제거해주는 수단을 제공하는 것이다.

이종현T의 독해 Point

3번의 "강제적으로 분배를 했다."는 공평하고 윤리적인 방식이라는 말과 맞지 않는다. 계속 나오는 문제들처럼 보기의 형용사/부사의 의미를 대충 파악하지 말고 확실하게 구분짓는 연습을 하도록 노력하자!

① 포틀래치는 서로 다른 사회집단들 사이의 관계를 존중했다.

② 포틀래치는 사람들의 삶에서 주요한 사건을 기념하기 위해 열렸다.
③ 포틀래치는 부유층이 강제적으로 그들의 귀중품들을 분배하도록 했다.
④ 포틀래치는 소유권의 변동을 공개적으로 알리는 역할을 했다.
⑤ 포틀래치는 사회적 유대관계를 공개적으로 보여주었다.

19.

해석 : '타이타닉'에 관한 모든 것은 원래의 배만큼이나 웅장했다. 우선, 예산은 그 당시 어떤 영화보다 최대였다. 작가와 감독이었던 'James Cameron'은 2억 달러를 가지고 무엇을 하였나? 첫째, 그는 원래 (타이타닉호가) 난파된 지점까지 11번에 걸친 심해탐사를 했다. 그 다음, 그는 'Leonardo DiCaprio'와 'Kate Winslet'에 의해 이끌어진 모든 인기배우들을 총출연시켰으며, 이들(디카프리오와 윈슬렛 및 모든 인기배우들)을 1,700만 갤런의 물탱크 속으로 몰아넣었다. 갑판 위에서 호화로운 무대장치를 만들었으며, 타이타닉호의 원본 청사진을 본떠 웅장한 계단에서 중국 상표에 이르기까지 꼼꼼하게 만들었다. 영화에 쓴 돈이 잘 쓰였나? 타이타닉을 촬영하는 것은 악명높게 거친 항해였지만, 타이타닉은 Best Picture과 Best director(작품상, 감독상)을 포함하여, 후보에 오른 11개 부문에서 11개의 오스카상을 휩쓴 최고의 작품이 되었다. 타이타닉은 또한 엄청난 돈을 벌어들였으며, 10억 달러의 흥행수익을 기록한 최초의 영화가 되었다.

이종현T의 독해 Point

'Above deck a sumptuous set was built, meticulously modeled after the Titanic's original blueprints, down to the grand staircase and the logo on the china.' 이 부분을 보면 meticulously modeled after를 보고 모든 부분에 세심하게 관심을 기울였다는 것을 알 수 있다. 그러므로 3번이 올바른 진술이다.

① 타이타닉호의 운항과 관련된 위험들
② 타이타닉호가 난파된 본래 위치
③ 사소한 것까지 꼼꼼하게 신경을 쓴 제임스 카메론 감독
④ 영화 『타이타닉』의 전 세계 DVD 판매 실적

20.

해석 : 23년 동안, 'Maryland'주의 수천 명의 가족들과 방문객들은 'Chesapeake Bay Bridge'에 해마다 봄에 열리는 행사에 참여하기 위해 모여왔다. 오직 하루 동안 — 올해의 경우, 5월 4일 — 그 다리의 동쪽 구간이 보행자들에게만 유일하게 개방되어, 모든 연령의 보행자들이 4.3마일에 이르는 멋진 길을 산책할 수 있도록 해준다. 경치가 좋은 산책로는 약 1시간 30분정도가 걸리지만, 대부분의 가족들은 다리 위에서 소풍을 즐기고 지나가는 배들을 보기 위해 시간을 들이면서 하루 종일을 보낸다. 보행자들은 트레킹(도보여행)을 오전 9시에서 오후 2시 사이에 시작할 수 있다. 아기 유모차는 괜찮지만, 애완동물과 인라인 스케이트는 집에 두고 오길 바랍니다. 걷기 행사에 참여하는 것은 무료이지만, 교통 당국에서는 가족들을 출발지점까지 데려다 주는 셔틀버스의 운영비를 충당하기 위해 1인당 1달러의 기부를 청하고 있다.

이종현T의 독해 Point

"Baby strollers are welcome, but please leave your pets and in-line skates at home."

위 문장을 보면 유모차는 괜찮지만, 인라인 스케이트와 애완동물은 안된다는 말을 하고 있다. 이에 따라 1번이 올바르지 않은 진술이다.

① 사람들은 산책하는 동안 애완동물을 데려갈 수 있다.

② 사람들은 1년에 단 하루 동안만 산책에 참가한다.

③ 교통 당국에서 셔틀버스를 제공한다.

④ 산책은 아침에 시작할 수 있으며 1시간 이상 걸릴 수 있다.

21.

해석 : 나는 처음에는 이것(아직 알 수 없다.)이 참가자 각각의 스타일을 분석한 것이 되도록 의도하였으나, 대화 그 자체가 이것(스타일 분석)을 불가능하게 만들었다. 뉴욕시민이 아닌 참가자들은 그 대화가 '뉴욕'다운 특성을 갖고 있다고 생각했고, 그리고 그들(뉴욕시민이 아닌 참가자)은 자신에게 맞지 않는 환경이라고 느꼈다. 참석한 뉴욕시민들은 이야기를 나눌 때 말하는 사람들 사이에서 잠깐 멈추는 것이 더 짧은 경향이 있기 때문에, 뉴욕시민이 아닌 사람들은 더 빨리 말하는 사람이 이야기를 시작하기 전에 무언가를 말하기를 힘들어 했다. 뿐만 아니라, 뉴욕시민들은 이야기의 주제가 어떻게 흘러가는가에 대해 다른 생각을 갖고 있었기 때문에, 뉴욕시민이 아닌 사람들은 종종 어떻게 말하는 것이 적절한지 또는 다른 사람들이 말한 것에 대해서 어떤 것이 적절했는지에 관해 혼란을 겪었다. 그러므로, 이 책은 내가 '높은-관여' 스타일이라 부르는 것에 대한 연구가 되었는데, 이 스타일(높은-관여)은 뉴욕 출신의 사람들이 말하는 특징을 규정하는 경향이 있는 것으로, 내가 '높은-신중함(동정심)' 스타일이라 부르는, 뉴욕 출신이 아닌 사람들의 스타일과 대조를 이룬다. (참가자들의 스타일의 측면들이 그들을 이런 식(높은-관여/높은-신중함)으로 분류하는 것을 정당화시켜주지만, 말하는 사람 각각의 스타일은 독특하다는 것을 다시 한 번 명심해라! : 즉 이 연구에서 나루고 있는 뉴욕 출신의 사람들과 스타일이 매우 다른 뉴욕 출신의 사람들도 많이 있으며, 뉴욕 출신이 아니지만 이들 뉴욕 출신의 사람들과 스타일이 비슷한 사람들도 많이 있다.)

이종현T의 독해 Point

"the New Yorkers present tended to expect shorter pauses between speakers' turns at talk, the non-New Yorkers had a harder time saying something before a faster speaker had begun to talk." 이 문장을 보면 뉴욕시민들은 말을 하면서 멈추는 것이 더 짧고, 뉴욕시민들이 아닌 사람들은 말하기 힘들어 한다고 한다. 결국 이 말은 뉴욕사람들은 다른 사람들이 이야기 할 틈을 잘 주지 않는다고 말 할 수 있다. 그러므로 1번이 올바른 진술이다.

① 그들은 뉴욕 출신이 아닌 사람들보다 더 빨리 이야기를 하기 시작했다.

② 그들이 다른 사람의 이야기를 중간에 끊는 일은 뉴욕 출신이 아닌 사람들보다 덜 자주 있었다.

③ 그들은 자신들의 의견이 다르다는 것을 뉴욕 출신이 아닌 사람들만큼 자주 표현하지 않았다.

④ 그들은 뉴욕 출신이 아닌 사람들보다 새로운 화제에 대해 말하기 시작하는 데 더 많은 어려움을 겪었다.

UNIT 2 추론 (inferred / cannot be inferred)

1.

해석 : 현대 컴퓨터에서 2진법 코드의 존재와 작업은 사용자의 사용자에 보이지 않는다. 개인용 컴퓨터는 여러 가지 기능(음악을 듣고, 사진을 편집하고, 문서를 작성하고, 또는 재무 회계를 수행)으로 사용될 수 있다. 사용자는 서로 다른 소프트웨어 프로그램에 관계없는 명령어들은 입력함으로써 각각의 활동들을 수행한다. 그러나, 이런 각각의 응용 프로그램(소프트웨어 프로그램)들은 컴퓨터에서 각자의 기능을 수행하기 위해서 같은 요소를 사용한다. 이것(기능 수행)을 성공하기 위해서는, 각 프로그램의 기능들은 컴퓨터의 프로세서, 메모리, 그리고 저장 하드웨어에 사용되는 2진법 코드로 변환되어야 한다.

이종현T의 독해 Point

"The presence and operation of the binary code in a modern computer are not apparent to the user." 첫 문장을 보면 not apparent와 1번의 not visible이 같은 말이라는 것을 알 수 있다.

① 명령어를 2진법 부호로 변환하는 것은 컴퓨터 사용자의 눈에 보이지 않는다.
② 서로 다른 응용 프로그램의 명령어 이면의 기능은 실제로 상당히 비슷하다.
③ 중앙처리장치와 저장 컴포넌트는 비슷한 기능을 수행한다.
④ 응용 프로그램은 사용자가 2진법 부호를 입력하면 더 효과적으로 수행할 것이다.
⑤ 비슷한 코드체계는 일정한 수행을 위한 필수 요소이다.

2.

해석 : 미국의 몇몇 주들은 국가에서 가장 혼잡한 고속도로들의 일부(고속도로)에서 한 개의 차선을 유로차선으로 전환하고 있다. 이러한 선불노선(유료차선)들은 운전자들이 교통체증 없는 길을 돈으로 사고 교통체증에 갇힌 돈을 지불하지 않은 운전자들 옆을 지나갈 수 있도록 해준다. 몇몇 주들은 민간 기업들이 새로운 유료차선들을 건설하고 그 대가로 그들(새로운 유료차선들)로부터 발생되는 수익을 갖게 해준다. 다른 주들은 단순히 기존 차선들을 유료차선으로 지정하고 있다. 그러나 많은 사람들은 이러한 유행(차선 유료화)을 불공평하다고 생각한다. 몇몇 운전자 시민단체들은 통행료가 운전을 해야만 하는 사람들에게는 또 다른 세금에 달한다고 주장한다. 미국자동차서비스협회(AAA) 대변인인 'Mantill Willians'는 "통행료는 운전자들에게 역진세라는 것이 우리의 전반적인 생각입니다."라고 말한다. 다른 사람들은 새로운 차선(유료차선)들을 'Lexus Lanes'라고 불렀고 이 차선(Lexus Lanes)(유료 차선)들을 오직 돈을 낼 형편이 있는 사람들만을 위하는 사치품이라고 비난한다. 그러나 유료차선의 지지자들은 그들(Lexus Lanes)이 어떤 사람들은 편리를 위해 비용을 지불하는 선택을 하고, 다른 사람들은 그렇게 하지 않는 편리한 것에 불과하다고 주장한다. 미국 주도로 및 교통 공무원 협회의 'John Horsley'는 "유료차선은 운전자들에게 개인적으로 선택하는 한 가지 모델을 제공한다." "만약 당신이 기꺼이 조금 더 돈을 낸다면, 당신은 목적지에 좀 더 빠르게 도착할 수 있다."라고 말한다.

이종현T의 독해 Point

"Others have dubbed the new routes "Lexus Lanes" and criticize them as a luxury for only those who can afford to pay." 이 부분을 보고 'Lexus Lanes'는 부자들을 위한 사치품이라는 것을 알 수 있다. 그러므로 1번이 올바른 추론이다.

① 유료차선들은 부자들만을 위한 것이다.
② 유료차선들은 렉서스에 의해 자금을 제공받아 왔다.
③ '렉서스 차선'이라는 용어는 미국자동차서비스협회(AAA)에 의해 만들어졌다.
④ 렉서스를 소유한 사람들만이 유료차선을 이용할 수 있다.

3.

해석 : 교리 문답서(catechism)의 말을 빌려서, 인간의 주된 목적은 무엇이며, 인생에서 진정으로 필요한 것들과 수단이 무엇인가를 생각해볼 때, 그(사람)들이 일반적인 생활방식을 다른 어떤 방식보다 더 선호했기 때문에 의도적으로 그것(아직 알 수 없다.)을 선택한 것처럼 보인다. 그러나 사람들은 솔직하게 선택의 여지가 없다고 생각한다. 하지만 기민하고 건강한 본성을 가진 사람들은 태양이 분명히 떴음을 기억한다. 우리의 편견을 포기하기에는 결코 늦지 않았다(포기하자). 아무리 오래되었을지라도, 어떤 사고나 행동도 증거 없이 신뢰되어서는 안 된다. 오늘날 모두가 울리거나 또는 침묵한 채로 진실로 통하는 것이 내일에는 거짓(일부 사람들이 그들의 땅에 단비(fertilizing rain)를 뿌려줄 구름이라고 믿었던 단순한 연기 같은 의견)으로 판명될지도 모른다. 옛날 사람들이 당신은 할 수 없다고 말하는 것에 대해, 당신은 그것을 당신이 할 수 있다는 것을 발견하고 노력한다. 옛날 사람들에게는 옛날 행동이 있고 새로운 사람들에게는 새로운 행동이 있다. 옛날 사람들은 아마도 새로운 연료(땔감)를 가져와서 불이 계속 타오르게 할 만큼 충분히 알지 못했다; 새로운 사람들은 아궁이(pot) 밑에 약간의 마른 나무를 넣고, 말 그대로 옛날 사람들의 생각을 없애는 방법으로 온 세상을 새의 속도로 돌아다니는 것이다. 연륜은 젊음보다 교육자로의 자격이 더 낫지 않고, 못한 것은 연륜으로 인해 얻은 것이 아니라 잃었기 때문이다. 가장 현명한 사람조차도 삶을 통해 절대적 가치가 있는 무언가를 배웠을지는 거의 의심할지도 모른다. 실제로, 노인들은 젊은 사람들에게 줄 그다지 중요한 충고는 갖고 있지 못하고, 그들(노인들)의 경험은 편파적이며, 그들의 삶은 사적인 이유로, 그들(노인들)도 반드시 그렇게 믿고 있듯이 비참한 실패였다; 그리고 그들에게는 그 경험이 거짓임을 나타내는 약간의 믿음이 남아있을지도 모르며, 그들은 단지 예전보다 덜 젊을 뿐이다.

이종현T의 독해 Point

"it appears as if men had deliberately chosen the common mode of living because they preferred it to any other. Yet they honestly think there is no choice left." 사람들은 일반적인 생활방식을 선호하고 다른 선택의 여지가 없다고 생각한다. 그 뒤에서 '이러한 편견은 포기할 수 있다'로 글이 전개가 된다. 그러므로 our prejudice가 암시하는 내용은 현재 주어진 방식대로 살아가는 것을 말한다. 4번이 일치한다.

① 우리는 자유롭게 태어난다.
② 우리는 자연의 법칙을 따른다.
③ 우리에게 미래는 없다.
④ 우리는 이런 식으로 살 수밖에 없다.
⑤ 우리는 우리가 할 수 있는 것은 무엇이든지 할 수 있다.

4.

해석 : 안전과 시민의 자유 사이에서 이루어져야 한다고 하는 우리가 들어온 균형에 대해 고려해 보자. 추상적으로, 이러한 주장에는 일리가 있다. 그러나 특정 정책 영역에서 올바른 균형은 저울을 완전히 한쪽으로 기울게 하는 것을 의미할지도 모른다. 예를 들어, 재판 없이 몇 년을 계속해서 사람들을 투옥하는 것과 국가 안보사이에는 아마도 틀림없이 균형을 이룰 필요가 없을 것이다. 전자(재판 없이 투옥)는 결코 일어나선 안 되는 일이기 때문이다. 저울이 한쪽으로 확실하게 기우는 경우에는 균형을 맞추는 것은 필요하지 않다.

이종현T의 독해 Point

본문의 내용은 균형을 맞추는 것이 중요하다는 내용이 아니라 계속해서 한쪽으로 기우는 결과, 균형을 맞추는 것이 필요하지 않은 일 등을 설명해주고 있다. 그러므로, 1번의 "하나의 관심은 다른 하나를 무시한다."를 추론할 수 있다.

① 하나의 관심사가 다른 하나의 관심사를 무시하게 만든다.
② 안전이 확보된 상황에서의 가난이 불확실한 가운데의 풍요보다 낫다.
③ 자유의 토대는 서서히 얻어내야 한다.
④ 공정한 저울과 정확한 측정에 다치는 사람은 아무도 없다.
⑤ 진실은 피난처를 찾지 않는다.

5.

해석 : 분명히, 싼 에너지 가격은 귀중한 에너지를 낭비하고 싶은 마음을 점진적으로 늘어나게한다. 이 더 싸면, 귀중한 에너지원을 조금씩 허비하고픈 마음(자동차 엔진을 공회전하도록 내버려 두는 것, 또는 불을 끄기 위해 위층으로 올라가지 않는 것)도 점차적으로 늘어난다. 사소한 습관이 중요하다. 왜냐하면 기후의 재앙을 향해 무자비하게 시간이 흘러가고 있는 상황에서 사소한 모든 것들이 상처를 줄 수 있기 때문이다. 유가폭락(oil crash)이 여기에 얼마나 많은 피해를 입히는지는 다음에 발생하는 일에 달려있다. 과거에는, 세계는 가격의 하락뿐만아니라 (가격)상승에 의해서도 영향을 받았다. 만약 하락하던 것(가격)이 곧 회복한다면, 그러한 직접적인 영향은 크지 않은 것으로 증명될 지도 모른다. 장기적인 관점에서 더 중요하게 될 것은 에너지 기반시설에 대한 엄청난 영향이다.

이종현T의 독해 Point

If what comes down soon goes back up, such direct effects may not prove so profound.

마지막에 이 문장을 보면 내려갔던 것이 다시 올라가면 영향력은 심각하지 않을 것이라고 나와 있다. 그렇다면 가격이 내려가는 것은 어떤 영향을 준다는 걸 추론할 수 있다. 그리고 이 글에서는 오일 가격이 싸지면 사람들이 오일을 더 쓴다는 것이므로 정답은 1번이 된다.

① 값싼 석유로 인해 대체 에너지에 대한 투자는 위축될 것이다.
② 비싼 에너지 가격은 물가를 더 낮추는 데 도움이 될 것이다.
③ 전기자동차 제조업체들은 생살라인을 확장할 것이다.
④ 석유 수출업체들은 유가하락으로부터 분명히 수혜를 입을 것이다.
⑤ 화석연료를 뽑아내는 가장 착취적인 계획이 더 경제적인 것이 될 것이다.

6.

해석 : 모든 과학은 인간의 편견의 영향을 받기 쉽다. 이것(앞 문장)은 특히 사회과학자들에게 해당한다. 인간의 행동이 그들(사회과학자)의 연구 분야이기 때문에, 그들은 실제로 연구 대상의 일부인 것이다. 더욱이, 인간의 행동모형은 장소마다 다르고 또한 집단마다 다르다. 이것(행동모형이 다르다는 것)은 자연과학의 연구 대상과 대조를 이룬다. 화학자가 수소를 연구할 때, 그는 하나의 수소원자는 어디서 발견된 것이든 다른 수소 원자와 아주 비슷하다(고 가정할 수 있고), 그것(수소원자)을 둘러싸고 있는 환경이 상당히 정확하게 통제될 수 있다고 가정할 수 있다. 물리학자가 금속 막대를 측정할 때에도 마찬가지이다. 그는 자연환경이 똑같다면, 그 금속 막대의 길이가 늘어나거나 줄어들지 않다는 것을 상당히 확신할 수 있다. 'Earl Babbie'가 경제학자 'Daniel Suits'(연구 대상의 예측가능한 속성 때문에 자연과학을 '쉬운 과학'이라고 부르는)의 말을 인용하는 까닭도 이것(자연환경이 같다면 금속막대의 길이가 수축하지 않다는 것) 때문이다.

이종현T의 독해 Point

"it will not stretch or shrink in length as long as natural conditions are the same." 이 문장을 보면 자연환경이 동일하다면 수축하지 않는다고 한다. -> 이 말은 자연환경이 변한다면 수축할 수 있다는 의미를 내포한다. 그러므로 5번이 올바른 추론이다.

① 인간의 선입견은 사회 과학자들의 주된 연구대상이다.

② 인간의 행동을 둘러싸고 있는 환경은 정확하게 통제될 수 있다.

③ 사회과학은 연구 대상이 다루기 힘들다는 점 때문에 어려운 것으로 간주될 수 있다.

④ 'Daniel Suits'의 말을 인용하는 것은 자연과학이 선입견의 영향을 받는다는 점을 뒷받침하기 위함이다.

⑤ 금속막대는 자연조건에 따라 길이가 변할 수도 있다.

7.

해석 : 곧, 미국 'Iowa'주에서 스마트폰 어플은 많은 사람들을 위한 공식적인 운전면허증 역할을 하게 될 것이다. 주 교통부 'Paul Trombino'는 "이것(어플의 역할)으로 인해 우리는 정말로 발전해가고 있습니다."라고 이번 주의 부서 예산 청문회에서 발표했다. "일이 진행되는 걸 보면, 우리가 미국에서 처음일지 모른다." 그 새로운 면허증은 주 공항뿐만 아니라 교통단속 때에도 경찰에 의해 인정된다. 경찰은 그 새로운 면허증을 아이오와 주의 공항에서뿐만 아니라 교통단속 때에도 인정할 것이다. 신문보도에 따르면 "그것은 본질적으로 전화기 안에 있는 면허증입니다."라고 그는 말했다. 'Pin number'는 증명과 보안을 위해 필요로 된다. 아이오와 주의 주민들(Iowans)은 기존 면허증을 유지할 수 있는 선택권을 여전히 갖게 될 것이다. 그 새로운 어플 면허증은 2015년에 운전자들의 추가적인 비용 부담 없이 이용할 수 있게 될 것이다.

이종현T의 독해 Point

"We are really moving forward on this." 이 문장을 보면 우리는 점점 발전하고 있다 그 뒤에 계속 어플 면허증의 긍정적인 부분만을 언급을 한다. 그러므로 3번이 올바른 추론이다. 나머지 보기는 금방 소거할 수 있는 내용이다.

① 어플 면허증을 가지려면 운전자들이 등록비를 부담해야 한다.

② 전화기 속의 새로운 면허증은 신원 도용에 취약하다

③ 아이오와 주 정부는 새로운 기술을 적극적으로 활용하고 있다.

④ 아이오와 주의 주민들은 공항에서는 기존 면허증을 갖고 다녀야 한다.

8.

해석 : 경제 자료들을 비교하는 동안, 한 사회학자 연구팀은 특정 소득 수준의 모든 사람들 가운데, 시골 지역 사람들이 도시나 교외지역에 사는 사람들 보다 구매력이 더 높다고 결론지었다. 그 연구팀은 도시 중심부 특정 반경 내의 인구밀도, 가구당 인구 수, 맞벌이 가구의 비율 등 몇 가지 자료 측정값을 계산에 넣었다, 그러나 결국, 주된 전제는 도시와 교외 거주자들의 기본적인 필요한 음식과 거주에 쓰인 돈은 시골가정에서는 선택적 소비재의 구입에 쓰인다는 것이다.

이종현T의 독해 Point

the money spent by urban and suburban dwellers on their fundamental need for food and shelter could be spent by rural households on discretionary items. 도시와 교외지역 가정이 음식과 거주에 돈을 쓸 때 시골 가정은 선택적 소비재의 구입에 돈을 쓴다고 한다. 이 점으로 4번의 시골 가정은 도시나 교외지역 가정보다 음식, 거주에 적은 돈을 쓴다는 올바른 추론이다.

① 교외 지역 가구는 도시 가구보다 구매력이 더 크다.

② 시골 가구는 도시 중심에서부터 더 멀리 떨어져 있을수록, 더 작은 구매력 을 가진다.

③ 보통의 도시 혹은 교외 지역 가구의 인구는 보통의 시골 지역 가구의 인구보다 적다.

④ 시골 가구는 도시나 교외지역 가구보다 식품과 주택에 더 적은 돈을 쓴다.

9.

해석 : 'Bohr'와 'Einstein'이 함께 대화를 이어가는 것의 궁극적인 실패는 오늘날 물리학 분야에 존재하는 분열의 정도를 상징한다. 그들의 친밀한 우정과 그들의 만남 때마다 상기 된 에너지에도 불구하고, 그들은 결국 서로에 대해 더 이상 할 말이 없을 지경에 이르렀다. 이런 의사소통의 중단은 물리학의 비공식적인 용어의 사용법이 서로 다르고 양립할 수 없었던 것의 결과였다. 각각의 주창자(Bohr와 Einstein)는 특정한 용어를 특정한 방식으로 사용하고 있었고 서로 다른 해석적 측면을 강조하고 있었다. 이 전체적인 질문의 깊은 분석은 정말로 문제가 된 것은 관련된 차수(order)에 대한 생각의 차이를 보여준다. 물리학과 자연의 차수에 대한 미묘하게 다른 생각을 가지고 있었던 'Bohr'와 'Einstein' 둘은 그들의 대화는 필연적으로 중단되었는데, 이 중단은 오늘날 존재하는 상대성이론과 양자이론 사이의 거리가 잘 반영해준다. 특히 'Bohr'는 소립자운동의 차수는 모호성을 인정할 것이라고 믿었지만, 'Einstein'는 그러한 가능성은 너무나 터무니없어서 생각할 필요도 없다고 느꼈다. 그러므로 현대 물리학의 두 거장 사이에 의사소통 실패 원인은 차수에 대한 그들의 양립할 수 없는 견해에 놓여있다.

이종현T의 독해 Point

'Bohr'와 'Einstein'의 불화는 서로 다른 해석적 차이에서 비롯된 것이다. 이로 인해 1번의 추론은 올바르다. 2번은 차수가 다른 것이 아니라 차수에 대한 견해가 다른 것이므로 올바르지 않다.

① 아인슈타인의 상대성 이론과 보어의 양자론은 차수에 대한 두 가지 서로 다른 해석으로 이해할 수 있다.

② 두 과학자들 사이의 의사교환의 단절은 그들 이론에 포함된 서로 다른 차수들 때문이었다.

③ 오늘날 과학은 실체를 파악할 수 있는 타당한 도구가 아닐지 모른다고 일반적으로 인정된다.

④ 물리학 연구방법론에 있어 보어와 아인슈타인은 근본적으로 달랐다.

10.

해석 : 필리핀에서 텔레비전은 모든 사람들에게 모든 것이 되었다. (모든 것)친구, 선생님, 연인, 어머니가 된 것이다. 이 지역(필리핀)에서 제작하는 영화의 수가 줄어들면서, 시청자들은 필리핀 영화에서 가장 인기 있는 스타를 매일 집에서 만나고 있다. 현재 가장 큰 두 TV 방송사는 시청자들과 그들의 친밀한 관계를 강조하면서 스스로를 'kapuso(한 마음)', 'kapamilya(한 가족)'으로 선전한다. 뉴스 앵커는 단지 그 날의 뉴스를 읽는 것이 아니고, 그들(뉴스 앵커)은 또한 오류 범한 정부 관료를 비난하기도 하는데, 종종 아무런 조사도 없이 이루어진다. 그들은 의료지원에서부터 장학금과 노래방 기계에 이르는(분명히 기본적인 필수품) 모든 것들을 제공하는 공익 프로그램을 진행한다.

대략 인구의 절반이 빈곤 속에서 살고 있는 나라에서, TV는 가장 쉬운 탈출구이다. TV는 버라이어티쇼, 드라마 그리고 슈퍼히어로 판타지뿐만 아니라, 게임 쇼와 경연 프로그램에서 수백만의 현금을 기부하고 있다. 물론, 궁극적인 탈출은 시청자들이 문자메시지 투표에 의해 우승자를 선택하는 'American Idol'류의 새로운 쇼를 통해서이다. 이것은 거르지 않고 즉흥적으로 활동을 하는 민주주의이다.

이종현T의 독해 Point

두 번째 단락의 중심적인 내용은 TV를 통해 빈곤에서 탈출할 수 있다는 것이다. 주제를 계속 생각을 하면서 문제를 푼다면 일치하는 것은 4번의 부자가 되는 것(=빈곤에서 탈출하는 것)과 일맥상통한다.

① 믿을만한 변명
② 최종 목적지
③ 안전한 비상구
④ 부자가 되는 것

11.

해석 : 글은 우리가 생각을 기록하고 의사소통하도록 도와준다. 글은 인간의 일상적인 경험의 분명하고 필수적인 부분이다. 우리가 쇼핑목록을 쓰든 훌륭한 소설을 쓰든, 우리는 만약 그것(도구)이 없다면 우리 자신이 고립되는 것을 알 수 있는 도구를 이용하고 있다. 글이 없다면, 우리는 정치적 견해의 표현, 응급상황에 대한 묘사, 그리고 일기와 편지에서의 우리의 감정을 검사하는 것과 같은 중요한 과정들을 할 수 없게 된다.

글은 여러 문화를 교차한다. 우리가 역사적인 동굴 그림을 보든 세계무역센터 참사 후의 팩스 메시지 전송을 떠올리든, 우리는 다른 사람들에게 정보를 전달하고자 하는 인간의 본능에 대한 증거를 발견하게 된다.

과거에는, 글은 변화를 야기했다. 미국 흑인 노예들은 빈번하게 읽고 쓰는 법을 배우는 것이 금지되었지만, 일부는 어떻게든 읽고 쓰는 방법을 찾았다. 노예들의 삶의 이야기들은 노(노예제도)폐지 운동에 불을 붙이는 데 도움을 주었다. 19세기에 열정적인 연설과 신문에 실린 기사를 통해 투표권을 얻은 여성들은 글을 참정권 운동(cause)을 발전시키기 위해 사용하였다. 이민자들은 신세계에서 더 나은 삶을 찾기 위해 영어를 배우려 노력했다.

이종현T의 독해 Point

본문의 마지막을 보면 19세기에 여성들이 투표권을 얻고 참정권 운동을 했다고 언급되어 있다. 이에 따라 19세기 이전에는 여성들의 투표가 허용되지 않았다고 하는 4번이 올바른 추론이다.

① 우리가 무언가를 쓸 때 우리는 대개 다른 사람들과 떨어진 채 혼자 있다.

② 노예제도가 폐지되기 전에는, 글을 읽거나 쓸 줄 아는 흑인이 한명도 없었다.

③ 그림은 여러 문화를 망라하는 보편적인 의사소통 수단인데 반해, 글은 특정 문화에 국한되어 있다.

④ 19세기 전에는, 여성들의 투표가 허용되지 않았다.

⑤ 짧은 메모나 긴 산문을 쓰기 위해 우리는 도구가 필요하다.

12.

해석 : 외국인들이 계속 들어오도록 하는 것에 대해 경비 요원들이 꺼려하는 것은 이해할만하다(당연한 것이다). 'Hanle'에 위치한 정부 관측소를 향해 가는 소수의 과학자들 이외에, 대부분의 서양인들은 1962년 중국과 인도의 전쟁이 끝난 이래로 접근이 금지되어왔다. 중국 스파이가 국경을 넘어 분쟁중인 국경으로부터 12마일 떨어진 곳에 위치한 'Hanle'로 몰래 잠입할 것을 두려워한 인도 정부는 그 지역에 대해 출입금지를 선언했다.

이종현T의 독해 Point

두 번째 문장을 보면 소수의 과학자를 제외한 대부분의 서양인들은 1962년 전쟁 이후로 접근이 금지되어 왔다고 한다. 이로 인해 4번의 많은 사람들이 머물고 있다는 추론은 옳지 않다.

① 한레는 인도의 영토에 속한다.

② 한레는 국경선 부근에 위치해 있다.

③ 한레 사람들은 중국인들을 좋아하지 않는다.

④ 한레에는 많은 서양인들이 체류하고 있다.

⑤ 한레에는 국영 천문대가 있다.

13.

해석 : 지하철 시스템의 유명한 안내방송인 "지하철 문이 곧 닫힙니다. 한 걸음 물러 서 주세요(의역)."가 사라질 수도 있다. 도시교통당국(MTA)은 2호선에서 승객들에 대한 익숙한 경고 방송을 보다 간결한 문구인 "한 걸음 물러 서 주세요."로 바꾸기 시작할 것인데, 이는 도시교통당국(MTA)의 대변인에 따르면, 간결함이 열차 운행이 빨라지게 되는지를 알아보기 위한 것이라고 한다. "지하철 문이 곧 닫힙니다. 한 걸음 물러 서 주세요."와 새로운 "한 걸음 물러 서 주세요."의 안내방송 사이의 네 단어 차이는 약 1초를 절약할 수 있다. 마찬가지로 수정할 예정인 다른 안내방송과 합칠 때, 지하철은 약 3, 4초 더 빠르게 움직일 수 있다. 새로운 단어들(지하철 안내방송)은 곧 다른 노선으로 확대될지도 모른다.

많은 뉴욕 시민들은 지하철 문이 닫히고 열차가 움직이는 순간에 들리는 "지하철 문이 곧 닫힙니다. 한 걸음 물러 서 주세요."라는 말을 그리워하지만, 그 단어들(기존 안내방송)을 말하던 남자는 이러한 변화에 냉정하다. 2001년에 그 안내방송을 녹음했던 'Bloomberg'라디오의 기자 'Charlie Pellett'는 "뉴욕에서 엄청나게 오래 공연했네요." "브로드웨이 연극 공연도 그렇게 오래 가지 못하죠."라고 말했다. 그는 그 지하철 안내방송이 뉴욕에서 가장 유명한 (유명)문구 중의 하나지만, 그는 녹음으로 인해 돈을 받지 않았다고 말했다. "만약 매 방송마다 1페니씩 번다면, (더 이상 돈을 벌 필요가 없어서)은퇴할 수 있을 겁니다."라고 그는 농담을 하였다.

이종현T의 독해 Point

"to see if brevity will speed rail traffic" 1단락 중간부분을 보면 방송 길이를 줄이는 이유는 지하철 운행속도 증진을 위한 것이라 하였다. 그러므로 3번은 올바론 추론이다.

① 새로운 안내방송을 현재 모든 지하철 노선에서 들을 수 있다.

② 찰리 펠레는 안내방송이 나올 때마다 돈을 지급받았다.

③ MTA는 더 짧아진 새로운 메시지가 지하철이 역에 정차해 있는 시간을 줄여주기를 바라고 있다.

④ 뉴욕시 지하철 승객들에게는 열차를 더 빨라지게 하기 위한 교육이 더 많이 필요하다.

⑤ 대중교통 이용자들은 오래된 안내방송에 싫증이 났으며, 그로 인해 안내 방송이 바뀌게 되었다.

14.

해석 : 속박되지 않은 주권의 신성불가침적인 지위가 점점 더 의문시 되고 있다. 비난의 일부는 주권의 전통적인 비판자로부터 왔다; 예를 들어, 전쟁을 반대자들은 무력 충돌은 주권이 지배하는 세상에서 필수적이고 불가피하고 그리고 유감스러운 세계의 결과라고 주장한다. 이런 관점으로부터, 주권을 해체시키는 것은 세계 평화에 반드시 필요한 전제조건이다. 동시에, 인권과 같은 다른 관심사들의 발생은 국가 주권과 충돌한다. 왜일까? 그것은 국가 안에서 개인들과 집단들의 학대에 대한 주요 역사적인 정당화는 주권국가는 자국 시민들에 대한 절대적인 권위를 소유하고, 그리고 국가가 주권 관할구역 안에서 어떻게 행동하는지는 엄밀히 말해 국가가 알아서 결정해야 할 문제라는 것이기 때문이다.

이종현T의 독해 Point

"dismantling sovereignty is the necessary prerequisite for world peace." 이문장을 보면 주권을 해체하는 것이 세계 평화의 전제조건이라고 말한다. 글의 주제는 주권을 해체하는 것을 주장한다. 그러므로 4번의 국가에게 무제한적인 자유를 준다는 말은 글의 전체 흐름에 부합하지 않는다.

① 전쟁을 반대하는 이들은 무력 분쟁과 주권 사이의 연관성을 지적한다.

② 인권과 국가 주권 사이에 분쟁이 가끔 발생한다.

③ 주권에 대한 비판론자들은 세계 평화는 주권 폐지에 의해 더 증진될 수 있다고 주장한다.

④ 저자는 주권국가는 시민들의 권리를 제한할 수 있는 무제한적인 자유를 가져야 한다고 제안한다.

15.

해석 : 어느 사회에서든, 특권의 전달이 '잘못 인식되고'있다. 개인들은 그들 사회의 사회적 배치를 정당한 것으로 간주하는 경향이 있다. 신분, 특권, 그리고 유사한 사회적 보상들은 주장한 바에 이르면 개인들에 의해 '얻어졌다고'한다; 다시 말해, 그것(얻어진 것)들이 지능, 재능, 노력, 그리고 다른 전략적으로 보여 진 능력들의 결과로서 얻어지는 것으로 간주된다는 것이다. 'Pierre Bourdieu'는 개인들의 사회적 지위는 노력 또는 지능과 같은 개인적 속성의 결과가 아니라는 것을 분명히 하고 있다. 특히, 그는 특권적인 사회적 지위에 있는 개인들은 그들의 문화적인 경험의 본질적인 장점의 결과가 아닌 방식으로 유리한 위치에 놓인다고 주장한다. 오히려, 특권층 가정에서의 아동 양육의 기준과 이러한(지배적인) 제도들에 제안 된 기준 사이의 밀접한 양립성 때문에, 가정에서의 문화적 교육은 지배적인 제도들에서 불공평한 가치를 부여받고 있다는 것이다.

이종현T의 독해 Point

"Pierre Bourdieu makes clear that individuals' social position is not the result of personal attributes such as effort or intelligence." 이 부분에서 'Pierre Bourdieu'는 개인들의 사회적 지위는 노력 또는 지능과 같은 속성의 결과가 아니라는 것을 분명히 하고 있다. 4번의 진술은 정반대의 진술이므로 옳지 않다.

① 개개인들은 그들의 사회적 지위를 정당한 것으로 잘못 받아들이는 경향이 있다.

② 부르디외는 사회구조의 중심에 지배와 불평등의 패턴이 있음을 알아본다.

③ 부르디외는 특권층 가정의 아이들의 경우 가정에서의 문화적 교육과 지배적인 제도 사이에 밀접한 관계가 있음을 지적한다.

④ 부르디외는 개개인의 사회적 위치는 그들의 지성, 재능 그리고 노력으로부터 비롯된다고 주장한다.

16.

해석 : 심지어 그것(현대화)의 목적이 예상하지 못하거나, 의도하지 않거나 또는 환영받지 못한 결과들 없이 성취된다는 좁은 의미에서 성공적일 때조차, 현대화는 모든 합리적인 관점에서 확실한 이익은 아니다. 독재자들이 그들의 억압적인 장치 또는 군사력을 현대화할 때, 아무도 환영하지 않는다.; 심지어 완전히 시민 차원 활동들의 성공적인 현대화조차도 낭비적인 막다른 길임이 입증될 수 있어서, 지속적인 개발을 위한 보다 더 견고한 플랫폼인 것으로 입증될지 모르는 다른 현대화로 대체되어야 할 수도 있다. 비록 현대화는 다양한 시기에 걸쳐 정책입안자들에게 매우 매력적일지라도, 그것(현대화)은 항상 비장의 카드로 간주되어 온 것은 아니고, 다른 수사학적 정당화들이 광범위한 개혁을 위해 사용되어 왔다.

이종현T의 독해 Point

이 전체적인 글은 현대화는 모든 합리적인 관점에서 확실한 이익은 아니다. 라고 진술되었다. 이 말은 양면적인 모습을 보여주는데, 2번의 일방적인 부정은 올바르지 않다.

① 근대화 개혁은 종종 모종의 의도치 않거나 예상치 못한 결과를 낳았다.

② 근대화는 실망, 실패, 그리고 좋지 않은 놀라움으로의 일방통행로다.

③ 때때로 한때 성공적이었던 근대화가 좀 더 지속적인 개혁에 의해 대체될 필요가 있다.

④ 독재자들의 억압적인 장치와 군사력은 근대화의 달갑지 않은 결과가 될 수도 있다.

17.

해석 : 질서에 관한 매우 다른 개념이 사회주의자들과 무정부주의자들의 글에서 등장했다. 예를 들어, 무정부주의자들은 국가와 모든 형태의 정치권력의 폐지를 옹호하는데, 여기에는 물론, 법과 질서라는 장치의 폐지도 포함한다. 마르크스주의 사회주의자들 또한 이러한 이상적인 시각에 공감해왔다. 마르크스 자신은 국가는 — 그리고 국가와 함께 법과 또 다른 형태의 사회통제들은 — 일단 사회적 불평등이 없어지고 나면 점차 '시들' 것이라고 믿었다. 의회 사회주의자들과 현대 자유주의자들은 좀 더 신중한 제안을 했지만, 그럼에도 불구하고 그들은 질서는 단지 엄격한 법과 처벌에 의해서만 유지될 수 있을 뿐이라는 비판적인 믿음을 가져왔다. 비록 그러한 견해들이 '법과 질서'에 대한 전통적인 견해에 비판적일지라도, 그것(견해)들이 '질서' 그 자체에 대한 완전한 거부인 것은 아니다. 오히려 그것(견해)들은 사회질서란 개인들 자신의 타고난 분별력에 의해서만 통제되는 자발적인 조화의 형태를 취할 수 있다는 대안적인 믿음을 기초로 하고 있다.

이종현T의 독해 Point

마지막 문장을 보면 자발적인 조화의 형태를 기초로 하고 있다고 한다. 3번은 비판적이라고 하였으므로, 반대되는 진술이다.

① 마르크스주의자들은 사회질서의 개념에 대한 무정부주의자들의 주장에 공감한다.

② 무정부주의자들은 모든 형태의 정치적 권위는 사회 불평등의 문제를 해결하기 위해 폐지되어야 한다는 것을 지지한다.

③ 사회주의자들은 사회질서는 자발적인 개개인들의 조화를 장려하는 사회 에서 좀 더 쉽게 유지될 수 있다는 믿음에 비판적이다.

④ 무정부주의자들과 마르크스주의자들은 질서의 개념에 대해 의회 사회주의자들과 근대 진보주의자들보다 더 급진적인 견해를 갖고 있다.

18.

해석 : 어느 날 아침 내가 운영하는 주유소에 45분 늦게 도착한 나는 손님들을 향해 소리쳤다. "지금 바로 가스펌프를 킬게요." 내가 모르고 있었던 것은 야간 직원이 밤새도록 가스 펌프를 켜뒀다는 것이었다. 이것은 어떤 차라도 공짜로 기름을 가득 채우고 갈 수 있었다는 것을 의미한다. 내가 사무실에 도착했을 때, 대부분의 차들이 이미 기름을 넣고 떠난 뒤였다. 오직 한 명의 손님만이 돈을 지불하기 위해 남아 있었다. 심장이 내려앉았다. 그때 그 손님은 주머니에서 현금 한 다발을 꺼내고 내게 건네주었다. "우리는 마지막 사람에게 돈을 계속 전해줬어요. 우리는 당신이 곧 올 거라고 생각했거든요." 라고 그가 말했다.

이종현T의 독해 Point

돈을 지불하지 않고 그냥 떠나도 되는 상황에서 손님들은 뒤의 손님에게 돈을 전달하여 나중에는 주인이 받을 수 있도록 하였다. 그러므로 2번의 손님들은 정직했다가 맞는 추론이다.

① 기름펌프는 밤새도록 고장 나 있었다.

② 손님들은 글쓴이만큼 정직했다.

③ 마지막에 있던 손님은 다른 손님들의 기름 값을 자신의 돈으로 지불했다.

④ 일단 기름펌프를 열면, 어떤 차도 공짜로 기름을 채울 수 있다.

⑤ 몇몇 차의 기름 값을 글쓴이는 받았다.

19.

해석 : 진보주의 패러다임의 규범적 입장은 그것의 설명적인 이론들로부터 곧바로 나온다. 진보주의자들은 국제문제에서의 진보는 불가능하다는 현실주의자의 의견을 거부한다. 그들은 협동이 참여자(국가)들을 더 부유하게 만들 수 있고, 따라서 협동(that)이 국제문제에서 우선사항이 되어야 한다고 주장한다. 현대 국제 정치의 이슈들에 대한 실질적인 토론의 상당 부분은 국가들이 문제점들을 해결하기 위해 서로 협력해야 할 필요가 있다는 것을 인식하는 것과 관련되어 있다. 보안, 경제, 건강, 그리고 환경문제에서, 토론의 상당 부분은 국제적인 협동의 모습과 협동을 촉진시키기 위한 최고의 방법에 관련되어 있다.

이종현T의 독해 Point

이 글의 주제는 협동을 통해 국제적인 문제를 개선할 수 있다는 것이다. 하지만 4번의 진술은 변하지 않는다고 하므로 주제와 일치하지 않다.

① 진보주의자들은 국제 정치에서 진보가 가능하다는 점을 시사한다.
② 진보주의들은 공동협력은 국제문제에서 우선사항이어야 된다고 주장한다.
③ 진보주의자들은 국제문제에서 현실주의자들보다 훨씬 덜 비관적인 견해를 제공한다.
④ 진보주의자들은 국제관계의 기본 특징은 많은 세월이 지나도 바뀌지 않았다고 믿는다.

20.

해석 : 실제로, 각 세대는 과거가 남겨준 전통적인 환경에서 자신의 삶을 시작하고, 자신의 이미지의 배경을 만들려고 아무리 노력할지라도, 심지어 자신의 삶이 끝날 때조차, 그 배경을 완전히 현대화하는 데 결코 성공하지 못할 것이다. 따라서 장소들은 과거로부터 물려받은 주된 건축 환경에 놓여있고, 우리가 좋아하든 싫어하든, 그것을 현존하는 요인들로 받아들이고 발전시킬 차례이다. 따라서, 어느 인간의 정착지든 반드시 과거와 미래 사이의 공존을 의미하고, 이러한 공존은, 시기와 장소에 따라 다르겠지만, 한 장소 내에서 지리적, 사회적, 역사적으로 결정된 후자(미래)의 성격을 변함없이 반영할 것이다. 이 성격의 가장 두드러진 특징들은 그 장소의 역사적 기념물에 구현될 것이고, 그것들(기념물들)은 과거부터 미래까지 이어지는 그 공간 구조의 본질적인 부분이고 그런 본질적인 부분으로서 그것(구조물)과 함께 보존되고 존속되어야 한다.

이종현T의 독해 Point

이 글의 주제는 과거와 미래 사이의 공존을 주장한다. 그러므로 3번의 과거의 역사적 기념물을 장애물로 취급한다는 진술은 올바르지 않다.

① 우리는 기념물들을 소생시키는 수단을 찾음으로써 그 기념물들을 보호할 필요가 있다.
② 과거의 건축 배경들을 완전히 현대화시키는 일은 불가능하다.
③ 역사적 기념물들은 진보에 대한 장애물로 취급되어야 한다.
④ 현대 지역사회는 과거와 현재의 계속되는 공존으로 인식된다.

UNIT 3 지칭 추론

1.

해석 : 미국 독립 혁명이 있기 전, 북미대륙의 영국 식민지에 살고 있던 대부분의 사람들은 자신들을(Colonialist) 영국 사람들과 똑같은 권리와 의무를 가진 영국 왕실의 충성스러운 백성들로 여겼었다. 그러나 중상주의에서, 영국 사람들은 식민지들을 그들(영국 국민)의 경제적 이익을 위해 이용될 수단으로 더 여기고 있었으며, 식민지 주민들을 거의 존중하지 않았다. 그러한 인식의 차이는 식민지 주민들의 악순환으로 이끌었다. 그 악순환은 자신들(Colonialist)이 불공평한 정책으로 간주하는 것에 대항하여 행동을 하고, 이에 대해 영국이 거칠게 대응하고, 이어서 식민지 주민들이 더 강하게 대응하고, 또 이것은 더 거친 영국의 반응을 이끌었으며 그리고 이 모든 것들은 결국 혁명을 낳았다. 식민지 주민들이 영국을 거부하기 시작하면서, 그들(Colonialist)은 또한 다른 길에서도 더 급진적으로 되기 시작했으며, 넓은 의미에서의 민주주의에 대해 더 많은 관심을 갖게 되었다.

이종현T의 독해 Point

대명사를 확실히 확인하며 꼼꼼히 읽어나가는 버릇을 들이자. 위에 해석처럼 2번은 영국 국민, 그 외는 식민지 주민들을 가리킨다.

2.

해석 : 소설의 여주인공 'Isobel'은 지난 10년을 장애가 있는 아버지를 간호하며 보냈는데, 그 소설책의 시작에서 아버지의 천주교 장례식으로 발생하였다. 그녀(A-Isobel)의 유일한 경쟁상 대는 그들의 과거 가정부였던 'Margaret'이었는데, 'Margaret'은 'Isobel' 아버지의 아내가 되기를 바랬었다. 그러나 그녀의 속셈을 간파한 'Isobel'은 그녀(B-Isobel)의 아버지를 설득해 그녀(C-Margaret)를 해고하고 승리자가 되었다. 아버지의 장례식 이후, 'Isobel'은 처음에는 평온해 보인다.: 그녀는 자신이 입을 옷들을 사고, 아버지와 살던 집을 팔고 어떤 유부남과 간통을 시작한다. 그러나 새로 발견된 행복은 유부남의 아내로부터의 갑작스러운 장황한 비난으로 산산조각 나고 만다. 깊은 슬픔으로 좌절하여, 'Isobel'이 그녀(D-Isobel)의 잘못에 대해 생 각할 수 있는 유일한 속죄는 그녀가 혐오했던 'Margaret'에게 그녀의 남은 일생을 헌신하는 것이었다.

이종현T의 독해 Point

위의 해석처럼 A, B, D는 모두 'Isobel'을 가리키는 데 반해, C는 'Margaret'을 가리킨다.

3.

해석 : 육로로 여행할 때, 경치가 연속되며 인물과 사건도 서로 연결되어 연속적으로 일어나는데, 인생 이야기는 계속되고 부재와 이별의 영향은 줄어든다. 사실, 우리는 우리의 순례에서의 각 이동에서 '늘어나는 사슬'을 끌고 다니지만, 그 사슬은 끊어지지 않는다: 그 사슬을 하나씩 더듬어서 우리는 왔던 길을 추적할 수 있다; 그리고 우리는 그 마지막 사슬이 여전히 우리를 붙잡고 집으로 데려간다고 생각한다. 그러나 광활한 바다 여행은 한 번에 우리를 단절시킨다. 광활한 바다를 여행은 우리를 정착된 삶이라는 안전한 정박지로부터 풀려나 의심되는 세계로 표류하게 됨을 인식하게 한다. 그것은 단지 가상의 것이 아니라 우리와 고향사이에 실제 큰 간격을 두는데, 이 간격은 소동, 두려움, 불확실성에 쉽게 영향을 받아 (우리와 고향 사이) 거리를 명백하게 만들며, (고향으로)돌아가는 것을 불확실하게 만든다.

이종현T의 독해 Point

the last는 앞에 언급된 it(사슬)을 가리킨다.

① 마지막 이야기

② 마지막 사슬

③ 마지막 세상

④ 마지막 인물

4.

해석 : 과학자가 자연을 들여다보려고 시도하는 통찰력은 무엇일까? 그것(통찰력)은 정말로 상상력이 풍부하거나 창의적인 것으로 불릴 수 있을까? 문학인에게, 그 질문은 그저 어리석은 것으로 보일지도 모른다. 그(문학인)는 과학은 사실들의 거대한 집합체라고 배워왔다. 그래서 만약 이것이 사실이라면, 그러면 과학자들이 해야 할 필요가 있는 유일한 관찰은, 그(문학인)가 가정하건데, 사실들을 관찰하는 것이다. 그(문학인)는 과학을 전문으로 하는 중립적인 사람들이 아침에 중립적이고 노출되지 않은 상태로 일(연구)을 하러 대학교로 가는 모습을 상상한다. 그런 다음, 그들(과학 전문가)은 사진 건판(photographic plate)처럼 자신을 노출시킨다. 그러고 나서 어두운 방 또는 실험실에서, 그들은 영상을 현상하며, 그 결과 갑작스럽고 놀랍게도 그것(영상)은 대문자로 인쇄되어 원자에너지를 위한 새로운 공식이 된다.

이종현T의 독해 Point

사람은 문학인과 과학자만 언급이 되었다. 앞 문장부터 과학자들에 관한 이야기이며, 그 뒷문 장도 실험, 원자에너지 등으로 과학자임을 유추할 수 있다.

① 학자들

② 교수들

③ 과학자들

④ 사진작가들

5.

해석 : 젊은 잠재적 지도자들은 글쓰기와 말하기 모두에서 그들의 언어를 구사할 수 있는 비범한 능력을 갖추어야 한다. 추가로, 그들은 제2언어에 대해 실행 가능한 지식을 가지고 있어야 한다. 리더십은 강력한 대중연설 능력을 필요로 한다. 오늘날 대중연설 교육과정은 학계에서 높은 지위를 누리지 못하고 있다; 더군다나, 많은 젊고 뛰어난 젊은 사람들은 서투른 연설을 구사하며, 그리고 뛰어난 젊은이들 가운데 상당수가 연설을 하는 데 서투르며, 따라서 그들은 이 분야에서 그들의 능력을 계발해야만 한다.

이종현T의 독해 Point

이 글의 주제는 대중연설의 필요성과 중요성에 대한 글이다. 그들이 계발해야 하는 분야는 따라서 대중연설이 옳다.

① 제2언어

② 리더십

③ 대중연설

④ 높은 지위

⑤ 학계

6.

해석 : 25살 때, 2008년 여름 나는 한 청년회의에 참석했다. 나는 그 청년회의를 도시에서 신선한 주말을 보내는 것 정도로 생각했다. 첫째 날, 청년들이 수영을 하러 갔을 때 나는 약간 긴장을 했다. 4년 전에 발생한 맹장파열은 나의 배에 12cm의 흉터를 남겼고, 사람들이 내 배를 응시하며 무슨 일이 일어났었는지 궁금해 하는 것을 참을 수 없었다. 내가 거기서 만난 한 남자가 흉터를 볼지도 모른다는 것을 알고서 이것(감정)은 더 심해졌다. 그 남자도 또한 수영하는 것에 긴장을 하고 있다는 것을 나는 알지 못했다. 그가 17살 때, 심각한 자동차 사고를 당했고, 그의 배에 15cm의 흉터가 있었던 것이다. 어색함을 깨기에 좋은 소재였다. 거의 동일한 흉터와 너무 많은 공통점, 우리는 결혼할 운명이었다. 이제 우리는 결혼 6주년을 맞이했다

이종현T의 독해 Point

It was meant to be는 그럴 의도(운명)이었어. 정도로 해석 할 수 있다. 그 뒤의 내용인 결혼 6주년을 참고한다면 3번의 결혼할 운명이었다가 적당하다.

① 우리가 마치 쌍둥이 같다는 느낌이 들었다

② 그것은 우리 모두에게 많은 것을 의미했다

③ 우리는 서로 결혼할 운명이었다

④ 우리는 심지어 말없이도 서로를 이해할 수 있었다

7.

해석 : 사회의 열등한 구성요소로 간주되는 사람들이 역사의 형성하는 데 있어 중요한 역할을 할지도 모른다. 그들의 중요성은 그들(열등한 구성요소)이 어떤 방향이든지 집단적으로 움직이는 것이 쉽다는 것에 있다. 그들(열등한 구성요소)은 위험을 무릅쓰고 어떤 통합된 행동에 돌진하도록 쉽게 설득된다.

이종현T의 독해 Point

이 글은 열등한 구성요소의 역할과 중요한 이유에 대한 글이다. 그러므로 대명사도 열등한 구성요소 말고는 선택할 또 다른 대안이 없다.

8.

해석 : 과학은 종종 조직화된 지식의 체계로 부적절하게 정의된다. 이것(부적절한 정의)은 요리책, 카탈로그, 그리고 전화번호부도 과학으로 만드는데, 이것들은 과학이 아니다. 가끔, 과학은 단순히 합리성으로 정의된다. 그러나, 그것(합리성으로 정의)은 많은 신학과 형이상학을 과학으로 만드는데, 이것들은 과학이 아니다. 합리성은 논리적인 일관성이 있으며, 모순이 없다. 그것(합리성)은 사리분별과 구별되어야 하는데, 사리분별은 정신의 믿음에 반대되는 주장과 증거에 열려있는 논쟁에 열려 있는 정신의 특성 : 즉 기꺼이 다시 생각하려는 것이다. 합리 주의자들은 꽤 비합리적이거나 독단적일 수 있다.

이종현T의 독해 Point

문법적으로도 쉽게 접근할 수 있는 문제다. which 앞에 선행사는 science가 적당하다.

9.

해석 : 'Claudia', 'Christy', 'Kate'와 같은 슈퍼모델들을 숭배하는 사회에서, 백인 10대들은 날씬한 몸매 유지에 사로잡혀 있다. 그러나 흑인 여학생과 백인 여학생들은 그들의 몸을 극적으로 매우 다르게 본다는 증거가 점점 늘어나고 있다. 올해 봄 'Arizona'대학의 흑인과 백인 연구원으로 이루어진 연구팀에 의한 최신 연구의 결과물이 'Human Organization'지에 발표 될 예정이다. 연구대상 중 90%의 백인 중, 고등학교 여학생들은 그들의 몸무게에 불만을 표출한 반면, 70%의 흑인 10대들은 그들의 몸무게에 만족하고 있었다. 사실, 심지어 상당히 뚱뚱한 흑인 10대들도 스스로에 대해 행복하다고 표현하고 있다. 이러한 자신감이 또 다른 흑인 10대들의 삶에까지 미치지 않을지도 모르지만, 연구는, 적어도 여기에서 만큼은, 그것이 평생의 자신감의 근원임을 보여준다. 나이가 드는 여성에 대해 묘사해보라고 요청받는다면, 흑인 10대의 3분의 2가 그들은 더 아름다워지고, 많은 사람들이 그들의 어머니를 예로 들었다. 백인 소녀들은 그들의 어머니가 젊었을 적에는 아름다웠을지 모른다고 응답했다. 그 연구의 공동저자 중 한명인 인류학자 'Mimi Nichter'는 "백인 문화에서는, 아름다움의 창이 너무 작다."라고 말한다.

이종현T의 독해 Point

마지막 문장의 인류학자가 말한 글이 A부분에 해당한다. 이 글 전체는 흑인과 백인들의 서로 다른 미의 기준에 대해 언급하고 있다. "백인문화에서, 미의 창이 너무 작다."라고 말한 것은 엄격한 기준을 가지고 있다고 받아들일 수 있다. 그러므로 3번이 올바른 표현이다.

① 대체로, 흑인 여학생들은 백인 여학생들보다 더 날씬하다.

② 백인들은 흑인들보다 외모에 관심이 적다.

③ 백인 10대들은 아름다움에 대해 보다 엄격한 기준을 갖고 있다.

④ 대부분의 아름다운 여성들은 백인 소녀들로 묘사된다.

⑤ 흑인 소녀들은 백인 소녀들보다 더 아름다운 것으로 인식된다.

10.

해석 : 시간이 오래 지났을지라도, 'Amherst'대학에 입학허가를 받았다는 사실을 알게 됐을 때 내가 보였던 반응을 나는 생생하게 기억한다: 입학처에서 중대한 실수를 저지른 것이 틀림 없다는 것이다. 대부분의 학생들이 대학에 진학하지 않는 'Long Island'고등학교를 졸업했고, 그래서 나는 'Amherst'대학에서 더 나은 교육을 받고 더 수준 높은 학우들에게 압도당할 것 이고 훌륭한 교수들에 의해 찢기고 말 것이라 확신했다. 놀랍게도, 나는 꽤 좋은 성적을 냈다. 하지만 내가 사기꾼이라는 생각을 완전히 극복할 수 없었다. 단지 몇 십년 후 동창회에서, 나는 많은 내 학우들도 나와 같은 기분을 느꼈다는 사실을 발견하였다. 성적증명서와 관계없이, 많은 신입생들은 대학에서 성공하기 위해 필요한 지적능력 또는 사교성을 가지지 않았다고 생각한다. 이러한 실패의 두려움은 가난하고, 소수이고, 1세대 이민자 학생들에게 큰 영향을 미친다. 만약 그들이 시험에서 낙제하거나 교수가 찾지 않으면, 대학이 그들이 속할 곳이 맞는지에 대한 그들의 두려움은 확신된다. 의심의 굴레는 스스로 강화되고, 학생들은 자퇴를 할 확률이 높다.

이종현T의 독해 Point

밑줄의 앞부분 내용은 저자의 고등학교는 대학에 대부분 진학하지 않고, 입학처에서 실수를 저지른 것이라고 생각하고 있다. 그러므로 사기꾼이 의미하는 바는 실력이 아니라 운 또는 입학처의 실수로 입학했다는 것으로 이해할 수 있다. 그러므로 운이 좋아 입학허가를 받았다는 3번이 올바르다.

11.

해석 : 요리가 어떻게 그리고 어떤 방식으로 다르거나 비슷한지, 그리고 시간이 흐르면서 어떻게 변하는지를 설명하기 위해, 나는 요리가 언어와 같다는 것을 암시하는 '요리의 문법'을 제안한다. 그 은유는 언어의 문법에서 유래한 것이다. 예를 들어, 영어의 문법은 명사 앞에 형용사가 오는 경향(우리는 'fudge hot'이라고 말하지 않고, 'hot fudge'라고 말한다.)이 있다던가 동사 뒤에 목적어가 온다(우리는 "chocolate eat'이라고 말하지 않고, 'eat chocolate'이라고 말한다.)는 암묵적인 규칙들로 이루어져 있다. 문법은 어떻게 언어적인 부분들이 전체의 언어로 구조화되는 방법을 정의한다. 언어가 원어민들이 설명하지는 못하더라도 알고 있는 암묵적인 문법을 가지듯이, 요리도 암묵적인 규칙(어떤 음식들이 서로 어울리는지, 그 요리에서 무엇이 '문법적인' 음식이나 식사를 구성하는지에 대한 규칙들의 구조)을 가지고 있다. 요리의 이러한 암묵적인 체계는 어떻게 재료들로부터 음식이 만들어지고, 음식들로부터 식사가 구성되는지, 특별한 맛의 조합과 필요한 요리 기술로부터 전체 요리가 구성되는지에 대한 규칙들로 이루어져 있다. 이러한 종류의 구성 각각은 요리들의 성격과 유사점과 차이점을 설명하는 데 도움을 준다.

이종현T의 독해 Point

본문은 요리와 문법을 은유적으로 설명하고 있다. 그러므로 요리에 있어서의 grammatical은 '문법적인'이 아니라 '올바른, 적당한' 정도로 이해할 수 있다. 그러므로 3번이 올바르다.

① 맛있는

② 언어학의

③ 적절한

④ 고전적인

UNIT 4 주제 / 제목 / 요지

1.

해석 : 육로로 여행할 때, 경치가 연속되며 인물과 사건도 서로 연결되어 연속적으로 일어나는데, 인생 이야기는 계속되고 부재와 이별의 영향은 줄어든다. 사실, 우리는 우리의 순례에서의 각 이동에서 '늘어나는 사슬'을 끌고 다니지만, 그 사슬은 끊어지지 않는다: 그 사슬을 하나씩 더듬어서 우리는 왔던 길을 추적할 수 있다; 그리고 우리는 그 마지막 사슬이 여전히 우리를 붙잡고 집으로 데려간다고 생각한다. 그러나 광활한 바다 여행은 한 번에 우리를 단절시킨다. 광활한 바다를 여행은 우리를 정착된 삶이라는 안전한 정박지로부터 풀려나 의심되는 세계로 표류하게 됨을 인식하게 한다. 그것은 단지 가상의 것이 아니라 우리와 고향사이에 실제 큰 간격을 두는데, 이 간격은 소동, 두려움, 불확실성에 쉽게 영향을 받아 (우리와 고향 사이) 거리를 명백하게 만들며, (고향으로)돌아가는 것을 불확실하게 만든다.

이종현T의 독해 Point

이 글은 육로여행과 바다여행을 비교하며 육로여행보다는 바다여행의 중점을 두는 글이다. 그러므로 4번의 바다여행이 초래하는 불확실성의 의미가 글 내용에 부합한다.

① 정착하는 것의 장점

② 육로로 여행하는 것의 단점

③ 사람의 인생에서 긴 여행의 의미

④ 바다여행이 초래하는 불확실성의 의미

2.

해석 : 우리의 계층 구조에 대한 조사는 도박이 중산층보다는 하위계층과 상류층의 관심사라는 것을 드러내고 있고, 만약 우리가 도박을 기본적인 사냥 욕구를 표현하는 것으로 받아들이면 이것(계층에 대한 도박선호)에 대한 합당한 이유가 있게 된다. 일(노동)은 원시 사냥의 주요한 대체물이 되었지만, 그러한 것(사냥 대체물)으로서의 노동은 중산층에게 가장 큰 이득을 주었다. 일반적인 하위계층의 남자에게, 그가 해야 하는 일(노동)의 성격은 사냥 욕구라는 요구에 적합하지 않았다. 그 일(노동)은 지나치게 반복적이고, 예측 가능한 것이다. 사냥하는 남성에게 너무나도 중요한 도전, 행운, 그리고 위험이라는 요소들이 부족하다. 이러한 이유로, 하위계층의 남성들은 일을 하지 않는 상류층 남성들과 함께 그들의 사냥 욕구를 표현하려는 필요성을 중산층보다는 더 많이 갖게 되는데, 그것은 중산층이 하는 일의 성격이 사냥 대체물로서의 역할에 훨씬 더 적합하다.

이종현T의 독해 Point

첫째 줄부터 계층구조에 대한 도박의 선호도라고 글을 시작하였다. 그 뒤로 계속 중산층과 상, 하류계층으로 비교하면서 그 이유에 대해 설명하는 글이다. 그러므로 4번의 계층별 도박 성향 수준의 이유가 본문의 주제로 적합하다.

① 인류 역사상 사회구조에 대한 진화론적 견해

② 사냥과 도박의 공통점과 차이점

③ 사회계층과 노동 분업 사이의 관계

④ 사회계층별 도박 성향 수준의 이유

3.

해석 : 실시간 자동 번역의 정확성과 속도는 틀림없이 가까운 미래에 급격하게 향상될 것이지만, 이 수단이 전 세계적으로 퍼지고 모든 사람들이 경제적으로 이용할 수 있을 때까지 훨씬 더 많은 시간이 걸릴 것이다. 이것(자동 번역)은 세계 공용어의 현재 이용성과 인기에 위협을 제기한다. 모든 증거는 세계 공용어로서의 영어의 위치가 더 강해질 것이라고 주장한다. 자동 번역이 대중적인 의사소통 수단으로 성숙해질 때면, 그것(영어)의 위치가 확고해질 가능성이 매우 높다. 그때 어떤 일이 발생할지 보는 것은 매우 흥미로울 것이다. — 세계 공용어의 존재가 세계 번역 서비스의 수요를 없앨 것인지 — 아니면 자동 번역의 경제성이 세계 공용어를 학습하는 데 드는 비용을 낮추어 세계 공용어가 쓸모없게 되는 것이다.

이종현T의 독해 Point

이 글은 자동번역 기술이 발전하였을 때 세계 공용어인 영어의 위치에 대한 논쟁에 대한 글이다. 그러므로 3번의 기술과 세계 공용어의 전쟁이라는 3번이 올바르다.

① 세계 공용어를 위협하는 것은 무엇인가?

② 컴퓨터가 영리한 번역가가 절대 될 수 없는 이유

③ 기술과 세계 공용어 사이의 전쟁

④ 자동 번역과 언어 학습의 종말

4.

해석 : 미술은 장식 이상의 것인데, 담겨 있는 내용이 비록 피상적이거나 모호하더라도 미술은 의미를 담고 있기 때문이다. 미술은 우리가 이해하는 것을 달리 표현될 수 없는 방식으로 소통할 수 있게 해준다. 정말로, 그림은 그 묘사적인 가치뿐만 아니라 상징적인 중요성에서 천개의 말만큼 가치가 있다. 언어에서와 같이, 인간은 특히 복잡한 생각을 새로운 방식으로 전달하는 상징의 발명가이다. 우리는 미술을 일상적인 산문의 관점에서 생각하지 않고, 새롭고, 종종 다양한 의미와 분위기를 전달하기 위한 전통적인 어휘와 구문을 재배열하는데 자유로운 시라고 반드시 생각해야 한다. 마찬가지로 그림도 그것(그림)이 주장하는 것보다 훨씬 더 많은 것을 주장한다. 시처럼, 미술의 가치는 그것(미술)이 말하는 것과 그 내용을 말하는 방식에 똑같이 존재한다. 미술은 부분적으로 우화, 자세, 얼굴표정 그리고 기타 등등(and the like)을 통해 의미를 암시하고, 또는 선, 형태, 색깔 그리고 구성과 같은 시각적 요소를 통해 그것(의미)들를 환기시키는 방법으로 그렇게 한다.

이종현T의 독해 Point

이 글은 미술과 시를 비교하는 글이다. 그 자체의 의미보다는 표현하는 방식으로 많은 것들을 보여줄 수 있다고 말한다. 그러므로 4번의 표현이 의미만큼 중요하다가 정답이다.

① 미술의 궁극적 가치는 표현의 아름다움이다.

② 미술 감상에서 의미는 구문보다 우선한다.

③ 미술 작품은 복잡한 시라기보다 개인적인 에세이와 유사하다.

④ 시에서처럼, 미술에서도 표현은 의미만큼 중요하다.

5.

해석 : 전통적인 교배육종보다 유전공학을 선택한 식물 육종가들은 원하는 특성을 더 빠르고 더 일관성 있게 얻을 수 있게 되었다. 그러나 유전자 변형 식품의 안전성은 이 생산물들을 시장에 가져올 때 중요한 문제가 되어왔다. 음식 알레르기가 있는 소비자들은 유전자 변형 식품들이 알레르기 반응을 일으킬 것이라고 걱정했다. 예를 들어, 만약 밀로부터의 유전자가 옥수수의 질병을 막는 데 사용된다면, 밀 상품에 알레르기가 있는 사람이 유전적으로 변형 된 옥수수를 먹은 후에 알레르기 반응을 보일 것인가? 라는 걱정이다.

이종현T의 독해 Point

유전자 변형 식품을 소개하면서 알레르기 반응에 대한 걱정 등을 나타낸 글이다. 그러므로 3번의 유전자 변형식품의 잠재적인 위험성이 올바르다.

① 최근에 이뤄진 유전공학의 발전

② 유전공학 기술의 이점

③ 유전자 변형 식품의 잠재적인 위험성

④ 소비자들과 식품 시장 사이의 갈등

⑤ 밀과 옥수수 사이의 유전적 유사성

6.

해석 : 과제를 다시 돌려받을 때, 선생님이 적어준 지적을 검토하는 데 시간을 들여라. 지금이 당신이 원본과 수정본 사이에 변경된 점들을 고려하면서 당신의 학우들의 반응과 선생님의 지적을 비교해보기 좋은 시기이다. 당신의 원본 중에서 급우들이 당신에게 수정하도록 추천한 부분을 고쳤는가? 당신의 과제 중에 급우들이 지적하지 않은 측면들에 대해 선생님이 지적을 해주셨는가? 동료 간 상호편집을 했던 급우들과 이런 정보를 공유해 보라. 당신이 살펴본 각각의 과제마다, 당신이 했던 지적을 선생님의 지적과 비교해 보아라. 각각의 과제에 대해 당신과 선생님이 공통으로 가지고 있던 생각을 명심하라. 또한, 선생님이 지적하였지만 당신이 놓친 지적에 주목하여라. 이것(놓친 지적)은 귀중한 정보이다. 너는 이 정보를 다음에 글을 쓰고 동료 간 상호편집을 할 때 사용할 것이다.

이종현T의 독해 Point

이 글은 과제에 있어서 선생님과 동료 간의 상호편집에 지적을 현명하게 사용하라는 글이다. 그러므로 4번이 주제로 적절하다.

① 동료 피드백의 장단점

② 효율적인 초안 작성과 교정을 위한 몇 가지 비결

③ 동료 간 상호 수정 프로젝트에서 의견을 공유하는 것의 중요성

④ 글쓰기에서 선생님과 동료의 피드백을 현명하게 사용하는 것
⑤ 동료 간 상호 수정에서 다른 사람들의 기분을 고려해야 하는 이유

7.

해석 : 한 매혹적인 실험에서, 연구원들은 실제로 일어났던 사건에 대한 아이들의 기억(진실 된 기억)과 절대 일어나지 않은 사건에 대한 아이들의 기억(거짓 된 기억)에 관한 사진들의 영향을 조사했다. 세 차례에 걸친 인터뷰에서, 10살 아이들에게 4장의 사진을 보여주었다: 부모들에게 받은 세 장의 진짜 사진은 아이들이 대략 6살 쯤 되었을 때 일어난 사건을 묘사하고 있었으며 한 장은 열기구가 찍힌 가짜 사진이었다. 절반의 아이들에 있어서, 그 사진은 열기구의 바구니에 한 무리의 모르는 사람이 있었다(아이가 부재한 상황). 또 다른 절반의 아이들은, 그 사진은 'Adobe Photoshop'으로 조작되어 있어서 가족들과 함께 있는 아이의 이미지가 열기구 바구니 속에 다른 사람들 사이에 삽입되어 있었다(아이가 있는 상황). 물론 실제로는, 이 아이들 중 누구도 실제로 열기구를 탄 사람은 없었다. 연구원들은 거의 모든 아이들이 진짜 사진 속의 사건들에 대해서는 기억이 있다는 것을 발견했다. 보다 중요한 것은, 많은 아이들이 또한 자신의 모습이 사진에 나와 있든 아니든, 열기구를 탄 기억이 있다고 보고했다는 사실이다. 그러나 아이들이 사진 속에서 자신들의 모습을 보지 못했을 때(약 18%)보다 보았을 때(약 47%) 거짓 기억들은 현저하게 더 자주 발생했다.

이종현T의 독해 Point

이 글에서 실험의 핵심은 아이들이 일어나지 않는 일에 대한 사진을 봤을 때 거짓 기억을 하는지를 확인하는 것이 핵심이다. 따라서 정답은 4번으로 가야한다. 2번이 헷갈릴 수 있는 선지지만 사진으로 기억하는 것에 대해서 말하는 것이 아닌 거짓기억이 발생할까에 대해서 말하는 것이므로 정답은 4번으로 가야한다.

① 열기구 타기
② 사진 속의 사건을 기억하기
③ 사진으로 아이들을 인터뷰하기
④ 아이들에게 거짓 기억을 만들기
⑤ 기술로 사진을 조사하기

8.

해석 : 우리가 숨을 쉬기 위한 산소나 마실 물은 왜 고갈되지 않는 것일까? 많은 유기체들은 광합성이라고 불리는 과정 중에 산소를 발생시킨다. 광합성은 모든 호기성(유산소)의 유기체들에 의해 소비되는 산소를 지속적으로 재 보충한다. 생물이 의존하는 물질들은 현재 지구에 존재하는 것으로 한정되어있다. 예를 들어, 물은 대기에서 지구의 표면으로, 먹이 사슬을 통해 대기로 자연스럽게 순환된다. 질소, 탄소 그리고 다른 중요한 물질들도 유사한 방법으로 순환된다. 자연적인 과정에 의해 대체되거나 재순환되는 천연자원은 재생 가능한 자원이라고 불린다. 재생 가능한 자원들의 다른 예들은 식물, 동물, 식용 작물, 햇빛과 토양을 포함한다.

이종현T의 독해 Point

산소나 물들의 천연자원들이 고갈되지 않는 이유는 유기체 등을 통해 순환하면서 재공급된다고 설명한다. 그러므로 3번의 천연 자원의 재순환이 제목으로 적절하다.

① 자연 과정의 한계

② 보존 혹은 소비

③ 천연 자원의 재순환

④ 만약 산소가 고갈된다면

⑤ 생명에 중요한 물질

9.

해석 : 코르크 마개가 펑 하고 터진다. 샴페인 병 안에서 생긴 갑작스러운 압력 변화는 이산화탄소를 방출한다. 거품이 일어난다. 일단 유리잔 안에 있으면, 수백만 개의 거품은 컵의 가장자리에 붙어서 위로 떠올랐다가 터진다. 그 폭발은 너의 혀를 가로질러 가는 작은 물방울들을 방출한다. 연구원들은 이산화탄소가 처음으로 형성되는 수확된 포도에서 그것(이산화탄소)이 너의 유리잔 속에서 터질 때까지 추적한다. 각 거품의 물보라는 강한 향과 맛이 가득한 물방울들을 가지고 있다.

이종현T의 독해 Point

이 글은 샴페인 병을 여는 순간부터 그 후 이산화탄소의 방출과정을 설명한다. 그러므로, 4번의 샴페인 병 안에서의 거품의 역동성이 올바르다.

① 샴페인 병을 여는 방법

② 샴페인 속 거품의 보존

③ 이산화탄소가 거품을 만드는 과정

④ 샴페인 속 거품이 가진 역동성

⑤ 거품의 향과 맛을 최대한도로 올리기

10.

해석 : 4차 산업혁명 그것이 인간에 미치는 영향

이 혁명은 우리가 하는 것뿐만 아니라 우리가 어떤 사람인지도 변화시킬 것이다. 그것(혁명)은 우리의 정체성, 그리고 우리의 정체성과 관련된 모든 문제(프라이버시 감각, 소유권에 대한 개념, 소비 패턴, 일과 여가에 바치는 시간, 그리고 우리가 경력을 개발하고, 기술을 연마하고, 사람들을 만나고, 인간관계를 키우는 방법)에 영향을 끼칠 것이다. 그것은 이미 우리의 건강을 변화시키고, '계량화된(적격의)' 자아를 이끌고 있다. 우리의 상상에만 얽매이기 때문에, 목록은 끝이 없다. 새로운 정보기술에 의해 제기되는 가장 심각한 개인적인 문제들 중 하나는 사생활이다. 우리의 정보에 대한 통제력 상실이 우리의 내적 삶에 미치는 영향과 같은 근본적인 문제들에 대한 논쟁은 오직 향후에 강력해지기만 할 것이다. 이와 유사하게도, 생물공학과 인공지능(AI) 분야에서 발생하고 있는 수명, 건강, 인지 그리고 능력의 현재 한계들을 뒤로 밀어냄으로써 인간이라는 것의 의미를 재정의하고 있는 혁명들은 우리를 도덕적, 윤리적 경계를 재정의하도록 강요할 것이다.

이종현T의 독해 Point

이 글은 전체적으로 4차 산업혁명이 우리의 외적뿐만 아니라 내적에도 영향을 미친다는 것을 나열하고 있는 글이다. 그러므로 1번이 적합하다.

① 그것이 인간에 미치는 영향
② 계량화된 자아를 향하여
③ 새로운 정보기술
④ 인간의 삶에 대한 논쟁
⑤ 생물공학과 인공지능

11.

해석 : 말과 동반하는 제스처들 안에서, 우리는 말하는 메시지의 내용을 나타내는 제스처와 언급되고 있는 무언가를 가리키는 제스처를 구분할 수 있다. 상징적 (제스처)는 우리가 "나는 작은 상자를 찾고 있어." 라고 말하면서 손가락으로 허공에 사각형을 그리는 경우에서처럼, 말하고 있는 것의 의미의 반영처럼 보이는 제스처이다. 그 자체로서, 상징적 제스처는 말하고 있는 것과 똑같은 '의미'를 갖지는 않지만, '의미'를 더할지도 모른다. 예를 들어, 한 여성이 "나 또 그 개를 쫓아냈어."라고 말하면서 마치 무기를 들고 있는 것처럼 주먹을 쥔 상태로 팔뚝을 위아래로 움직이고 있었다. 무기를 포함한 전달되는 메시지는 말과 제스처의 결합을 통하여 성취했다. 또 다른 흔한 종류의 제스처는 지시적 제스처로서 묘사될 수 있다. '지시적'이라는 용어는 '가리킨다'는 의미이고, 우리는 종종 말을 하면서 사물이나 사람을 가리킬 때 제스처를 사용한다. 한 손을 사용하여 (케이크가 놓여 있는)식탁을 가리키면서 누군가에게 "케이크 좀 드실래요?"라고 묻는 경우에서처럼, 우리는 일상에서 '지시적 제스처'를 사용할 수 있다. 우리는 또한 나중에 "그 케이크는 정말 맛있었어."라고 말할 때, (더 이상 케이크가 없는)식탁을 가리키며 같은 제스처를 사용할 수도 있다. 이 경우에는, 제스처와 말은 성공적으로 결합하여 현재 물리적인 공간에 있는 것뿐만 아니라 공유된 기억 에만 존재하고 있는 것을 효과적으로 가리킬 수 있다.

이종현T의 독해 Point

이 글은 말과 함께 사용하는 상징적 제스처와 지시적 제스처를 설명하는 글이다. 그러므로 2번의 말과 함께 사용하는 제스처의 종류가 적당하다.

① 인간이 사용하는 제스처의 본질

② 말과 함께 사용하는 제스처의 종류

③ 의사소통에 있어서의 물리적 공간의 역할

④ 과거에 관해 이야기할 수 있는 인간의 능력

12.

해석 : 시간의 성질은 우리가 인식하는 방법과 매우 밀접하게 연관되어 있는 것처럼 보인다. 가장 기본적인 측면에서, 우리가 인식하고 있는 우주는 우리의 감각기관의 창조물이다. 당신이 손가락 끝으로 목재 테이블 위를 만질 때, 당신은 실제로 무수히 많은 전자들의 작은 반발력을 '느낀다'; 즉, 당신은 실제로는 아무것도 '만지고' 있지 않은 것이다. 당신이 물체를 '바라볼' 때, 당신은 단순히 반사되고 방출된 광자들을 지각하고 있다. 그 광자는 당신의 뇌가 아마도 꽤 임의적이고 우발적인 방식으로, 밝고 어두운 색깔 등으로 해석할 수 있도록 진화한 것이다. 시간에서도 마찬가지이다. 지각된 시간의 이상하고 유연한 성질은 'Albert Einstein'으로부터 인용구에 의해 잘 설명된다: '한 남성이 예쁜 여자와 한 시간 동안 앉아 있을 때, 그것(1시간)은 1분 같이 느껴진다. 그러나 그를 뜨거운 난로 위에 1분동안 앉아있게 시키면, 그것(난로위의 1분)은 어느 한 시간보다도 길게 느껴진다. 그것이 바로 상대성이다.'

이종현T의 독해 Point

이 글은 우리가 인식하는 방법에 따라 시간의 성질이 달라지는 상대성에 대한 글이다. 전체 글과 부합하는 제목은 2번의 '시간은 당신이 인식하는 방법에 달려있다'가 적당하다.

① 무(無)에서 유(有)로

② 시간은 당신이 그것을 인식하는 방법에 달려 있다.

③ 당신이 인식하는 것은 지금의 우주이다.

④ 우리의 감각기관의 발달

⑤ 시간의 직선 개념: 하나의 시간에는 하나의 길만 존재한다.

13.

해석 : 1986년, 음악가 'Paul Simon'은 매일 아침 뉴욕에 있는 그의 녹음실로 걸어가다가 본 'Marie'라는 이름의 한 노숙자 여성과 친구가 되었다. 그러던 어느 날, 'Marie'가 그곳에 없었고 — 그리고 그는 그녀가 무사한지를 알아낼 방법이 없었다. 그는 노숙자들의 문제에 관심을 가지게 되었고, 아동 옹호자이자 'Columbia University' 소아과 교수인 'Irwin Redlener'를 만났다. 'Simon'은 그와 함께 하루 동안 노숙자 보호시설을 찾아 다녔고, 그들은 충격적인 또 다른 사실을 발견하였지만 'Marie'는 발견하지는 못했다: (또 다른 사실) "우리는 집이 없는 천 명의 아이들과 그들의 가족들을 위한 본질적으로(원래는) 창고였던 것을 보았습니다." 'Redlener' 박사는 기억한다. "그리고 심지어 그들이 가장 기본적인 의료 서비스는 받고 있는지에 대해 아무도 관심을 기울이지 않았습니다." 'Redlener'의 아내 'Karen'과 함께, 그들은 최첨단 이동식 진료소를 갖춘 '파란색 대형버스'에서 아동건강모금을 시작했다. 오늘날, 그 단체는 지정장소에서 운영되는 서비스가 충분하지 못한 200개 이상의 의료 센터뿐만 아니라 50개의 이동식 진료센터 네트워크를 전국의 저소득 지역에서 운영하고 있으며, 지금까지 35만 명의 가난하고 집 없는 아이들에게 도움을 주었다.

이종현T의 독해 Point

이 글의 전체적인 흐름은 'Simon'이 노숙자 여성과 친해지고 그러면서 그 쪽에 관심이 생기고 'Redlener' 박사와 아동건강모금을 시작했다는 이야기이다. 그러므로 1번의 '아동건강모금'의 설립이 적당하다.

① 아동건강기금의 설립

② 노숙자 가족을 위한 법률 제안

③ 노숙자 보호시설을 개조하는 방법

④ 빈곤에 처란 아이들의 원인과 결과

⑤ 아동 진료소를 통한 의료 서비스 개발

14.

해석 : 'Occam'의 면도날(법칙)은 단순한 것이 완벽한 것이라는 개념을 기본으로 하고 있다. 그것(면도날 법칙)은 과학적인 방법과 완벽하게 들어맞는다. — 과학자들이 무언가의 옳고 그름을 증명하기 위한 일련의 단계들 — 사실은, 당신은 과학적 방법이 'Occum'의 면도날(법칙)을 바탕으로 하고 있다는 가정을 할 수 있다. 그것(면도날 법칙)은 체험적인(스스로 발견하게 하는) 장치역할 — 지침 또는 제안 — 로서의 역할을 하는데, 이 장치는 동일한 것에 대해 두 개의 설명이 주어졌을 때, 더 단순한 설명이 옳다는 것이다.

'Occam'의 면도날 법칙에 대한 전형적인 예를 들어보자. 두 명의 물리학자 — 'Lorentz'와 'Einstein' — 는 모두 물체들이 시공간 연속체 안에서 약간 불안정해지는 경향이 있다는 결론을 수학적으로 이끌어 냈다. 예를 들어, 우리가 빛의 속도에 가까운 속도로 움직일수록, 우리는 더 느려진다. 비록 두 사람 모두 이러한 방정식을 통해 같은 결론에 도달했을지라도, 'Einstein'과 'Lorentz'는 다른 결론에 대해 다른 설명을 가지고 있었다. 'Lorentz'는 그것(다른 설명을 가진 것)을 '에테르'에서 발생하는 변화 때문이라고 말한다. 문제는 '에테르'가 존재한다는 것을 과학자들이 지지하지 않고, 그로 인해 방정식의 문제가 되는 요소를 집어넣지 않는다는 것이다. 문제가 되는 요소 하나가 방정식에 들어가게 된다는 것이었다. 'Einstein'의 설명은 에테르를 언급하지 않았고, 그러므로, 그의 설명은 결국 'Lorentz'의 설명을 이기게 되었다.

이종현T의 독해 Point

제목문제의 정답을 찾기 위해서 가장 중요한 점들 중 하나는 그 글의 key-word가 들어가 있어야 한다는 점이다. 2번의 아인슈타인과 로렌츠의 설명을 비교하는 것이 헷갈릴만한 선지이지만 4번의 오컴의 면도날 법칙을 언급해준 것이 답으로 더 적절하다.

① 단순함을 지향하는 완벽함

② 아인슈타인의 설명과 로렌츠의 설명 비교

③ 현대 과학의 기초

④ 과학적 방법으로서의 오컴의 면도날 법칙

⑤ 문제해결의 도구의 중요성

15.

해석 : 'Westbury' 교수는 언어장애와 뇌 기능 사이의 연관성을 탐구하면서 중요한 연구를 해오고 있다. 자신의 연구의 일부분으로, 'Westbury'는 실어증환자들 — 글과 말의 표현에 대한 이해력이 종종 손상된 사람들 — 에게 일련의 문사를 세시하고 그것(문사)이 신싸 영어 난어에 속하는 것인지 아닌지를 물어본다. 어느 날, 한 대학원생이 신기한 점을 지적했다: 어떤 무의미한 단어들이 지속적으로 환자들을 웃게 하고 가끔은 큰 소리로 웃게 만든다는 것이다. 'Westbury'는 특히 "snunkoople"이라고 말한다. 그는 친구들과 동료들에게도 똑같은 반응을 보이는지 확인해 보았는데, 그 반응은 거의 일치했다. 'snunkoople'은 재미있다는 것이었다. 하지만 왜일까? 'Westbury'는 그가 대답이라고 믿고 있는 것을 제시한다: 단어의 내재적인 재미, 또는 적어도 문맥에서 자유로운 무의미한 단어들이 자격이 있고, — 그리고 무의미한 말은 평등한 상태로 만들어진다는 것은 아니다. 'Westbury'에 따르면, 특정 문자들의 조합이 통계적으로 영어에서 실재하는 단어를 형성할 가능성이 적을수록, 더 재밌게 된다. 1972년, 극작가인 'Neil Simon'은 그의 작품, 'The Sunshine Boys'에서 이러한 함축적인 의미를 파악한 것처럼 보였다. 그 작품에서는 한 늙은 등장인물이 그의 조카에게 "만약 그것(알파벳)에 'k'가 없다면 그건 재미가 없을 거야! — 'k'는 알파벳에서 가장 적은 빈도로 사용되는 문자들 중 하나이다. —

이종현T의 독해 Point

이 글은 무의미한 단어들의 조합이 실어증 환자들을 웃게 만든다는 글이다. 그 예시로 snukoople을 예로 들며 k가 없는 단어는 재미가 없는 단어라는 설명을 해준다. 이런 내용들을 모두 포함할 수 있는 2번이 제목으로 적절하다.

① 실어증: 우리가 웃는 방식
② 왜 특정 단어들은 우스꽝스러울까?
③ 한 가지 모호함의 기술로서의 유머
④ 여러 문자들의 보기 드문 결합인 "Snunkoople"

16.

해석 : 세계 시장에 참여하고 있지 않은 기업들과 산업체들은 오늘날의 무역환경에서 고립은 불가능해졌다는 것을 깨달아야 한다. 좋든 싫든, 점점 더 많은 기업들은 세계적 사업에 참여하고 있는 중이다. 비록 선택에 의해서가 아닐지라도, 대부분의 기업들과 개인들은 직접적 또는 간접적으로 국제 시장에서 발생하는 경제적, 정치적 발전의 영향을 받고 있다. (국제 시장) 참여를 거부하는 기업들은 국제 시장에 반응하는 처지가 되고 따라서 해외로부터의 강력한 경쟁에 대비가 되어있지 않다.

몇몇 산업체들은 국제 시장 적응의 필요성을 깨달았다. 농부들은 극심한 국제 경쟁을 고려하였을 때 높은 생산성의 필요성을 이해한다. 컴퓨터 제조업체와 다른 기술적으로 발전된 산업에 있는 기업들은 경쟁에서 뒤쳐지지 않기 위해 국제적인 관계를 형성하는 것을 배운다. 철강, 직물, 가죽 분야의 기업들은 생산량을 변화시키고, 해외로부터의 압도적인 공격에 반응하여 주요 사업을 조정했을 것이다. 몇몇 국가의 다른 산업체들은 (이것들을) 인식하지 못하고 적응할 수 없었다. 그 결과는 미국의 VCR산업과 다른 국가들의 탄광업이나 철강 제련업과 같은 기업들이나 전체 산업체들이 소멸하게 된다.

이종현T의 독해 Point

이 글의 주제는 국제적인 경쟁이 불가피하고 그로인해 기업들이 인식해야 할 여러 가지 사항을 다루고 있다. 그러므로 2번의 국제시장에서 다가오는 난제들이 적당하다.

① 가지 않은 길: 미래의 기업가 정신

② 세계 시장에서 떠오르고 있는 새로운 난제들

③ 비즈니스 세계에서의 서로 다른 선수들과 서로 다른 규칙들

④ 글로벌 비즈니스의 두 얼굴: "글로벌/로컬"의 딜레마

17.

해석 : 성격 특징의 지위는 기준점에 달려있다. 예를 들어, 유인원에게 있어서 손톱은 모든 다른 영장류들이 손톱을 가지고 있기 때문에 다른 영장류들에 비해 원시적인 것으로 여겨진다. 따라서, 예를 들어, 손톱은 유인원가 원숭이를 구별하는 것을 돕지 못한다. 그러나, 손톱은 다른 어떤 포유류들도 그것들을 가지고 있지 않기 때문에, 전체적으로 영장류에게서만 파생된 특징이다. 따라서 손톱은 영장류와 다른 포유류들을 구별하는 것에 도움이 된다. 여기에서 설명되는 두 번째 특징은 - 눈두덩이 - 다른 영장류들이 아닌 오로지 직립보행 영장류들에게서만 발견된다, 따라서 직립보행 영장류에 의해서 파생된다. 이 특징은 유인원과 원숭이들을 구별해준다. 그러나, 침팬지에 있어서, 눈 두덩이는 다른 직립보행 영장류에 관련해서는 원시적인 것으로 여겨진다; 즉, 예를 들어, 그 특징은 침팬지와 고릴라를 구별해주지는 않는다.

이종현T의 독해 Point

본문은 첫 번째 문장 "성격특성 상태는 기준점에 달려있다."가 주제문이다. 나머지는 주제를

뒷받침하는 문장이며, 기준점에 따라 구분할 수 있고 없고를 말한다. 그러므로 3번의 특징의 상대적인 상태가 올바르다.

① 종의 상대적인 지위

② 종의 절대적인 지위

③ 형질의 상대적인 지위

④ 형질의 절대적인 지위

18.

해석 : 미국의 오케스트라들은 삭막한 현실에 점점 직면하고 있다: 지금은 미국의 오케스트라들은 그들의 힘이 되어주었던 티켓 판매보다는 평균적으로 자선금에 더 의지하고 있는 자선단체가 되었다. 업계 협회인 미국 오케스트라 협회에 의해 화요일에 발표된 한 보고서에 따르면, 오케스트라들은 — 항상 군주, 교회, 정부 또는 후원자에게 — 보조금을 요구해왔지만, 균형은 일반적으로 티켓 판매보다는 기부금에서 더 많은 수익을 얻는 수준으로 움직이게 되었다. 이 보고서는 또한 오케스트라들의 티켓 판매가 판매방식에 있어서 분기점에 도달했다는 것을 발견했다: 2013년, 합창단들은 처음으로 티켓 판매 수익금의 대부분을 더 이상 수십 년 동안 의지해 왔던 사전 예약 패키지에서 얻지 못했다. 이러한 변화들은 오케스트라들을 그들의 구성에서부터 그들의 임무 규정에 이르기까지 모든 것에 변화를 강요하였다.

이종현T의 독해 Point

마지막 문장을 보면 이제 오케스트라들은 조직 구성부터 규정에 이르기까지 모든 것에 영향을 받았다고 하였다. 그러므로 4번의 오케스트라에 부는 변화의 바람이 적당하다.

① 증가추세인 미국 관현악단들의 사전 예약 패키지 상품

② 증가추세인 미국 합주단들의 예산삭감 요구

③ 미국에서의 클래식 음악의 몰락

④ 미국의 관현악단들에 부는 변하의 바람

19.

해석 : 대부분의 산업 집중성에 관한 이야기는 내가 '블랙박스 오류'라고 부르는 것에서 시작하고 끝난다: 조만간 모든 미디어는 거실에 있는 하나의 블랙박스를 통해 흐르게 될 것이고, 우리가 해야 할 일은 그것이 어떤 블랙박스가 될 것인지를 알아내는 것이다. 미디어 집중성은 끝나는 지점이 아니다; 오히려, 그것(미디어 집중성)은 미디어 기술, 산업, 컨텐츠, 그리고 청중 사이의 다양한 교차점에서 일어나고 있는 진행중인 과정이다. 채널의 확산과 점점 더 만연해진 컴퓨터 사용과 전자통신의 성격 덕분에, 우리는 어느 곳에나 미디어가 존재하고 모든 종류의 미디어를 서로 관련시켜 사용하게 될 시대에 들어가고 있다.

미디어 집중성은 단순한 기술적 변화 그 이상이다; 그것(미디어 집중성)은 현재 존재하는 기술, 산업, 시장, 장르와 청중 사이의 관계를 변화시킨다. 미디어 변화의 초기 물결은 불안정한 영향을 주어서, 흥분과 공포 사이에 일련의 요동을 낳는다. 그러나 미디어 집중성은 또한 대중문화의 거의 모든 부문에서 창의적인 혁신을 일으키고 있다; 우리의 현재 미디어 환경은 차이의 확산에 의해 특징지어져 있다.

이종현T의 독해 Point

이 글의 첫 단락에서는 미디어 집중성에 대한 일반적인 내용을 기술하고, 두 번째 단락에서는 변화하는 내용을 기술한다. 그러므로 부정적인 영향과 긍정적인 영향이 둘 다 기술되었으므로 4번이 정답이다. 3번은 부정적인 측면만 이야기하므로 정답이 될 수 없다.

① 블랙박스 오류: 미디어 컨버전스의 시작과 끝

② 블랙박스 오류와 기술의 변화

③ 미디어 컨버전스와 그 불안정한 영향

④ 미디어 컨버전스와 변화하는 환경

⑤ 미디어 교차점과 컨버전스의 오류

20.

해석 : 식물들은 독소를 생산함으로써 초식동물들의 약탈로부터 스스로를 보호한다. 예를 들어, 'Madagascar' 숲에는, 매우 독성이 강한 대나무가 있다. 그 죽순 끝부분은 가장 내성이 강한 채식주의자들조차 단념시킬 양의 청산가리를 포함하고 있다. — 그 양은 대략 대나무 1파운드당 1/500 온스 정도 된다. 그러나 이 대나무를 먹는 동물이 있다. — 그 동물은 대나무를 먹는 것으로 알려진 세 종류의 여우원숭이들 가운데 하나인 황금대나무 여우원숭이다. 다른 두 종류의 회색 온화한 여우원숭이와 큰대나무 여우원숭이는 대나무 잎과 두꺼운 대나무 줄기는 먹으면서, 독성이 있는 죽순은 황금대나무 여우원숭이에게 남겨준다. 이 동물(황금대나무 여우원숭이)은 매일 17.5파운드의 죽순을 먹는데 이것은 인간 치사량의 12배에 해당하는 양이다. 몇 가지 가능한 설명이 있지만, 어떻게 이런 일이 가능한 지는 수수께끼이다. 그 중 하나는 그 여우원숭이(황금 대나무)는 아마도 몇몇 시행착오의 과정을 거치면서 그들의 서식지에 있는 철분이 풍부한 토양을 섭취함으로써 독성을 중화시키는 법을 터득하였다는 것이다. 토양 속의 철분은 독소의 형성을 막기 위해 청산가리와 결합한다. 토양 안의 점토 역시 인간 의약품의 카올린 역할을 한다. 그것은 내장 속에서 그것들의 해로운 영향을 감소시키기 위해 물질들과 결합한다.

이종현T의 독해 Point

독성에 대해 내성을 가진 여우원숭이 3종류를 소개하면서, 이 원숭이들이 어떻게 내성을 가졌는지에 대한 가설을 소개하는 글이다. 그러므로 1번이 정답이 된다.

① 마다가스카르 여우원숭이가 청산가리를 섭취하고도 생존할 수 있는 이유에 대한 가능성이 있는 설명

② 마다가스카르 숲의 대나무 독소가 지닌 방어적 역할

③ 인체용 신규 천연약제로서 죽순의 발견

④ 황금대나무 여우원숭이들의 신비로운 학습

UNIT 5 빈칸 유형

1.

해석 : 비록 국경은 강인하게 생기고 터프한 사람들을 미국의 위대한 영웅이라고 우상화 할지라도, 국경 지역에서 자급자족에 대한 욕구는 발명에 대한 영혼을 장려했다. 국경 지역의 남성과 여성은 그들의 매일의 삶의 필수품들을 제공해야만 했을 뿐만 아니라 그들은 또한 지속적으로 창의적인 해결책을 요구하는 상황과 문제들을 마주했다. 다른 나라에서의 관찰자들은 국경지역 남자들의 새로운 농사 도구를 만드는 능력에 매우 감명을 받았다. 그들은 동등하게 국경지역의 여성들이 독특한 의상, 초, 비누, 그리고 다른 그녀의 가족의 매일의 생활을 위해 필요로 되어지는 품목들을 만드는 능력에도 감동을 받았다.

① 모험심이 강한 삶의 방식
② 발명에 대한 영혼
③ 성 평등의 개념
④ 개인주의에 대한 강한 인식

이종현T의 독해 point!

빈칸 뒷 문장에서 무엇을 장려하는지를 보면 된다. 그리고 빈칸 문장 뒤를 보면 frontierman들이 뭔가를 만드는 능력과 pioneer woman들이 뭔가를 만드는 능력에 감명을 받았다고 나왔으므로 빈칸에도 만들고 발명하는 것과 관련된 내용이 들어가야 한다. 따라서 정답은 2번이 된다.

2.

해석 : 일본인들은 신선한 음식에 대해서 광신도이다. 결과적으로, 일본의 음식을 처리하는 회사들은 지역 독점을 즐긴다. 북일본 지역의 우유 제작자들은 남일본에서 경쟁하기를 희망할 수는 없다, 왜냐하면 거기에 우유를 운반하는 것은 하루나 이틀 더 걸리기 때문이고, 이것은 소비자들의 눈에는 치명적인 결함이다. 이런 지역별 독점적 지위는 일본 정부에 의해 강화되고 있는데, 일본 정부는 다른 제한들 중에서도 특히 10일간의 검역제도를 시행함으로써 외국산 가공식품의 수입을 막고 있다. 따라서 일본의 식품 생산업체들은 국내 또는 외국 상품과의 경쟁에 노출돼 있지 않다.

① 수입 식품에 크게 의존할 수밖에 없다.
② 전략적으로 운영을 세계적인 수준으로 최적화하다.
③ 유통기한을 늘리기 위한 방법들에 몰두한다.
④ 국내 또는 외국 상품과의 경쟁에 노출되어 있지 않다.

이종현T의 독해 Point

두 번째 줄에 독점을 즐긴다는 결론이 나와있고 따라서 마지막 문장의 결론에도 독점을 즐긴다는 얘기가 필요하다. 독점인 상황에 있다 = 경쟁에 노출되지 않는다 이므로 정답은 4번이 된다.

3.

해석 : 낮은 기업 활동률과 높은 실업률에 대처하는 정책을 사용함으로써 이 두 문제를 해결할 수 있는 방법이 있는가? 그에 대한 답은 사업상의 모험을 장려하기 위해 실업보험을 조정하는 것에 있을지도 모른다. 이런 생각을 뒷받침하는 사례는 2002년 프랑스에서 시행된 대규모의 개혁조치에서 찾을 수 있다. 그 개혁은 사업을 시작한 자영업자들이 사업상의 모험이 실패할 경우에 3년 동안 실업 수당 프로그램을 이용할 수 있도록 했다. 그 프로그램은 성공적이었다. 전반적인 긍정적 혜택에는 더 짧아진 실업 기간과 더 생산적이고 보수가 많은 직업으로 노동이 재분배되는 것이 포함되었다.

① 신생 기업을 위해 세금 감면 계획을 도입하는 것
② 사업상의 모험을 장려하기 위해 실업보험을 조정하는 것
③ 생산적인 기업 활동을 자극하기 위해 기술 교육 프로그램을 제공하는 것
④ 초기 벤처 창업 개발 단계에서 정부 기금을 제공하는 것

이종현T의 독해 Point

뒤의 프랑스 사례의 핵심적인 내용이 빈칸에 들어간다고 생각해야 한다. 프랑스 사례에서 사업을 시작한 사람들이 3년 동안 실업 수당 프로그램을 받을 수 있다고 했으므로 그 얘기가 그대로 들어간 선지가 정답이 되어야 한다. 따라서 실업 보험을 조정한다는 2번이 정답이 된다.

4.

해석 : 핵실험 금지와 관련한 미국과 소련 사이의 회담이 1950년대 중반에 시작됐다. 두 나라의 관료들은 핵무기 경쟁이 위험한 수준에 이르고 있다고 믿게 됐다. 게다가, 대기권 내 핵무기 실험에 반대하는 대중의 항의가 점점 힘을 얻고 있었다. 그럼에도 불구하고, 두 나라 사이의 회담들은 수년 동안 이어졌으며, 대개 사찰 문제가 제기되면 회담이 결렬됐다. 미국은 소련이 격렬하게 반대하는 현장 검증을 원했던 것이다. 1960년 양측의 협상이 거의 합의점에 도달한 듯 보였지만, 그해 5월에 미국 정찰기가 소련에서 격추되자 협상이 끝나게 되었다.

① 방사능 낙진의 영향이 의문시되었다.
② 강경파들이 협상에서 과도한 요구를 했다.

③ 소련이 지하 핵실험을 고집했다.
④ 사찰 문제가 제기되었다.

이종현T의 독해 Point
빈칸 바로 뒷 문장에서 미국은 현장 조사를 원했고 소련은 그것을 엄청나게 반대했다고 써있다. 따라서 현장 조사의 부분이 맞지 않는다는 것을 알 수 있고 빈칸에도 그 얘기가 들어가면 된다. 따라서 정답은 4번이 된다.

5.
해석 : 정수에 배료된 피타고라스학파 사람들은 다른 모든 수들은 물론이고 만물이 정수에서 파생되어 나올 수 있다고 생각했다. (그러나) 그들이 2의 제곱근(정사각형의 한 변에 대한 대각선의 비율)이 무리수이고, 루트2가 그 어떤 두 정수의 비율로도 정확히 표현될 수 없다는 것을 발견했을 때, 학설에 위기가 발생했다. 아이러니하게도, 이 발견은 피타고라스의 정리를 도구로 하여 이루어졌다. '무리수'는 원래 수가 비율로 표현될 수 없다는 것만을 의미했다. 그러나 피타고라스학파들에게 그것은 어떤 위협적인 것, 즉 그들의 세계관이 이치에 맞지 않을 수도 있다는 암시를 의미하게 되었으며, 이것이 오늘날 '무리수'의 또 다른 의미(불합리한 것)이다.

① 대중들은 의심했다.
② 학설에 위기가 발생했다.
③ 그들은 훨씬 더 확신하게 되었다.
④ 불확실성이 마침내 해결되었다.

이종현T의 독해 Point
첫 문장에서 만물이 정수에서 나오고, 그 뒤에서 그러나 라는 이야기가 나오고 정수로 표현할 수가 없다는 이야기가 나왔다. 즉 앞의 결론과 반대되는 상황이므로 이와 관련 얘기가 빈칸에 들어가야 한다. 따라서 정답은 2번이다.

6.

해석 : 사람들은 서기 476년에 있었던 로마의 멸망과 14세기 르네상스 시대의 시작 사이의 유럽을 설명하기 위해 '중세시대'라는 용어를 사용한다. '중세시대'라는 용어는 그 시대 자체에 대해서보다도 그 시대에 뒤이은 르네상스 시대에 대해 더 많은 것을 우리에게 말해준다. 14세기경부터 유럽의 사상가들, 작가들, 그리고 예술가들은 고대 그리스와 로마의 예술과 문화를 되돌아보고 기리기 시작했다. 이에 따라, 이들은 로마의 멸망 이후의 시기를 그 어떤 과학적 성과도 없었고, 그 어떤 위대한 예술 작품도 나오지 않았으며, 그 어떤 지도자도 태어나지 않았다고 여겨 '중간의' 시대 또는 심지어 '암흑의' 시대로 무시해버렸다. 중세시대에 대한 이러한 사고방식은 비교적 최근까지도 널리 퍼져 있었다. 그러나 오늘날의 학자들은 이 시기가 다른 어떤 시기보다 복잡하고 활기찼다는 것에 주목한다. 실제로 르네상스 시대의 대단히 지적이고 예술적인 발전은 중세 시대에 뿌리를 두고 있었다.

① 이 시기의 출발점은 수정될 필요가 있다.
② 이 시기가 다른 어떤 시기보다도 복잡하고 활기찼다.
③ 르네상스 시대는 현대 역사로 이어지는 문화적인 가교였다.
④ 이 시기에 대한 용오는 우리가 유럽 역사 전체를 이해하는 데 도움을 준다.

이종현T의 독해 Point

However라는 그러나로 글이 뒤집어지고 있다. However 위에는 중세 시대를 무시한다는 얘기고 However로 뒤집어지므로 중세시대는 무시할 수 없는 좋은 시대라는 얘기가 와야 한다. 따라서 정답은 2번이다.

7.

해석 : 상투적인 복장이 너무 표준화되어서 '유니폼'이라고 말해지는 일이 종종 있다. 예를 들면, 이런 종류의 옷에는 런던의 신사가 입는 가느다란 세로줄 무늬의 정장과 중산모와 검정 우산 또는 고등학교 학생들의 청바지와 티셔츠가 있다. 그러나 일반적으로 이런 옷들은 외부인들에게는 유니폼처럼 보이지만, 동료들은 중요한 차이를 알아차릴 것이다. 런던의 사업가의 넥타이는 그가 어느 학교에 다녔는지 동료들에게 알려줄 것이며 그의 양복의 재단 상태와 옷감이 동료들로 하여금 그의 수입에 대해 추측할 수 있게 할 것이다. 고등학생들은 새 청바지를 유행에 맞게 해서 입는 청바지와 한 눈에 구별할 수 있는데, 유행하는 청바지는 기능적이로나 장식으로 덧대거나 아니면 아무렇게나 누더기가 된 청바지이다. 그들은 일자바지, 나팔바지, 부츠컷, 팽이 모양 바지가 의미하는 미세한 차이를 이해할 수 있다.

① 우리 모두는 복장에 굉장히 신경을 쓴다.
② 이러한 표현의 범위는 상당히 제한되어 있다.

③ 동료들은 중요한 차이를 알 것이다.
④ 그런 옷들은 대도시에서 흔하다.

이종현T의 독해 Point
빈칸 문장 앞에선 표준화된 복장에 대한 얘기이고 빈칸 뒤에는 지역 사람들은 그 중에서도 차이를 구별한다는 내용이 나온다. 따라서 정답은 3번이 된다.

8.
해석 : 1918년 봄에, 치명적인 독감 바이러스가 세계를 강타했다. 그 바이러스는 전 세계 인구의 40% 정도에 이르는 사람들을 감염시켰다. 그 전 세계적 유행병은 미국과 유럽에서 '스페인 독감' 또는 '스페인 아가씨(Spanish Lady)'로 널리 알려지게 되었다. 많은 사람들은 이렇게 알려지게 된 이유가 그 병이 이베리아 반도에서 생겼기 때문이라고 추정하지만, 그 별명은 실제로는 널리 퍼진 오해에서 비롯된 것이었다. 스페인은 1차 세계대전에서 중립을 지켰던 소수의 주요 유럽국가 가운데 하나였다. 전시에 사기에 영향을 끼치는 것을 피하기 위해 독감과 관련된 뉴스를 검열한 연합국과 동맹국과는 달리, 스페인 언론 매체는 자유롭게 바이러스에 대해 매우 세세한 부분까지 보도할 수 있었다. 언론을 통제한 나라들은 스페인 뉴스를 통해서만 자세한 내용을 읽어볼 수 있었기 때문에 그들은 일반적으로 스페인이 전염병의 시초라고 추정했다.

① 그 나라가 전염병의 시초였다.
② 스페인은 전쟁이 끝날 때까지 중립을 유지했다.
③ 스페인의 언론매체는 다른 어떤 나라보다 좀 더 많은 자유를 누린다.
④ 그 나라는 독감을 대류모로 퍼뜨리는 보급자로 잘못 낙인찍혀버렸다.

이종현T의 독해 Point!
빈칸에 들어갈 내용은 다른 나라 사람들이 생각한 내용이 들어가야한다. 따라서 정답은 1번이 되어야 한다. 4번을 헷갈리기 쉬운데 4번이 들어가게 되면 다른 나라의 사람들이 스페인이 낙인찍힌 것은 잘못되었다는 것을 아는 것이므로 글 내용 자체가 스페인을 그렇게 생각하지 않았다는 얘기가 와야 한다. 그런 얘기가 아니므로 정답은 1번이 된다.

9.

해석 : 8명이 청산가리가 첨가된 타이레놀 캡슐을 복용해서 사망했던 비극적인 약품 변조 사건을 생각해 보사. 그 약이 공장이 아니라 극소수의 매장에서 변조가 이뤄졌다고 생각했음에도, 존슨 앤드 존슨은 모든 타이레놀 제품을 재빨리 회수했다. 그 리콜 조치로 인해 2억 4천만 달러의 소득 손실을 보았다. 그러나 결국 타이레놀을 빨리 회수한 존슨앤드존슨의 조치는 소비자의 신뢰와 충성도를 강화시켰고, 타이레놀은 여전히 미국의 대표적인 진통제로 남아있다. 존슨앤드존슨의 경영진은 올바른 일처리가 고객들과 회사 모두에게 이롭다는 것을 알게 됐다.

① 새로운 고객들을 유치하는 비용이 빠르게 증가하고 있다.
② 고객의 욕구를 만족시키는 것은 마케팅에서 최우선 사항이다.
③ 고객들과 수익성이 있는 관계를 형성하는 것이 중요하다.
④ 올바른 일처리가 고객들과 회사 모두 이롭다.

이종현T의 독해 Point
위 지문의 핵심은 손해를 봤지만 회수를 했고 결국 충성도를 강화시켰다는 얘기가 된다. 따라서 빈칸에는 손해를 보더라도 올바른 일을 해야 이득을 볼 수 있다 같은 얘기가 필요하게 된다. 따라서 정답은 4번이 된다.

10.

해석 : 우리는 현대 문명의 문화와 학문을 전달하는 매우 많은 이미지 속에서 살고 있다. 전례가 없을 정도로 대중매체가 확대됨으로써 촉진된 이런 시각적인 배경의 잡음은 일상의 삶에 너무나 많은 부분을 차지하고 있어서 우리는 그것을 당연하게 여긴다. 이 과정 중에 우리는 예술에 대해 둔감해지게 되었다. 누구나 방을 꾸미기 위해서 값싼 그림이나 복제품을 구입할 수 있다. 방에 있는 그림들은 종종 실제로 눈에 띄지 않는 곳에 걸리는데, 어쩌면 당연한 일일 것이다. 또한, 우리가 이와 똑같이 무심하게 박물관에 있는 예술작품을 보는 것도 놀랄 일이 아니다. 우리는 한 작품에서 다른 작품으로 빠르게 스쳐 지나가며 스모가스보드의 음식을 시식하듯이 작품을 감상한다. 우리는 우리가 감탄해야 하는 유명한 걸작 앞에서 짧게 머물고는 그 작품 주위에서 미술관을 가득 채우고 있는 똑같이 아름답고 중요한 작품들은 모른 체하는지도 모른다.

① 예술에 대해 둔감해졌다.
② 여러 차원에서 예술에 반응했다.
③ 예술의 진정한 의미를 이해하게 된다.
④ 의미 있는 개인적 선택을 하는 법을 배운다.

이종현T의 독해 Point!

앞에서 시각적인 배경을 너무나 당연하게 여긴다 라고 되어있고 지문의 끝 부분에 보면 우리는 걸작을 그냥 지나친다고 나와있다. 따라서 우리는 예술 작품을 잘 감상하지 못한다는 얘기가 빈칸에 들어가야 하고 정답은 1번이 된다.

11.

해석 : 물론, 두려운은 위험, 즉 실질적 위험에 대한 정상적 반응으로, 도피, 불안, 주의 등과 같은 조건 반사적인 방식의 반응들을 초래한다. 그러나 어린아이는 실질적 위험들에 대해서는 물론이고 많은 가상의 위험들에 대해서도 강렬한 두려움을 보인다. 어린이에게 두려움을 불러일으키는 상황을 구성하는 요인들에 대해 심리학자들 사이에 많은 논쟁이 있어왔다.

① 두려움을 불러일으키는 상황
② 애매한 상상력
③ 마음의 의식적 수준
④ 내적 자극들에 대한 반응

이종현T의 독해 Point!

빈칸 앞까지의 내용이 아이들은 여러 요인에 두려워한다는 얘기가 계속 나오므로 빈칸에도 두려움에 관련된 내용이 빈칸에 들어가야 한다. 따라서 정답은 1번이 된다.

12.

해석 : 기생 식물들은 태양에너지로부터 직접 양분을 생산하기보다는 숙주 식물들이 생산한 양분을 활용함으로써 생존하는 식물들이다. 생존하기 위해 햇빛을 필요로 하지 않기 때문에, 기생 식물들은 햇빛에 식섭 노출된 지역보다는 그늘진 지역에서 일반적으로 발견된다. 기생 식물들은 흡수근이라는 뿌리를 이용해 주로 숙주 식물의 줄기나 뿌리에 들러붙는다. 기생식물들은 숙주 식물의 양분 통로 속으로 자신의 흡수근을 뻗어 자신의 생존에 필요한 양분을 숙주 식물로부터 흡수한다. 세상에서 가장 무거운 꽃인 라플레시아는 밀림의 덩굴 식물들의 뿌리에 의지해 살아가는 기생 식물이다. 이 육중한 꽃의 무게는 15파운드까지 나가고 폭이 3피트까지 이르기도 한다.

① 비옥한 - 부피가 큰
② 몹시 건조한 - 활기넘치는, 무성한
③ 충적토의 - 빈약한
④ 그늘진 - 육중한

이종현T의 독해 Point!

빈칸이 두 개일 땐 하나에 집중해서 보는 것이 중요하다. 첫 번째 빈칸을 보면 rather than으로 연결되어 있으므로 빈칸에는 than 뒤의 속성과 반대되는 것이 들어가야 한다. 따라서 than 뒤에 햇빛에 노출된 지역이 나와있으므로 빈칸에는 노출되지 않은 지역이 들어가야 한다. 그리고 두 번째 빈칸은 문장의 소재가 무게에 관련된 것이므로 관련 내용을 맞추면 정답은 4번이 된다.

13.

해석 : 오늘날 법률은 젊은이들의 근로 조건은 물론 근로 시간까지 규정해놓고 있다. 그러나 항상 그랬던 것은 아니었다. 예를 들어, 20세기까지만 해도 영국의 가난한 가정들의 아이들은 종종 싸구려 노동력으로 착취되곤 하였다. 이러한 착취는 형태가 다양했다. 아홉 살의 어린 아이들이 하루에 14시간에서 16시간까지 일해야 했다. 열악한 작업 환경은 아이들의 건강을 심하게 해쳤다. 비록 많은 부모들이 자신들의 자녀들을 보호와 보살핌으로 감싸려고 노력했지만, 그 가족들은 돈이 필요했고 공장주와 광산주들에게 저항할 수 없었다. 많은 아이들은 버림받았다고 느꼈음에 틀림없다. 영국의 작가들은 이러한 아동학대를 비판했다. 가령, 유명한 소설가였던 찰스 디킨스는 아이들의 생명이 비인간적으로 낭비되는 모습을 종종 묘사하였다.

① 방자한, 제멋대로 하는 - 잔혹한
② 버림받은, 고독한 - 비인간적인
③ 구원된 - 중요한, 비판적인
④ 버려진 - 재미없는

이종현T의 독해 Point!

빈칸 앞까지의 내용은 아이들을 보호해줄 수 없다는 내용이 나오고 아이들의 노동력이 착취되었다는 내용이 나오고 이에 대한 결론에 해당하는 부분이다. 따라서 빈칸 모두에 그런 내용이 들어가야 하고 정답은 2번이 된다.

14.

해석 : 정부의 지출 삭감과 높은 이자율이 지속되면서 인플레이션은 줄어들었지만, 그러한 '치료법'은 1979년 이래 겪고 있었던 경기후퇴를 가속화시켰고, 1930년대 이래 최악의 경기침체를 불러왔다. 공장들이 문을 닫았고, 기업들이 도산했으며, 담보대출을 갚지 못한 농장들의 압류 비율은 점점 높아졌다. 1982년 말에는 이미 1200만 명 이상의 미국인들이 실직 상태였는데, 이는 전체 노동력의 10퍼센트 이상에 달하는 규모였다. 두 자릿수 인플레이션은 두 자리 수 실업이라는 대가를 치르고 종식되었던 것이다.

① 발생되다 - 악화시키다.
② 줄어들다, 가라앉다 - 촉진시키다.
③ 물결을 이루다 - 파기하다.
④ 감소하다 - 달래다, 요구를 들어주다.

이종현T의 독해 Point!

두 번째 줄에서 그러한 '치료법'이라는 단어를 잘 봐야 한다. 즉 앞 문장의 내용을 한 단어로 치료법이라는 단어로 받아준 것이다. 따라서 첫 문장의 내용은 무엇인가 나쁜 상황을 좋게 만들어주려는 치료법 같은 내용이 필요하다. 그렇다면 인플레이션(물가상승)은 줄어야 해결되는 것이므로 첫 번째 빈칸에는 줄다가 들어가야 한다. 그리고 but으로 이어져있으므로 뒤에는 그 치료법이 좋지 않은 결과를 내야 한다. 따라서 정답은 2번이 된다.

15.

해석 : 정치경제학 즉 경제학은 일상적인 인생사 속의 인간에 관한 연구이다. 경제학은 개인적, 사회적 활동들에 있어서 행복의 물질적 필수요건들을 성취하고 활용하는 것과 가장 긴밀하게 관련된 부분을 연구한다. 그러므로 경제학은 한편으로는 부에 관한 학문이요, 다른 한편으로 더 중요하게는 인간에 관한 학문이다. 왜냐하면 인간의 특성은 자신의 종교적 이상에 영향을 미치는 요인이 아니라면 다른 어떤 요인들보다, 자신의 일상적 노동과 노동함으로써 얻게 되는 물질적 자원에 의해 형성되었기 때문이다.

① 부 - 인간
② 복지 - 자본주의
③ 사회 - 종교
④ 계급 - 동등함

이종현T의 독해 Point!

첫 번째 빈칸은 빈칸 앞에 근거가 있고 두 번째 빈칸은 빈칸 뒤에 근거가 있다. 일단 앞에선 물질적 요건에 대한 얘기이므로 부가 들어가고 뒤에는 인간이 가진 위상과 연결시켜야 하므로 인간에 대한 내용이 들어가면 된다. 따라서 정답은 1번이 된다.

16.

해석 : 많은 언어학 학자들은 인간이 언어를 사용하여 동물 세계에서 인간의 가까운 친척되는 침팬지와 의사소통이 가능할 것이라는 사실에 대해 들떠 있다. 몇몇 과학자들은 침팬지, 그리고 특히 보노보 침팬지가 2살 반 된 어린이의 이해력을 가지고 있을지도 모른다고 믿고 있다. 맞춤 훈련을 거치는 경우, 이 침팬지가 복잡한 문장을 이해하고 인간과 높은 수준의 의사소통을 하는 것이 가능하다고 과학자들은 주장한다. 예를 들어, 최근에 있었던 다소 놀라운 한 사건에서, 보노보 침팬지는 별도의 시설에 있던 두 침팬지 간의 싸움에 대해 트레이너에게 알리려고 특수 키보드에 있는 기호를 눌렀다.

① 예를 들어
② 게다가
③ 그럼에도 불구하고
④ 대조적으로

이종현T의 독해 Point!

빈칸 앞에는 보노보 침팬지의 일반적인 특성, 그리고 빈칸 뒤에는 그런 보노보 침팬지의 특수한 행동에 관련된 얘기가 나오고 있으므로 정답은 1번이 된다.

17.

해석 : 인간의 뇌에는 약 1조 개의 신경세포가 있으며, 따라서 우리 자신이 하는 행동의 신경 기제를 이해하려고 노력하는 것은 우리 능력으로는 불가능한 작업으로 보일 수도 있을 것이다. 다행스럽게도 신경세포는 전체 동물계에 걸친 작동 방식에 있어서 모두가 현저하게 서로 유사하다. 이것은 이 흥미롭고 빠른 속도로 달라지고 있는 동물행동 분야에서 현재 이루어지고 있는 신경생물학적/기술적 돌파구가 우리 자신의 행동 기제를 이해하는 데 실질적인 영향을 줄 수 있을 것임을 의미한다.

이종현T의 독해 Point!

앞으로의 일에 대해서 얘기해야 한다. 따라서 did have가 들어간 것은 정답이 될 수 없다. 그리고 영향을 줄 것이라는 내용이어야 하기 때문에 2번과 4번은 정답이 될 수 없다. 고로 정답은 3번이 된다.

18.

해석 : 개복치는 지느러미를 이용하여 다소 어색한 모양의 몸이 물을 헤쳐 나아가게 한다. 개복치의 몸은 횡단면이 매우 좁다. 개복치는 기본적으로 평평한 타원체로, 머리가 앞에 있고 높은 등지느러미와 뒷지느러미는 뒤쪽에 있다. 사실 개복치의 높이는 종종 그 길이와 동일하며, 이는 일반적으로 가늘고 긴 어류에서는 보기 드문 경우에 해당한다.

이종현T의 독해 Point!

빈칸에는 물고기의 특징에 관련된 얘기가 필요한데 빈칸 앞 문장을 보면 개복치의 횡단면이 좁다는, 즉 크기에 관련된 얘기가 들어가있다. 따라서 정답은 2번이 된다.

19.

해석 : 미국 자동차 산업의 지난 기록적인 매출액과 이익을 감안하면, 현 세계는 디트로이트에게 행복한 한 세기였어야 했다. 그러나 "세상에 완전한 행복이란 없으며"이 말이 나에게는 슬픈 현실이다. 자동차 산업은 여전히 번창하고 있지만, 점점 더 많은 미국산 자동차들이 미국 밖에서 만들어지고 있다.

① 가시없는 장미는 없다.(완전한 행복은 없다)

② 쇠가 달았을 때 두드려라.(기회를 놓치지 말라는 뜻)

③ 명수도 때로는 실수가 있는 법

④ 울타리 저 편 잔디가 더 푸르다.(남의 떡이 커보인나.)

이종현T의 독해 Point!

빈칸 앞에는 자동차 산업의 매출이 올라갔다는 좋은 얘기이고 빈칸 뒷 내용은 미국 밖에서 만들어지고 있는 현실이 슬프다는 안좋은 얘기를 하고 있다. 따라서 정답은 좋기도 하지만 안좋은 점도 있다는 1번이 된다.

20.

해석 : 하이데거는 이해하기 어렵기로 악명이 높은 철학자다. 그가 글을 썼던 방식은 부분적으로는 그가 의도적으로 철학적 전통과 결별하고자 노력하고 있었다는 사실이 가져온 결과물이었다. 전통과 결별하는 한 가지 방법은 신조어를 만들어내는 것, 다시 말해 그 독창성으로 인해 그 어떤 철학적인 인습에도 구애받지 않을 단어들을 고안해내는 것이다. 이것은 하이데거가 빈번하게 사용한 방법이긴 하지만, 이해가능성을 희생하게 만든다. 게다가, 하이데거는 자신의 임무가 잘 정의된 문제에 대한 쉬운 대답을 제공하는 것이 아니라 깊이 생각하도록 독자를 자극하는 것이라고 믿었다.

① 독창성 - 독창성
② 독창성 - 명료함, 이해가능함
③ 명료함, 이해가능함 - 명료함, 이해가능함
④ 명료함, 이해가능함 - 독창성

이종현T의 독해 Point!

첫 번째 빈칸 앞을 보면 신조어를 만들어내는 것이란 얘기가 나온다. 따라서 첫 번째 빈칸에는 신조어를 만드는 것과 관련된 의미가 들어가있어야 한다. 두 번째 빈칸은 뒤에 보면 쉬운 대답을 제공하는 것이 아니라는 얘기가 나온다. 즉 쉬운 대답을 제공하는 것에는 관심이 없다는 뜻이고, 빈칸에 희생하는 명사도 쉬운 대답에 관련된 표현이어야 한다. 따라서 정답은 2번이 된다.

21.

해석 : 수화에 관한 근거 없는 통념 중의 하나는 수화가 보다 큰 범위의 사회에서 사용하고 있는 음성 언어와 똑같은 언어이며, 단지 그것을 손과 얼굴을 통해서 하는 것일 뿐이라는 것이다. 이것은 사실이 아니다. 실제 수화에는 그것이 맞닿아 있는 음성언어와는 현저하게 다른 문법이 있다. 사실, 본질적으로 같은 음성언어를 사용하는 국가들이 반드시 상호간에 이해가 가능한 수화를 갖고 있는 것은 아니다. 예를 들어, 미국, 영국, 아일랜드에서 사용하고 있는 수화는 서로 상당히 다르다. 수화는 해당 지역에서 사용하고 있는 음성언어의 문법 규칙에 따라 발전하지 않는다. 대신에, 수화는 그 나름의 복잡한 형태론, 음운론, 구문론, 그리고 의미론적 규칙을 가지고 있다.

① 대신에 - 그럼에도 불구하고
② 대신에 - 사실
③ 사실 - 그럼에도 불구하고
④ 사실 - 대신에

이종현T의 독해 Point

첫 번째 빈칸은 빈칸을 중심으로 같은 말이 이어져있으므로 재진술이 될 수 있는 in fact가 들어가야 한다. 그리고 두 번째는 앞 문장이 부정문이고 ~가 아니라 대신에 ~다 같은 말이 되기 때문에 정답은 4번이 된다.

22.

해석 : 올해, 북극해의 표면을 덮고 있는 얼음은 북극이 가장 많은 태양에너지를 받는 달인 6월에 상대적으로 녹는 속도가 느렸다. 그러나 태양이 여전히 강한 7월 동안에는 얼음이 녹는 속도가 빨라졌다. 정상보다 빨리 얼음이 녹는 것은 8월 내내 계속됐는데, 8월은 얼음이 녹는 것이 전형적으로 느려지기 시작하는 과도기에 해당하는 달이다. 8월에는 알래스카 북부의 유방에 큰 '구멍'이 생겼는데, 이 시기에 더 두껍고 더 오래된 얼음으로 둘러싸여 있던, 계절적으로 나타나는 더 얇은 얼음이 녹아내렸기 때문이다. 그 거대한 구멍은 바다가 더 많은 태양에너지를 흡수하도록 하여, 그러한 과정을 가속화시켰다.

이종현T의 독해 Point!

첫 번째 빈칸을 중심으로 앞 뒤의 내용이 속도가 느리고 빠른 반대 얘기이다 따라서 However가 들어가야 한다. 그리고 두 번째 빈칸은 구멍이 생겼다고 했으므로 얼음은 녹아야 한다. 따라서 1번이 정답이 된다.

UNIT 6 무관한 문장

1.

해석 : 곳곳에 흩어져 있던 지방의 항공사들이 일찍이 1913년에 승객들에게 항공편을 제공하기 시작했지만, 미국에서 국내선 정기 항공편을 널리 이용할 수 있게 된 것은 1920년대에 접어들면서부터였다. A. 상업 비행이 이뤄지던 초기의 경우, 미국의 항공 여행은 비싼 항공요금을 지불할 여유가 있던 소수의 비즈니스 여행객과 부유한 개인들에게 한정돼 있었다. B. 도시와 도시 사이를 오가야 하는 경우, 대부분의 여행객들은 비행기 대신에 보다 적당한 가격의 가치에 일존하고 있었다. C. 95년이 넘는 세월이 흐른 뒤에, 미국의 비즈니스와 레저 여행객들에게 항공편을 가장 중요하고 또 가장 많이 이용하는 운송 수단 중의 하나로 성장했다. D. 1978년에 미국 정부가 항공 산업에 대한 규제를 철폐한 뒤에, 항공 노선은 늘어났고, 항공요금은 내려갔으며, 저가 항공사가 호황을 누리게 되었다. 이로 인해 더 광범위한 계층의 미국인들이 항공 여행을 할 수 있게 되었다. (E. 비행기 티켓은 대체로 먹지를 이용해서 손으로 써서 준비했고 승객이 공항에 도착하면 곧바로 주었다.) 2008년 한 해에만도, 6억 4990만 명의 긍객들의 미국 항공사의 국내선을 통해 여행한다.

이종현T의 독해 Point!
전부다 국내 여행 시작의 기원에 대한 얘기가 쭉 나와있는데 E는 비행기 티켓 얘기가 나온다. 따라서 정답은 5번이 된다.

2.

해석 : 2012년~13년 독감 유행 철에 가정에서 많은 희생자가 나왔다. 158명의 어린이 — 대부분이 11세 이하였다 — 가 목숨을 잃었다. 가슴 아픈 것은 숨진 아이들 가운데 약 90%가 자신들을 살릴 수도 있었을 한 가지를 하지 않았다는 사실이다. 그것은 바로 독감 예방접종이었다. ⓐ 독감 예방접종이 생명을 구한다는 사실을 입증하는 여러 연구결과에도 불구하고, 미국의 모든 어링니들 가운데 매년 예방주사를 맞는 것은 절반에 미치지 못한다. ⓑ 한 사회조사 회사에서 최근 실시한 조사에 따르면, 16%의 미국인들이 예방접종을 안전하지 않다고 여기고 있으며 35%는 예방접종을 하면 독감에 걸린다고 믿고 있다. ⓒ "충분히 예방할 수 있는 질병으로 아이들이 계속해서 죽는다는 것은 비극적인 일입니다."라고 블룸버그 박사는 말한다. (ⓓ 의사들은 생후 6개월에서 5세까지의 어린이들은 설사와 탈수증 같은 심각한 질병에 걸릴 위험성이 높다는 사실을 부모가 이해하길 바라고 있다.) ⓔ 가족의 건강에 대해 현명한 결정을 하는 비결은 인식과 교육에 있기 때문에, 아이와 함께 있는 부모들이 독감과 백신접종에 관해 명확한 지식을 갖는 것이 무엇보다도 중요하다.

이종현T의 독해 Point!

d번을 제외하곤 전부 독감과 관련된 현상에 대해 말하고 있는데 d는 그냥 독감이 아닌 다른 질병에 대해 얘기하고 있으므로 정답은 4번이 된다.

3.

해석 : 노예 출신의 존 헨리는 체사피크 & 오하이오(C&O) 철도 부설사로서 철도 건설 현장에서 일하게 되었다. 그가 맡은 일은 강철에 대못을 바위 속에 박아 넣는 것이었는데, 그는 자신이 속한 조에서 가장 강하고 빠르게 일을 해냈다. ⓐ C&O 철도회사의 소유주들이 웨스트버지니아 주의 빅 밴드 산을 둘러 가는 대신 그 산을 곧바로 관통하는 철도를 건설하기로 결정했을 때, 위험한 작업으로 인해 많은 노동자들이 목숨을 잃었다. 그러나 존 헨리는 아니었다. (ⓑ 수천 명의 흑인들이 철도 건설 현장에서 일을 했는데, 수백 명이 그레이트 벤드 터널을 뚫는 과정에서 목숨을 잃었다.) 그는 계속해서 못을 박아 나갔고, 마침내 산을 파헤쳐 뚫어냈다. ⓒ 하루는 한 세일즈맨이 와서 새로 나온 증기동력 드릴의 효율성과 속도를 입에 침이 마르도록 칭찬했다. 노동자들은 존 헨리와 그 기계의 시합을 주선했다. ⓓ 먼지가 걷혔을 때, 존 헨리는 14피트(4미터)의 구멍을 파낸 반면, 기계는 9피트(거의 3미터)의 구멍을 파내는 데 그쳤다. ⓔ 철도 건설 노동자들이 축제 분위기에 휩싸였을 때, 존 헨리는 기진맥진하여 쓰러져 죽고 말았다.

이종현T의 독해 Point!

b 문장 앞 뒤로는 존 헨리의 얘기인데 B 혼자서 그냥 일반적인 흑인들 이야기를 하고 있으므로 정답은 2번이 된다.

4.

해석 : 활기차게 움직이는 것은 대개 건강에 좋은 일이지만, 극단으로 치닫는 경우에는 부적응 상태가 될 수도 있다. ⓐ 예를 들어, 운동을 강박적으로 하는 것을 이용해서 생활의 다른 측면들에 대한 책임을 회피하고, 그 결과 가족, 친구 혹은 부가적인 관심사에는 시간을 거의 허용하지 않는 달리기 선수나 보디빌딩 선수들이 있다. ⓑ 몸을 단련시키는 노력들을 즐겁게 하는 대신, 그들은 자신들의 정해진 일상에 다른 조정을 하는 데에는 무기력함을 느끼고 오로지 더 많은 운동을 하려고만 한다. (ⓒ 즐겁게 신체 단련을 하는 노력을 기울이는 것은 일상에서 겪는 압박감들을 완화시키기 위한 훌륭한 대응 전략이 될 수 있다.) ⓓ 불행하게도, 일부 청소년들과 어른들이 운동을 하는 방식은 뿌리깊은 심리적 문제들을 나타내 보이고 있다. ⓔ 그들은 몸을 지치게 만드는 운동과 다이어트를 통해 몸을 변화시키는 데에 위험할 정도로 사로잡혀서, 약물 남용과 섭식 장애를 비롯한 심각한 건강상의 문제를 겪게 될 위험을 높이고 있다.

이종현T의 독해 Point!

이 글 전체가 과도하게 운동하는 것에 대해서 걱정하는 이야기인데 C번만 즐겁게 신체훈련하는 것의 좋은 점에 관한 이야기이므로 정답은 3번이 된다.

5.

해석 : ⓐ 테오티우아칸은 서반구에 건설된 진정한 의미에서의 최초의 도시들 가운데 하나였으며, 전성기에는 면적이 거의 8평방마일에 이르렀다. ⓑ 달의 피라미드와 그 외 다른 구조물에서 발견된 귀중한 인공물들은 이곳이 여러 지역들과 광범위하게 연결된 부유한 무역 중심지였음을 보여준다. ⓒ 설명할 수 없는 일이지만, 테오티우아칸은 서기 600년경에 갑작스럽게 맹렬히 몰락하고 말았으며, 많은 사람들이 그곳에서 달아났다. (ⓓ 몇몇 건물을 무덤이라 여기고 그들은 그 대로를 죽음의 거리라고 불렀다.) ⓔ 그들은 문서로 된 기록을 거의 남기지 않았으며, 그들이 살던 도시의 잔해와 한때 강력했던 문화였음을 보여주는 흥미로운 단서만이 남아있을 뿐이다.

이종현T의 독해 Point!

d 문장 앞에 있는 c 문장 도시가 없어졌다는 얘기이고 e도 도시가 없어졌다는 얘기인데 d만 건물과 도로에 대한 얘기이므로 정답은 4번이 된다.

6.

해석 : 학습 전문가들에 따르면, 시험을 잘 보기 위한 비결 가운데 하나는 매일 그리고 매주 규칙적으로 공부하는 것이다. 또 다른 비결은, 당신이 공부하는 시간에 교사가 수업 중에 강조했던 개념들을 집중적으로 공부하는 것이다. ⓐ 더불어, 시험 전날 밤에는 스트레스를 많이 받는 벼락치기가 아니라 면밀한 복습을 해야 한다. ⓑ 그런 다음, 시험 당일 아침에는 조금 일찍 일어나서 노트를 한 번 더 복습하도록 하라. (ⓒ 공부하는 기술은 학습을 보다 효과적이고, 조직적이고, 성공적이도록 만들기 위해 이용되는 도구이자 전략이다.) ⓓ 끝으로, 일단 시험이 시작되면, 전문가가 해줄 수 있는 조언은 가장 쉬운 문제를 먼저 풀고, 그런 다음 다시 돌아가 어려운 문제에 매달리라는 것이다.

이종현T의 독해 Point!

나머지 전부는 시험을 잘 보는 방법에 대한 이야기인데 c번은 공부하는 기술에 대한 이야기이므로 정답은 3번이 된다.

UNIT 7 문장 삽입

1.

해석 : 동전은 사용하기에 매우 편리하지만, 무겁다. 10세기 중국에서, 철로 만든 동전은 가운데에 네모난 모양의 구멍이 있었고, 사람들은 끈을 사용하여 동전들을 묶어, 동전 100개씩의 무거운 꾸러미를 만들어 냈다. 사람들은 이 동전 꾸러미들을 상인에게 맡기고 그 대신 영수증을 받기 시작했다. 이 영수증은 상인들로부터 물건을 구입하는 데 계속해서 사용될 수 있었다. (11세기에 중국 정부는 세계 최초의 지폐가 된 이런 영수증을 발행하기 시작했다.) 돈은 정부가 그 가치를 보증하지 않으면 아무런 쓸모가 없을 것이다. 사람들이 그것이 가진 가치를 신뢰하지 않는다면 지폐는 아무런 가치가 없다.

이종현T의 독해 Point!

제시문 앞에는 영수증 얘기고 뒤에는 지폐 얘기가 와야 한다. 따라서 정답은 4번이 된다.

2.

해석 : 스마트폰이 널리 쓰이고 통신기술이 발달함에 따라 페이스북과 같은 소셜 미디어가 급속도로 퍼져나갔으며, 소셜 미디어는 뉴스 플랫폼으로서 여론을 형성하는 데 있어 영향력이 커졌다. (소셜 미디어의 영향력이 커지면서 우려의 목소리도 높아지고 있다.) 소셜 미디어를 통해 거짓 정보가 생산되어 유통되고 있기 때문이다. 미국 대통령 선거에서는 교황이 후보들 가운데 한 사람을 지지하고 있다는 것과 같은 가짜 뉴스가 논란이 됐고, 가짜 뉴스로 인해 발생하는 문제들은 여전히 만연하고 있다. 페이스북과 같은 소셜 미디어 사이트에서 공유되는 뉴스는 걸러내기가 어려우며, 따라서 가짜 뉴스는 언제든 문제가 될 수 있다. 표현의 자유를 최대한 보장하면서도 가짜 뉴스와 가짜 정보의 유통과 확산에 대한 대응과 그런 뉴스 정보의 영향은 연구되어야 할 필요가 있다. 뉴욕의 스토니브룩 대학은 사실과 허구를 구별하기 위한 6주간의 무료 온라인 강좌를 제공하고 있다.

이종현T의 독해 Point!

앞에는 소셜 미디어의 영향력이 커진다는 얘기가 있어야 하고 뒤에는 우려, 걱정에 대한 이야기가 와야 한다. 따라서 정답은 3번이 된다.

3.

해석 : 화가들은 이탈리아의 르네상스 기간 동안 사람들의 나체를 그리기 시작했던 것으로 추정된다. 이 기간 동안, 화실의 견습생들은 그들의 임무들 중 하나로 포즈를 취했다. 그림들은 보통 남성의 나체를 대

상으로 그려졌는데, 이는 교회의 심기를 건드리지 않기 위해서였다. 여성의 몸을 그린 르네상스 시대의 그림들을 자세히 살펴보면 대부분의 그림들이 실제로는 젊은 남성들을 그린 그림에 약간의 수정을 가한 것임을 알게 될 것이다. 이 시기 동안 화가들은 또한 인체의 이상적인 비율들을 정의하려 노력했다. 레오나르도는 원과 정사각형 안에 인간을 넣어 그렸던 반면, 뒤러는 인체의 이상적인 비율에 대한 연구를 한 층 더 깊이 들어갔다. 뒤러는 신체의 미수한 치수에도 완벽을 추구한 다음, 삽화에 설명이 들어가있는 책 네 권을 발견했다. 절개해부로부터 해부학을 공부한 르네상스 시대의 화가들은 그 당시 의료진들보다 수십 년 앞서 있었다. (미켈란젤로는 인간의 외형을 완벽하게 이해하기 위해 절개 해부를 참관했던 반면, 레오나르도는 우리 신체의 구조를 보고 이해하기 위해 직접 개복을 했다.) 레오나르도는 심지어 뇌 아래, 눈 뒤에 있는 뇌하수체와 영혼입서다고 믿어, 눈이 영혼의 창이라는 이론에 물리적인 기반을 마련해주었다.

이종현T의 독해 Point!

제시문이 부사절과 주절로 구성되어있고 부사절은 레오나르도 얘기 주절은 미켈란젤로의 이야기이다. 부사절 앞에 콤마가 있으므로 뒷 내용에 레오나르도 얘기가 있고 앞에 미켈란젤로 얘기가 있음을 추측할 수 있다. 따라서 정답은 4번이 된다.

4.

해석 : 1890년대 후반에, 두 명의 독일 심리학자 케오르크 뮐러와 알폰소 필체커는 뇌 속에서 기억이 고정되기 위해서는, 즉 '강화되기' 위해서는 한 시간 정도가 걸린다는 사실을 발견했다. 후속 연구들을 통해 단기기억과 장기기억이 존재한다는 점이 확인되었고, 단기기억이 장기 기억으로 전환되는 강화단계가 중요하다는 증거가 추가적으로 확인되었다. 1960년대에, 펜실베니아 대학의 루이 플렉스너는 매우 흥미로운 발견을 했다. 생쥐에게 세포의 단백질 생성을 방해하는 항생제를 주입하였더니, 그 동물들이 장기기억은 형성하지 못하지만 단기기억은 여전히 저장할 수 있다는 것을 알게 되었다. 그것이 함축하고 있는 의미는 분명했다. 장기기억은 단기기억보다 더 강력한 형태의 기억에 불과한 것이 아니라는 것이다. (그 두 유형의 기억에는 서로 다른 생물학적 과정이 수반된다) 장기기억을 저장하려면 새로운 단백질의 합성이 필요하다. 단기기억의 저장은 그렇지 않다. 좀 더 최근의 연구들은 단기기억과 장기기억의 물리적 작용이라는 문제에 관심을 돌렸다. 그 결과, 어떤 경험을 더 많이 반복할수록 그 경험에 대한 기억은 더 오래 지속된다는 사실이 입증되었다. 반복이 강화를 촉진하는 것이다. 특히, 반복이 신경신호에 미치는 생리적 영향을 조사한 과학자들은 놀라운 사실을 발견하였다. 신경세포 접합부의 신경전달물질 농도가 변화하여 신경세포 간의 기존 연결 강도가 변화했을 뿐 아니라, 신경세포들이 완전히 새로운 신경세포 접합부 말단들을 생성시키는 것이었다. 달리 말해, 장기기억의 생성은 생화학적 변화뿐만 아니라 해부학적 변화까지 수반하는 것이다. 이는 기억강화에 왜 새로운 단백질이 필요한지를 설명해준다. 단백질은 세포의 구조적 변화를 발생시키는 데 필수적인 역할을 수행한다.

이종현T의 독해 Point!

앞에는 두 유형의 기억이 어떤 종류인지 나와야 하고 뒤에는 각각의 차이에 대한 설명이 필요하다. 따라서 정답은 1번이 된다.

5.

해석 : 독서를 진정으로 즐기기 위해서는, 그건이 제2의 천성이 되어야 한다. "어린이들은 소리를 내지 않고서도, 또 큰 소리로도, 책을 읽어야 합니다."라고 주디 치텀은 말한다. 바로 거기서 아이의 유창성 — 부드럽고 표현력 있게 읽는 능력 — 이 길러진다고 치텀 박사는 말한다. 아이들은 친숙한 글을 연습함으로써 유창성을 얻게 되므로, 아이가 같은 책을 반복해서 선택한다고 해서 걱정할 필요는 없다. 만약 아이가 당신에게 큰 소리로 책을 읽는 것을 걱정하면, 조용히 혼자서 읽거나 녹음기에 대고 읽도록 한 다음, 녹음된 것을 자신이나 어린 동생에게 들려주게 하라. (아니면 훨씬 더 너그럽게 들어주는 사람에게 돌려주어 즐겁게 해주라고 장려해라.) 캘리포니아 대학 데이비스 캠퍼스의 한 연구에 의하면, 집에서 키우는 개에게 큰 소리로 책을 읽어준 2학년 학생들이 10주 만에 읽기 능력이 12% 향상되었다.

이종현T의 독해 Point!

제시문에 Or이 있고 명령문이 있으므로 앞에는 또 다른 명령문이 있어야하고 그건 아이에게 뭔가 행동을 하게 만드는 이야기어야 한다. 따라서 정답은 5번이 된다.

6.

해석 : 선물을 주는 것에 대한 기존 연구를 바탕으로 2016년에 작성된 한 논문에서는 선물을 주는 사람과 받는 사람이 선물에 대해 생각하는 방식에 차이가 있다고 기록하고 있다. 선물을 주는 사람은 일반적으로 그 선물을 상대방이 어떻게 받을지를 상상하면서 종종 '와우'하고 깜짝 놀랄 반응을 얻어내려고 선물을 선택한다. 그러나 받는 사람은 선물을 열어볼 때 보다 실용적인 입장을 보이며, 그 선물의 유용성과 장기적인 면에서의 만족도에 초점을 맞춘다. 예를 하나 들어보겠다. 남편은 아내를 위해 값비싼 다이아몬드 귀걸이를 구입한다. 바로 그 '깜짝 놀랄' 반응을 노린 것이다. (그는 아내가 박스를 여는 순간 기쁨의 탄성을 자그맣게 내지를 것을 상상할 수 있다.) 그러나 아내는 그렇게 하지 않는다. 아내는 슬리퍼, 믹서, 또는 가죽장갑을 달라고 부탁했었으며, 아무리 아름다운 다이아몬드 귀걸이라고 해도, 다이아몬드 귀걸이보다 그것들을 더 좋아했을 것이다. 또 다른 시나리오도 있다. 한 여성이 커피를 좋아하는 아빠에게 커피숍에서 쓸 수 있는 기프트 카드를 사 주면서, 매우 사려깊은 선물이라고 생각한다. 그녀의 아빠는 커피를 무척 즐기기는 하지만, 그는 더 다양한 용도에 쓸 수 있는 신용카드 기프트 카드를 받았으면 좋았을 거라 생각한다.

이종현T의 독해 Point!

앞에는 그의 예상에 대한 이야기이고 뒤엔 아내의 반응에 대한 이야기가 시작된다. 따라서 정답은 4번이 된다.

7.

해석 : 물론, 국가 자체도 오랜 시간에 걸쳐 그 형태가 바뀌어 왔다. 유럽에서, 초기의 국가는 15세기 즈음 나타났다. 그리고 19세기에 거의 완전히 성장한 형태를 이뤘다. 그때 이후로 만들어졌던 나라는 주로 자기결정에 대한 권리와 주권 영토 내에서의 권리를 표현하는 사람들이나 부족들이었다. 더욱이 그들은 실제로 그들을 통치하는 사람들을 무시하면서 실제 혹은 허구의 공격자들에 대항해서 특정한 지리적인 경계를 보호할 권리를 주장했다. (더욱이, 현대 국가 내에서, 정부는 지역에 대한 권한을 가지는 것으로 보여지고 그 내에서 궁극적인 힘을 가지고 있다.) 현대 국가들은 관료주의에 의해 운영되는 일련의 규칙에 의해 절대적인 통치자들의 교체를 특징으로 한다. 여기에서 국가는 타당성을 성취하는 것으로 보여진다.

이종현T의 독해 Point!

앞 내용엔 권리에 대한 요구가 있어야 한다. 그리고 뒷 내용이 추론이 어려울 땐 뒤에는 새로운 소재가 나온다고 생각을 하면 된다. c의 앞에는 권리를 표현하는 얘기가 있고 c 뒤에는 새로운 정부의 역할에 대한 얘기가 있으므로 정답은 3번이 된다.

8.

해석 : Norman French의 침략은 모든 것들을 바꿨다. 1066년 헤스팅스 전투에서 헤롤드 왕의 패배는 런던의 왕좌에 프랑스 왕국의 건립을 야기시켰다. (처음에는, 헤스팅스 전투인 William 1, 실제로는 영국에서 거의 시간을 보내지 않았다.) 그리고 그 이후 300년동안 프랑스는 영국의 모든 문화, 힘, 통치의 모든 영역에 영향력을 행시했디. Norman French는 영국 행정부의 언이가 되었고 나라의 공식직인 인어의 형태로 정착했다. Old English는 잠깐 경멸 되었고, 농부와 서민들의 언어로 여겨졌다. (그러나, 많은 것들이 변했을지라도, Old English는 사실 날아남았다.) 아무도 그 언어에 무슨 일이 발생했는지 확실하지 않은 언어적인 미스테리가 있고 한세기 반 후에, Old English 기적적으로 살아남았다, 스스로를 Middle English라고 불리는 것으로 변화시키고, 수많은 단어들을 프랑스어로부터 빌렸고 그렇게 함으로써 더 강력해졌다. 마침내, 고대영어는 완전하게 확립된 채 모습을 드러내게 되었고, '초기 영국 문학계에서 가장 인상적인 인물이었던 제프리 초서의 글에 나타나 항상 가장 큰 유익을 주었다.

이종현T의 독해 Point!

앞 내용인 많은 것들의 변화에 대한 얘기가 나오고 뒤에 Old English가 살아남았다는 얘기가 나오는 부분이 정답이 된다. 따라서 정답은 4번이 된다.

9.

해석 : Aeschylus가 쓴 오레스테아이아의 결말 부분에서, 등장인물들의 고대 세계에 두 가지 변화가 일어난다. 그 유명한 변화에서, 아테네 여신은 끝없이 반복되는 것으로 보이는 피의 복수를 대체하고 끝내기 위해 법 제도를 도입한다. 이성에 바탕을 둔 주장을 하고 증거에 대한 평가를 내리는 절차가 확립돼 있고, 독립적인 제 삼자인 재판관, 그리고 아테네 시민들로 구성된 배심원을 갖춘 법원을 설립함으로써, 그녀는 살인죄는 고대의 목수의 여신들인 Furies에 의해서가 아니라 법에 의해 해결될 것이라고 선언한다. 그러나 그 복수의 여신들이 그냥 퇴출된 것은 아니다. (대신에, 아테네 여신은 그들이 이 동일한 법률제도와 아테네시의 미래의 안정을 위해 중요하다는 것을 인식하고서 그들에게 대지 아래의 명예로운 사리르 제공하면서 그들을 설득해서 도시에 동참하게 한다.) 전형적으로 아테네 여신의 이러한 조치는 법률제도가 어두운 보복성 감정들을 통합하고 존중해야 한다는 것을 인정한 것으로 이해된다. 따라서 그리스 문명학자인 휴 로이드-존스는 아테네 여신은 복수의 여신들의 특권들을 없애길 원하기는커녕 그것들을 보존하고 싶은 것이라고 결론을 내리고 있다.

이종현T의 독해 Point!

제시문에 Instead가 있으므로 앞에가 부정문이어야 한다. 따라서 정답은 3번이 된다.

10.

해석 : 1916년, 스웨덴 지질학자인 레나트 본 포스트는 스웨덴의 토탄 늪지에 서로 다른 깊이로 보존되어 있는 꽃가루를 확인하고 그 수를 헤아림으로써 시간 경과에 따른 숲 구성의 변화를 추정할 수 있음을 보여주었다. 그의 선구적인 연구 이후, 꽃가루 분석은 과거의 식물, 기후, 그리고 생태계를 이해하는 데 있어서 중요한 도구로 재빨리 자리 잡게 되었다. 오늘날, 그것은 과거의 생태계를 재구성하고 생태계 변화의 동인에 대한 가설을 검증하기 위해 널리 쓰이고 있다. 꽃가루 분석을 사용하면서 본 포스트는 남부 스웨덴의 많은 곳에서 빙하기 이후 숲 구성의 일시적인 변화를 자세히 알아보았다. 그리고 나서 그는 선정된 여러 시기의 꽃가루 자료를 지도로 만들어 공간적 변화 패턴을 보여주었다. (그는 지역적 유사성이라는 개념을 공식화했는데, 그 개념에 따르면 기후 변화에 대한 식물의 반응들은 전 세계 여러 지역에서 비슷했다.) 그는 또한 꽃가루 분석을 빙하기 이후 해수면의 변화를 설명하기 위한 상대적 연대측정 기법으로 발전시켰다. 1930년대와 50년대 사이에, 전 세계적인 꽃가루 분석연구는 식물의 역사를 확립하고, 꽃가루 축적비율을 추정하고, 현대 꽃가루 스펙트럼과 식물과의 관계를 밝히고, 그와 더불어 시대에 따른 꽃가루 자료이 지도를 만들기 휘새 실험되었다.

이종현T의 독해 Point!

문장삽입에서 보기는 새로운 이야기의 시작점이거나 어떤 이야기가 끝나는점이다 따라서 정답은 3번이다. 앞에는 공간 변화에 대한 얘기고 뒤엔 시간적 변화에 대한 얘기이다.

11.

해석 : 센트럴 대학의 케이스 교수에 따르면, 희생자들은 소외감과 낮은 자존감을 경험한다. 그는 최근에 있었던 10대 소년 제롬 피싱의 자살사건을 지적하는데, 제롬 파싱은 뚱뚱하다고 놀리는 무수히 많은 협박성 문자메시지와 이메일을 받고 난 뒤에 자살했다. 그의 전화와 이메일 기록에 대한 조사 결과는 그를 놀리고 위협하는 자그마치 563건에 달하는 문자 메시지와 1,465건에 이르는 이메일을 보여주었다. (케이스 교수는 만약 학생들이 학교 상담전문가들과 후원단체게 더 잘 접근할 수 있었더라면 그의 죽음은 막을 수 있었을 것이라고 주장한다.) 통계자료에 따르면, 헌신적인 상담전문가와 사이버 왕따 정책이 있는 학교와 지역사회들의 경우, 사건이 보고되는 비율은 더 높지만 심각한 사건의 비율은 더 낮다.

이종현T의 독해 Point!

제시문 앞에는 죽음에 대한 얘기, 뒤에는 그의 죽음을 막을수 있었다는 얘기가 나와야 한다. 따라서 정답은 4번이 된다.

12.

해석 : 그 어느 유행병들과 마찬가지로, 에볼라도 초기에 진압하는 것이 최선이다. 에볼라는 사망할 때까지 바이러스로 가득 찬 체액을 매일 최대 10리터씩 배출하는 환자들에게 의료 인력들을 노출시킴으로써 그들의 목숨을 앗아가고 있다. 감염자의 수는 2~4주마다 두 배씩 늘어나는 경향을 보이고 있다. 의료 인력들이 감염되고 감염자의 수가 기하급수적으로 늘어남에 따라, 에볼라에 대한 사회의 방어체계는 급속도로 붕괴된다. (이번의 경우에는 대응이 치명적일만큼 느렸다.) 한 가지 이유는 아프리카의 그 지역에서 유행병이 돈 적이 한 번도 없었기 때문이다. 에볼라의 전파는 도시화와 개발에 의해서도 촉진되었을 것인데, 도시화와 개발로 인해 교통망이 발전됐고, 이 때문에 바이러스는 마을에서 도시로 그리고 감염되지 않은 시골 지역으로 오갈 수 있게 됐던 것이다. 슬럼지역은 너무 무질서하고 광범위해서 대처가 불가능하기 때문에, 그곳으로 에볼라가 흘러들어가는 것은 아마도 시간문제였을 것이다.

이종현T의 독해 Point!

제시문 앞에는 경우에 대한 얘기 뒤에는 반응에 대한 얘기가 나와야 하므로 정답은 3번이 된다.

13.

해석 : 많은 미국인들이 살이 찌는 이유는 그들이 너무 많은 탄수화물을 섭취하기 때문이라는 것이 일반적인 생각이다. 고탄수화물의 저지방 음식은, 고지방 음식과 칼로리는 같더라도, 체중을 늘어나게 하고, 인슐린과 혈당 수치를 끌어 올리며, 당뇨병도 더 많이 발병하게 만든다는 것이다. 연구 결과에 따르면 그런 일은 발생하지 않았다. 다른 사람들은 반대되는 의견을 내놓기도 했는데, 저지방 식사를 하면 자연스럽게 체중감량을 할 수 있다는 것이다. (그러나 그와 같은 생각도 연구 결과상의 수치가 뒷받침하지 못하는 것이었다.) 심장병의 위험 요소들에 대해 말하자면, 영향을 받은 유일한 요소는 LDL 콜레스테롤이었는데, 이것은 심장병 발병 위험을 증가시킨다. 그 수치는 고지방 음식을 섭취하는 여성들에서 약간 더 높게 나왔지만, 심장병 위험에 눈에 띄는 차이를 만들 만큼 높지는 않았다. 연구에 참여했던 사람들은 모두 여성이었지만, 결과는 남성에게도 적용된다.

이종현T의 독해 Point!

앞에 어떤 결론이 나오고 그게 연구의 뒷받침해주지 않는다 라는 내용이 필요하고 그 이후 또 다른 연구에 대한 얘기가 나오고 그 결과가 나와야 한다. 따라서 정답은 2번이 된다.

14.

해석 : 현대적인 기상 예보 방법들은 단기간의 날씨를 확정짓는 것과 관련해서는 꽤 정확하지만, 예보가 길어질수록 그 예보가 틀릴 확률은 더 높아진다. 수학적으로 계산하여 기상 상태를 확인하는 현재의 방법은 날씨의 급변하는 성질 때문에 정확한 예측이 약 5일 앞서 하는 것으로 제한된다. 기상학자들은 컴퓨터 데이터 수집 방식의 결과를 현재 일어나고 있는 실제 기상 조건과 합친다. 다양한 고도에서의 온도, 이슬점, 바람과 관련한 현재의 정보가 전 세계에서 온 종일 모아져서 여러 단서들을 제공하고 이 단서들을 과거의 상황에 근거한 컴퓨터 모형과 비교하여 개연성 있는 기후 패턴을 제시하게 된다. (그러나 기상 관측법의 과학과 방법이 향상되었음에도 불구하고, 대기와 날씨가 관련된 움직임을 이해하는 데는 여전히 큰 격차가 있다.) 결과적으로 다양한 기상 조건을 보아왔고 그러한 기상 조건이 가져올 변화와 추이에 대해 잘 알고 있는 경험 많은 기상학자가 컴퓨터에서 생성된 모형 못지않게 미래의 기상 상태를 정확히 예측할 수 잇다.

이종현T의 독해 Point!

제시문의 앞에는 과학과 방법론의 향상에 대한 얘기가 있어야 하고 뒤에는 이해도의 차이에 대한 얘기가 나오는 것이 좋다. 따라서 정답은 4번이 된다.

UNIT 8 순서 배열

1.

해석 : 만일 우리가 절대불변의 행성에 살고 있다면, 할 일이 정말 아무것도 없을 것이다. 아예 생각할 필요가 없기 때문이다. ⓓ 그런 세계에서는 과학을 위한 자극이 없을 것이다. ⓐ 그리고 모든 것이 무작위적이거나 매우 복잡한 방식으로 변화하는 예측할 수 없는 세계에서 산다면, 우리는 아무것도 이해할 수 없을 것이다. ⓑ 그런 세상 역시 과학이 존재하지 않을 것이다. ⓒ 그러나 우리는 모든 것이 변하긴 하지만 패턴이나, 규칙이나, 소위 자연 법칙에 따라 변하는 중간 세계에서 살아가고 있다. 허공에 막대기를 집어 던지면 막대기는 반드시 땅으로 다시 떨어진다. 태양이 서쪽에서 지면, 다음날 아침 동쪽에서 항상 다시 떠오른다. 그래서 모든 것을 이해하는 것이 가능해진다. 우리는 과학을 할 수 있고, 이를 통해 우리의 삶을 발전시킬 수 있다.

이종현T의 독해 Point!

제시문 뒤의 보기에서 a는 소재가 변화한다. 뒤에가 전부 예측할 수 없는 세계에 대한 얘기라면 d 다음에 a일 것인데 그렇지 않다. 그리고 b는 again 때문에 이와 관련된 첫 번째 결론이 앞에 있어야 한다. 그리고 그 역할을 d가 하므로 제시문 다음엔 d가 온다. 그리고 다른 입장인 a가 오고 그다음 a의 결론 b가 온다. 그 이후 이 둘의 중간을 얘기하는 c가 오면 둘을 합쳐줄 수 있다. 따라서 정답은 ③ d-a-b-c가 된다.

2.

해석 : 알츠하이머병은 아마도 전형적인 노인성 질환이다. 육체적으로 노쇠해지는 것은 예상해서 대처할 수 있지만, 정신적인 노쇠함은 환자에게도 훨씬 더 두려운 것이고 그 환자를 돌봐야 하는 사람들에게도 훨씬 더 벅찬 것이다. 그것은 또한 비용이 많이 든다. ⓓ 미국만 해도 알츠하이머병으로 인해 매년 1,700억 달러가 들 것으로 보인다. ⓒ 게다가, 평균 수명이 늘어나면서 알츠하이머 병은 더 흔히 발생하고 있다. ⓐ 알츠하이머 병에 걸린 사람의 수는 2050년까지 3배 증가할 것으로 보인다. ⓑ 따라서 효과적인 치료법을 환자들과 사회가 모두 적극적으로 받아들일 것이다.

이종현T의 독해 Point!

제시문 끝에 비용 얘기로 끝나고 그게 d로 이어진다. 그리고 알츠하이머병이 흔해지고 있다는 얘기인 c와 a가 뒤에 이어지고 마지막 결론이 b가 나오면 정답은 ③ d-c-a-b가 된다.

3.

해석 : 말과 함께 사용되는 제스처들에서, 우리는 말하고 있는 메시지의 내용을 그대로 나타내는 제스처와 언급하고 있는 무언가를 가리키는 제스처를 구분할 수 있다. 상징적 제스처는 우리가 "나는 작은 박스를 찾고 있어." 라고 말하면서 손가락으로 허공에 네모를 그리는 경우에서처럼, 말하고 있는 것의 의미를 그대로 나타내는 것처럼 보이는 제스처다. 상징적 제스처 단독으로는 말하고 있는 것과 똑같은 '의미를 가지지는' 않지만, '의미'를 더해줄 수는 있다. 예를 들어, 한 여인이 "나 또 그 개를 쫓아냈어"라고 말하는 동안 마치 무기를 들고 있는 것처럼 주먹을 쥔 상태로 팔뚝을 아래위로 휘젓고 있었다고 해 보자. 무기를 떠올리게 하면서 메시지를 전달할 수 있었던 이유는 제스처와 말을 같이 사용했기 때문이다. 보편적으로 사용하는 또 다른 종류의 제스처는 지시적 제스처라고 할 수 있다. ⓑ '지시적'이라는 용어는 '가리킨다'는 뜻이며, 우리는 종종 말을 하면서 tanf이나 사람을 가리킬 때 제스처를 사용한다. ⓓ 한 손을 사용하여 (케이크가 놓여 있는) 식탁을 가리키면서 누군가에게 "케이크 좀 드셔보시겠어요?"라고 처하는 경우에서처럼 우리는 '지시적 제스처'를 현재 상황에 사용할 수 있다. ⓒ 또한 우리는 나중에 "그 케이크는 정말 맛있었어."라고 말하는 경우에, 더 이상 케이크가 있지 않은 식탁을 가리키며 같은 제스처를 사용할 수도 있다. ⓐ 이 경우에는, 제스처와 말이 결합하여 현재 물리적 공간에 있는 것이 아니라 상대방과 공유하는 기억 속에만 존재하고 있는 것을 효과적으로 가리킬 수 있다.

이종현T의 독해 Point!

지시적에 대한 얘기가 시작이 되고 지시적이라는 말의 정의가 시작되는 b가 가장 먼저 온다. 그리고 d와 c는 케이크를 가리키는 예시에 대한 얘기가 이어지므로 d c가 이어지고 마지막으로 그러한 경우의 결론을 나타내는 a가 오면 된다. 따라서 정답은 2번이다.

4.

해석 : 로렌스는 사람들이 발걸음을 내딛는 힘을 깨끗한 재생가능 에너지로 바꿔주는 포장용 타일인 'Pavegen'을 만든 사람으로, 그는 현재 이 제품에 대한 특허권을 갖고 있다. "저의 비전은 Pavegen과 도시의 관계가 'Intel Inside'와 PC의 관계와 같게 되는 것입니다. 저는 세계 모든 도시에 Pavegen을 깔고 싶습니다. 저는 모든 다리와 도로와 건물을 운동 에너지 장치로 만들고 싶습니다."라고 그는 말한다. 이런 발상은 그가 러프버러 대학에서 산업 디자인과 기술을 공부하고 있던 도중에 떠올랐다. 그는 교육과정의 한 부분으로 에너지 회사 E.ON으로 파견되었다.

ⓑ 사람들은 "로렌스, 태양 에너지나 풍력 에너지로 작동하는 신호등을 설계할 수 있겠어요?"라고 제게 말했죠. 하지만 햇빛이 비치지 않고 바람이 불지 않으면 전기를 얻을 수 없죠. 그래서 1년 동안 시도하다가 실패했습니다"라고 그는 회상한다.

ⓐ "정말 속상했습니다. 그러던 어느 날 런던의 빅토리아 역을 걸으면서 지나가다가 거기에 있던 수많은 사람들에 대해 생각하게 되었어요. 한 시간에 3만 8천명의 사람들이 그 역을 걸어서 지나간다는 것을 읽은 적이 있었어요. 만약 그 에너지를 전력 공급원으로 이용할 수 있다면 어떨까 하고 생각했죠."

ⓓ 로렌스는 인정한다. "발걸음을 내딛는 힘으로부터 에너지를 생산하는 것은 새로운 것이 아닙니다. 다른 사람들도 시도한 적이 있어요. 그들은 라이터에서 볼 수 있는 압전결정체와 같은 것들을 이용하여 전기를 만들고 있습니다. 하지만 전력이 너무 적어서 그 에너지로는 의미 있는 일을 저혀 할 수 없습니다.

ⓒ 로렌스는 다른 길을 선택했다. 그가 발명한 타일에 가해지는 발걸음의 무게는 타일 속에 들어 있는 수평 플라이휠을 회전하게 만든다. "사람들이 더 많이 걸을수록, 이 플라이휠은 더 많이 회전하죠."라고 그는 설명한다 | "그러면 우리는 플라이휠에서 필요할 때 전기를 거둬들이는 거죠. 우리는 조금씩 전기를 얻을 수 있습니다."

타일 위로 지나가는 모든 보행자는 약 7와트의 에너지를 만들어낸다. 이 타일들은 압전효과, 그리고 구리 코일과 자석을 이용한 유도 방법을 포함하는 복합적인 메커니즘을 통해 전기를 생산한다.

이종현T의 독해 Point!

EON회사 파견 이후의 얘기가 이어진다. 여기서 일단 발걸음 에너지가 아니라 그 이전에 실패했던 에너지에 대한 이야기인 B가 먼저 오고 그 이야기 이후 이어지는 A가 온다. A가 오는 이후는 실패 이후 발걸음 에너지에 대한 얘기가 시작되는 시작점이다. 그리고 발걸음 에너지에 대한 접근 방식을 이야기하는 시작점이 D이므로 D가 먼저 와야 한다. 따라서 정답은 3번이 된다.

5.

해석 : 아기들과 유아들의 미각을 연구하는 생물학자인 줄리 메넬라는 종종 자신의 실험을 비디오로 녹화한다. 최근에 내가 필라델피아에 위치한 모넬 화학감각연구소에 있는 그녀를 만났을 때, 그녀는 아기용 식탁 의자에 앉아 있는 한 아기에게 엄마가 더 단 것을 먹여주고 있는 동영상을 나에게 보여주었다.

ⓑ 숟가락이 아기의 입에 들어가자마자, 아기의 얼굴은 매우 기뻐하며 빛이 나면서 빨고 싶은 듯이 입술을 오므렸다. 그런 다음에 메넬라는 또 다른 동영상을 내게 보여주었는데, 그 동영상에는 많은 녹색 채소들과 같이 약간의 쓴맛이 있는 브로콜리를 처음 맛보는 다른 아기의 모습이 있었다.

ⓐ 그 아기는 얼굴을 찡그리고 메스꺼워하면서 몸서리쳤으며, 아기용 식탁의자의 앞부분을 쾅쾅 쳤는데, 이것은 "그만해!"라는 말을 손짓으로 표현한 것이다. 인간의 모유에는 당분인 유당이 들어있다 "우리가 아기에 대해 알고 있는 것은 단 것을 좋아하는 것이 타고난 것이라는 거예요."라고 메넬라가 주장했다.

ⓒ 메넬라는 쓴 음식을 혐오하는 것 역시 타고난 것이라고 말했는데, 이 쓴 음식을 혐오하는 것도 생존을 위해 가치 있는 것이다. 쓴 음식을 혐오하는 것은 식물들이 우리 인간을 포함한 동물들에게 먹히지 않기 위해 진화시킨 독소들을 우리가 먹지 않도록 도와준다.

이종현T의 독해 Point!

제시문이 단 것을 먹고 있는 아기의 비디오에 대한 얘기이므로 단 것에 대한 이야기가 이어지는 것이 b이다. 그리고 b에서 쓴 것을 먹는걸 보여주는 아기에 대한 이야기가 시작이 된다. 그 이야기가 이어지는 것이 a이고 a번에서 단 것과 쓴 것에 대한 결론이 시작이 된다. 시작인 걸 알 수 있는 장치는 c에 있는 too라는 것이다. 따라서 정답은 2번이 된다.

6.

해석 : [A] 샬롯 퍼킨스 길먼은 작품을 읽는 모든 독자들은 그녀가 같은 이야기를 반복해서 한다는 것을 알고 있다. [D] 그녀의 글이 가진 이러한 특징을 나는 유사어의 글쓰기라 칭하고 싶다. [B] 길먼의 소설에서, 유사어의 사용은 특정 플롯이나 테마를 단순하게 반복하는 것 이상이다. [E] 그것은 그녀가 자신의 예술과 이데올로기를 체계적으로 표현한 방식을 이해하는 데 있어 매우 중요하다. [C] 예를 들어, 그것은 그녀가 개인과 사회의 건강 사이의 관계를 다루고 있을 때 특히 효과적이다.

이종현T의 독해 Point!

A번 다음에 이어질 걸 찾아야 하는데 그녀의 글쓰기의 특징을 정의하는 D가 이어진다. 그리고 D에 대한 얘기가 이어지는 B가 오고 그 얘기에 대해서 진짜 의미를 설명하는게 E가 오고 E의 예시인 C가 오게 되면 정답은 4번이 된다.

7.

해석 : 고대 그리스인들이 수학과 천문학을 추구한 것은 그 학문들 자체를 위한 것이었다. 그들이 그 학문들을 연구한 것은 회계사가 된다거나 계절을 예측하는 사람이 되기 위해서가 아니었다. 그들의 유일한 갈망은 세상에 대한 더 나은 이해를 얻는 것이었다. 우리는 셰익스피어의 '햄릿'과 월트 휘트먼의 시를 읽는다. 그 구절들은 하늘을 가로지르는 혜성처럼 아름답게 다가오기에 우리는 그 유명한 모든 구절들을 암송할 수밖에 없는 것이다.

(C) 다시 현실로 돌아와 보자. 그런 구절들이 무슨 소용인가? 아름답게 쓴 셰익스피어의 구절을 암송하는 것이 우리에게 최신 벤츠를 구해주는가? 그렇게 하는 것이 자본주의의 병폐를 강조하는 데 도움이 되거나, 사회적 계층의 정상으로 우리를 데려다주는가? 유감스럽지만 그렇지않다. 지식은 우리에게 좋은 직업을 가져다주는 도구에 불과하다고 나는 들었다. 그래서 나는 필경 실용적 지식의 필요성은 인정하고, 예술과 인문학은 그 무용성 면에서 무시하고 만다.

(A) 그러나 나는 그리스인들에게는 칭찬할 만한 뭔가가 있다고 여긴다. 그들은 호기심이 요구할 때면 괴짜가 되는 것을 부끄러워하지 않았다. 그들은 언제나 지식의 물질적 이득보다는 지식의 본질적인 재미를 더 중시하였다. 그들이 수학적 지식을 철저히 검토할 때나 우리가 어떻게 살아야 할지에 관한 지식을 추구할 때조차 거기에 실용적인 이유는 전혀 없었다. 그들은 쓸모없는 지식이 인생에 바람직한 것들을 계발함으로써, 문명을 가능케 하는 데 필수적임을 넌지시 말해주고 있다.

(B) 그렇다면 과연 별들에 관한 연구나 여타 쓸모없는 지식들이 어떻게 문명을 가능하게 만드는가? 별들에 관한 연구는 도시의 불빛 외에도 저 밤하늘에 본질적으로 우아하고 아름다운 뭔가가 있다는 것을 시사한다. 아마 몇 백만 년 전에 생겨났을 빛의 장관을 연출하는 별들을 우리로 하여금 자연이 빚어낸 예술작품과 직면하게 한다. 그러나 별들에 관한 연구는 우리로 하여금 자연의 아름다움을 감상하도록 할 뿐만 아니라 우리들 안에 사색하는 마음의 습관을 만들어 준다.

도시 생활은 빠르고 사람들을 초조하게 만든다. 비즈니스맨의 하루는 회의로 빽빽이 채워져 있다. 그는 고요함을 누리거나, 자신과 자신을 둘러싸고 벌어지는 모든 것들에관해 면밀히 검토할 시간이 없다. 별을 바라봄으로써, 그는 그가 예전에 등한시하였던 아름다움을 발견하게 된다. 별들이 고요히 그를 내려다볼 때, 그는 까마득한 아름다움 속에서 경외감을 느끼며 관조에 필요한 마음의 평화를 얻게 된다. 별들을 연구함으로써, 우리가 세상을 이해함으로써 얻게 되는 즐거움은 더욱 충만해지고 풍요롭게 된다. 그것은 우리의 감수성을 풍부하게 하고 우리의 영혼을 정화함으로써 우리를 문명화시켜준다.

이종현T의 독해 Point!

제시문에서는 긍정적인 면을 말하고 있으므로 같은 긍정적인 면을 말하는 A가 제시문 다음에 but으로 이어질 수가 없고 but이 나오려면 부정적인 면에 대한 얘기가 있어야 한다. 따라서 부정적인 면에 대한 얘기가 나오는 (C)가 먼저 오고 그 다음 (A)가 온다. 그리고 쓸모없는 지식에 대한 이어지는 (B)가 오면 된다. 따라서 정답은 4번이 된다.

8.

해석 : 전쟁이 끝난 후에, 그리고 루스벨트가 세 번째와 네 번째 임기의 대통령으로 선출된것에 대응하여, 1951년에 22차 헌법 수정안이 채택되었다. © 그 수정안에서는 그 누구도 세 번째 임기의 대통령직에는 선출되지 못하도록 하고 있다. 그것은 또한 이전에 대통력으로서 봉직한 적이 있거나 대통령 권한 대행으로 다른 사람의 대통령 임기를 2년 이상 대행한 사람의 경우도 한 번에 한해서만 중임을 할 수 있도록 하고 있다. ⓐ 수정안이 채택된 이래로, 두 번의 임기를 모두 채웠던 대통령은 4명, 즉 드와이트 D. 아이젠하워, 로널드 레이건, 빌 클린턴, 조지 W. 부시였다. 지미 카터와 조지 H.W. 부시는 두 번째 임기에 도전했으나 패하고 말았다. 리처드 닉슨은 두 번째 임기에 선출되었으나, 임기를 마치기 전에 사임했다. ⓑ 이 수정안이 채택될 당시의 대통령이었던 해리 S. 트루먼은 수정안의 제한 규정을 적용 받지 않았는데, 그는 1952년 선거에서 세 번째 임기(완전한 임기로서는 두 번째 임기)를 노렸으나, 곧 불출마를 선언했다.

이종현T의 독해 Point!

제시문 다음에 수정안에 대한 설명이 이어지는 C가 먼저 오고 그 수정안이 적용된 이후 대통령들에게 어떻게 적용되는지가 시작되는 A가 그 다음에 오고 마지막으로 대통령에 대한 사례가 이어지는 B가 오면 정답은 4번이 된다.

9.

해석 : 루이스 멈퍼드가 지적했듯이, 기술에 미친 영향의 측면에서나 인간의 습관에 미친 영향의 측면에 있어서 시계는 기계 시대의 핵심적인 기계라고 할 수 있다. © 기술적인 면에서 볼 때, 시계는 인간의 생활에서 중요한 의미를 갖게 된 최초의 실질적인 자동 기계였다. 시계가 발명되기 전의 일반적인 기계들은 인간이나 동물의 근육, 물이나 바람과 같은 외부적이고 신뢰할 수 없는 힘에 의지해서 작동하는 성격의 것들이었다. ⓐ 그리스인들이 원시적인 자동 기계들을 많이 발명했던 것은 사실이지만, 이것들은 헤론의 증기기관처럼 사원에서 '초자연적인' 효과를 얻기 위해서나 레반트의 도시에 있던 폭군을 즐겁게 하기 위한 목적으로 사용되었다. ⓑ 그러나 시계는 대중적인 중요성과 사회적 기능을 갖게 된 최초의 자동 기계였다. 시계 제작은 사람들이 기계 짝의 여러 요소들을 배우고 산업혁명 때에 복잡한 기계들을 만들 수 있게 해줄 전문 기술을 습득하는 산업이 되었다.

이종현T의 독해 Point!

제시문에서 시계가 가진 의의에 대한 이어지는게 c가 되고 c에서 시계 이전 시대에 대한 이야기가 나오기 시작한다. 그 시계 이전에 대한 이야기가 연결되는게 a가 되고 그 이후 다시 시계가 가진 의의에 대해서 나오는 b가 나오면 c-a-b가 된다. 따라서 정답은 4번이 된다.

10.

해석 : 1950년, 2년에 걸친 훈련을 끝낸 후에, 플로렌스 채드윅이라는 32세의 장거리 수영선수는 프랑스에서 영국 방향으로 영국 해협을 13시간 20분만에 헤엄쳐 건넘으로써, 거트루드 에덜 리가 갖고 있던 24년 된 세계 기록을 경신했다. 얼마 지나지 않아 그녀는 영국 해협을 양쪽 방향으로 — 프랑스에서 영국으로 뿐만 아니라 영국에서 프랑스로도 — 헤엄쳐 건넌 최초의 여성이 되었다. 그런 다음 그녀는 카타리나 해협을 헤엄쳐 건넌 최초의 여성이 되려고 시도했다.

ⓒ 카타리나 해협을 헤엄쳐 건너기로 예정돼 있던 날, 채드윅은 격랑과 맞닥뜨렸다. 그러나 그녀는 페르시아 만에서 훈련을 해 왔었기 때문에, 컨디션은 최고조에 달해 있었고 높은 파도와 맞서 싸울 준비가 돼 있었다. 채드윅은 또한 쌀쌀한 추위에도 직면했다. 그것은 문제가 됐지만, 다시 한 번, 그녀가 받은 훈련이 큰 차이를 낳았다. 그녀는 차가운 물에 익숙해져 있었고, 코치들은 그녀의 몸에 기름을 발라서 그녀가 비바람으로부터 차단되도록 도움을 줬다. 게다가, 채드윅의 코치들은 나란히 배를 저어 가면서 그녀가 거친 바다의 추위와 싸우고 있을 때 용기를 북돋워 주는 격려의 말을 해줌으로써 그녀가 기운을 낼 수 있도록 했다.

ⓓ 그러나 그녀의 계획과 우수한 훈련에도 불구하고, 채드윅과 코치들이 예상하지 못한 한 가지가 있었으니, 그것은 바로 안개였다. 짙은 안개가 내려앉자, 그녀가 볼 수 있는 거리는 불과 몇 피트로 줄어들었고, 수평선과 먼 곳의 해안이 보이지 않게 되었다. 채드윅은 허둥대기 시작했다. 시야를 잃게 되자, 얼음같이 차가운 큰 파도가 높이 솟아오르는 것처럼 보였다. 채드윅은 매서운 추위로 인해 팔, 다리, 빨, 손에 경련을 일으키기 시작했다. 거대한 파도와 싸울 때, 그녀의 근육은 매우 고통스러웠다. 마침내, 그녀는 코치들에게 자신을 배에 태워 해변으로 데려다달라고 부탁했다.

ⓑ 나중에, 그녀가 몸을 데워 말리고 나자, 신문기자들은 기록을 경신하고자 하는 용기 있는 도전을 포기했을 당시에 해변으로부터의 거리가 얼마 남지 않았던 것을 알고 있느냐고 그녀에게 물었다. 그녀는 코치들이 그와 똑같은 말을 했었지만, 자신에게는 아무런 영향을 주지 못했다고 대답했다. "보다시피, 저는 목표가 시야에서 사라졌어요. 제 맘속에 목표가 분명히 있었는지도 확신할 수 없습니다."라고 그녀는 말했다. 그러나 두 달이 지난 어느 맑은 날에, 플로렌스 채두윅은 카타리나 해협을 헤엄쳐 건넜는데, 이로써 27년 된 기록을 2시간 이상의 차이로 경신했으며, 카타리나 해협을 헤엄쳐 건넌 최초의 여성이 되었다.

이종현T의 독해 Point!

제시문에서 건너기 시도한 얘기가 나왔고 그 도전을 처음으로 시작한 얘기가 c에 나온다. 그리고 그 과정에서의 어려운 점이 d가 나오고 그녀가 포기한 것에 대한 이야기가 나오는 b가 마지막으로 나오면 c-d-b가 된다 따라서 정답은 3번이 된다.

11.

해석 : 추운 겨울 아침에는 많은 사람들이 자동차의 시동을 거는 데 어려움을 겪는다. 차갑게 식어 있는 자동차의 경우, 엔진의 시동이 더 천천히 걸리며, 때로는 전혀 시동이 걸리지 않는다. 자동차 소유주들은 차가운 엔진 탓을 하겠지만, 실제로 문제가 되는 것은 시동 모터에 동력을 공급하는 차가운 배터리이다. 이 모터는 일반적으로 배터리를 사용하여 회로에 연결된다. ⓑ 모터가 배터리를 통해 회로에 연결되면, 전자는 회로를 통해 이동하여 전류를 생성한다. ⓐ 이동하는 전자의 수를 늘리면 전류가 증가하므로 모터가 사용할 수 있는 전력량이 늘어가게 된다. ⓒ 마찬가지로, 이동하는 전자의 수를 줄이면 사용 가능한 전력량이 줄어들 것이다.

이종현T의 독해 Point!

전류 얘기가 처음 시작되는 b가 먼저 와야 한다. 그리고 c의 likewise를 받아주기 위해선 a가 필요하다. 따라서 정답은 b-a-c가 되고 3번이 된다.

12.

해석 : 많은 질병이 결함이 있는 유전자로 인해 발생한다. 유전자 치료법의 목표는 그러한 질환을 치료하기 위해 환자의 세포에 올바른 유전자를 삽입하는 것이다. 초기 치료 가운데 일부는 성공적이었다. 그러나 유전자 치료에는 몇 가지 단점이 있다. ⓐ 우선 그 중 한 가지를 예로 들면, 치료를 반복적으로 해야한다는 것이다. ⓒ 뿐만 아니라, 인체의 면역 체계가 거부반응을 나타내고 치료를 받아들이지 않음으로 인해 환자가 사망하게 될 가능성이 있다. ⓑ 이러한 난관에도 불구하고, 과학자들은 유전자 치료법이 개별 환자의 필요에 맞춘 의학적 치료의 잠재력을 제공한다고 믿고 있다. 최근에는 많은 노력을 기울여 망막 질환을 가진 환자의 시력을 회복시키는 데 성공했다.

이종현T의 독해 Point!

단점에 대한 이야기가 처음으로 이어지는게 a이고 이와는 다른 또 단점이 나오는 c가 그 뒤로 이어진다. 그리고 이런 난관들 이라는 표현으로 앞의 단점들을 받아주는 b가 오면 정답은 2번이 된다.

13.

해석 : ⓑ 우리가 '크레올'이라는 단어를 들을 때, 우리들 중 많은 이들은 먼저 자이데코를 생기게 한 남부 루이지애나 고유의 민속음악 양식을 떠올리는 경향이 있다. ⓓ 또 다른 사람들은 이해할 만한 일이긴 하지만 종종 '크리올'을 아이티의 민족 언어 두 가지 가운데 하나라고 착각한다. ⓒ 그러나 크리올은 그 참된 의미에 있어서는 훨씬 더 일반적이고 포괄적인 용어로, 멕시코 만 연안이나 카리브해 지역을 넘어서는 역사를 지녔다. ⓐ 유럽의 식민지 건설이 한창이던 시절, 크리올은 서부 아프리카 지역에서부터 오스트레일리아에 이르기까지 전 세계에서 발견될 수 있었다.

이종현T의 독해 Point!

b와 d는 크레올 단어에 대해서 잘못 생각하고 있는 이야기에 대한 것이고 c와 a는 퍼진 것에 대한 이야기이다. 따라서 b d 그리고 c a가 묶이게 되고 b가 크레올에 대한 통념에 대한 얘기이고 c엔 however가 있으니 b가 먼저 오게 된다. 따라서 정답은 b-d-c-a 4번이 된다.

14.

해석 : ⓓ 확률론은 애초부터 실질적인 응용을 지향했던 수학 분야들 중 하나이다. ⓒ 확률론은 실제로 도박에서의 가능성에 관한 질문에서 발달하였다. ⓐ 일반적으로 말해서, 확률론은 미래 사건의 결과를 측정해야 할 경우의 의사결정을 위해 사용된다. ⓑ 예를 들어, 상해보험의 비용은 너무 높지는 않아야 하지만 보험업자의 비용을 충당할 만큼은 되어야 한다.

이종현T의 독해 Point!

a와 b는 예상되는 비용에 대한 얘기이고 c와 d는 확률론의 정의에 관한 얘기이다. 따라서 a, b 그리고 c, d가 먼저 나오게 되고 이 용어의 정의가 먼저 나와야 하므로 정답은 d-c-a-b 3번이 된다.

15.

해석 : 컴퓨터 마우스는 1964년에 더글러스 엥겔바트가 발명한 것으로, 나무로 만든 몸체, 회로기판, 그리고 위에 놓고 사용하는 표면과 접촉하게 되는 두 개의 금속 바퀴로 이루어져 있었다. ⓒ 8년 후에 빌 잉글리시는 "볼 마우스"로 알려져 있는 것을 발명하여 기존 마우스의 설계를 발전시켰다. 볼이 바퀴를 대체했으며 어느 방향으로도 움직임을 모니터할 수 있었다. 볼은 두 개의 롤러와 닿게 돼 있었고, 이번에는 이 롤러들이 눈금이 새겨져 있는 바퀴를 돌려 방향과 속도를 나타내는 전기신호로 바꿔줄 수 있었다. ⓑ 광학 마우스는 8년 후인 1980년에 개발되었는데, 데스크톱 컴퓨터 주위에서 움직이는 경우 종종 더러워져서 동작에 나쁜 영향을 주었던 볼을 제거한 채로 나왔다. 다시 8년이 지난 후, 리사 윌리엄스가 발명한 광학 마우스에 미국 특허 번호 4751505가 발행되었다. ⓐ 이 마우스는 17달러에 생산되어 35달러에 팔렸

다. 이런 사실에도 불구하고, 광학 마우스가 볼 마우스를 대신할 상업적 성공 가능성이 있는 대안이 되어 일반 소비자 시장에 침투한 것은 10년이 지난 후이 1998년 무렵이었다.

이종현T의 독해 Point!

b와 a에는 the ball 이라는 표현이 있으므로 ball 마우스라는 용어가 처음 등장하기 전까진 절대 나올 수 없다. 따라서 보기 다음엔 C가 먼저 오게 되고 optical mouse가 개발되었다는 얘기가 먼저 와야 하므로 b가 그 다음 온 후에 마지막으로 optical mouse가 퍼지게 된 A가 오면 정답은 c-b-a 3번이 된다.

16.

해석 : 12월이 왔다. 가게 앞은 크리스마스 장식들로 꾸며지고, 추위가 시작되며, 또 한 해가 저물어간다. 고대 로마인들이 그들의 첫 번째 달력을 확립한 이래로, 12월은 한해의 끝과 겨울의 시작을 나타내 왔다. 어원에서 알 수 있듯이, December는 '10'을 의미하는 라틴어 어근 'decem-'으로부터 만들어졌지만 December는 12번째 달이다. ⓑ 숫자가 어색하게 어긋난 것은 september, October, November도 마찬가지인데 이들은 각각 '7', '8', '9'를 의미하지만, 각각 9번째, 10번째, 11번째 달이다. ⓐ 이렇게 된 이유는 고대 로마의 달력은 1년이 열 달로 이루어져 있었고, 1년의 시작이 march였기 때문이다. 늦어도 기원전 45년에 율리우스력이 제정되기 이전이었지만 결국 January와 February가 1년의 끝인 December 다음에 추가되었다. ⓒ January와 February는 한 해가 시작되는 곳에 나타나게 되었고, 원래 있던 달들을 두 달씩 뒤로 밀어냈으며, 이름은 처음에 정해진 그대로 두었다.

이종현T의 독해 Point!

일단 이 문제에선 a에서 1월과 2월 얘기가 시작되고 그 뒤에 1월과 2월 얘기가 이어지는 c가 와서 a-c가 되어야 한다. 그리고 12월과 비슷한 다른 사례에 대한 얘기인 b가 제시문 다음에 이어지면 된다. 따라서 정답은 b-a-c로 3번이 된다.

17.

해석 : 여성과 남성이 서로에 의해 방해받는다는 느낌을 받는 것은 이야기를 통해 이루려 하는 것이 다르기 때문이다. ⓒ 남성은 대화를 하나의 경쟁으로 간주하고 다가가기 때문에, 상대방의 이야기를 지지해주려고 노력하는 것이 아니라 대화를 다른 방향으로 이끌어가려고 노력할 가능성이 높은데, 그 방향은 아마도 이야기를 하거나 지식을 드러냄으로써 자신이 대화의 중심 무대를 차지할 수 있는 방향일 것이다. 그러나 그와 같은 행동을 하면서, 그들은 대화 상대가 이에 대해 저항을 할 것으로 예상한다. ⓐ 여성은 이러한 노력들에 굴복하고 마는데, 이는 여성이 유약하거나 자신이 없거나 공손해서가 아니라, 대화의 핸들을 잡으려는 시도를 빛나가게 만드는 경험이 거의 없기 때문이다. ⓑ 남성과는 달리, 여성은 대화를 다른 방향으로 돌리는 것을 게임에서 자기 차례를 행하는 것으로 보지 않고, 게임의 규칙을 위반하는 것으로 여긴다.

이종현T의 독해 Point!
일단 남성 얘기인 c가 나오고 a의 여성 얘기에서 these efforts가 앞의 남성들에 대한 얘기를 받아줄 수 있다. 그리고 주어를 일치시켜야만 하므로 b는 a 뒤에 와야 한다. 따라서 정답은 c-a-b 5번이 된다.

18.

해석 : 역사상 최초로, 세계적 경제번영 덕분에 세계는 극단적 빈곤을 완전히 제거할 수 있는 길에 들어서게 되었다. 어떤 이들에게는 이러한 예상이 상상에 불과하겠지만, 중국, 인도 및 여타 아시아의 저소득 지역들이 지난 25년간에 걸쳐 이룩해낸 놀라운 경제발전은 이것이 현실이 될 수 있음을 증명하고 있다. 경제성장이 대다수의 사람들을 극단적 빈곤에서 벗어나게 하는 탁월한 능력을 보여주긴 했지만, 발전이 저절로 일어나거나 필연적인 것은 아니다. 시장의 힘과 자유무역만으로는 충분하지가 않다.
ⓒ 가장 가난한 지역들의 상당수는 여전히 빈곤의 덫에 붙잡혀 있다. 그들은 사회 기반시설과 교육, 의료체계 및 여타 필수적인 요구들에 충분한 투자를 할 만한 재정적 수단을 갖고 있지 못하다. 부유한 국가들의 여론은 종종 극단적 빈곤의 책임을 가난한 사람들 스스로의 잘못이거나, 적어도 그들 정부의 잘못으로 돌린다. 한때는 종교적 분열과 금기, 카스트 제도, 기업가 정신의 결여, 성 불평등 등 문화가 결정적 요인으로 생각되기도 하였다.
ⓐ 그런 설명들은 날로 다양해져 가는 종교와 문화를 가진 사회들이 상대적 번영을 성취함에 따라 약해졌다. 더욱이, 사회가 도시화되고 경제적으로 발전함에 따라 바뀔 수 없는 것으로 여겨졌던 문화의 측면들이 종종 극적으로 변화하고 있다. 최근에, 논객들은 '열악한 통치', 즉 부패에 초점을 맞추어왔다. 그들은 정부가 자신들의 시장을 개방하지 않고 공공서비스를 제공하지 않으며, 뇌물 수수를 제거하지 않아 극단적인 빈곤이 지속된다고 주장한다.
ⓑ 논쟁이 아직 끝나진 않았지만, 통치가 영향을 미치기는 하나 경제성장의 유일한 결정 요인은 아니라는 증거가 압도적으로 많다. 국제 투명성 기구에서 실시한 조사연구에 따르면, 기업의 지도자들은 실제로 성

장이 부진한 아프리카 국가들보다 빠르게 성장하는 일부 국가들이 더 부패했다고 인식하고 있다. 두 번째 흔한 오해는 부패로 인해 기부된 돈이 횡령되는 정도에 관한 것이다. 과거 해외원조금의 일부가 실제로 그런 식으로 빼돌려진 적이 있었다. 냉전 기간 동안 정치적 이유로 자금이 제공되었을 때 그런 일이 있었다. 이와 달리, 정치적 목적보다는 개발에 목표를 둔 지원의 경우, 그 결과는 좋았다.

이종현T의 독해 Point!

a와 b가 governance의 측면을 다루고 있으므로 소재가 이어지고 있다. 따라서 a와 b를 묶어줄 수 있고 a의 그런 설명에 대한 얘기를 c에서 하고 있으므로 정답은 c-a-b 4번이 된다.

19.

해석 : 1900년대 초, 런던 위생 열대 의과대학의 교육과정은 말라리아의 원인을 연구하기 위해 수개월 동안 이탈리아의 임시막사로 여행가는 것을 의미했을지도 모른다. ⓑ 아니면 그 교육과정에는 서인도제도로 배를 타고 가서 모기에 의해 확산되는 것으로 보이는 병원균인 필라리아증으로 불리는 어떤 것을 연구팀이 조사하는 것을 돕는 것이 포함되어 있었을지도 모른다. 심지어 그 교육과정은 흑사병이나 이질과의 전쟁을 돕기 위해 아프리카로 향하는 것을 의미했을 수도 있다. ⓒ "식민지의 유산으로 열대 의과대학이 창립되었습니다. 벨기에, 독일, 프랑스, 포르투갈은 식민 강대국으로 이들 국가들에는 모두 열대 의과대학이 있었습니다."라고 2010년 이래 런던 위생 열대 의과대학장을 맡아온 피터 피오트 박사가 말했다. 피오트 박사에 따르면 그런 위생 열대 의과대학의 주요 목적은 해외영토의 풍토병들이 귀국하는 선원들을 통해 유럽국가로 유입되기 전에 그 풍토형을 연구하는 것이었다고 한다. ⓐ 오늘날, 의과대학 교수들은 상호 연결된 세상에서 그런 질병전구가 보다 복잡해졌다고 주장한다. 연구원들은 생물학 이외의 요인들이 환자의 행복에 기여한다는 것을 깨달았다. 공중위생을 다루는 것은 미생물과 병원균을 넘어 사회경제적 지위와 정치까지 망라한다고 연구원들은 주장한다.

이종현T의 독해 Point!

말라리아에 대해 연구하는 얘기가 b로 이어지고 그 이후 c에서 열대 의과대학이 창립되어있는 얘기가 시작된다. 그리고 그 의과대학에 대한 얘기가 이어지는 a가 오면 b-c-a로 3번이 된다.

20.

해석 : ⓒ 소셜 네트워킹은 매우 많은 친구를 쉽게 사귈 수 있도록 해준다. ⓐ 수억 명의 사람들이 페이스북, 카카오톡, 그리고 그 밖의 다른 사이트에 가입했으며, 그 결과 사람들은 친구들과 온라인상에서 대화를 할 수 있다. ⓑ 그러나 '친구'라는 단어의 의미는 변한 것처럼 보인다.

과거에는, 친구란 당신과 가까운 인간관계에 있던 사람이었다. 현재는, 세계의 누구든 온라인에서 당신의 친구가 될 수 있다! 어떤 사람들은 수천 명의 친구가 있다. 그렇지만, 당신이 그렇게 많은 친구를 원하지 않는다면 어떻게 하겠는가? 그것은 쉬운 일이나. 손가락으로 한번만 눌러서 원치 않는 친구를 버릴 수 있다.

이종현T의 독해 Point!

c에서의 friends가 a에서 those friends로 이어지고 지문의 마지막 부분의 얘기가 친구라는 것의 의미가 변한 얘기이므로 b가 마지막으로 온다. 그래서 정답은 4번이 된다.

21.

해석 : 미국의 군대는 역사를 거치면서 많은 적들과 싸워왔다. 이런 모든 적들이 인간이었던 것은 아니다. 군대의 가장 힘든 적들 중에는 질병을 일으키는 미세한 생물체들도 있었다. 1898년 당시 군대는 쿠바에서 스페인-미국 전쟁을 치르고 있었다. 그곳은 지내기에 좋은 곳이 아니었다. 많은 병사들이 노랗게 하기 때문이었다. 그 병은 스페인 병사들보다 더 무서운 적이었다. 어떤 조치가 취해졌어야 했고, 군대에는 마침 그 병을 해결할 적임자가 있었는데, 그는 뛰어난 내과의사인 월터 리드 소령이었다.

ⓑ 리드는 20살이 되기 전에 의학 학위를 받았다. 그러고는 입대했다. 군에서 복무하는 동안, 그는 어떻게 장티푸스가 전염되는지에 대한 실마리를 푸는 데 도움을 주었다. 파리가 그 병을 전염시켰다는 것이다.

ⓐ 그의 능력을 믿은 군대에서는 리드 소령에게 황열병을 연구하고 그 병이 어떻게 전염되는지 알아내도록 명령했다. 황열병이 감기처럼 사람을 통해서 전염이 됐는가 아니면 다른 매개체가 있었던 것인가?

ⓒ 리드는 황열병 환자들을 치료하는 위생병을 관찰했다. 그들은 그 병에 거의 걸리지 않았다. 그래서 리드는 황열병이 사람을 통해 직접 전염되지 않는다는 것을 알게 되었다. 그렇다면 다른 어떤 것이 그 질병을 옮길 수 있었을까?

정답은 모기였다. 모기는 황열병을 일으키는 바이러스는 옮겼다. 리드는 지원자들에게 실험을 했을 때 모기가 그 질병을 전염시켰다는 것을 발견했다.

이종현T의 독해 Point!

일단 리드에 대한 설명이 나온 b가 가장 먼저 나오고 그 병을 연구하는 시작이 a고 결론을 내는 c가 a 뒤에 오면 정답은 b-a-c로 2번이 된다.

UNIT 9 어휘 유형

1.

해석 : 과학적 증거에 따르면, 인간은 낯선 사람을 비롯하여 다른 사람들을 도우려는 생물학적인 욕구가 있다고 한다. 낯선 사람들에 대한 이타적인 행동은 인간만이 가진 자질이며 매우 어린 나이에도 관찰된다. 연구원들은 18개월 남짓한 아이들도 낯선 사람들을 돕기 원한다는 것을 보여주었다. 이 연구원들의 실험에 참가한 18개월 된 아이들은 낯선 사람이 바닥에 연필을 던지는 것을 보았을 때, 어느 누구도 연필을 줍지 않았다. 그러나 그 동일한 실험 참가자들이 누군가가 '실수로' 연필을 떨어뜨리는 것을 보았을 때에는, 거의 모든 아이들이 첫 10초 안에 연필을 주웠다. 연구원들은 이 아이들이 너무나도 어리기 때문에 이같은 연구결과는 당연한(→ 놀라운) 것이라고 말한다. 그들은 여전히 기저귀를 차고 있고 거의 말을 할 수 없지만, 이미 남을 돕는 행동을 보여주고 있다. 이타적인 행동이 아주 어린아이들에게도 나타날 수 있기 때문에 연구원들은 인간의 뇌가 이타적인 행동을 하도록 만들어져 있다는 가설을 세우고 있다.

이종현T의 독해 Point!
3번 선지의 다음 문장에서 아기가 어린 것과 다른 사람을 돕는 것의 관계가 but으로 연결되어 있으므로 아기들이 도움을 주는 행동을 할 수 있는건 당연한 행동이 아니라 뜻밖의 행동이라는 것을 알 수 있고 따라서 정답은 3번이 된다.

2.

해석 : 한 사람은 열띤 토론에서 토론 상대방의 성격을 비난하도록, 그들의 지능이나 합리성을 부정하도록, 그들의 이해도나 진지함 혹은 그들의 통합성까지도 전부 의심하도록 유혹받는다. 그런데, 상대방의 성격은 논리적으로 그사람이 주장하는 것 혹은 이용된 추론의 정확성의 참과 거짓과는 논리적으로 관련이 있다.(→ 없다.)

이종현T의 독해 Point!
첫 번째 문장과 but으로 연결되어 있으므로 but 뒤의 내용은 다른 상대방을 비난하는 것은 좋지 않다는 얘기가 나와야 한다. 그러려면 이런 성격은 주장의 참 거짓과는 관련이 없다고 해야하므로 정답은 4번이 된다.

3.

해석 : 몇몇 역사학자들은 역사에 대한 연구가 종교적이든 자연주의적이든지간에 단 하나의 거대한 목적이나 패턴의 존재를 밝혀줄 것이라고 믿는다, 그리고 그것은 전체 역사의 과정을 설명해줄 것이라고 믿는다. 다른 사람들은 어떤 그러한 거대한 계획의 존재를 부정하지만 역사에 대한 연구가 과거 사건의 실제 연속성을 설명해줄 법칙들을 밝혀줄 것이라고 주장하고 미래를 예측하기 위해 사용될 수 있을 것이라고 주장한다. 두 관점 모두에서, 역사학자는 과거 역사의 기록에 의해 확인되어져야 하고 설명해야만 하는 이유들을 찾는다. 그러므로, 두 관점 모두에서, 역사는 단순히 설명하는 과학이라기 보단 이론적이다, 그리고 역사학자의 일에서 가설의 역할은 사소한(→ 중요한) 걸로 여겨져야만 한다.

이종현T의 독해 Point!

이 글의 핵심적인 내용은 역사는 이론적이고 무엇인가 법칙은 있다는 얘기가 된다. 따라서 가설들의 역할은 사소한 것이 아니라 중요한 것이 되어야 하고 정답은 5번이 된다.

4.

해석 : 원인들의 사슬이 보상이 필요한 부상과 같은 사건들을 야기시킬 때, 그 부상에 가장 가까운 실제 사슬의 요소들은, 즉 가장 근접한 원인들은, 그 결과에 대한 법적인 책임을 부여받을 가능성이 가장 높다. 인과관계의 사슬에서 더 뒤쪽인 행동을 지니고 있는 사람들 그러므로 부상의 결과를 예측할 수 없었던 사람들은 여기에 더 책임을 질 가능성이 높다(→ 낮다.) 그런데 얼마나 멀리 우리는 인과관계의 사슬을 추적해서 뒤로 거슬러 올라가야하는가?

이종현T의 독해 Point!

인과관계에서 뒤쪽에 위치한 것들이므로 사건에 책임을 가능성은 낮아져야하므로 정답은 4번이 된다.

UNIT 10 연결사 유형

1.

해석 : 여행자가 전략적인 구매자가 되기는 어렵다. 구매자는 항공사와 독립(개인) 소매업자가 제공하는 다양한 여행 시간대나 티켓 가격에서 선택을 하므로 인터넷을 통해 경쟁업체들의 티켓 가격을 비교해서 잘 살펴볼 수 있다고 생각한다. 그러나 그 시스템은 겉보기처럼 투명하지 않다. 대부분의 이용자들은 항공 업계에서 고객이 아니라 항공사에게 이익이 되도록 하는 정교한 수익관리 시스템을 사용하고 있다는 것을 알지 못한다. 이러한 시스템에서 사용하는 가격 책정 알고리즘을 통해 항공사들은 이용자들의 행동을 예측할 수 있고 여행자들이 전략적인 구매를 하지 못하게 할 수도 있다. 예를 들어, 항공사들은 인터넷을 활용하여 다양한 항공운임별로 이용 가능한 좌석의 수를 끊임없이 조절할 수 있으며, 그 결과 최대 수익을 확보할 수 있다. 1977년에, 유나이티드 에어라인 한 곳에서만 1,000만 번이 넘는 운임 변경이 이루어졌으며, 오늘날에는 인터넷을 이용한 가변적 가격 정책을 항공사들이 적극적으로 활용하고 있다.

이종현T의 독해 Point!

첫 번째 빈칸 앞 얘기는 잘 비교할 수 있고 잘 볼 수 있다는 것이고 뒷 얘기는 투명하지 않다. 즉 잘 비교하기 어렵다는 것이므로 반대로 뒤집어지는 얘기가 들어가면 된다. 그리고 두 번째 빈칸은 뒤에 실제로 항공사들이 하는 전략에 대한 얘기가 나오므로 예시가 된다. 따라서 정답은 2번이 된다.

2.

해석 : 연구원들에 따르면, 잡담에는 몇 가지 이점이 있다고 한다. 정보를 교환하는 것은 건전한 관계를 형성할 수 있다. 잡담은 받아들일 수 있는 행동과 받아들일 수 없는 행동에 대한 규칙을 만들 수 있다. 잡담은 사회를 개선시킬 수 있다. 마찬가지로, 잡담은 사업계에서도 유용하다. 잡담 연구가인 프랭크 맥앤드류(Frank McAndrew) 교수는 "만일 사람들이 다른 사람들이 하는 좋은 행동들에 대해 말을 하고 있으면, 우리는 그 좋은 행동을 모방하기를 원합니다. 이것은 사람들을 사회적으로 제어하는 좋은 방법입니다."라고 주장한다. 회사가 힘든 시기를 겪을 때, 직원들의 앞날에 대한 잡담은 두려움과 불확실성을 줄일 수 있으며. 동료의식 또한 생기게 할 수 있다.

그러나 다른 사람들의 생활에 대한 부정적인 대화인 나쁜 잡담(험담)은 해로울 수 있다. 매우 실망스럽게도, 연구원들은 이런 형태의 악의(험담)에 대해서는 거의 시간을 들이지 않는다. 사람들은 몇 가지 이유로 부정적인 잡담을 한다. 사람들은 다른 사람과 친밀한 관계를 형성하기 위해 험담을 한다. 사람들은 시간을 때우기 위해서나 (당면한) 문제를 거부하기 위해 험담을 한다. 사람들은 다른 사람과의 비교를 통해 자신을 치켜세우기 위해 또는 다른 사람들을 해할 목적으로 잡담을 할지도 모른다.

이종현T의 독해 Point!

첫 번째 빈칸 뒤를 보면 in business world라고 했으므로 상황이 바뀌었기 때문에 소재가 바뀌었다. 그런데 내용은 같은 내용이므로 similarly가 된다. 그리고 두 번째 빈칸은 bad gossip으로 바뀌었으므로 대조가 된다. 따라서 정답은 4번이 된다.

3.

해석 : 물리적인 우주에 대한 우리의 이해는 지난 세기 동안 매우 깊어졌다. 양자역학과 일반 상대성 이론이라는 이론적인 도구를 통해 우리는 원자와 아원자 영역의 물리적 현상에서부터 은하계와 그 너머에서 일어나고 있는 현상들과 우주전체의 구조에 이르기까지 모두 이해할 수 있게 되었다. 이것은 기념비적인 성취이다. 은하계의 먼 가장자리에 위치한 작은 행성에 갇혀 있는 존재들이 물리적 우주의 가장 신비한 특징들을 확인하고 이해할 수 있게 된 것은 매우 고무적인 일이다. 그럼에도 불구하고, 물리학자들은 천성적으로 우주에 대한 가장 깊고도 가장 근본적인 이해가 드러났다고 느껴질 때까지는 만족하지 못할 것이다. 이것은 스티븐 호킹(Stephen Hawking)이 "신(神)의 마음"을 알기 위한 첫걸음이라고 암시해온 것이다.

이종현T의 독해 Point!

빈칸 앞은 아주 훌륭한 일이고 빈칸 뒤는 아직 만족하지 못한다는 것이므로 내용 관계가 반대가 된다. 따라서 정답은 2번이 된다.

4.

해석 : 특이한 유형의 금융거래는 수사관들에게 테러 용의자에 관한 단서를 줄 수 있다. 그러나 이런 유형에는 항상 예외가 있으며, 잠재적인 테러리스트들은 단지 수상쩍어 보이는 것을 피하기 위해 특이한 행동을 할지도 모른다. 마찬가지로, 당신이 '일반적으로' 테러리스트라고 생각하는 프로필이 항상 정확한 것은 아닐지도 모른다. 가난하고 교육을 받지 못한 사람들이 테러리스트가 될 가능성이 가장 높다고 여기지만, (실제로) 미국에서 크리스마스에 테러를 감행하려다 미수에 그쳤던 사람은 저명한 나이지리아 가문의 아들이었다

이종현T의 독해 Point!

예외에 대한 1번 예시와 2번 예시이므로 같은 내용이지만 다른 소재를 가지고 말하고 있다. 따라서 정답은 4번이 된다.

5.

해석 : 피부색이 자외선 수준에 적응한다는 이론은 일면 타당하다. 아프리카의 적도 근처에 주로 거주했던 현대 인류의 조상들의 피부색은 현대 인류보다 거무스름했는데, 왜냐하면 거무스름한 피부색이 열을 반사하는 데 보다 효과적이어서 몸을 시원하게 해주고 피부가 해로운 자외선을 받지 못하도록 해주었기 때문이다. 그러나 자외선에 적게 노출됨으로써 '햇빛 비타민'으로도 알려져 있는 비타민 D의 결핍을 초래할 수 있다. 이것이 바로 흑인들이 비타민 D 결핍으로 인한 류머티스성 관절염에 걸릴 위험이 보다 높은 주요 이유이다.

이종현T의 독해 Point!

해로운 자외선을 막아주는 긍정적인 역할이 빈칸 앞이면 그것 때문에 생기는 부정적 상황이 빈칸 뒤 이므로 역접의 연결사가 들어가면 된다. 따라서 정답은 3번이 된다.

UNIT 11 Test 1

1~2.

복제에 관한 대중매체가 과장하는 것과 관련된 가장 중요한 문제는 보통 '유전 본질론'이라 불리는 견해인, 인간은 단순히 그들의 유전자의 산물이라는 손쉬운 가정일 것이다. 텔레비전 진행자와 라디오 출연인사들은 전체 농구팀을 마이클 조던의 복제 인간으로 채우는 것이 가능할 지를 질문해왔다. 그에 대한 대답으로, 철학자, 신학자, 그리고 다른 전문가들은 비록 인간의 행동이 유전적 구성요소를 부인할 수 없이 가지고 있지만, 많은 다른 요소들, 예를 들면 자궁의 환경, 가정의 역동적 환경, 사회 배경, 식사, 그리고 다른 개인사들이 개인의 발전에 중요한 역할을 한다는 말을 지루하게 반복해왔다. 그러므로 탁월한 운동선수의 DNA로부터 복제된 사람이 스포츠에 관심을 가지지 않을 수도 있다. 더욱이, 복제 문제는 대중매체가 과학의 '발전'은 중단될 수 없음을 암시함으로써 과학과 기술 결정론의 태도를 조장하는 방식을 보여주고 있다. 두 말 할 필요 없이, 많은 과학자들이 이러한 태도를 공유하고 있으며, 너무나 자주 그들은 인간의 고통을 야기할 수도 있는 연구에 참여하는 것에 대해 도덕적 책임을 수용하기를 거부한다.

이종현T의 독해 Point!

1. 핵심소재가 매체와 복제에 관한 이야기가 된다 따라서 이 얘기가 들어간 선지가 정답이 되어야 한다. 5번 선지같은 경우는 해결책이 등장하지는 않으므로 정답은 2번이다.

2. 글의 주제를 생각하면서 접근하면 되는 문제이다. 2번의 경우는 대중매체는 복제에 대해서 복제가 모든 것을 할 수 있다고 믿고 있다는 내용이 첫 문장에 '인간은 단순히 유전자의 산물이다'라고 나와 있으므로 정답은 2번이 된다.

3~5.

카메라는 이미 전문 사진가들에 의해 멋지게 기록되어 모든 골목의 책방과 신문 가판대에서 판매되고 있는 세계의 경이로움을 기록한다는 핑계로, 우리가 보는 모든 것에 우리 자신의 흔적을 찍어 넣는 수단이다. 그러나 우리에게 완벽한 사진 도감이 무슨 소용인가? 귀국해서 우리의 친구들에게 타지마할, 콜로세움, 피사의 사탑 사진 엽서를 보여주는 것도 우리가 그 사진에 없으니 무슨 소용이겠는가? 그 어떤 사원도 그 옆에 씩 웃는 우리의 얼굴이 없다면 흥미롭지 않다. 대부분의 아마추어 사진가는 있는 그대로의 세상에 관심을 보이지 않고, 이상적으로 있어야할 세상에 관심을 갖는다. 예를 들면 당신은 진정한 모로코의 사진, 즉 매우 오랜 역사를 보여주는 장면을 원한다. 불행히도, 한 현대식 유리 건물이 그 회교 사원에 인접해 있다. 사원의 뾰족탑 뒤에는 텔레비전 안테나가 하늘 높이 솟아있다. 낙타 옆에는 상황에 안 어울리는 서양 정장을 입은 두 명의 모로코인이 사업 이야기를 하며 서있다. 그래서 나머지는 그대로 유지하면서 사진 속에 그 건물만 들어오지 않게 하기 위해, 안테나와 전선만을 잘라내기 위해, 그리고 사업가들만을 제외하기 위해, 당신은 당신의 카메라를 세우고 비틀고 옆으로 들고, 당신의 위치를 바꾼다. 그리고 이 모든 낯선 요소들이 귀중한 한 순간에 삭제되었을 때, 셔터를 눌러라. 거기에 진정한 모로코가 있다. 그것은 아마추어 사진 예술의 극치이다. 완전한 비현실이자, 있는 그대로가 아닌 세상이다.

이종현T의 독해 Point!

3. 결론이 나오고 있는데 그 결론이 좋은 듯 썼지만 좋지 않은 결론이므로 정답은 4번이다.

4. 빈칸에는 뒷 문장의 without our face를 보고 우리의 얼굴이 없다는 의미가 들어가면 되므로 정답은 3번이다. 2번 선지 내용을 보면 그 장소에 가지 않는다는 것인데 가서 찍지 않으면 의미가 없다는 내용이므로 글의 내용과 맞지는 않다.

5. 이 글의 핵심적인 내용이 아마추어 사진사들은 카메라를 가지고 보고 싶은 것들만을 본다는 내용이므로 그 핵심내용을 담은 5번이 정답이 된다.

6~8.

고객 회사의 한 상무이사가 두 명의 중간 관리자에게 팀 형성 세미나에 참가하도록 예약을 해주었다. 이 유명한 행사는 호화로운 맨해튼 호텔의 풍요 속에서 개최되었다. 그들이 참석한 시간의 기회비용 외에도, 참가비가 일인당 1,000달러 가까이 되어, 직접 비용만 2,000달러에 달했다. 그는 그 두 사람이 자기 개발의 아이디어를 몹시 원하고 잘 받아들였으며, 열심히 일하는데다 야망이 컸고, 또한 자신이 그들의 성과에 대해 얼마나 만족하고 있는지에 관해 분명한 메시지를 전달하고 싶었기 때문에 그들을 선발했다. 그가 그들에게 표를 건네 줄 때, 그들은 좋게 말해서 미적지근하다고 말할 수 있는 정도의 반응을 보였으며, 그가 그 행사 후에 그들한테서 들은 말은 그 행사가 '괜찮았다'는 정도의 말이 고작이었다. 더 자세히 조사했을 때, 그는 두 중간 관리자의 끓어오르는 분노를 발견했는데, 그것은 "우리는 회사에서 최고이며, 가장 잘 나가는 두 개의 팀을 이끌고 있다. 왜 우리를 제물로 선택하는가? 우리가 무엇을 잘못했는가?"라는 말로 해석될 수 있었다. 그러한 배은망덕을 좀처럼 잊을 수가 없는 우리 상무이사는 분노를 터뜨리고 앞으로는 덜 관대해지겠노라고 조용히 결심하게 되었다. 무엇이 잘못된 것이었을까? 그 대답의 주요한 부분은 "아무도 내게 묻지 않았다"는 것이다. 그것은 평등주의에 영합하는 문제가 아니라 상식이다. 이러한 접근은 단지 "가능하면, 의사 결정으로 영향 받는 모든 사람을 참여시켜라"라는 일반적인 원리의 특별한 사례에 불과하다. 우리는 협의가 우리가 하는 일의 구조 가운데 일부이자 혹은 그렇게 되어야 하는 시대에서 일하고 있다. 이 사례는 아무리 불공정하게 보이더라도, 단지 우리가 무언가 '좋은' 일을 하고 있다는 이유로 협의가 무시될 수 있다고 생각하는 것은 끔찍한 실수라는 것을 보여준다.

이종현T의 독해 Point!

6. 직원들이 분노한 것을 보고 덜 관대해지겠다고 결심했단 얘기가 있으므로 정답은 4번이 된다.

7. 빈칸은 주제와 관련이 깊고 이 지문의 핵심은 결정에 관련된 사람들을 가능하면 포함시켜서 생각하자는 얘기이다. 따라서 빈칸에도 결정에 관련된 모든 사람들을 포함시켜 얘기하는 것과 관련이 있어야 한다. 그에 맞는 선지는 4번이 된다.

8. 마찬가지로 모든 사람을 포함시켜서 결정하는 것은 서로 결정을 얘기하는 것이고 정답은 1번이 된다.

9~11.

문자 상징체계의 흥미로운 측면 하나는 글자 구조 내의 다양한 글자체들을 얼마만큼 신뢰성 있게 해석할 수 있느냐 하는 문제이다. 필체의 심리연구를 지칭하는 필적감정은 백년이 넘는 세월동안 행해져 왔다. 필적학을 최초로 본격 학문분야로서 정립한 사람은 프랑스의 수도원장 장 이폴리트 미숑(Jean Hippolyte Michon)이었다. 필적 감정가들의 주장에 의하면 한 개인의 필적을 주의 깊고 면밀하게 분석하면 그의 인성에 대해 중요한 정보를 밝힐 수 있다. 예컨대 필적을 분석하면 특정 직업에 그 사람이 어울리는지 여부를 알 수 있다는 것이다. 최근 몇 년간 필적 감정가들은 필적 관련 신원과 모방을 중요하게 취급하는 여러 전문 분야와 과학수사에 고용되어 일해 왔다. 필적 감정은 분명히 과학으로서 발전할 수 있는 여지가 있다. 필적의 크기, 모양, 각도, 선의 방향, 필적의 농도 같은 변수들을 원칙상 과학적으로 엄밀하게 기술할 수 있기 때문이다. 그러나 필적 감정은 의심을 받아왔는데, 이는 휘갈겨 쓴 서명 따위에 근거하여 성격을 말해 주고 운명을 예측하는 필적 감정이 시골 농산물 품평회나 해변의 휴양지에서 누린 인기 때문이었다. 필적 감정은 또한 평판이 좋거나 나쁜 사람들 위주로만 이루어져 왔다. 즉, 성공의 기초를 필적 하나에서 식별은 하지만, 이에 대한 객관적 대조군은 없다.

이종현T의 독해 Point!

9. 필적 분석에 대한 얘기가 글의 핵심소재이므로 정답은 1번이다.

10. 빈칸 앞 내용은 필적 분석이 가치가 있다는 이야기이고 빈칸 뒷 내용은 필적 분석에 관한 의심을 다루는 이야기이므로 흐름이 반대가 된다. 따라서 정답은 5번이 된다.

11. 마지막 부분에 필적 분석은 의심을 받아왔고 휴양지에서 휘갈겨쓴 글씨로 예측하고 운명을 예측하는 정도라고 했으므로 이를 받아주는 정답은 5번이 된다.

12~14.

이 나라는 지금까지 50년 이상 텔레비전과 함께 살아왔다. 예전의 예측과는 달리 우리는 타문화나 지구 생명의 기원에 대해 잘 알지 못한다. 사람들은 텔레비전 다큐멘터리가 얼마나 좋았는지 이상의 내용은 기억하지 못한다. 다큐멘터리가 다루는 주제에 관해 애초부터 얼마간 알고 있던 사람들만이 내용을 기억한다. 어쨌거나 다큐멘터리는 대부분의 사람들이 보고 싶어 하는 프로그램도 아니다. 텔레비전이 가장 인기를 끄는 것은 현재를 찬양할 때이다. 이상적인 텔레비전의 주제는 기억하지 않아도 되고 즉시 대체가능한 것들이다. 텔레비전에서 가장 중요한 것은 지금 벌어지고 있는 일과 다음에 일어날 일이다. 스포츠, 뉴스, 퀴즈프로, 경찰 드라마, 롱런하는 연속극, 시트콤 등의 프로그램들은 방영되는 동안에만 우리를 사로잡는다. 내용이 좋든 나쁘든 심야 프로는 정말 잊기 쉽다. 심야프로는 수면용이고 오락물이다. 우리의 도덕성은 자극 받지 않은 채 여전히 그대로이다. TV는 사람들이 시청하는 양에 의해 더 중성화된다. 물론 일부 프로그램은 다른 프로그램보다 훨씬 가치가 있다. 뛰어난 사람들이 텔레비전에서 일한다. 그러나 좀 더 거리를 두고 바라보면, 다시 말해서 3개월간 매일 밤 4시간 TV를 본 관점에서 보자면 개별 프로그램의 질이 지니는 가치는 교통 혼잡 때 막혀 있는 차 한 대 정도이다(그만큼 가치가 떨어진다는 뜻).

이종현T의 독해 Point!

12. 단락 나누기 문제는 소재가 바뀌는 점을 찾는 것이 중요하다. 소재가 바뀌는 점을 찾아보면 ⓑ를 기준으로 앞은 TV를 통해 정보를 얻지 못한다는 소재이고 뒤는 TV가 다루는 주된 소제와 그냥 잊기 쉬운 오락물에 대한 얘기이므로 소재가 바뀐다. 그리고 ⓔ를 기준으로 뒷 내용은 TV가 별 가치가 없다는 내용이므로 정답은 3번이 된다.

13. 이 글의 주제는 텔레비전은 볼수록 그냥 오락거리이고 어떤 것도 잘 기억 못한다는 내용이다. 따라서 정답은 5번이 된다.

14. 이 글의 핵심소재는 TV가 아무 쓸모가 없다는 것이다. 따라서 정답은 3번이 된다.

15~16.

현대 선진 사회에서는 다른 언어보다 상위에 위치하는 한 언어의 종류가 있다. 이 상위에 위치한 종은 정부와 커뮤니케이션 매체들에 의해 선택되고, 교육 기관에서 사용되고 가르쳐지며, 주된, 혹은 유일한 문자언어이다. 이 언어의 종은 사회 속에 있는 다른 모든 품종들보다 고정되어 있고, 변화에 저항하며, 다른 모든 종들을 평가하는 기준이기도 하다. 다른 사람들이 언어를 이용하는 방식을 규제하려고 애쓰는 규범 문법학자들이 몇몇 용례들을 부정확하고, 부적절하고, 심지어는 야만적이라고 비난할 때, 이들은 이러한 문자 기준에 호소한다.

이종현T의 독해 Point!

15. 이 글의 핵심소재는 기준이 되는 언어에 대한 것이므로 그 기준이 되는 언어라는 표현이 정답에 있어야 한다. 따라서 정답은 2번이 된다.

16. 이 글에선 정보를 전달하고 있는 설명문이므로 정답은 2번이 된다. 주관이 개입해서 필자가 잘난척한다는 생각이 들어 1번으로 정답이 가지 않게 조심해야 하는 문제이다.

17.

히스토리시즘(역사주의)은 모든 종류의 텍스트를 해석할 때 역사적 맥락의 중요성을 주장하는 하나의 중요한 운동이다. 이것은 사상의 많은 분야에서 오랫동안 전통적인 영향력을 행사해 왔으며 최근에 현대 문학비평분야에서 활기찬 부활을 경험하고 있다. 가장 현저한 20세기 후반의 중요한 유행사소들인 탈구조주의와 포스트모더니즘은 결국 그들이 암시하는 역사의 이미지를 통해 이해되었다. 그러나 이러한 역사적 전환은 히스토리시즘의 진부한 전통 속으로 합류해 들어가고, 현재, 히스토리시즘은 문학이론을 발전시키는 가장 최신의 방식으로서 '새로운' 모습을 보이고 싶은 유혹을 받고 있다.

히스토리시즘은 사람들이 어떻게 정치적·사회적으로 그들 스스로를 조직할 수밖에 없는지에 관한 진실을 제일(근본) 원리로부터 연역해 내는 관행에 대한 반동으로 등장하고 있다. 항상 인간의 행동을 다스리는 자연법들이 공식화되고, 문화들이 이러한 이상적인 패턴과 어느 정도로 유사한가에 의해 평가된다. <역사주의자들은 이런 전통에 반대한다.> 그들은 인간의 본성은 너무나 다양해서 그러한 법칙들이 보편적으로 적용될 수 없다고 주장하고 있다. 따라서 그들은 과학적이고 법칙에 지배되는 계몽주의적 패러다임과는 다른 사회적·문화적 다양성을 이해할 수 있는 하나의 모델을 발전시켜야 한다.

이종현T의 독해 Point!

17. ⓒ를 기준으로 앞에는 공식화된다는 얘기가 되어있고 ⓒ 뒤에는 보편적으로 적용할 수가 없다는 얘기가 나온다. 따라서 ⓒ를 기준으로 갑자기 글이 뒤집어진다는 것을 알 수 있고 정답은 3번이 된다.

18.

ⓑ 산림파괴가 현재 열대지역 전역에서 숲속의 야생동물들을 위협하고 있다. ⓓ 세계의 본래 열대우림 중 거의 절반이 지난 40년 동안 파괴되어 왔다. ⓒ 산림을 보호하려는 국제적인 노력이 이루어지고 있다. 예를 들면 코스타리카에서는 그 나라의 거의 30%가 국립공원으로 지정되었다. ⓐ그러나 많은 나라에서는 산림벌채가 빠른 속도로 계속되고 있다.

이종현T의 독해 Point!

ⓑ와 ⓒ, ⓓ가 현상에 대한 이야기고 ⓐ가 속도에 대한 이야기 이다. 따라서 먼저 ⓑ, ⓒ, ⓓ를 배열하면 ⓑ-ⓓ-ⓒ가 된다. 그리고 ⓐ는 ⓒ의 얘기가 뒤집어지는 것이므로 정답은 2번이 된다.

19.

ⓓ 후두는 우리가 흔히 성대라고 부르는 두 개의 조직 띠를 가지고 있는 연골 조직이다. ⓒ 성대는 기도(氣道)의 상부 끝에 있는 기류에 위치하고 있다. ⓑ 그 기류가 성대 사이를 통과할 때 마치 깃발이 바람에 펄럭이듯 성대가 진동하게 되어 있다. ⓐ 성대는 또한 기도를 수축시키는데, 이것은 발성에 중요한 개념이다.

이종현T의 독해 Point!

ⓒ, ⓓ는 성대의 위치에 대한 소재로 묶이고 ⓐ, ⓑ는 성대가 하는 행동과 역할에 대한 소재로 묶인다 그리고 성대라는 개념이 처음 등장한 곳이 ⓓ이므로 정답은 4번이 된다.

20.

ⓐ 고틀리브 미텔버거(Gottlieb Mittelberger)는 1740년대에 수천 명의 다른 독일인들과 함께 펜실베이니아로 이주한 루터교회 목사였다. ⓓ 식민지 주민들이 신앙에 독실하지 못하고 종교적 권위에 대한 국가의 지지가 부족한 것에 실망한 그는 몇 년 뒤 고향으로 돌아갔다. ⓑ 1750년에 독일에서 출간된 『미국으로의 여행(Journey to America)』이라는 책에서 그는 비판적인 눈으로 미국을 관찰했다. ⓒ 그는 독자들에게 이주의 어려움, 약정된 강제노역의 위험, 경쟁사회에서의 삶의 위험성 등을 경고했다.

이종현T의 독해 Point!

미텔버거라는 인물에 대한 소재로 ⓐ, ⓓ가 묶이고 그 사람이 쓴 책에 대한 이야기로 ⓑ, ⓒ가 묶인다. 인물 소개가 먼저이므로 정답은 3번이 된다.

UNIT 12 Test2

1~2.

아동기 초기에 우리는 세상과 접하는 과정에서 우리를 돌보는 이들이 정성을 다해 중재자로 나서서 때때로 직접 가리키면서 말하는 실물지시라는 방법으로 생애 최초의 단어들의 의미를 알게 된다. 그러나 일단 어떤 언어를 사용하기 시작하면, 다른 사람이 해주는 설명을 듣거나 단어들이 구성되어 있는 구조로부터 추론을 해서, 대부분의 단어들의 의미를 언어 그 자체를 통해 배운다. 언어연구의 초점 중 하나는 어떤 언어 안에서 표현의 느낌들 사이의 의미관계들을 체계적으로 기술하는 것이다. 그 목적은 어느 표현들이 어느 다른 표현들과 의미적으로 같은지 또는 그것들과 대조를 이루는지를 그 언어에 능숙한 사람들의 언어지식에 따라 다양한 방식으로 경제적으로 통찰력 있게 진술하는 것이다.

이종현T의 독해 Point!

1. 이 지문의 핵심소재는 언어들 간의 의미 관계를 파악할 수 있다는 얘기이므로 이 얘기가 들어간 3번이 정답이 된다.

2. 위 글에서 말하길 언어를 시작하면서 언어들 간의 관계를 파악한다는 얘기가 But 뒤에 나와 있으므로 빈칸에도 언어를 할 수 있는 같은 의미가 될만한 말이 들어가야 한다. 그렇게 봤을 때 정답이 1번과 2번이 될만한데 이 중 capable은 of라는 전치사와 결합하므로 in과 결합할 수 있는 2번이 정답이 된다.

3~4.

문학연구에서 상식은 결코 제자리를 벗어나지 않는다. 어떤 교수가 전에 한 시간 수업의 대부분 동안 오든(W. H. Auden)의 『시모음집(Collected Poems)』의 내용의 배열에 관해 열광적으로 강의했다. 교수는 오든이 주제의 지속정의 대가이며 시들을 서로를 가장 잘 보완해 주는 순서로 탁월하게 배치했다고 주장했다. 수업 시간이 거의 끝나갈 무렵 한 학생이 수줍게 손을 들며 오든이 그 책속의 시들을 주제별이 아니라 각 시의 첫 번째 단어에 따라 알파벳순으로 배열했다고 지적했을 때, (학생들 사이에서) 들리지는 않지만 풋 하는 소리가 터져 나오며, 그의 이론들이 망쳐졌다. 그 교수는 입이 떡 벌어지며 말했다. "왜 더 빨리 말하지 않았지?" 그 학생은 사죄를 구하며 말했다. "저, 저는 제 말이 너무 정상적으로(상식적으로) 들릴 것으로 걱정했어요."

이종현T의 독해 Point!

3. 빈칸이 세 개인 문제이므로 빈칸 하나에 중심을 두고 가면 된다. 여기선 두 번째 빈칸에 중심을 두면 좋고. 두 번째 빈칸의 앞에는 교수님이 순서에 대해 극찬을 한 것이고 두 번째 빈칸 뒤로는

학생이 이에 반박해서 그냥 알파벳 순이라고 반박하고 있으므로 둘의 관계는 반대가 되고 교수의 이론은 뒤집힌다는 것을 알 수 있다. 따라서 정답은 1번이 된다.

4. 이 글의 핵심소재는 common sense이고 이 common sense는 옳다는 얘기이다. 이 관점으로 봤을 때 1, 3, 4번이 절대 정답이 되기가 어렵고 old ideas가 그나마 common sense를 받아줄만하므로 정답은 2번이 된다.

5.

소고기와 닭고기가 많은 뉴멕시코 지역의 요리법에 등장하지만, 매사추세츠는 바다에서 가깝기 때문에 생선이 아주 흔하다. 뉴잉글랜드는 크램 차우더, 랍스터, 대구, 가리비, 생선튀김으로 유명하다. 영국의 허브와 양념이 뉴잉글랜드 지역에서 양념으로 사용된다. 따라서 이 지역의 음식은 맵고 자극적인 뉴멕시코 지역 음식에 익숙한 사람들에게는 다소 밍밍하게 느껴질 수 있다. 미국의 각각 지역들은 특이하다. 루지아나는 프랑스의 영향을 받았다. 많은 독일인들이 중서부 지방에 모여 살고 있다. 미국을 이리저리 여행하다보면 여행객들은 다양한 장소를 보고 다양한 풍경을 볼 수 있는 기회는 물론 다양한 음식도 맛볼 수 있는 기회를 가질 수 있다.

이종현T의 독해 Point!

뉴잉글랜드에서 소고기가 어떤지에 대한 이야기는 나와있지 않으므로 정답은 3번이 된다.

6.

바이오연료 산업에 규제가 가해져야 한다. 열대가 좀 더 많은 햇빛과 비와 경작 가능한 땅이 있다는 이유로 지구의 북쪽 위도에 살고 있는 나라들이 과소비의 책임을 남쪽으로 전가해서는 안 된다. 바이오연료가 숲 친화적이고 음식 친화적이려면, 곡물과 수수와 팜오일 산업들이 규제되어야 할 필요가 있다. 그것도 적지 않은 규모로 말이다. 바이오 연료를 위해 생물들을 심는 땅을 제한하는 강력하고 집행 가능한 기준들이 당장 필요하다. 시장의 힘이 한 기업에 집중되는 것을 막는 트러스트 규제법만큼이나 강력한 법이 필요하다. 바이오연료가 지속 가능한 농촌 발전을 위한 계획에서 중심적인 것이 아니라 보완적인 것일 때만 시골 지역의 지속 가능한 혜택은 가능할 것이다. 바이오연료에 대한 전 세계적인 확산의 일시적 중단이 필요하다. 그래서 그 동안 규제의 틀을 만들고 보호의 틀을 만들고 바이오연료 전환에 대한 대안을 만들어야 한다. 우리는 음식과 연료의 주권으로 더 나은 전환을 이루기 위한 시간이 필요하다.

이종현T의 독해 Point!

독점 금지법은 기업의 시작 집중도를 촉진시키기 위해가 아니라 약화시키기 위해 있는 것이므로 정답은 1번이 된다.

7~9.

그렇다면 진리란 무엇인가? 유동적인 한 무리의 은유, 환유, 의인화들이다. 간단히 말해서, 시적·수사학적으로 고양되고 전용되고 장식되어 이를 오랫동안 사용한 민속에게는 확고하고, 표준적이며 구속력이 있는 것으로 여겨지는 인간적 관계의 총체이다. 진리는 환상이다. 진리들은 마멸되어 감각적 힘을 잃어버린 은유들이라는 사실을 망각해 버린 그런 환상들이며, 문양이 사라질 정도로 표면이 닳아버려 더 이상 동전이라기보다는 그저 쇠붙이로만 여겨지는 그런 동전들이다. 오직 저 원시적 비유 세계의 망각을 통해서만, 인간적 환상의 근원적 능력으로부터 본래 뜨거운 액체의 형태로 뿜어 나오는 영상들 덩어리가 돌처럼 굳어지고 경직됨으로써만, 이 태양과 이 창문과 이 책상이 진리 자체라는 정복될 수 없는 믿음을 통해서만, 간단히 말해서 인간이 자기 자신이 예술적으로 창조하는 주체라는 것을 망각함으로써만, 그는 어느 정도 평온과 안정과 일관성을 가지고 살아간다.

이종현T의 독해 Point!

7. 첫 부분에 오랫동안 사용한 민족에게는 확고하고, 표준적이며, 구속력이 있다고 했고 그게 굳어짐으로써만 평온하게 살 수 있다고 했으므로 진리는 굳어지는 것이라는 얘기가 들어간 2번이 정답이 된다.

8. 이 글의 핵심소재는 Truth이므로 Truth가 들어간 내용을 찾으면 되는데, 이 글에서 Truth에 대한 해결책을 필자가 제시하고 있으므로 정답은 1번이 아닌 4번이 된다.

9. fiery liquid라는 액체의 표현이 있으므로 액체가 굳어진다는 표현이 될 수 있는 1번이 정답이 된다.

10~12.

역사는 현재의 사건들을 설명하는 것을 돕기 때문에 필요하다. 문화가 어떻게 흥하고, 어떻게 망하는가? 역사는 우리에게 답을 주지 않을 것이지만 그러나 역사는 우리의 문제와 오늘날 세상에서 작용하고 있는 힘들의 이해에 초점을 맞추는 것을 분명히 도울 것이다. 물론 역사가 쉽게 조작된다는 사실이 실재 발생한 사건을 우리들이 아는 것을 훨씬 더 중요하게 만들지라도, 역사는 쉽게 조작된다. 우리는 지도자들과 그리고 미디어의 현혹을 알아내기 위해 역사의 지식을 필요로 한다. 유권자와 시민으로서, 우리는 이러한 위험한 왜곡을 꿰뚫어 볼 수 있어야 한다. 뿐만 아니라, 역사는 흥미가 있고 — 혹은 흥미가 있어야 한다. 세부 사항이 매혹적인 것처럼, 원인과 결과의 연쇄관계도 매혹적이다. 역사에 관한 훈련을 받지 못한 많은 교사들은 이것을 회피하면서 자연적으로 수세적인 태도를 취하며, 자신들의 과목이 학생들을 지루하게 할지 모른다고 두려워한다. 나는 역사가들이나, 역사교사들이 도덕적인 역할을 갖고 있다고는 결코 주장하지 않을 것이다. 그들의 주된 의무는 시대의 정신을 이해하고 그 이해를 전해주는 것이다. 그들은 도덕적인 효과를 위해 역사를 단순화시켜도 안 된다. 역사는 도덕적인 사례와 도덕적인 딜레마의 상상할 수 있는 가장 풍부한 원천을 제공하며, 그 자체가 위대한 소설의 본질, 위대한 드라마, 그리고 삶 자체의 원천이 된다. 역사에 대한 이해가 없다면 우리는 정치적으로, 문화적으로, 그리고 사회적으로 빈곤하게 된다.

이종현T의 독해 Point!

10. 이 글은 과거의 사건들의 도덕을 교훈으로 도덕적인 딜레마를 해결할 수 있는 방법을 찾을 수 있다는 얘기의 글이므로 과거 사건들의 도덕성들이 열어진다고 하는 2번이 정답이 된다.

11. 선생님들은 역사에 관한 훈련을 받지 못한 것과 비슷한 얘기가 들어가야 하므로 정답은 4번이 된다.

12. 핵심 소재가 역사이므로 역사이고 역사에 대해 긍정적인 글이다. 따라서 정답은 역사를 통해 알 수 있다는 3번이 정답이 된다.

13~15.

마카리(Makari)의 대단히 매력적인 이야기는 르네 데카르트(Rene Descartes)에게서 시작된다. 그리스 칠학이 그리스도교와 통합된 이후, 영혼은 '자연, 인간 그리고 하느님 사이를 통합하는 연결고리'로 간주되어왔다고 마카리는 쓰고 있다. 그러나 17세기에 이미, 그리스도교는 위기에 처해 있었고, 많은 사람들은 무형적인 영혼의 개념을 물질로 이루어진 것으로 점점 더 이해되고 있던 기계적 세계와 조화시키기가 어렵다고 여기게 되었다. 데카르트는 영혼의 개념을 '사고하는 존재'로 좁힘으로써 의심 많은 박물학자들의 요구를 충족시키고자 했지만 그것은 육체와는 분리된 것이었다. 그 프랑스의 철학자는 그리하여 불멸의 영혼에 대한 그리스도교 신앙에 새로운 생명력을 불어넣었다. 전체 범위의 반대 극단(데카르트와 정반대 쪽)에 토머스 홉스(Thomas Hobbes)가 있었는데, 그는 '비물질적 실체'같은 것은 없다고 생각했다. 영혼에 대한 그의 견해에 따르면, 영혼은 합리적이고 신을 닮은 어떤 것이라기보다는 '물질적이고, 질병에 걸리고, 오류를 범하기 쉬운' 존재였다. '사고하는 존재'의 본성에 대한 이처럼 본질적으로 다른 견해들은 엄청나게 큰 내포적 의미들을 가질 운명이었다. 그리고 그 견해들은 마카리의 담화가 단지 하나의 지적 운동(저술행위) 이상의 것으로서의 중요성을 지나고 있음을 보여줄 운명이었다. 인간은 불가피하게 갈등을 낳을 수밖에 없는 동물적 감정에 지배된다고 홉스가 결론을 내린 이후, 그가 제안한 해결책은 권력을 절대군주에게 넘겨주자는 것이었다.

이종현T의 독해 Point!

13. 이 글은 마카리가 현대 철학에 대해 쓰는 글이고 뒤에 나오는 홉스를 더 중점적으로 쓴 글이다. 따라서 현대철학은 종교와는 반대되는 개념의 철학이므로 세속적인 철학이라고 할 수 있고 정답은 2번이 된다.

14. 홉스와 데카르트가 서로 다르다는 얘기만 찾아주면 된다 정답은 3번이 된다.

15. 빈칸은 문장을 보충해줄만한 말이 들어가면 된다. 따라서 정답은 4번이다.

16~19.

문화의 장(場)을 기존에 이미 확립한 보편성 개념에 대한 확고한 믿음을 보여주는 이런저런 증거를 찾기 위해 들어가 볼 수 있는 장(場)으로 떠올리는 것은 거의 이치에 맞지 않다. 만약 누군가가 세계시민의 예를 찾기 위해 문화의 다양한 영역 속으로 들어간다면, 그는 그 다양한 사례들로부터 똑같은 교훈, 똑같은 보편적 의미들을 골라 모을 것이다. 그러나 문화와 보편적인 것들과의 관계를 어떤 예와 그것이 지지한다고 말해지는 도덕적 언명 간의 관계라고 해석하는 것이 적절한가? 그런 경우에, 그 예들은 보편적인 것들에 종속된 것이고, 따라서 그것들은 모두 똑같은 방식으로 그 보편적인 것들을 나타낼 것이다. 그러나 그 보편적인 것들 가운데 어떤 것들이 제시되고 있고, 그것들은 어떤 것들을 배제한 토대 위에 있는지, 그리고 그렇게 배제된 것들이 보편적인 것들의 영역 속으로 들어올 수 있으려면 보편성에 대한 우리의 사고가 어떻게 근본적으로 변해야 하는지를 이해하기 위해 다양한 문화적 예들 간의 문화적 번역(변환)을 낳게 할 방법들을 찾을 경우에야 비로소 보편적인 것들에 대한 분명한 미래적 표현이 가능하다. 보편적인 것들에 관한 주장들이 상충할 때, 논쟁의 대상이 되는 문화적 순간들이 기성의 보편성을 예시하는 것이라고는 간주하지 말아야 할 것 같다. 그러한 주장은 보편성에 대한 지속적인 문화적 표현의 일부이고, 그러한 주장을 해독하는 방법을 배우는 복잡한 과정은 우리들 중 그 누구도 문화적 번역의 어려운 과정을 벗어나 해낼 수 있는 것이 아니다. 이러한 번역은 모든 문화적 사례들을 전제된 보편성으로 환원시켜버리는 쉬운 번역이 아닐 것이고, 서로 어떤 소통도 불가능한 급진적인 개별주의들을 열거하는 것도 아닐 것이다.

이종현T의 독해 Point!

16. abiding이 영속적인, 지속적인 이란 뜻이므로 정답은 확고한 이라는 1번이 된다.

17. 여기서 핵심은 보편성이라는건 문화적 해석을 통해 발생한다는 것이고 문화적 해석은 다양하다는 것이어서 제외된 것들이 계속 들어가면서 바뀔 수 있다는 얘기이다. 따라서 보편성이라는 것이 분화적 해석을 통해서만 될 수 있다고 하는 2번이 정답이 된다.

18. 보편성이라는 것은 계속 변하는 것이라는 얘기를 찾아주면 된다. 따라서 정답은 2번이 된다.

19. 첫 번째 빈칸에는 앞 문장과 이어질 대 같은 교훈, 즉 보편성을 찾는다의 find같은 말이 필요하고 두 번째 빈칸에는 미리 정해진이라는 presupposed같은 말이 필요하므로 정답은 1번이 된다.

UNIT 13 Test3

1~4.

성역할은 변하지 않는 안정된 정체성으로 해석되어서는 안 된다. 오히려 성은 '행동의 양식화된 반복'을 통해 외부 공간에서 시행되면서, 시간 경과에 따라 희미하게 형성되는 정체성이다. 성의 효과는 신체의 양식화를 통해 만들어지고, 그렇기 때문에 다양한 신체의 제스처, 움직임, 스타일이 영속적인 성별화된 자아라는 환상을 형성하는 일상적인 방법이라고 이해되어야 한다. 이러한 공식화는 성의 개념을 실체적인 정체성 모델이라는 근거에서 하나의 확립된 사회적 일시성으로서의 성의 개념을 요구하는 정체성 모델이라는 근거로 옮겨 놓는다. 의미심장하게도, 성이 내면적으로는 계속되지 않는 행동에 의해 시행된다면, 실체의 외양은 정확히, 행위자 자신을 포함한, 일상적인 사회의 구성원들이 믿고 그렇게 믿는 방식으로 행하게 되는 수행적 성취물인 하나의 구성된 정체성이다. 성은 또한 완전히 내면화될 수 없는 규범이다. "내면적인 것"이라는 것은 표면적인 의미이고 성 규범은 결국 유령 같은 것이고 구현하기가 불가능하다. 만약 성 정체성의 근거가 시간에 따른 행동의 양식화된 반복이고, 일견 완벽해 보이는 정체성이 아니라면, "근거"라는 공간적인 은유의 표현은 제자리를 잃고 밀려나고 양식화된 형태, 실제로는 시간의 성별화된 유형화로서 나타내어지게 될 것이다. 그러면 영속적인 성별화된 자아는 정체성의 실체적 근거라는 이상에 가까워지려 하지만, 이 "근거라는 것"의 일시적이고 우연한 근거 없음을, 가끔 불연속적으로, 보여주는 반복된 행동에 의해 구조화되는 것으로 드러날 것이다. 성별 변환의 가능성은 정확히 말해 그런 행동들 사이의 자의적 관계에서 발견될 수 있다.

이종현T의 독해 Point!

1. 이 글의 핵심은 성별은 딱 정해진 것이 아니라는 것이다. 그와 관련한 답들이 중요하다. 지금 첫 번째 빈칸은 뒤에 rather가 있으므로, 빈칸에는 rather 뒷 문장과 반대가 될만한게 와있어야 한다. 따라서 정답은 성별은 안정된 정체성으로 해석되면 안된다는 3번이 정답이 된다.

2. 첫 번째 빈칸이 핵심이다. 마찬가지로 성별이 하나로 딱 정해진 것이 아니라는 얘기를 찾아야 한다. 따라서 정답은 사회적인 일시성이라는 얘기가 첫 번째 빈칸에 들어간 4번이 된다.

3. 뒤의 impossible to embody를 받아줄 만한 표현이 빈칸에 들어가야 한다. 따라서 정답은 2번이 된다.

4. 추론할 수 없는 문제이므로 주제와 정반대가 되는 것을 찾아보면 된다. 주제가 성별은 딱 정해진 것은 아니라고 했으므로 성별의 개념이 딱 정해졌다는 의미가 될만한 선지를 찾아보면 정답은 1번이 된다.

5~7.

많은 초기 실험가들은 후천적인 지식에 의존하지 않고, 타고난 정신적 능력을 본질적으로 측정할 수 있는 테스트를 고안했다고 믿었다. 이처럼 그들은, 이와 같은 테스트에 대한 개인들의 점수가 환경 속에 존재하는 평범한 그 어떤 차이들에 의해서 영향 받지 않을 것이라고 생각했다. 그러나 다양한 연구들과 실험들은, 가족 환경과 학교교육의 차이 등과 같은 요소들이, 개인들이 표준적인 지능 테스트에서 얻는 점수에 중대한 영향을 미친다는 합리적인 의심 너머까지를 설명해주고 있다. 예를 들어, 일란성 쌍둥이가 어렸을 때 헤어져서 서로 다른 가정에서 키워진다면, 우월한 사회적, 경제적, 교육적 지위에 있는 부모들에 의해서 키워진 쌍둥이는 지능 테스트에서 다른 쌍둥이보다 항상 더 좋은 점수를 얻는다. 그리고 때로 그 차이는 상당이 크게 나기도 한다.

또 다른 예는 고등학교에 들어가고 나서 30년이 지난 후에 동일한 테스트를 본 사람들이, 그 기간 동안 그들이 받는 교육의 정도와 직접 관련이 있는 점수를 얻게 된다는 것이다. 그러나 지능 테스트의 무오류성이라는 갑옷에 나 있는 또 다른 틈은, 여러 선생님들에게 특정 학생들이 더 재능이 있다는 사실을 성공적으로 확신시켜 준 하버드대의 로버트 로젠탈(Robert Rosenthal)과 샌프란시스코에 있는 초등학교 교장 르노 제이콥슨(L enore Jacobsen)으로부터 나온다. 연구가 발표된 '교실의 피그말리온'에 따르면, 무작위적으로 선택된 학생들이 그들의 급우들을 추월했고 높은 수준의 성취도를 보여주었다. 이들 보다 더 똑똑한 학생들은, 학기 초와 학기 말에 실시된 성취테스트에서 평균 12.22포인트 더 높은 점수를 얻었다. 그리고 이는 그들 급우들이 보인 8.42 포인트의 성적 향상과 비교된다. 이 두 집단 사이에 존재하는 유일한 차이는 그들의 학습요구에 대해 교사들이 어떻게 반응하는가의 정도이다.

이종현T의 독해 Point!

5. Intelligence Test는 후천적인 요소에 영향을 받을 수 밖에 없다는 문제를 제기하고 있는 글이므로 정답은 2번이 된다. 또는 Intelligence test에 대한 통념을 반박하는 글이므로 2번이라고 볼 수도 있다.

6. 첫 번째 빈칸이 핵심이고 acquired의 반대가 들어간다고 생각하면 된다. 후천적인의 반댓말이고 선천적인 이라는 말이 들어가 있는 2번이 정답이 된다.

7. 여기서 핵심은 타고난 지식에 상관없이 후천적인 요소에 많은 영향을 받는다는 얘기가 된다. 따라서 학생들도 지식에 따라서가 아니라 누구든 후천적인 요소에 많은 영향을 받을 수 있다는 얘기가 들어가야하고 아무나 라는 의미가 빈칸에 필요하다. 따라서 정답은 4번이 된다.

8.

아이스킬로스(Aeschylus, 그리스 비극시인)가 쓴『오레스테이아(Oresteia, 3부작으로 구성된 비극작품)』의 결말 부분에서, 등장인물들의 고대세계에 두 가지 변화가 일어난다. 그 유명한 변화에서, 아테네 여신은 끝없이 반복되는 것으로 보이는 피의 복수를 대체하고 끝내기 위해 법 제도를 도입한다. 이성에 바탕을 둔 주장을 하고 증거에 대한 평가를 내리는 절차가 확립돼 있고, 독립적인 제 삼자인 재판관, 그리고 아테네 시민들로 구성된 배심원을 갖춘 법원을 설립함으로써, 그녀는 살인죄는 고대의 복수의 여신들인 Furies에 의해서가 아니라 법에 의해 해결될 것이라고 선언한다. 그러나 그 복수의 여신들이 그냥 퇴출된 것은 아니다. <대신에, 아테네 여신은 그들이 그 동일한 법률제도와 아테네시의 미래의 안정을 위해 중요하다는 것을 인식하고서 그들에게 대지 아래(지하세계)의 명예로운 자리를 제공하면서 그들을 설득해서 시에 동참하게 한다.> 전형적으로 아테네 여신의 이러한 조치는 법률제도가 어두운 보복성 감정들을 통합하고 존중해야 한다는 것을 인정한 것으로 이해된다. 따라서 그리스 문명학자인 휴 로이드-존스(Hugh Lloyd-Jones)는 아테네 여신은 복수의 여신들의 특권들을 없애길 원하기는커녕 그것들을 보존하고 싶은 것이라고 결론을 내리고 있다.

이종현T의 독해 Point!

8. 제시문에 Instead가 들어가 있다. 따라서 앞에는 부정문이 필요하다. 정답은 3번이 된다.

9.

12월이 왔다. 가게 앞은 크리스마스 장식들로 꾸며지고, 추위가 시작되며, 또 한 해가 저물어간다. 고대 로마인들이 그들의 첫 번째 달력을 확립한 이래로 , 12월은 한해의 끝과 겨울의 시작을 나타내 왔다. 어원에서 알 수 있듯이 , December는 '10'을 의미하는 라틴어 어근 decem - 으로부터 만들어졌다. 하지만 December는 12번째 달이다. Ⓑ 숫자가 어색하게 어긋난 것은 September, October, November도 마찬가지인데, 이들은 각각 '7,' '8,' '9'를 의미하지만, 각각 9번째, 10번째 , 11번째 달이다. Ⓐ 이렇게 된 이유는 고대 로마의 달력은 1년이 열 달로 이루어져 있었고, 1년의 시작이 March였기 때문이다. 늦어도 기원전 45년에 율리우스력이 제정되기 이전 이었지만 결국 January와 February가 1년의 끝인 December 다음에 추가 되었다. Ⓒ (그 후 기원전 45년 율리우스력 제정으로) January와 February 는 한 해가 시작되는 곳에 나타나게 되었고, 원래 있던 달들을 두 달씩 뒤로 밀어냈으며, 이름은 처음에 정해진 그대로 두었다.

이종현T의 독해 Point!

9. A에서 January와 February 얘기가 시작되고 C도 그에 관한 얘기이므로 A-C는 무조건 묶여야 한다. 그 상태에서 (B)는 제시문과 같은 소재이므로 A 앞에 오면 된다. 따라서 정답은 3번이 된다.

10~12.

서방은 지하드 테러와의 싸움에서 승리하고 있다고 생각했다. 몇 개월 전에 버락 오바마 대통령은 알카에다가 "패배의 길 위에" 있다고 선언하였다. 그는 생존한 알카에다 구성원들이 서방에 대한 공격을 획책하는 것 보다는 자신들의 안위에 더 관심을 갖고 있다고 말했다. 그는 미래의 테러 공격은 1990년대의 공격들과 유사해서, 국제적인 테러보다는 국지적인 테러의 성격을 띨 것이며, "쉬운 목표물"에 초점이 맞춰질 것이라고 주장했다. 그가 전반적으로 말하고자 한 것은 이제 조지부시가 이끈 세계 테러리즘과의 전쟁을 축소시키기 시작할 때라는 것이었다. 오바마는 알카에다 소말리아 지부인 샤바브가 자행한 나이로비의 웨스트케이트 쇼핑몰에 대한 공격이 바로 자신이 말하고 있는 종류의 테러, 즉 치명적이고 충격적이지만, 미국으로부터 멀리 떨어진 곳에서 이뤄진 테러라고 주장할지도 모른다. 그러나 불편한 진실은 지난 18개월간 알카에다는 무자비한 타격과 패배를 겪었음에도 불구하고, 알카에다와 그 지하드 동맹군들은 비범하게 재기를 했다는 사실이다. 현재 그 테러 조직은 25년의 역사상 그 어느 시기보다도 더 많은 영토를 지배하고 있으며 더 많은 전사를 모집하고 있다.

이종현T의 독해 Point!

10. 이 글의 핵심은 마지막에 새로운 테러를 조직하고 있다는 얘기이므로 정답은 5번이 된다.

11. 이 글의 핵심은 아직 테러가 끝난 것이 아니니 안심하면 안된다는 이야기이므로 정답은 3번이 된다.

12. 테러 조직은 이전과 비슷한 테러가 아닌 새로운 테러를 준비하고 있다고 되어 있으므로 과거와 비슷한 테러를 준비하고 있다고 하는 4번이 정답이 된다.

13~15.

대부분의 나라에서, 유족이 된 배우자나 동거인들은 사망자의 공적연금의 일부, 보통은 절반만을 기대할 수 있는데 그것도 부양자녀가 있거나 당사자가 은퇴 연령에 가까워야 한다는 조건들이 종종 붙어 나온다. 브라질의 경우, 유족은 나이와 상관없이 남은 생애 동안 거의 전액의 연금을 받는다. 사망자가 아직 은퇴하지 않았다 할지라도 연금은 즉시 시작된다. 그 결과 브라질은 다른 나라에서 유례를 찾아보기 힘든 수준인 GDP 의 3%를 유족들의 연금에 쓰고 있다. 부유한 OECD국가들은 평균적으로 1% 미만을 유족연금에 지출하고 있다.

연금가입자도 상당히 잘 살 수 있다. 15년 동안 연금을 들기만 하면, 남성은 65세에 여성은 60세에 퇴직하여 상한선까지 연금을 전액 지급 받을 수 있다. 최근에 고용된 경우를 제외하면 모든 공무원들은 상한선 없이 연금 전액을 지급받으며 은퇴할 수 있다. 가난한 가정의 65세 이상 남성과 60세 이상의 여성은, 비록 연금을 부어오지 않았다 할지라도, 현재 678 레알인 최저 임금에 상응하는 연금을 매달 받는다. 가난하든, 그렇지 않든, 농촌의 노동자들은 다섯 살 더 일찍 동일한 특권을 누린다. 조기 은퇴에 대한 조건은 특히 관대하다. 연금 제도가 국가를 거의 파산시켰던 그리스인들은 평균 61세까지 일을 한다. 브라질 사람은 평균적으로 54세에 최종 급여의 70%에 해당하는 연금을 받는다.

이종현T의 독해 Point!

13. 마지막 문장에서 그리스의 안좋은 사례보다 더 심하다는 문장이 있으므로 정답은 2번이 된다.

14. 15년만 일하면 받을 수 있다고 중간 부분에 있으므로 정답은 3번이 된다.

15. cap이 한도라는 뜻이 있으므로 정답은 4번이 된다.

16~18.

암 유전학자 보겔스타인(Vogelstein)과 응용수학자 크리스티안 토마세티(Cristrian Tomasetti)는 연구 논문에서 암의 발병을 설명할 수 있는 수학적 공식을 발표했는데, 그 원리는 다음과 같다. 어떤 장기 속에 있는 세포의 숫자를 헤아린 후에, 그 중에서 오래 된 줄기세포가 몇 퍼센트인지를 확인하고, 그 줄기세포가 몇 번 분열하는가를 측정하는 것이다. 분열이 일어날 때마다, 딸세포에서 암을 유발하는 돌연변이가 발생할 위험이 있다. 그래서 토마세티와 보겔스타인은 줄기세포 분열이 가장 많은 횟수로 일어나는 조직이 암에 가장 취약하다고 판단했다. <암이 무작위적으로 발생하는 면은 놀라울 정도지만, 현장의 과학자들 또한 긍정적인 측면을 발견하고 있다.> 그 숫자를 계산해서 그것을 실제 암 관련 통계자료와 비교한 후에, 토마세티는 이 이론을 통해 모든 암의 2/3를 설명할 수 있다고 결론을 내렸다.

"진화의 수학을 이용하면, 그 질병을 명확하게 이해할 수 있습니다. 그것은 분열해야 할 필요가 있는 세포를 가진 동물이 가진 근원적인 위험입니다." 라고 노웍(Nowak)은 말한다. 노웍은 토마세티와 보걸스타인과 함께 공동연구를 해왔다. 이런 생각은 보겔스타인의 연구실에서 가졌던 두 사람의 주간 아이디어 회합에서 떠올랐다. 그들은 얼마나 많은 암이 환경적인 요인들에 의해 발병하고, 얼마나 많은 암이 유전적인 요인들에 의해 발병하는가라는 오래된 질문으로 돌아갔다. 그 문제를 해결하기 위해서 토마세티는 "우선 먼저 어느 만큼이 운에 의한 것인지를 이해하고, 그 만큼을 전체 정황에서 빼야겠다."라고 판단했다.

토마세티에 따르면, "우연"이라는 것은 유해한 유전자 혹은 흡연이나 방사능 노출과 같은 환경적인 요인들의 영향은 배제한 가운데, 매번의 세포분열이 나타내는 확률을 의미했다. 그가 줄기세포에 가장 큰 관심을 가졌던 이유는 줄기세포는 계속 지속되기 때문인데, 줄기세포가 계속 지속된다는 것은 줄기세포에서의 돌연변이가 보다 빨리 죽는 세포에서의 돌연변이보다 문제를 유발할 가능성이 더 크다는 뜻이다. 토마세타는 논문들을 검색해서 각각의 세포조직 안에 있는 줄기세포 "구획"의 크기와 같이 그가 필요로 하던 수치를 찾았다. 31개의 서로 다른 장기 안에서 평생 동안의 줄기세포 분열 횟수를 평생 동안의 암 발병 위험에 견주어 계산해보니 상관관계가 밝혀졌다. 세포분열의 횟수가 증가할수록, 암 발병의 위험도 증가했던 것이다.

예를 들어, 대장암은 소장(小陽)에서 처음 뻗어나가는 부분인 십이지장의 암보다 훨씬 더 빈번하게 발생한다. 이것은 장(腸) 전체를 위험하게 하는 돌연변이 유전자를 갖고 있는 사람들에게조차 사실이다. 토마세티는 평생 동안 십이지장에서 약 번의 줄기세포 분열이 일어나는 데 반해, 대장에서는 줄기세포 분열횟수가 번이라는 사실을 발견했다. 이와는 대조적으로, 쥐의 경우에는 대장에서보다 소장에서 줄기세포의 분열이 더 많이 발생하고, 그리고 암도 더 많이 발생한다. 돌연변이와 암의 관계가 반드시 직접적이라고 할 수는 없다. "암은 단순히 돌연변이가 일어나느냐 아니냐의 문제가 아닐지도 모릅니다."라고 장기간 암을 연구해 온 브루스 폰더(Bruce Ponder)는 말한다.

이종현T의 독해 Point!

16. (B) 혼자서 긍정적인 면에 대해 이야기하고 있으므로 정답은 2번이 된다.

17. 수명이 긴 세포들이 암을 더 잘 유발시킨다고 했으므로 반대로 쓴 3번이 정답이다.

18. 위 글은 첫 번째 문장에서 수학적 공식을 발견했다고 했으므로 수학적 공식으로 암이 어떻게 발생하는지를 말하는 글이다. 따라서 정답은 1번이 된다.

19~20.

어떤 베스트셀러 책은 "더 나은 사람이 되기 위한 일곱 가지 방법"을 제시한다. 어느 라디오 광고에서는 약간의 알약을 먹기만 해도 30일이 채 되지 않아 희열을 맛볼 수 있을 것이라고 약속한다. 어떤 TV 광고는 만약 당신이 우리의 운동 장비를 구입한다면 당신이 항상 원해왔던 몸을 갖게 될 것이라고 보장한다. 오늘날의 사회에서, 우리는 더 나은 우리를 만들기 위한 최신 기법들의 공세를 끊임없이 받고 있는데, 어떤 이들은 이러한 집중은 건강에 해롭다고 생각한다. 더 나은 접근법은 사람들이 인격을 도야하는 것을 돕는 것이다. 인격을 도야한다는 것은 그 사람의 장점을 취하여 그것을 키워주는 것과 관련 있다. 사심 없는 마음과 같은 장점들은 평생 동안 관대함을 보이는 습관을 갖도록 발전시킬 수 있으며, 긍정적인 정신은 타인에 대해 한결같은 연민을 갖도록 발전시킬 수 있다. 모든 이들은 인격적인 면에서 장점을 갖고 있으며, 자기계발을 통해 이러한 장점들을 키울 수 있는 능력을 갖고 있다. <약점은 결함이 아니라 단지 부정적인 특성이며, 이는 자기계발을 거쳐 좀 더 긍정적인 특성으로 발전시킬 수 있다.> 예를 들면, 조급함은 목표 성취를 위한 결단력으로 변화시킬 수 있다. 의지가 완고한 특성은 인내심으로 변화시킬 수 있다. 만약 어떤 사람이 약점을 활용할 수 있는 길을 찾을 수만 있다면, 그 약점은 장점으로 변할 수 있다. 자기계발이 그렇게 할 수 있는 최선의 방법이다.

이종현T의 독해 Point!

19. 뒤에 부정적인 특징을 긍정적인걸로 바꾼다고 갑자기 시작되는 부분이 (C) 뒤이므로 정답은 3번이 된다.

20. 다음에 나올 내용을 묻는 문제는 지문의 핵심소재와 주제를 생각하면 된다. 이 글은 약점과 강점을 통해 성격을 개발하자는 글이므로 정답은 4번이 된다.

21~23.

우리는 일반적인 지적 능력은 평균보다 훨씬 낮지만; 특정한 분야의 재능은 뛰어난 사람들을 이따금씩 볼 수 있다. 그들은 종종 '서번트'라 불린다. 서번트의 가장 흥미로운 예는 '언어 서번트'이다. 크리스토퍼(Christopher)는 낮은 지능 때문에 일상생활을 하는 데 많은 어려움이 있었다. 그는 셔츠의 단추를 잠그거나 진공청송기로 카펫을 청소하는데조차 도움이 필요했다. 그러나 그는 매우 뛰어나게 잘하는 것이 하나있었는데 그것은 바로 10개 이상의 언어를 말하고 쓸 수 있었다는 것이다. 그는 언어 교사나 어떤 전문가로부터도 이들 언어를 배우지 않았다. 오히려 그는 혼자서 문법책을 읽는 것과 같은 자신만의 방식으로 그런 언어들을 습득했다. 어떻게 우리는 낮은 지능과 뛰어난 언어 능력 사이의 불일치를 일치되게 적절히 설명할 수 있을까? 한 가지 가능성은 언어 능력이 일반적인 지능과 관련이 없다고 제안하는 것인 듯하다. 다른 말로 하면, 언어 능력은 일반적인 지적 능력을 반영하지도 않고 미리 가정하는 것도 아니라는 것이다. 실제로 이와 같은 주장이 일부 언어학자들과 심리학자들에 의해 제기되어 왔다. 그러나 언어 서번트가 뛰어난 재능을 갖는 것이 어떤 것 때문에 가능하게 되었는지에 대해서는 지금까지 알려진 바가 없다. 진실을 알기 위해서는 서번트의 능력에 대한 많은 연구가 필요할 것이다.

이종현T의 독해 Point!

21. 빈칸 앞은 어떤 주장이 되어진다는 얘기이고 뒤에는 아직 알 수 없다는 얘기이므로 내용상의 관계가 반대가 된다. 따라서 정답은 1번이 된다.

22. 이 글은 savant들이 낮은 지능을 갖고 있는데 특정한 분야에는 재능을 가지고 있다는 얘기인데 그 이유는 알 수 없다는 것이므로 정답은 4번이 된다.

23. 크리스토퍼는 책으로 스스로 공부했다는 얘기가 있으므로 정답은 3번이 된다.

24~25.

우리 모두는 동물들이 놀고 있는 것을 본 적이 있다. 그러나 동물들이 재미를 느끼고 있는가? 이전에 대부분의 과학자들은 인간만이 재미를 느낄 수 있다고 생각했다. 그러나 현재 이런 생각들이 변하고 있다. 점점 더 많은 과학자들이 동물의 감정과 놀이를 연구하고 있다. 그리고 그들이 찾아내고 있는 것은 당신을 깜짝 놀라게 할지도 모른다. 예를 들면, 과학자들은 그 중에서도 침팬지, 개, 쥐가 모두 웃는다는 사실을 알게 되었다. 그러한 동물들의 웃음이 인간의 웃음처럼 들리지 않을지도 모르지만, 그 동물들은 웃고 있는 것이다. 웃고 있는 침팬지와 개라는 개념은 상상하기 어렵지 않을지 모른다. <우리는 인간과 침팬지 사이에 많은 공통점이 있다는 것을 알고 있다. 그리고 개를 키우고 있는 사람이라면 개가 노는 것을 좋아한다는 것을 알고 있다. 그러나 쥐는 어떤가? 당신은 쥐와 놀아본 적이 있는가? 당신은 쥐를 간질여 본적이 있는가? 오하이오 주의 한 대학의 과학자들이 쥐를 간질여 보았다. 무슨 일이 일어났을까? 쥐들이 웃었던 것이다. 실제로 쥐들은 찍찍 소리를 냈는데 이것은 쥐들이 내는 소리이다. 인간과 같이 쥐들은 그들이 알고 있고 알고 있고 좋아하는 사람이 간질였을 때에만 찍찍 소리를 냈다. 그러나 과학자들은 쥐가 실제로 웃고 있었다는 것을 어떻게 아는가? 그들은 쥐의 두뇌를 연구했다. 인간이 웃을 때 뇌의 한 영역이 활발히 반응한다. 쥐가 찍찍 소리를 낼 때 쥐의 뇌도 그 영역이 반응한다.

이종현T의 독해 Point!

24. 침팬지와 인간의 소재가 이어질 수 있는 부분이 (C)밖에 없다. 따라서 정답은 3번이 된다.

25. 이 글의 핵심소재는 동물이 웃는지 아닌지에 대한 얘기이다. 따라서 정답은 5번이 된다.

UNIT 14 Test4

1~2.

어느 누구도 미디어 그 자체가 공격성을 조장한다고 생각하지는 않는다. 그러나 미시건 대학교의 레오나르도 에론과 로웰 후스만은 3학년 아이들이 성인기에 이르기까지의 22년에 걸친 연구를 통해, 나중에 나타날 공격성의 가장 중요한 예측변수는 가난, 학업 성적, 한부모 가정 또는 실제 폭력에의 노출보다는 TV에 등장하는 대량 살상을 즐겨보는 어린 시절의 습관이라는 사실을 발견했다. "물론 모든 청소년들이 영향을 받는 것은 아닙니다. 폐암에 걸린 모든 이들이 담배를 피웠던 것은 아니지요, 그리고 담배를 피우는 모든 사람들이 폐암에 걸리는 것도 아니고요, 하지만 담배업계 밖에 있는 그 어떤 사람도 담배가 폐암의 원인이라는 것을 부인하지 않습니다."라고 에론은 말한다. 가장 효과적인 많은 연구가 아이들을 대상으로 행해졌는데, 이들이 가장 취약한 것으로 여겨지기 때문이었다. 센터월이 말한 바와 같이 "나중에 청소년기와 성인기가 되어서는 TV 폭력에 대한 노출에 변화를 주어도 더 이상의 추가적인 효과를 낳지 못한다." 60년대 스탠포드 대학교의 앨버트 밴두러는 아이들이 부모뿐만 아니라 TV로부터도 행동을 배운다는 사실을 처음으로 보여주었다. 심리학자들은 TV 폭력이 아이들에게 어떻게 영향을 주는지 설명하기 위해 다음의 네 가지 학습이론을 사용했다. 즉 아이들은 특히 그들의 행동이 보상받을 때 TV에서 본 것을 모방할 줄 알게 된다는 것, TV에 폭력이 자주 나온다는 것으로부터 폭력이 정상적이라고 알게 된다는 것, 아이들은 사람들의 실제 고통에 대해 둔감해 진다는 것, 그리고 아이들은 TV에 나오는 영상에 자극되어 폭력적인 반응을 일으킨다는 것이다.

이종현T의 독해 Point!

1. 아이들이 TV영향을 받아 모방할 수 있다는 얘기가 이 지문의 핵심적인 부분이므로 정답은 1번이 된다.

2. 빈칸 뒷 내용을 보면 아이들이 가장 잘 따라한다라는 얘기가 있고 청소년기나 성인기엔 영향을 별로 안받는다고 되어 있으므로 정답은 1번이 된다.

3~4.

감상적인 태도가 잔혹한 취향과 양립 가능하며 그보다 더할 수 있다는 것은 주지의 사실이다. (아우슈비츠의 사령관이 저녁에 귀가하여 자신의 부인 및 아이들과 포옹하고 저녁 식사 전에 피아노 앞에 앉아 슈베르트의 곡을 연주했다고 하는 전형적인 예를 떠올려 보라.) 사람들이 그들 앞에 보이는 것에 단련되는 것은 — 만약 단련이라는 표현이 이 상황을 기술하는 적절한 방식이라고 한다면 — 단지 그들에게 쏟아지는 이미지들의 양 때문이 아니다. 감정을 무디게 하는 것은 수동성이다. 흔히 냉담함,

도덕적 또는 감정적 무감각으로 기술되는 상태들은 감정들로 가득 차 있다. 그 감정들은 분노와 좌절이다. 그러나 만약 우리가 어떤 감정들이 바람직할까 생각해보면, 너무나 쉽게 동정심을 꼽는 것 같다. 타인들에게 가해지는 고통을 이미지를 통해 보게 될 때 느끼는 그들과의 가상의 근접성은 TV의 근접 촬영으로 비춰지는 먼 곳의 고통 받는 이들과 그것을 지켜보는 특권적 시청자들 사이에 하나의 연결을 암시하지만 그것은 분명히 허구적인 것이며, 우리가 권력과 맺고 있는 실질적 관계들에 대한 또 하나의 신비화이다. 우리가 동정심을 느끼는 한, 우리는 그 고통을 야기한 것들과 공범이 아님을 느낀다. 우리의 동정심은 우리의 무력함과 더불어 우리의 결백을 분명히 보여준다. 그런 만큼, 동정심은 (우리의 선한 의도에도 불구하고) 비록 부적절한 반응은 아닐지라도, 무례한(뻔뻔스런) 반응이다. 전쟁과 폭정으로 괴로워하고 있는 타인들에 대한 우리의 동정심을 한쪽으로 제쳐두고, 어떤 이들의 부가 다른 이들의 궁핍을 의미할 수도 있기에, 우리의 특권이 그들의 고통과 같은 지도 위에 어떻게 위치해 있는지, 그리고 우리의 특권이 그들의 고통과, 어쩌면 상상하고 싶지 않을 방식으로, 어떻게 연결되어 있는 지를 성찰해보는 것이 우리의 과제이며, 고통스럽게 우리를 동요시키는 저 이미지들은 이 과제를 시작하도록 첫 점화를 시켜줄 뿐이다.

이종현T의 독해 Point!

3. moral or emotional anesthesia와 동격의 내용이 와야하므로 정답은 3번이 된다.

4. 이 글의 핵심은 모든 인간에게는 다 폭력적인 성향이 있고 우리에게도 이런 성향이 있다는 얘기이므로 정답은 2번이 된다.

5.

모든 인간들이 스스로를 이해하는 과정에서 자아를 보호하기 위한 일련의 방어기제를 구축한다. 신생아는 자아에 대한 개념이 없다. 그러나 점차 타인과 구별되는 자아를 확인하는 것을 배우게 된다. 아동기에는, 인지, 반응, 그리고 가치판단의 정도가 커지면서 개인들이 자신과 동일시하는 정서적 특성 체계를 구축하기 시작한다. 청소년기에는, 사춘기 직전의 아동과 10대의 신체적, 정서적, 인지적 변화가 방어적 금지사항들을 증가시키는데, 이는 취약한 자아를 보호하고, 자존감 평가의 기초가 된 가치와 믿음의 조직을 무너뜨릴 위험이 있는 생각과 경험과 감정을 피하기 위함이다. <방어기제 구축의 과정은 다음 단계로 계속 이어진다.> 높은 자존감과 자아강도를 가진 일부 사람들은 그들의 존재에 위협이 되는 것을 더 잘 견딜 수 있으며 따라서 그들의 방어기제는 낮다. 약한 자존감을 가진 사람들은 약하거나 취약한 자아라고 인식되는 것, 즉 상황이나 과업에 있어 자신감의 부족을 보호하기 위한 금지의 벽을 유지한다.

이종현T의 독해 Point!

5. 앞에서 방어기제 구축에 관한 이야기가 나오고 뒤에는 그 이후의 새로운 소재가 나오는 점을 찾는 것이 필요한 문제이다. 따라서 정답은 3번이 된다. 3번 앞은 방어에 대한 얘기이고 뒤에는 사람들의 방어기제 구축 성향에 대한 얘기가 이어지므로 소재가 바뀌는 점이다.

6.

1979년, 켄 로스(Ken Ross)가 8살이던 해에, 그의 가족은 IBM에서 일하고 있던 아버지의 직장일 때문에 스코틀랜드에서 프랑스로 이사를 가게 되었다. Ⓑ 컴퓨터 회사인 IBM은 파리영어학교(ESP)에 수업료를 지불해 주었는데, 이 학교의 반 친구들은 주로 영국과 세계 여러 나라에서 온 경영자, 군 장교, 외교관 등 국외거주자들의 자녀들이었다. 그 중 2명은 사우디아라비아의 왕자들이었다. 가장 최근에 있었던 동창회 때에는, 남녀 졸업생들이 중국과 남아프리카 공화국처럼 멀리 떨어진 곳에서도 날아왔다. Ⓒ 그 때 이후, 그런 '국제학교들'이 급격히 증가해 왔는데, 이 국제학교들은 비영어권 국가들에서 영어로 수업을 하며, 주로 영국의 A-level, 미국의 AP와 SAT 또는 International Baccalaureate를 위한 강좌를 제공한다. Ⓐ 영국 소재의 국제학교자문그룹 (ISG)에 따르면, 지난 25년 동안, 국제학교의 수는 1,000개 이하에서 7.300개 이상으로 증가하였다. 2013~2014 학년도에서, 국제학교는 416억 달러의 총수입을 벌어들였으며, 전 세계적으로 375만 명의 학생들을 가르쳤다. 100개 이상의 국제학교가 있는 국가는 22개인데, UAE가 478곳으로 가장 많으며, 중국이 445 곳으로 뒤를 이었다.

이종현T의 독해 Point!

6. 컴퓨터 회사의 소재가 이어지는 B가 제시문 다음에 오고 학교에 대한 얘기가 이어지는 A, C가 그 뒤에 와야한다. A, C 중에선 국제학교에 대한 얘기 중 붐이 일었다는 얘기가 시작되는 점이 C이므로 A보단 C가 먼저 오게 된다. 따라서 정답은 3번이 된다.

7~9.

올해 가장 많이 팔린 크리스마스 선물 중 하나는 드론이다. 50달러면, 비디오카메라를 장착한 아주 작은 쿼드콥터를 살 수 있으며, 이것은 정원 조감도를 촬영하기에 안성맞춤이다. 700달러면, 회전운동 중에도 평형을 유지하는 카메라가 장착된 드론을 살 수 있는데, 손목에 무선 추적 장치를 착용할 경우, 이것은 당신이 스키나 자전거를 타거나 카이트 서핑을 하는 동안 당신의 모습을 촬영해 줄 것이다. 더욱 의미심장하게도, 드론은 온갖 종류의 사업 영역에 대변혁을 일으킬 수 있다. 본래 군사용으로 개발된 드론은 민간영역으로도 활동을 시작하고 있는데, 대체로 (드론의) 전자 물품 비용이 줄어든 덕분이다. 스마트폰에는 자이로스코프, 가속도계, 무선 송수신기, 신호처리기 , GPS 장치 등 드론에 효율적으로 사용될 수 있는 많은 기기들이 들어있다.

드론을 즉시 쓸 수 있는 상업적인 용도 가운데 하나는 토지를 저렴하고 효과적으로 측량하는 것이다. 위성의 촬영해상도가 30cm인 것에 비해 드론은 도로를 2cm 해상도로 촬영할 수 있으며, 동일한 촬영을 1/3의 비용으로 할 수 있다. 이미 농부들은 드론을 이용해 농작물의 발육상태를 살펴보고 있으며, 이렇게 해서 현대적인 농기계가 정확한 양과 정확한 종류의 비료를 살포할 수 있다. 드론은 또한 안전성을 향상시키기 때문에, 현재는 헬리콥터에서 매달린 채 작업을 해야 하는 전선 점검과 같은 일들을 하는 데 사용될 수 있다. 그리고 드론은 상품을 보다 빨리 전달할 수 있다. 물류회사인 DHL은 이미 '파슬콥터'를 이용해 의약품을 독일 해안에서 멀리 떨어져 있는 작은 섬인 주이스트(Juist)로 배달하고 있다.

그러나 드론의 잠재력은 규제에 달려있다. 드론은 위험할 수 있기 때문에 - 주변에서 하늘을 날고 있는 드론으로 인해 걱정을 하는 항공기 조종사들로부터의 보고가 점점 늘어나고 있다 - 각국 정부들은 드론 사용에 대한 규정을 정할 필요가 있다. 그리고 상업용 드론에 대한 취급이 나라마다 상이하다.

미 연방항공국(FAA)은 거의 모든 상업용 드론의 사용을 금지하고 있다. 이 조치는 곧 변경될 것인데, 왜냐하면 의회가 미 연방항공국에게 2015년 9월 30일까지 상업용 드론의 비행에 대한 법령을 마련하라고 명령했기 때문이다. <그러나 앞으로 몇 주 뒤에 나올 제안서의 초안들은 미연방항공국이 계속해서 제한적인 입장을 취하리란 것을 보여줄 것으로 예상되는데, 왜냐하면 초안에서는 드론 조종사들로 하여금 유인항공기 조종 능력을 갖추도록 요구하고 있고, 드론이 항상 보이는 곳에 있게 하도록 하고 있기 때문이다.> 드론 업계는 이것에 규제포획이라고 의심을 하는데, 즉 미 연방항공국이 (유인 항공기) 조종사들을 위한 압력단체의 역할을 하고 있다는 것이다.

안전과 혁신 사이에 균형을 잡기 위한 올바른 방법은 크기, 용도 등에 따라 상업적인 드론에 대해 일련의 규정들을 만드는 것이다. 이 규정들은 또한 위치에 따라서도 달라야 하는데, 왜냐하면 도시에서 건물 외부를 측량하는 것이 들판 위를 나는 것보다 더 위험하기 때문이다. 모든 파괴적 기술처럼, 상업용 드론은 기존 사업에 피해를 줄 것이다. 더 많은 농부들과 물류회사들이 헬리콥터가 비행기를 사용하는 대신 드론을 사용함에 따라 일부 조종사들은 직장을 잃게 될 것이다. (그래서) 드론산업에 대한 현직 조종사들의 반대는 이해할 수 있다. 그러나 미연방항공국의 반대는 이해할 수 없다. 연방항공국은 보다 객관적으로 바라봐야 하며, 상업용 드론을 자유롭게 풀어주어야 한다.

이종현T의 독해 Point!

7. 의약품을 배달한다고는 했지만 누가 가장 먼저 했는지에 대한 얘기는 없으므로 정답은 3번이다.

8. 앞에는 FAA에 대한 얘기가 있어야 하고 But이 있으므로 앞에는 제한하지 않는다는 의미가 있을거고 뒤에는 제한한다는 얘기가 있어야 한다고 생각을 하고 접근하면 정답은 4가 된다.

9. 결국 필자가 원하는 것은 상업용 드론을 자유롭게 풀어주는 것이라는걸 알 수 있다. 따라서 정답은 2번이 된다.

10.

행복해야 할 의무만큼 우리가 과소평가하고 있는 의무는 없다. 행복해짐으로써, 우리는 이 세상에 이름 모를 좋은 일의 씨앗을 뿌리게 된다. 이 좋은 일에 대해서는 우리 자신조차도 알지 못하고 있거나 아니면 이 좋은 일이 드러났을 때에는 누구보다도 베푼 사람이 가장 놀라게 된다. Ⓑ 일전에, 누더기 옷을 입은 맨발의 소년이 구슬을 쫓아 거리를 달려 내려 온 적이 있는데, 그 소년은 너무나도 즐거워 보여서 그가 지나치는 모든 사람들의 기분이 좋아졌다. Ⓐ 그 가운데 한 명은 평상시보다 더 음울한 생각에서부터 벗어나게 되었는데, 그는 그 작은 아이를 멈춰 세운 뒤 약간의 돈을 주면서 이렇게 말했다. "즐거운 표정에서 때때로 어떤 일이 생겨나는지 너는 아는구나." © 만약 그 아이가 전에는 즐거운 표정이었다면, 이제는 즐거운 표정과 동시에 당황한 표정을 지을 수밖에 없었다. 나로서는, 울고 있는 아이들보다는 웃고 있는 아이들을 이렇게 격려해주는 것이 옳다고 본다. Ⓓ 나는 무대 위가 아닌 그 어디에서도 눈물을 흘리는 것에 대해 돈을 지급하지 않는다. 그러나 나는 정반대의 상품(웃음)은 크게 거래할 준비가 되어있다. 5파운드짜리 지폐보다 행복한 사람을 발견하는 것이 더 좋은 일이다.

이종현T의 독해 Point!

10. A, C가 제시문 뒤에 나오려면 제시문에 남자아이에 대한 얘기가 있어야하는데 없다. 따라서 A, C는 제시문 다음에 올 수 없고, D가 제시문 다음에 오기엔 주어가 I가 아니므로 역시 이어지기 어렵다. 따라서 제시문 다음엔 B가 오게 된다. 그리고 그 이후에는 C가 바로 오기엔 과거와 현재를 비교할만한 사건이 없으므로 그 사건이 되는게 A가 되고 C에서 I얘기가 시작 되고 D가 I 얘기로 이어진다고 볼 수 있다. 따라서 정답은 2번이다.

11.

미국 식품의약국(FDA)에서는 제약회사로 하여금 약품의 약효가 얼마나 지속 되는지를 실험한 후에 약품의 포장지에 유통기한을 포함시키도록 하고 있다. 그것이 그 약품이 유통기한 다음 날에는 약효가 전혀 없다는 것을 반드시 의미하는 것은 아니다. <그것은 적어도 유통기한까지는 그 약품들이 안전하고 약효가 있다는 것을 의미한다.> 대부분의 제약회사의 경우, 자사에서 만든 약품이 언제 약효를 잃는지를 알아보기 위한 실험을 무한정 계속하지 않는다. 제약회사는 오직 한두 해 동안만 실험을 할 것인데, 만약 그 약품의 승인이 나게 되면 제조일로부터 1년 혹은 2년 — 몇 년이 되었든 — 이라는 유통기한을 찍게 된다. 유통기한이 갖는 문제는 까다로워 보이지만, 소비자가 약품과 식품을 안전하게 보관하는 데 도움을 주는 지침들이 있다.

이종현T의 독해 Point!

11. It does not necessarily mean ~ 뒤에 It does mean ~ 으로 이어지는 문장이므로 정답은 2번이 된다.

12~13.

전직 대출 중개업자 크리스 일(Chris Ihle)은 지난 7월 아이오와 주(州) 에임즈(Ames)에 위치한 자신의 사무실 앞에 오토바이를 막 주차했을 때, 장애인 마크가 붙은 폰티악 본빌(Pontiac Bonneville) 승용차 한 대가 철로에 멈춰 서 있는 것을 보았다. 잠시 후에 그는 인접한 교차로에서 나는 기차 경적소리를 들었다.

크리스는 선글라스와 열쇠를 오토바이 가까이에 집어 던지고는 그 차를 향해 달렸다. 목 보호대를 하고 있는 나이가 지긋한 남자가 운전석에 앉아서 자동차 열쇠를 돌리면서 가속페달을 밟고 있었는데, 그는 84세의 장 패피치(Jean Papich)였다. 그의 아내인 78세의 매리언(Marion)은 조수석에서 초조하게 남편을 응시하고 있었다. 크리스는 건널목 차단기 아래로 몸을 숙이고 들어가, 자동차의 뒤쪽으로 간 다음, 차를 밀었다. 그러나 데워진 아스팔트에 그의 장화가 미끄러졌다. 그는 기차가 빠르게 다가오고 있는 것을 볼 수 있었다. <크리스는 차를 뒤로 미는 것이 더 쉬울 수도 있을 거라 생각했다.> 그는 차의 앞으로 뛰어갔고 장을 향해 차의 기어를 중립에 놓으라고 외쳤다. 크리스는 기관차가 끼익하는 브레이크 소리와 경적 소리를 내지르면서 자신들을 향해 밀어닥칠 때, 발밑에서 땅이 울리는 것을 느낄 수 있었다. 그는 자신의 장화를 철로의 홈에다 끼운 후 밀었고, 마침내 차는 철로를 빠져 나왔다. 크리스가 위를 올려다보았을 때, 유니온 퍼시픽 열차의 높게 솟은 방열판과의 거리는 몇 피트에 불과했다. 그는 그 승용차 옆에 바싹 엎드렸고 기차는 큰 소리를 내며 지나갔다. 아찔한 마음에 말을 잃은 크리스는 비틀거리면서 일을 하러 돌아갔고 커피 한 잔을 마셨다. 그러는 동안 많은 사람들이 현장에 모여들었다. 몇 주 후에 매리언이 크리스에게 감사하다는 말을 전하기 위해 방문했다. 그는 "말로 해야 될 때가 있고 행동해야 될 때가 는 법이죠."라고 대답했다.

이종현T의 독해 Point!

12. 제시문부터 차를 앞에서 뒤로 미는 얘기가 시작이 된다. 따라서 정답은 2번이 된다.

13. 주인공이 빠르게 행동해서 커플을 구한 이야기이므로 정답은 3번이 된다.

14.

진리가 사고체계의 첫 번째 덕목이듯이 정의는 사회제도의 첫 번째 덕목이다. 아무리 고상하고 간결하다 할지라도 이론이란 그것이 진리가 아니라면 거부하거나 바꿔야 한다. 마찬가지로, 아무리 효율적이고 정리가 잘되어 있다 할지라도 법과 제도는 만약 그것들이 불의하다면 개정되거나 폐지되어야 한다. 각 개인은 전체 사회의 복지라는 명분으로도 무효화시킬 수 없는 정의에 바탕을 둔 불가침성을 소유하고 있다. 이러한 이유로, 정의는 일부 사람들의 자유의 상실이 다른 이들이 공유하는 더 큰 선(이익)에 의해 정당화된다는 것을 부인한 다. 정의는 소수에게 강요된 희생들보다 다수가 누리는 더 큰 이익이 더 중요하다고 인정하지 않는다. 〈따라서 정의로운 사회에서는 평등한 시민의 자유가 이제 고정 불변의 것으로 여겨진다. 즉 정의에 의해 확보된 권리들은 이해관계의 계산이나 정치적 흥정의 대상이 아니다.〉 잘못된 이론을 묵인하게 허용해주는 유일한 것은 그것보다 더 나은 이론이 없는 경우이다. 마찬가지로 불의는 훨씬 더 큰 불의를 막기 위해 필요할 때에만 용납될 수 있다. 인간 활동의 첫 번째 미덕인 진리와 정의는 비타협적인 것이다.

이종현T의 독해 Point!

14. 제시문은 새로운 이야기의 시작점 혹은 그 이야기가 끝나는 지점이다. 지금 제시문엔 therefore가 있으므로 소재의 끝점이라고 생각하면 된다. 따라서 그 끝점이 될 수 있는 4번이 정답이 된다. D 다음부턴 우리가 허용할 수 있는 것에 대한 이야기가 나온다.

15~16.

설탕산업은 동양의 두 지역, 즉 인도와 남서태평양 군도에서 사탕수수가 도입되면서 발전했다. 사탕수수 재배는 마침내 서쪽으로 퍼져나갔고, 아랍인들에 의해 지중해 지역에 소개되었다. 서기 703년경에 설탕산업은 시실리(Sicily)섬에 자리를 잡았고, 755년경에는 스페인까지 퍼져나갔다. 이미 1150년에, 스페인에는 적어도 75,000에이커의 사탕수수 밭이 있었다. 설탕산업이 보다 더 확대되고 발전한 것은 부분적으로는 십자군운동 때문이었다. 초창기에 사탕수수는 지역의 수요를 충당하기 위해 주로 재배되었다.

사탕수수가 서아시아 여러 지역에서 아라비아로, 그리고 이후에 지중해와 인접한 여러 나라로 전파된 이후, 1500년대 후반까지 그곳에서 사탕수수를 이용한 설탕산업의 발전을 가져왔다. <사탕수수 용액을 기화해서 당밀을 만든 다음에, 설탕제조업자는 경험에 의거하는 방법을 통해 언제 설탕 결정을 만들지를 결정했다.> 1493년에, 콜럼버스는 두 번째 항해에서 사탕수수를 신대륙으로 가져갔으며, 그것은 히스파니올라(Hispaniola)섬에 최초로 심어졌다. 16세기와 17세기 기간 동안에, 스페인, 영국, 프랑스 인들은 카리브 해의 섬에 위치한 식민지에 설탕 생산 기지를 세웠다. 18세기 후반 무렵에는, 여러 나라에서 설탕 수요가 급격히 증가함에 따라, 프랑스 식민지 세인트 도미니크 (오늘날의 아이티 공화국)가 카리브 해 지역에서 가장 중요한 설탕 생산지 가운데 하나가 되었다.

1700년대 초반에, 아메리카 대륙의 여러 식민지에서는 세인트 도미니크에서 들여온 사탕수수를 남부 미시시피 강을 따라 두루 심었지만, 이런 시도는 성공하지 못했다. 그로부터 약 10년 후에, 프랑스령 루이지애나 식민지 초대 행정관이 마르티니크(Martinique)산 사탕수수를 반입해서 뉴올리언스 지역에서 재배하는 데 성공했다. 1750년대에 프랑스 예수회 소속 신부들도 세인트 도미니크산 사탕수수를 뉴올리언스 플랜테이션으로 도입해서 재배했다. 1750년대 말과 1760년대 초반에 몇몇 식민지 주민들이 세인트 도미니크나 예수회에서 가져온 사탕수수로 뉴올리언스 지역에서 상업용 설탕을 제조하는 데 성공했다.

이종현T의 독해 Point!

15. 전부 설탕이 퍼지는 이야기를 하고 있는데 B번 문장은 설탕이 만들어지는 과정에 대해서 이야기하고 있으므로 정답은 2번이 된다.

16. 이 글은 설탕이 어떻게 퍼져왔는지라는 것이 핵심소재이다. 따라서 정답은 1번이 된다.

17~19.

복제양 돌리(Dolly)의 탄생은 세상을 영원히 변화시킬 과학 연구의 중요한 순간들 중 하나처럼 보였다. 성인 세포로부터 처음으로 이루어진 동물 복제는 놀라운 과학적 성과였다. 그것은 중증 질병에 대해 새로운 치료의 희망을 주었다. 그러나 그것은 또한 복제된 인간, 맞춤형 아기 그리고 반(反) 이상향의 미래에 대한 두려움을 불러일으켰다.

돌리는 한 마리의 양에서 채취한 세포에서부터 추출한 DNA를 통해 만들어졌다. 돌리를 복제하기 위한 시도는 227차례 있었으며, 이 과정에서 유산이 된 경우가 매우 많았다. 복제된 인간들이 세상을 돌아다니는 것이 얼마 남지 않았다는 진심 어린 우려 또한 있었다. 방송은 이것이 인간에게 의미하는 것이 무엇인지, 복제된 인간이 복제의 원천인 사람과 정확히 같은지, 그리고 과학자들이 우리를 어떤 세상 속으로 몰아넣는지와 같은 대화로 넘쳐났다.

복제양 돌리를 탄생시킨 영국의 발생학자 이언 윌머트(Ian Willmut)교수는 대중의 의심을 정확히 인지하고 있었다. 그리고 그는 자신의 일에 관해 확실하고, 솔직하고, 정직한 것이 중요하다는 것을 알고 있었다. 그는 '치료 복제'라는 용어를 알렸으며, 그의 비전은 환자로부터 세포를 채취해서 환자의 손상된 세포를 치료하기 위해 이식될 수 있는 건강한 세포를 만드는 데 복제 기술을 사용함으로써, 심장병, 파킨슨병, 류머티즘의 치료제를 개발하는 것에 있었다.

이것은 일부 교회와 낙태 반대 단체들로부터 더 큰 우려를 불러 일으켰는데, 이 단체들은 인간 배아를 새로 만들고 파괴하는 것이 포함된 과정에 대해 우려를 나타냈다. 그들은 그 기술이 금지되길 원했으나, 의학 연구 단체의 강력한 로비에 따라 영국 의회는 치료 복제는 허용하는 한편, 인간의 복제는 금지했다.

그 이후로, 치료 복제를 통해 얻을 수 있을 것으로 기대했던 많은 혜택들이 실제로 드러나진 않았다. 그러나 과학자들은 동물 세포를 재프로그램할 수 있다는 것을 증명해 왔다. 이제는 동물세포를 다시 젊어지게 만들고 방향을 다시 정하여 인간의 몸에 있는 그 어떤 세포든지 만들어 낼 수 있다. 과학자들이 아직 임상적인 혜택을 거두진 못했을지도 모르지만, 돌리의 탄생으로 과학적인 사고를 단번에 영원히 바꾸었다.

이종현T의 독해 Point!

17. 바로 뒷 내용에서 그의 작품에 열리고 정직하고 명확해야한다고 되어 있으므로 그는 공개해야되는 걸 알고 있는거고 대중들에게 보여주고 싶은거고 따라서 대중들의 의심을 알고 있었다는 정답은 5번이 된다.

18. 이 글은 Dolly의 탄생 이후에 발생한 것이 핵심이므로 정답은 2번이 된다.

19. 영국 정부는 모든 복제를 금지한 것이 아니라 오히려 조금 더 풀어준 국가이므로 정답은 4번이 된다.

20~21.

사람과 실험용 동물의 본능적 두려움 및 학습된 두려움올 연구함으로써 우리는 사람에게서 일어나는 본능적 두려움 및 학습된 두려움의 행동 기제 및 생물학적 기제에 관한 많은 통찰을 얻게 되었다. 행동에 관한 첫 번째 통잘들 중 하나는 지그문트 프로이트(Sigmund Freud)와 미국의 철학자 윌리엄 제임스(William James)가 만들어낸 이론들에 자극받은 것이었는데, 이 두 사람은 두려움이 의식적인 구성요소와 무의식적인 구성요소 둘 다를 갖고 있다고 이해했다. (그러나) 분명하지 않은 점은 의식적인 구성요소와 무의식적인 구성요소가 어떻게 상호작용하는가였다. 전통적으로 사람들이 갖는 두려움은 자신의 집이 불에 타는 것을 보는 것처럼 중요한 사건에 대한 의식적인 인지에서 시작되는 것으로 여겨졌다. 이러한 인지는 대뇌피질에서 감정적인 경험을 만들어내는데, 이 경험이 바로 두려움으로 심장, 혈관, 부신, 그리고 땀샘에 신호를 일으켜 신체가 방어하거나 도망갈 대비를 하게 해준다. 따라서 이 견해에 따르면, 의식적이며 감정적인 사건은 나중에 신체에 반사적, 생물학적, 그리고 생리학적 방어반응을 일으킨다. 윌리엄 제임스는 이런 견해를 받아들이지 않았다. 1884년에 발간된 매우 영향력 있는 『감정이란 무엇인가?(What is Emotion?)』라는 제목의 논문에서, 그는 감정의 인지경험이 감정의 생리적인 표현에 부차적인 것이라고 주장했다. 그는 예를 들어 우리가 가는 길 한복판에 곰이 앉아있는 것과 같이 잠재적으로 위험한 상황에 직면할 때, 곰의 흉포함에 대한 우리의 평가가 의식적으로 경험된 감정 상태를 만들어내지는 않는다고 말했다. 즉, 우리는 곰으로부터 도망쳐 달아난 후에야 두려움을 경험하게 된다는 것이다.

이종현T의 독해 Point!

20. 빈칸에 들어갈 표현은 무의식적인 반응에 대한 얘기가 들어가야 한다. 따라서 반대말로 써있는 1번이 정답이 된다.

21. not A until B의 구조를 만들어주면 정답은 3번이 된다.

UNIT 15 Test5

1~3.

뇌의 정교함은 뇌가 어설프다는 사실에 있다. 수세기 동안, 신경과학은 뇌의 다양한 부위에 꼬리표를 적절하게 붙이려는 시도를 해왔다. 여기는 언어를 담당하는 영역, 여기는 도덕성을 담당하는 영역, 여기는 도구 사용을 담당영역, 여기는 색채 감지를 담당하는 영역, 여기는 얼굴 인식을 담당하는 영역 등으로 분류하는 식이었다. 질서정연한 뇌지도의 모색은 실행 가능한 시도로서 시작했지만, 그것은 오류인 것으로 드러났다.

뇌의 심오하고 아름다운 책략은 더 흥미롭다. 뇌는 이 세계를 다면적이고 중첩해서 처리하는 방식을 가지고 있다. 뇌는 서로 상충된 부품들로 구성된 기계이다. 또한 뇌는 문제 해결의 올바른 방법을 안다고 모두 확신하고 있는 여러 정당들 사이의 경쟁으로 작동하는 대의 민주주의제이다. 그 결과, 우리는 자신에 대해 분노하기도 하고, 자신과 다투고, 때로는 자신에게 욕설을 퍼붓거나 자신과 계약을 맺기도 한다. 우리는 (자신과) 갈등을 빚고 있다는 느낌을 받을 수 있다. 이런 유형의 신경증적 갈등이 혼외정사, 중독의 재발, 다이어트의 포기, 새해결심 위반 등의 이면에 있는데, 이 모두는 한 인간의 몇몇 부분들과 또 다른 부분들이 서로 별개의 것을 원하기 때문에 일어나는 상황들이다.

현대적인 기계는 이런 일들을 전혀 하지 않는다. 자동차는 어느 쪽으로 돌아야 하는지에 대해 갈등을 빚을 수 없다. 자동차는 하나의 핸들을 단 한명의 운전자가 통제하며, 자동차는 아무 불평 없이 그 지시에 따른다. 이와 달리, 뇌는 두 개의 마음, 그리고 종종 그보다 더 많은 수의 마음이 있을 수 있다. 우리는 케이크를 향해야 할지 혹은 외면해야 할지를 알지 못하는데, 그것은 행동의 핸들을 여러 개의 손이 잡고 있기 때문이다.

기억을 예로 들어보자. 정상적인 상황에서는 일상적인 사건에 대한 기억들이 해마(海馬)라고 불리는 뇌의 영역에 의해 통합된다. 그러나 자동차 사고나 강도사건과 같은 무서운 상황에서는, (소뇌) 편도체라고 하는 또 다른 영역 또한 독자적이고 부차적인 기억 통로를 따라 기억을 저장한다. 편도체에 저장된 기억은 다른 특성을 가지고 있다. 그 기억은 지우는 것이 어렵고, 강간 피해자나 참전용사가 공통적으로 설명하는 것처럼, 언제나 "플래시 전구"같이 다시 떠오를 수 있다. 다시 말해, 기억을 저장하는 데에는 한 가지 이상의 방법이 있는 것이다. 여기서 우리기 말하고 있는 것은 서로 다른 사건들에 대한 기억이 아니라 같은 사건에 대한 서로 다른 기억이다. 펼쳐지고 있는 정황에 따라 두 개 이상의 파당이 연관될지도 모르는데, 모든 파당들은 정보를 기록하고는 나중에 서로 자기 이야기를 하겠다고 경쟁을 벌인다. 기억의 통일성은 환상이다.

이종현T의 독해 Point!

1. 첫 번째 빈칸은 우리 얘기로 이어지고 있으므로 결론에 해당된다. 따라서 1번이나 4번이 적절하고 두 번째 빈칸은 앞의 두 가지 기억을 종합해서 한 가지 기억 이상이 있다고 했으므로

재진술이 된다. 따라서 정답은 4번이 된다.

2. 주제에 해당하는 걸 찾으면 된다. 하나의 기억도 여러 곳에 저장이 된다는 의미이므로 정답은 2번이 된다.

3. 뇌 지도에 대한 글이고 과거엔 딱딱 나눠진 줄 알았는데 그렇지 않았다는 얘기이므로 정답은 과거와 현재의 연구라고 하는 1번이 된다.

4~5.

세계에서 탄소를 가장 많이 배출하는 국가인 중국은 자국의 오염된 공기를 깨끗하게 할 수 있는 가장 좋은 방법 가운데 하나는 태양 에너지를 사용하는 것이라고 결론을 내렸다. 중국은 지난 2년간 태양광 발전소 부문에서 세계 1위 자리를 지켜왔으며 2015년에도 그 자리를 지켜낼 가능성이 높다. 현재 추세대로라면 중국이 2014년 말까지 33기가와트의 태양광 발전용량을 확보하게 될 것으로 블룸버그 뉴에너지 파이낸스(BNEF)는 내다보고 있는데, 이것은 2010년에 비해 42배 증가한 것이며, 현재 스페인, 이탈리아, 영국의 태양광 발전용량을 모두 합한 것보다도 더 많은 것이다. 중국의 경우, 태양광 발전을 통한 전기의 대부분은 서부의 농업지대에 퍼져나가고 있는 대규모 태양광 발전시설에서 만들어지고 있다. 이제 업무용 건물과 공장의 옥상에 태양 전지판을 설치하고 비용이 많이 드는 송전선을 길게 건설하는 일 없이 그 전지판들을 전력망에 연결시켜서, 태양 전지판을 도시 지역에도 퍼뜨리려는 계획을 갖고 있다. BNEF는 2015년에 중국이 15기가와트에 이르는 태양광 발전용량을 더 늘리게 될 것으로 전망하고 있는데, 이는 약 1600만 가구에 전기를 공급하기에 충분한 양이다. <늘어나게 될 발전용량의 반 이상은 상업용 건물 위에 설치한 저렴한 전지판으로부터 얻게 될 것이다> 2015년의 계획이 차질 없이 진행된다면, 중국은 세계에서 맑은 날이 가장 많은 나라 가운데 하나인 호주 전체에 현재 존재하고 있는 것보다 두 배 많은 태양광 발전시설을 1년 만에 공장과 사무실 건물에 설치한 셈이 될 것이다.

이종현T의 독해 Point!

4. 빈칸에는 앞 문장의 시골의 반대가 될만한 표현이 들어가야 하므로 정답은 1번이 된다.

5. 앞에 증가가 있어야 하고 빌딩에 대한 얘기가 있어야 한다. 따라서 정답은 4번이 된다.

6~8.

역사상 처음으로, 세계의 많은 곳에서 외국인인 것이 완벽하게 정상적인 상태가 되었다. 그것은 키가 크고 뚱뚱하고 혹은 왼손잡이인 것과 마찬가지로 특이한 것이 아니다. 베를린에 있는 프랑스 사람, 런던에 있는 짐바브웨 사람, 파리에 있는 러시아 사람, 뉴욕에 있는 한국 사람을 보고서 눈썹을 치켜 올리는 사람은 아무도 없다. 너무나도 많은 사람들이 기회가 주어진다면 모국이 아닌 나라에서 살고 싶어 한다는 사실은 정치학과 철학에서 오랫동안 확립되어온 "인간이라는 동물은 자기 집에서 가장 잘 산다"는 일치된 의견을 터무니없는 생각으로 만들고 있다. 철학의 오류는 인간이 사회적인 동물이기 때문에 어떤 특정한 사회에 속해야 한다고 가정한 것이었다. 확실히, 많은 사람들이 고향과 모국에 대해 가장 편안하게 느낀다. 그러나 모국이 억압적이고 외국인으로 지내는 것이 자유롭다고 생각하는 나머지 다른 사람들의 경우는 어떤가?

그들의 선택은 해가 갈수록 점점 쉬워지고 있고 동시에 점점 어려워지고 있기도 한 선택이다. 더 쉬워지고 있는 것은 산업과 교육의 세계화가 국경을 파괴하고 있기 때문이고, 더 어려워지고 있는 것은 이처럼 세계화된 세상에서는 그곳에 갔을 때 완전히 외국인이라는 느낌을 가질 수 있는 장소가 거의 남아 있지 않기 때문이다.

이종현T의 독해 Point!

6. 빈칸에는 no more 까지 합쳐서 보통이란 얘기가 되어야 하므로 빈칸엔 보통이 아닌 특별한, 뚜렷한 같은 얘기가 들어가야 한다. 따라서 정답은 3번이 된다.

7. 빈칸에는 다른 나라에 사는 것과는 반대가 될만한 얘기인 자기 나라가 최고다 같은 얘기가 들어가야하므로 정답은 1번이 된다.

8. 앞 문장의 many people과 반대되는 other people이므로 집을 싫어하고 외국을 좋아하는 사람들이다 따라서 정답은 4번이 된다.

9~10.

독재국가들을 살펴볼 때 우리는 이 모든 것을 충분히 잘 알게 된다. 그러나 우리가 대조의 방법으로 우리 자신의 체제를 그려보려고 할 때, 어떤 모습이 마음속에 떠오르는가? 키플링(Kipling)의 시에 나오는 사람들처럼 누구든지 자기주장을 내세울 수 있고 하고 싶은 말은 무슨 말이나 할 수 있는 그런 모습이지 않은가. 키플링의 시에 나오는 사람들은 각자의 별에 앉아서 있는 그대로의 사물들의 신을 위해 사물을 눈에 보이는 대로 그린다. 키플링은 아마 시인이었으니까 이렇게 할 수 있었을 것이다. 그러나 각자의 별에 고립된 보통 사람은 환각을 일으킬 것이고 (사물을 있는 그대로 보고 그리지 못할 것이고) 그래서 각자의 연단에서 변론을 펼치는 시민들은 격렬하고 터무니없는 혼란스런 말로 대기를 오염시킬 것이다. 누구든지 마음대로 연단을 세울 수 있고 마음대로 강당을 빌려 거기서 들으려고 하는 사람들에게 자신의 견해를 설명할 수 있을 때, 자유가 문명화된 사람들 사이에 발달한 것은 아니다. 오히려 반대로, 같은 강당에서 같은 청중들에게 서로 다른 여러 견해들이 설명될 때, 언론의 자유는 확립되는 것이다.

이종현T의 독해 Point!

9. 빈칸에는 not A but B 같은 형태를 만들어 줄 수 있는 연결사가 들어가야 한다. 따라서 정답은 4번이 된다.

10. 이 글의 주제는 민주사회란 같은 공간에서 모두가 다 다른 의견을 말할 수 있어야 한다는 것이므로 정답은 1번이 된다.

11~13.

자신의 소설에 몰두했던 작가로서 토마스 하디의 충동들은 분기하는 다양한 것들이었다. 그러나 그 충돌들이 항상 조화롭게 작동하는 것은 아니었다. 하디는 어느 정도까지 그의 소설 속에 등장하는 인물들의 심리학을 탐구하는 데 흥미를 가지고 있었다. 그리고 그 관심은 호기심보다는 공감에 의해서 촉진되었다. 때때로 그는 희극에 대한 충동(그의 모든 무심한 냉정함도 불구하고)은 물론이고 소극에 대한 충동도 느꼈다. 그러나 그는 더 자주 비극 쪽으로 기울어졌고 그 비극을 기록했다. 그는 또한 그 문구의 몇몇 의미에서 문학적인 사실주의에도 관심을 가졌다. 그는 평범한 사람들을 묘사하고 싶어 했다. 그는 그들이 처한 딜레마에 대해서 이성적으로 사유하기를 원했다 (그것도 불행하게, 심지어 개략적으로). 그리고 그는 물질적인 우주를 정확하게 기록하기를 원했다. 궁극적으로 그는 사실주의자 이상의 것이 되고 싶어 했다. 그는 단지 사건들을 정확하게 기록하는 진부함을 넘어서고자 했고, 더 나가 초자연적인 것과 낯선 것에 대한 그의 인식도 표현하고자 했다.

그의 소설들 속에서, 이 다양한 충동들은 자주 불가피하게 서로서로 희생당했다. 그 이유는 불가피하게도 하디가 플로베르나 제임스 같은 소설가들이 신경 쓰는 방식으로 신경 쓰지 않았고, 최소 저항선의 길을 택했기 때문이다. 이처럼 하나의 충동은 종종 더 새로운 충동에 굴복했고, 불행하게도 타협을 이끌어내는 대신에 단순하게 사라졌다. 현실을 향해 전례 없는 빛을 던지고 싶은 욕망은, 꽃의 구조와 질감을 정확하고 구체적으로 기록하는 소설가-과학자로서의 욕망에게 갑작스럽게 자리를 내주었다. 이런 경우에, 새로운 충동은 최소한 에너지 넘치는 것이었고, 그러한 충동에 대한 탐닉은 편안한 문체라는 결과를 초래하지 않았다. 그러나 다른 경우에, 하디는 추상적으로 분류하고 도식화하고자 하는 그의 치명적으로 편안한 (문체적) 충동을 선호해서 위험하고 에너지가 넘치는 (문체적) 충동을 포기했다. 편안한 충동에 빠져들었을 때, 그의 문체 - 작가의 문학적 가치에 대한 확실한 지표인 - 는 확실히 장황해졌다. 하디의 약점은 이들 분기하는 충동들의 오고감을 통제하는 그의 명백한 무능력과, 에너지 넘치고 위험한 충동을 구축하고 유지하고자 하는 의지의 부재로부터 비롯되었다.

이종현T의 독해 Point!

11. 하디의 충동에 대한 얘기고 그게 문제라는 문제로 끝나는 글이다. 따라서 정답은 3번이 된다.

12. cultivate를 같이 받아줄만한 표현이 들어가야 하므로 정답은 1번이 된다.

13. Flaubert와 James가 아닌 Hardy가 더 많은 충동을 가지고 있었으므로 정답은 4번이 된다.

14~15.

기계들이 숙련된 노동자들에 대한 수요를 감소시킨다는 믿음이외에도, 과거 경험 속에서 근거가 희박한 보다 지속적으로 제기되는 개념이 있는데, 그 개념은 기계 기술의 진보가 노동을 대체하는 것을 통해서 점진적으로 총 구직 기회와 총 고용을 감소시킬 것이라는 것이다. 이러한 믿음은 수백만이 일자리에서 쫓겨났던 1930년대에 강한 호소력이 있었다. 그 당시, 많은 저술가들은 우리 경제가 성숙하게 되었다고 주장했고 더 나가, 미래에 충분한 일자리를 제공하기 위해서, 노동시간을 점진적으로 줄이는 것을 통해 일자리를 확대하거나 정부로 하여금 공적인 일자리 프로그램을 확대하는 것을 통해 일자리를 지속적으로 창출할 수 있게 해야 한다고 주장했다. 노동시간을 단축하는 것 이외에도, 젊은이들이 보다 더 오래 학교에 다니고 나이 든 노동자들이 보다 일찍 은퇴해야 한다는 제안이 제기되기도 했다.

그 누구도 기계들이 개별적인 노동자들을 특정한 일자리에 빼앗고 단기적으로 이러한 현상이 어려운 문제를 야기 시킬 것이라는 사실을 의심하지 않았다. 예컨대 기차에 디젤 엔진과 전기 동력을 사용하는 것은 '철도 화부'의 직책을 쓸모없게 만들었는데, 철도화부란 기차의 증기 엔진을 위한 증기를 만들어주는 증기 기관차 보일러에 삽으로 석탄을 넣어주는 노동자다. 그러나 노조의 도움 때문에, 철도회사는 증기동력으로 작동하는 기차의 사용이 끝난 다음에도 수년 동안 그 직위를 유지했다. 그러나 그와 같은 문제들은 단기적인 것에 지나지 않았다. 궁극적으로 기계 기술의 진보는 비용과 가격을 내리게 하거나 혹은 비용과 가격을 억제하는 경향이 있고 더 나가 사람들로 하여금 더 많은 상품을 구입하도록 하는 것을 통해 새로운 고용기회를 창출한다. 만일 일부 산업들이 더 적은 노동자들을 고용한다면, 다른 산업들이 더 많은 노동자를 고용할 것이다. 동시에, 새로운 상품이 소개되고 새로운 산업들이 확립된다.

이종현T의 독해 Point!

14. 이 글의 핵심은 기술이 발달한다고 실업률이 올라가는건 아니라는 요지의 글이므로 정답은 4번이 된다.

15. 첫 번째 빈칸에는 fire man이 쓸모 없다는 것이고 두 번째 빈칸은 문제가 문제가 안된다는 것이므로 일시적이k는 말이 들어가면 정답은 3번이 된다.

16~18.

한강의 소설『소년이 온다(Human Acts)』는 주제의 중압감 때문에 쉽게 읽히지 않는 책이다. 오늘날의 유사한 사건들을 끌어들이지도 회피하지도 않은 채, 한강은 대량학살(1980년 광주 민주화 운동 때의 무력 진압) 이면의 사회, 정치적으로 촉매제가 된 사건들을 깔끔하게 풀어가면서, 그것이 가져온 오랜 동안의 해악한 결과를 정확히 서술하고 있다. 그러나 주목할 점은 작가가 그것(학살)을 피와 뼈의 (폭력) 소설로 만들면서도, 어떻게 이 작업을 완수하는가 하는 것이다. 작중인물들은 자주 무명의 '너'에게 말을 건다. 때때로 '너'는 죽은 사람이고 또 때로는 독자이지만, 그러나 종종 그리고 가장 심란하게도, '너'는 그 폭력사태(대량학살)가 있기 전의 사람들로, 이제는 추방되어 영영 돌아올 수 없게 된 사람들이다. 이런 전위의(자리가 옮겨진) 느낌이 가장 명확해지는 순간은 죽은 소년의 영혼이 썩어가는 자기 육신과 대화하는 장면이다. 바로 이 장면에서, 작품의 언어는 한강의 이전 소설,『채식주의자』의 고딕풍(괴기스러운 중세적 분위기)의 서정적 언어와 가장 가까워진다. 적어도 그 소년은 영혼이 있지만, 수많은 다른 희생자들은 자신에게 영혼이 있다고 더이상 확신하지 못하고 또한 (학살에서) 살아남았다는 치욕이 명확해진다. 소설을 자신의 문학표현 형식으로 선택한 다음, 소설로 하여금 소설이 가장 잘할 수 있는 일을, 즉 독자들을 그들 자신의 것이 아닌(다른 사람의) 삶의 바로 한가운데로 데려가는 일을, 하게 함으로써, 한강은 우리 시대의 가장 중요한 질문 가운데 하나에 대해 우리를 준비시킨다. 그것은 바로 "휴머니티(인간성)는 무엇인가? 휴머니티가 변질되는 것을 막기 위해 우리는 무엇을 해야 하는가?"이다. 한강은 이 질문에 결코 대답하지 않지만, 그녀의 이런 단호한 증언 행위가 가장 좋은 출발점으로 보인다.

이종현T의 독해 Point!

16. You라는 존재는 계속 바뀌어가는 존재이고 폭력 시대 이전의 사람이라고 나와 있으므로 이를 다 받아줄 수 있는 정답은 2번이 된다.

17. 첫 번째 빈칸에는 이것 저것으로 바뀐다는 얘기가 들어가면 되고 2번째 빈칸에는 보여준다는 말이 들어가면 된다. 따라서 정답은 3번이 된다.

18. Han은 정답을 내리지는 않았으므로 답을 내렸다고 하는 4번이 된다.

19~21.

우리는 'college'와 'university'란 용어를 상호교환해서 사용한다. 우리는 "그녀가 미시건 대학에 다녔다" 또는 "그가 오벌린 대학에 다닌다"라고 말을 할 때 마치 college와 university가 같은 의미를 가지고 있는 것처럼 이름 뒤에 오는 명사에 신경을 쓰지 않고 말한다. 두 용어는 같은 것이 아니지만, 확실하게 두 용어는 서로 관련되어 있으며 college는 university내의 '학부'로서 존재할지도 모른다. 그러나 college와 university에는 서로 다른 목적이 있다. college는 학생들이 미래를 살아가는 자원으로 지식을 이용하도록 과거의 지식을 대학생들에게 전하는 것과 관련되어 있다. university는 과거를 대체하기 위한 새로운 지식 창출을 목적으로 교수와 대학원생들이 하는 다수의 연구 활동이 주를 이룬다

이 둘은 모두 모두 가치 있는 목적이며, 대학생이 최첨단 또는 혁신적인 연구를 하는 학자 또는 과학자와 함께 연구를 할 때 때때로 이 둘의 목적이 수렴된다. 그러나 종종 이런 목적들은, 갈등은 아니라 하더라도, 경쟁에 놓이게 되는데, 연구의 수준이 높아질수록 특히 더 그러하다. 세계에서 가장 우수한 종합대학중 하나인 캘리포니아 주립대학교를 설립한 사람이 이례적으로 정직하게 인정했듯이, "(연구)수준이 높은 우수한 교수일수록 결과적으로 학부학생을 가르치는 데 대한 관심은 낮아지게 된다." 클라크 커(Clark Kerr)가 우리의 보다 절실한 문제 중 하나로 이런 '잔인한 역설'을 확인한 이후 이것은 거의 50년 동안 이어졌다. 오늘날은 그 어느 때보다 더 절실하다.

그러나 정확히 대학에서 문제가 되는 것은 무엇이고, 대학에서 얼마 만큼의 일이 이루어지고 있느냐 하는 것이 왜 중요한 것일까? 가장 중요한 점으로, 대학은 젊은이들이 청소년기와 성인기 사이에 있는 영역을 통과하는 데 도움이 될 수 있는 장소가 되어야 한다. 대학은 자기 인식을 위해 그런 험난한 상황을 건너기 위해 노력하는 학생들을 위해 강제가 아니라 안내를 해주어야 한다. 대학은 학생들이 사려 깊은 시민의 자질에 필요한 특정한 자질의 정신과 마음을 기르는 것을 도와야 한다.

이종현T의 독해 Point!

19. 1번과 헷갈릴 수는 있지만 보어 자리엔 목표라는 말이 있으므로 목표가 되는건 교육과 연구이다 따라서 정답은 3번이 된다.

20. 역설의 의미는 좋은 교수가 잘 못가르친다는 것이므로 정답은 2번이 된다.

21. B번부터 목표 얘기를 종합해서 다른 얘기로 이어지고 있고, E번부터 왜 그게 중요한지에 대한 얘기가 이어지므로 정답은 4번이 된다.

이것이 독해다

2023년 10월 10일 2판 2쇄 발행

저자 이종현
발행인 남승우

발행처 도서출판 상 학 당
신고 2-155호 (1968.11.29)
주소 서울특별시 동작구 사당로9가길 6
전화 02-595-1692~ 4
팩스 02-595-1394
이메일 shdbooks@naver.com
정가 35,000원

디자인 김마음
책의 표지는 Freepik.com의 이미지를 사용하여 제작되었습니다.

ISBN 978-89-6587-225-2 03740